WOMEN, SPORT AND PHYSICAL ACTIVITY

CHALLENGES AND TRIUMPHS

Second Edition

Sharon R. Guthrie
T. Michelle Magyar
Ann F. Maliszewski
Alison M. Wrynn

KENDALL/HUNT PUBLISHING COMPANY
4050 Westmark Drive   Dubuque, Iowa 52002

Cover image courtesy of Sandra Beckman, Shutterbug Art.

Foreword

I grew up in era where the effects of Title IX were beginning to take shape. I was fortunate enough to have the opportunity to participate in a wide variety of sports thanks to these opportunities and my parents' support. After having enjoyment and success at each level of volleyball (high school state championship, NCAA Championship at Long Beach State, and an Olympic gold medal in 2004), my wish is for every girl and woman to be able to experience the joy that comes from playing sport with great teams and teammates.

Of course, it hasn't always been easy, and I certainly have had challenges to overcome. I have battled through injuries, disappointment, and hard luck but through consistent training and sacrifice your goals are always within your reach.

I hope that readers of this book will understand and appreciate how hard girls and women work to become competitive athletes, the struggles female athletes have encountered and overcome to do something they love—and how much we can all gain from studying their experiences! I also hope that parents everywhere will encourage their daughters to participate in sport and physical activity because there are so many benefits to be gained for all. Despite the challenges that may have been placed before us, when given the chance, we are able to dig deep within ourselves, put it all on the line, and triumph in the world of sport, and, more importantly, in our lives.

Misty May-Treanor

Contents

SECTION 3
Psychological Perspectives on Women in Sport and Physical Activity

SECTION 4
Biomedical Issues

Introduction to the Second Edition

At the recently concluded 2008 Summer Olympic Games in Beijing, women made up nearly 50% of the competitors. This is a far cry from the first Modern Games held in Athens, Greece, in 1896 where there were *zero* women athletes! However, women have only recently moved toward equality in competitive opportunities in the Olympic Games compared to men. In 1988, women were still only 23% of the 7,000 competitors. Even today, in the Paralympics, women receive only about 40% of the competitive slots. When one examines the numbers of women in leadership positions in the Olympic movement in the United States and throughout the world, the numbers are much more sobering. The International Olympic Committee still has failed to reach its own recommended 20% minimal threshold for the inclusion of women in administrative structures [2008 representation = 15%] (Smith & Wrynn, 2008).

As a number of comprehensive reports have recently noted, sport is a valuable source of empowerment for girls and women, and by limiting their access to highly competitive sporting opportunities—and leadership roles—like those provided by international sporting competitions such as the Olympic and Paralympic Games, we are restricting their basic human rights (Oglesby, 2008; Tucker Center for Research on Girls and Women in Sport, 2007; United Nations Department of Economic and Social Affairs, 2008).

Why should girls and women participate in sport? Certainly all of the reasons that have been provided for the participation of boys and men over the past 100+ years apply in many ways to girls and women. If sports do provide the opportunity to learn about teamwork, good sportsmanship and leadership, why shouldn't we give girls and women the same opportunities that boys and men have been allowed? In addition, research has told us that girls and women can derive a number of other benefits from participation in a healthy and active lifestyle. In their book, *Raising Our Athletic Daughters: How Sports Can Build Self-Esteem and Save Girls' Lives*, Jean Zimmerman and Gil Reavill examined the research that was available on the ways that sport could benefit girls and young women. What they found was a powerful message about the importance of sport for girls and women:

> Girls who participate in sports are less likely to drop out of school, more likely to go on to college, and more likely to graduate from college. They tend to avoid a whole host of risk-taking and self-destructive behaviors. Girl athletes have one of the lowest rates of tobacco use among any sector of the high-school population; they are less likely to abuse drugs; they are less likely to get pregnant, more likely to delay their first sexual experience, and have, on average, fewer sexual partners than girls who do not participate in sports. In addition, girls derive benefits from athletics that are difficult to measure objectively, such as confidence and self-esteem; they score higher on tests designed to gauge positive body image. We spoke with girls all over the country in the course of doing

research for this book. The athletes we met were, on the whole, "achievers" who cited sports as an important strengthening factor in their lives. One characteristic we noticed over and over was a sense of focus and of being centered—these were, by and large, young women who knew where they were going with their lives.

The second edition of *Women, Sport and Physical Activity: Challenges and Triumphs* has a number of changes from the first edition. There are three new articles in the Historical Perspectives section, including a brand new article on Title IX by Sarah Fields, a leading researcher in this area. The second and third sections of the book, on the Sociological and Psychological Perspectives on women's participation, also include a number of newly written articles. Finally, the section on Biomedical Perspectives has been completely revised. These changes have come as a result of feedback from students like you in "Women in Sport" courses. If you have any comments or questions about the book, we hope that you will contact us!

Notes

"Interview with Jean Zimmerman and Gil Reavill, *Raising our Athletic Daughters*" on Family Education, *http://life.familyeducation.com/sports/girls-self-esteem/36266.html*

Oglesby, C. & the International Working Group on Women and Sport and WomenSport International. (2008). *Women 2000 and beyond. Women, gender equality and sport.* Retrieved April 1, 2008, from United Nations. Division for the Advancement of Women. Department of Economic and Social Affairs Web site: *http://www.sportsbiz.bz/womensportinternational/initiatives/documents/Women_2000_Report.pdf*

Smith, M., & Wrynn, A. (2008, July). Women in the 2000, 2004, and 2008 Olympic and Paralympic Games: An Analysis of Participation and Leadership Opportunities. *A Women's Sports Foundation Research Report.*

Tucker Center for Research on Girls & Women in Sport. (2007, December). *The 2007 Tucker Center Research Report. Developing physically active girls: An evidence-based multidisciplinary approach.* Retrieved April 10, 2008, from Tucker Center for Research on Girls & Women in Sport, University of Minnesota Web site: *http://www.tuckercenter.org/projects/tcrr/default.html*

United Nations Department of Economic and Social Affairs. (2008). *Article 30: Participation in cultural life, recreation, leisure and sport.* Rights and Dignities of Persons with Disabilities Convention. Retrieved April 24, 2008, from *http://www.un.org/disabilities/default.asp?id=290*

SECTION 1

Historical Perspectives on Women in Sport and Physical Activity

© Corbis

Section 1
Introduction

Alison M. Wrynn

Scholarly research into the field of women's history emerged, in large part, in the first half of the 1970s. Energized by the women's movement and the growth of social history, a variety of works on women in history appeared. Thanks to the diligent and insightful research of a substantial number of scholars, it was no longer possible to say that women were entirely "hidden from history" (Hartman and Banner, 1974).

Research on the history of women in sport also emerged in the 1970s. In 1974, Ellen Gerber, Jan Felshin, Pearl Berlin, and Waneen Wyrick's *The American Woman in Sport* was published. This ground-breaking volume presented, for perhaps the first time—and certainly to that point in time in the most comprehensive manner—a multi-disciplinary perspective of women in sport. In many ways the text you are now reading reflects this work from more than 30 years ago. We only hope that our text will serve students and scholars as well as *The American Woman in Sport* did for so many years.

In this section of the book you will be introduced to the history of women in sport. It is well beyond the scope of this text to tell you everything about women's sporting experience in the past. We won't be able to examine in detail the first women's intercollegiate basketball game, or the first women to compete in the Modern Olympic Games.[1] We also will not have the space to fully analyze significant female sporting pioneers like Eleonora Sears, Babe Didriksen, Wilma Rudolph, or Billie Jean King.[2] The following essays are designed to provide you with a broad picture of women's experiences in sport and physical activity in its historical context. In order to expand your knowledge on the history of women in sport, supplementary readings are listed following each reading. In addition, at the end of this *Introduction*, I have provided a list of general histories of women in sport that might be of interest to you.

The readings in this section begin with an article on *Pedestriennes*, long distance walkers of the nineteenth century. There were women who by the mid- to late-nineteenth century were undertaking intense physical contests for fame and fortune. This starting point certainly does not mean that interest in women's sport and physical activity did not exist before this point in history! Concern for issues of health and physical exercise had been a facet of American society prior to the end of the nineteenth century. In the 1850s Susan B. Anthony, Elizabeth Cady Stanton, and others labored to advance the cause of women's rights. Stanton, for example, raised the possibility that women might not be naturally physically weaker than men, but rather lacked the opportunity to develop physical strength and vigor since childhood, as had men (Stanton, 1850).

Women's rights advocates also called for equal opportunity to undertake training for, and be allowed entry into, various professions, especially law, medicine, and education. It was only in the second half of the nineteenth century, however, that women were allowed limited access to training and employment in these professions and others. When, for example, Elizabeth Blackwell was inadvertently granted admission to Geneva Medical College in 1846, against the objections of the all-male faculty, the field of medicine was all but closed to women. By the end of the nineteenth century, however, women had begun to make inroads into previously all male medical schools such as Johns Hopkins University, Tufts University, and the University of Michigan (Drachman, 1985).

Today physical education and sport have become separate entities on most college campuses. However, in the nineteenth century they were closely linked; in fact, it was the female physical educators who first organized sport for the young women under their charge. A concern for the health of young female students was evident at Vassar College, which opened in 1865. A medical doctor, Alida C. Avery, was hired as Professor of Physiology and Hygiene and resident physician in charge of the department of physical training (MacCracken, 1942).

These programs in physical training for women were emerging at a time when Victorian sensibilities endorsed, at least for the middle classes, the notion of separate spheres. The importance, indeed almost insistence, that most colleges and universities placed on appointing a woman physician to be in charge of departments of physical education for women is significant. This arrangement, whereby a medical doctor had overall responsibility for the department of physical education, the general health of the students, overseeing the work of the gymnasium, and serving as the resident physician, was a pattern that would continue at many women's colleges until the early 1900s. In the state universities, as young women lobbied for the right to utilize university gymnasia for exercise, universities grudgingly hired these women physicians to ensure the health and well-being of the young women under their care, and, in part, to fulfill their role *in loco parentis*.

In *Coming on Strong: Gender and Sexuality in 20th Century Women's Sport*, Susan Cahn argues that although women today have more opportunities for entering the sports world as participants, they still face numerous obstacles to success. Women's bodies continue to be controlled, while sport continues to focus on male dominance (Cahn, 1994). According to Cahn, early twentieth century directors of physical education used the weight of medical authority in directing their programs in the emerging field of women's physical education. While they were committed to improving women's health, and in some instances challenging the notion that menstruation periodically weakened their charges, they also "tended to" abide by medical concepts of ". . . the dangers of excessive physical activity" (pp. 23–25). They pursued the model of wide participation rather than the elite varsity model, and this choice was perhaps most fully developed in the credo that became the hallmark of the National Amateur Athletic Foundation in the late 1920s and early 1930s "play-day" movement: "a sport for every girl and a girl for every sport." And, in the case of basketball, they created, and for more than 60 years maintained, a markedly different form of basketball.

If the opportunities for women in sport have been limited in the past, women of color have been placed in what some scholars call a "double-bind." Sport not only excluded women until the last third of the twentieth century, but it has also restricted the opportunities for people of color as well. In the history of male sport, most people are familiar with the story of the re-integration of Major League Baseball by Jackie Robinson in 1947. But how many people are familiar with Althea Gibson, the first African American to win the singles titles at Wimbledon and the U.S. Open? The two articles presented in the text, one on the experiences of Olympic Track and Field star Alice Coachman and tennis great Althea Gibson, the other on Japanese American women's softball, will serve as a doorway to understanding the lives of those who have been excluded from the world of sport in America.

Finally, this section closes with an article on what is recognized as perhaps the most important moment for women's sport in America—the passage of Title IX of the Education Amendments of 1972. Although the law was designed to provide equal opportunities for males and females in educational settings, in the more than 30 years since it was enacted, one of its greatest influences has been the dramatic rise in the number of opportunities for women to compete in sport.

At the end of this section of the book are some activity worksheets that your instructor might have you complete, or you may choose to complete on your own. These activities are designed to give you the chance to explore in greater detail some aspects of women's sport history that interest you most. In addition, it gives you the opportunity to add your own sport history to the story of women in sport! It is vital to understand that many women in the past have sacrificed in order for contemporary American girls and women to have unprecedented opportunities in sport and physical activity. By analyzing their history we are able to honor them in ways that were perhaps not available to them in their own time.

References

Cahn, S. K. (1994). *Coming on Strong: Gender and Sexuality in Twentieth-Century Women's Sport*. New York: The Free Press.

Drachman, V. G. (1985). "Female Solidarity and Professional Success: The Dilemma of Women Doctors in Late 19th-Century America." In Judith Walzer Leavitt and Ronald L. Numbers, (Eds.) *Sickness and Health in America: Readings in the History of Medicine and Public Health* (1985). (2nd ed.) Madison: The University of Wisconsin Press.

Gerber, E., Felshin, J., Berlin, P., & Wyrick, W. (1974). *The American Woman in Sport*. Reading, MA: Addison-Wesley Publishing Co.

Hartman, M. S., & Banner, L., Eds. (1974). *Clio's Consciousness Raised: New Perspectives on the History of Women*. New York: Harper Torchbooks.

MacCracken, H. N., & Hazzard, Florence W. (10 November 1942), Biographical File, Vassar College Libraries, Special Collections.

Stanton, E. C. (1 April 1850). "Man Superior—Intellectually, Morally and Physically," *The Lily* 2, no. 4. As cited in Park, R. J. (1978). " 'Embodied Selves': The Rise and Development of Concern for Physical Education, Active Games and Recreation for American Women, 1776-1865," *Journal of Sport History* 5(2).

Further Reading

Birrell, S., & Cole, C. L. (1994). *Women, Sport and Culture*. Champaign, IL: Human Kinetics.

Boutilier, M. A., & SanGiovanni, L. F. (1983). *The Sporting Woman*. Champaign, IL: Human Kinetics.

Cahn, S. K. (1994). *Coming on Strong: Gender and Sexuality in Twentieth-Century Women's Sport*. New York: The Free Press.

Christensen, K., Guttmann, A., & Pfister, G. (2001). *International Encyclopedia of Women and Sports*. New York: Macmillan Reference.

Gerber, E., Felshin, J., Berlin, P., & Wyrick, W. (1974). *The American Woman in Sport*. Reading, MA: Addison-Wesley Publishing Co.

Guttman, A. (1991). *Women's Sports: A History*. New York: Columbia University Press.

Howell, R., Ed. (1982). *Her Story in Sport: A Historical Anthology of Women in Sports*. West Point, NY: Leisure Press.

Mangan, J. A., & Park, R. J., Eds. (1987). *From 'Fair Sex' to Feminism: Sport and the Socialization of Women in the Industrial and Post-Industrial Era*. London: Frank Cass and Co., Ltd.

Endnotes

1. The 1896 basketball contest between Stanford and the University of California is widely recognized as the first women's intercollegiate basketball game (Stanford won, 2–1). The first time women competed in the Modern Olympic Games was in the Games of the 2nd Olympiad held in Paris in 1900 when 22 women competed.

2. For more on these women and other sporting pioneers like them, see Christensen, K., Guttmann, A., & Pfister, G. (2001). *International Encyclopedia of Women and Sports.* New York: Macmillan Reference.

1

Pedestriennes: Newsworthy but Controversial Women in Sporting Entertainment*

Dahn Shaulis

© JupiterImages, 2009

*The author gratefully acknowledges James H. Frey and John A. Lucas for their reviews and suggestions, and Ed Sears, David Blaikie, Peter Lovesey, and John Cumming for locating historical materials.

In the nineteenth century, hundreds of women performed professional feats of strength and endurance. Endurance walkers and runners known as pedestriennes were particularly newsworthy, gaining metropolitan newspaper coverage in Britain and North America from the mid-1870s to the late 1880s. By the early twentieth century, however, historical recognition of these women was scarce.[1] Popular accounts of pedestrienne performances surfaced in the 1960s and 1970s, yet these women have received minimal scholarly attention.[2] Some sport histories do not even acknowledge women's participation in pedestrianism.[3] Others have recorded their performances as a single incident or a short-lived fad.[4] Contemporary texts that analyze women's roles in sport relegate the efforts of the pedestriennes to a few sentences.[5] Some histories briefly acknowledge the athletic endurance and significance of these women but include few if any sources.[6] Two sources recognize a history of women's footraces in England, but suggest that the phenomenon had died out by the mid-nineteenth century.[7] An overriding thesis in at least two other sources is that the pedestriennes were brazen entertainers violating Victorian moral standards who made little contribution, or even a negative contribution, to women's sport.[8]

In contrast to past accounts, this essay portrays women's footracing as an international phenomenon involving women of several nationalities and ethnic groups, with thread leading from medieval smock races to late-twentieth-century professional sports.[9] It is argued here that the pedestriennes were not universally marginalized during their era, nor was their form of entertainment short-lived. Some consciously strove for and for a time enjoyed a certain legitimacy despite relentless pressure to marginalize them. Their eventual marginalization, however, is significant because it allowed groups to continue to restrict women's activities. The story of the late-nineteenth-century pedestriennes should be of interest to contemporary sport historians because it illustrates how interest groups legitimize or marginalize cultural activity through the media and through government intervention. Powerful groups and their ideologies, then as now, are a major force for deciding what is newsworthy, profitable, revolutionary, or immoral, and ultimately how history is written. Interest group actions are interpreted here within the context of six ideologies: Victorian beliefs, capitalism, medicalization, suffrage feminism, popular culture, and physical culture.[10] In the see-sawing tension between legitimation and marginalization we discern a familiar pattern: the spectacular successes of a few promote legitimation and embolden so many others in such a short time to copy their activities that the social movement we call a "craze" develops. Often, as in this case, the craze leads to perceived excesses and abuses which erode legitimacy and provide a rationale for interference and suppression.

This essay focuses on two newsworthy performers, Madame Ada Anderson and Bertha Von Hillern, during the rise of American sporting entertainment in the 1870s. Based on hundreds of newspaper accounts that were written about them, I find that interpretations of the pedestriennes varied, and that several interest groups were politically or economically involved in their public approval and disapproval. On one side, women suffragists temporarily accepted the walkers as symbols for women's rights and health and business people fueled their popularity. On the other side, temperance and religious leaders labeled the pedestriennes as morally disreputable figures. Doctors and newspaper editors and reporters were divided in their opinions and interests, supporting or opposing activities as it fit their agendas. Later, the pedestriennes were identified by doctors and editors as exploited women in need of protection, stirring public disapproval of the events. Pressure to ban immoral and strenuous performances by women was followed by government action against such events. Women's pedestrianism eventually declined in popularity, allowing myths of female frailty to persist despite evidence to the contrary. This essay also attempts to understand the actions of women entertainer-athletes as they arranged their lives. Based on newspaper accounts of Von Hillern and Anderson, this study suggests that some pedestriennes desired moral respectability yet walked for economic necessity or future material comfort. This story of legitimation and marginalization has contemporary significance as women athletes of the 1990s face similar circumstances of being newsworthy but controversial people in international sporting entertainment.[11]

In the 1870s Americans were influenced by a number of restrictive ideologies. Victorian beliefs commanded that women and men maintain different social responsibilities. A woman's proper place was the home, a place to protect feminine virtue. This notion was particularly true for married women. Although women were expected to be morally superior to men, they were thought to be physically frail.[12] The emerging ideology of medicalization supported female frailty. Doctors who prescribed bed rest for the nervous and physically weak created a self-fulfilling condition that women were frail and dependent. Enterprising businesses disseminated this ideology by publishing books and newspapers in support of Victorian beliefs. Consistent with these beliefs, women were often restricted from public leisure, vigorous exercise, and sports.[13] Temperance groups supported Victorian beliefs by protesting against drinking, smoking, gambling, and Sunday public entertainment. In leisure, Victorian beliefs were restrictive for men as well. Professional sport was often located among the riff-raff who aggressively gambled, consumed alcohol, and smoked. Reading sporting and theatrical journals was considered immoral, and many women would not allow such material in their homes. Illicit reading was often restricted to barbershops or social clubs, and attending vulgar exhibitions in which scantily clad female entertainers performed was not done openly.[14]

The ideologies of capitalism and physical culture did not always match with Victorian beliefs. For some business people, Victorian beliefs regarding women were less important than their desire to maximize profits. As a cheap and efficient labor-pool, working class women and children toiled in factories or farms, at home in the needle trade, as domestic servants in wealthier homes, or as entertainers. For the women involved, Victorian beliefs gave way to economic necessity, sometimes even family survival.[15] The ideology of physical culture—a mixture of religion, diet, exercise, and alternative medicine—gained popularity in the early nineteenth century. Contrary to doctors who prescribed bed rest, doctors in favor of physical culture believed that women would be healthier and more productive if they engaged in physical activity. Many doctors and businesses profited from the prescription of gentle exercise for women with doctor-sponsored exercise equipment.[16]

While aspects of capitalism and physical culture conflicted with Victorian beliefs, suffrage feminism and popular culture directly challenged the restrictive ideology. Suffragists certainly did not agree on all issues. However, suffrage feminist ideology allowed a growing number of women to challenge the status quo by gaining education and employment. Most endured the hard labor of raising children and keeping house, but growing numbers of young women entered the work force. By 1880 approximately 2.6 million women were engaged in wage labor in the United States.[17] Popular culture also conflicted with Victorian beliefs. In leisure, it allowed young women and men to attend a variety of public and worldly pastimes and pleasures despite protests. By the 1870s popular culture and suffrage feminism helped establish an atmosphere for resisting Victorian beliefs. The public mingling of men and women of various social classes in professional sporting entertainment was one sign of this emerging resistance.[18]

American entertainment and newspapers were formidable industries by the 1870s. Thousands of customers flocked nightly to theaters and halls for plays, lectures, circus spectacles, and sporting events. Hundreds of thousands bought newspapers that promoted entertainment. The largest daily newspapers devoted regular space and occasionally accorded headline status to entertainment and sport celebrities. Some specialty weekly publications existed primarily by printing entertainment news.[19] A few thousand women worked in entertainment. Though women performers often played subordinate roles or were marked as less than moral women, some were materially successful. Some women were theater owners, writers, actresses, and singers. Higher-class women had greater opportunity for working in legitimate theater, but many working-class women performers made their wages working in a variety of "dive" or saloon acts as burlesque singers and actresses, chorus girls, or as performers of athletic feats. Women performed athletic feats as circus performers, swimmers, boxers, baseball players, wrestlers, bicyclists, and professional long-distance walkers. Although several athletic performers were highly skilled, many were portrayed as women with questionable reputations. Their activities were considered popular and vulgar entertainment.[20]

Women ran footraces for centuries in a tradition that would ebb and flow as a form of popular culture and entertainment. In England, smock races were popular contests for women beginning perhaps in the Middle Ages. Prizes for the victor of these half-mile to four-mile runs often included a garment or money. Contests were frequently held at fairs, yet they were presumably illegitimate for ladies. Participants were portrayed as nubile wenches, and spectators were portrayed as voyeurs.[21] In the nineteenth century, lower-class women's pedestrian efforts were described in sporting and local newspapers. In the 1820s the long-distance walking efforts of seven-year-old Emma Freeman and sixty-year-old Mary McMullen were reported. In the 1850s bloomer pedestrian Mrs. Dunne gained attention for her walks of several hundred miles. In 1864 Emma Sharp and Australian Margaret Douglas made even longer efforts that challenged men's records.[22] American women participated in smock races and pedestrian contests, though it is difficult to assess how frequently the events occurred. In 1851, bloomer pedestrian C.C. Cushman reportedly walked 500 miles. A year later, American Kate Irvine performed multi-day walks in England. Long-distance walking on a small wood surface, aptly called "walking the plank" became popular working-class entertainment. It is believed that American women performed these walks in saloons and at other exhibition sites, near or amid drinking, smoking, gambling, fighting, and prostitution. Though spectator crowds were sometimes large, the events were considered immoral by those holding Victorian beliefs. The walking track was not an acceptable place for a proper lady.[23]

Women's sporting entertainment gained greater newspaper attention despite Victorian beliefs. In 1875 *National Police Gazette* editor William E. Harding made a long-distance walk against lady pedestrienne Madame Lola as part of a circus attraction. Their records and average pace were newsworthy for the *New York Times*.[24] In 1875 and 1876 English swimmers Agnes Alice Beckwith and Emily Parker swam five to seven miles in the Thames, and gained thousands of spectators as well as international press coverage.[25] Six-day walking races in Chicago and New York between German Bertha Von Hillern and American Mary Marshall also attracted thousands of spectators. The editor of one sporting newspaper, however, displayed Victorian concern before the contest, remarking, "How do these ladies propose to walk? If in petticoats they will soon tire, if in bloomer costume they will not make very extraordinary time, but if they strip to tights and trunks, and go for putting on a record, they will expose themselves to criticism."[26]

Neither Von Hillern nor Marshall walked to openly contest Victorian morals. Both performers dressed in petticoats and neither attempted to run. The twenty-one-year-old Von Hillern was said to be from a respectable military family, but emigrated from Germany when her family experienced financial ruin. The thirty-year-old Marshall, a door-to-door bookseller, was hoping to improve her family's lot. According to the *Chicago Times* the contest was well managed, and "respectable and influential ladies and gentlemen" were present. The editor of *Chicago Field*, however, maintained his Victorian beliefs, stating, "It is not a woman's place— the walking path—least of all a married woman's. We can not look upon it as an athletic event, and give it notice to express our disapprobation of any such unfeminine display."[27]

Disapprobation notwithstanding, the ideologies of capitalism, popular culture, and suffrage feminism seemed to be holding sway. Crowds were so large that hundreds of potential spectators were refused at the ticket windows.[28] The women also received favorable coverage from metropolitan newspapers. A *New York Times* editorial even suggested that these pedestrians were pioneers for woman's rights. Noting that women had recently been denied the right to practice law before the U.S. Supreme Court but had been successful on the walking track, the editor remarked:

> The acclaim with which the victor was carried off the ground signalized the downfall of an ancient prejudice. . . . Obviously those who have aspirations above babytending, dishwashing, and writing for the magazines will refuse to accept walking matches in lieu of possible forensic honors, Let such be encouraged, however, by what has been accomplished. The world moves-is moving. To day it is the walking match, next it will be the coveted Bar. After that, who shah tell how soon the ballot will come.[29]

Newspapers continued to fuel the women's popularity as athletes, and their managers attempted to gain respectability, Mary Marshall's two victories against male athlete Peter Van Ness were news in the *New York Times*. Sporting newspapers reported that Marshall continued walking in New York, New England, and Pennsylvania. Millie Rose, a second attraction in the first Von Hillern-Marshall match, received star billing and local and sporting newspaper coverage in Cincinnati.[30] Von Hillern continued walking in New England, but in less controversial solo exhibitions. From 1876 to 1878 the German performed in at least 25 events in 13 different cities. Her many walks were billed as a symbol of physical culture for ladies.

New England suffragists supported and profited from Von Hillern's solo exhibitions, making her a symbol of women's capabilities. The leading women's suffrage newspaper *Woman's Journal* included four articles about Von Hillern from December 1876 to March 1877. [31] *Woman's Journal* acknowledged her accomplishments to refute Victorian beliefs and medical claims that women were too frail to be full citizens. "H.C.S." stated that "the remarkable feat of walking 350 miles in six consecutive days and nights . . . seems to me the most effective answer to Dr. Clarke's 'Sex in Education.' . . . She would certainly convince the strongest men who might undertake to walk with her, that the human female . . . is quite as enduring as the male."[32]

Businesses also profited from Von Hillern, treating her as a paragon of fashion and virtue. According to the *Boston Post,* two of her appearances at Music Hall drew daily crowds of 10,000 customers paying 50 cents-apiece. The *Post* remarked that "Miss Bertha Von Hillern appears to be the fashion, and her last remarkable feat will intensify the rage that her successes have excited." Newspaper advertisements noted that photographs of the pedestrienne would be sold at a local department store. Also banking on the performer's success, a hat seller in

Worchester advertised Von Hillern hats as the newest fashion. Bertha Von Hillern was considered a "household word" in several communities.[33] The *Worchester Evening Gazette* treated her as a symbol of physical culture and respectability, worthy of praise from all classes:

> She is not a mere professional intent only upon the pecuniary results and personal reputation to be secured by her efforts, but is doing her chosen work from a higher and nobler motive. She recognizes that fact, too often ignored, that women of today are too effeminate, and that each succeeding generation has less physical stamina than the last, and has determined in her own way to endeavor to incite women to self improvement in this direction. She is therefore an apostle of muscular religion, and so far as she brings light and health to the enfeebled and debilitated, she is a true evangel to her sex, and is worthy of their fullest respect, sympathy and countenance.[34]

Although the modest Von Hillern may have contested the belief of women's frailty, she did not try to threaten Victorian moral standards. Von Hillern worried what religious people thought about her. According to the *Worehester Evening Gazette*, "she is a regular attendant at church, and is conscientious and careful in her devotions. Her great fear is that in her contact with the public she may be suspected of evil, and she is every way circumspect and guarded. It is this natural modesty which prevents her exhibitions from turning into mere sporting affairs and which commend her to the confidence and good will of the best society."[35]

Von Hillern's performances continued to be supported by metropolitan newspapers and doctors. The *Washington Post* remarked that many of the 'elite" of the city visited Von Hillern's 100-mile walk, and doctors publicly appreciated her accomplishment.[36] As the front page headline in local news, the *Washington Star* noted that her audience "was composed of mainly leading citizens, ministers, lawyers, medical men and a large number of ladies, all showing interest in the performance."[37] In 1878, the *Washington Post* even published a letter signed by 33 Baltimore doctors requesting that the "lady of refinement" demonstrate her brand of physical culture in their city.[38] Although women sporting entertainers were often portrayed as inept sex objects, Von Hillern received favorable reviews. The *Washington Post* stated that Von Hillern's display of physical culture was "one of the wonders of the nineteenth century."[39] Another editorial favorably compared her to the famous male pedestrian Edward P. Weston, stating she was a fine tribute to "correct diet, strict temperance and systematic exercise."[40] Still another article noted that members of the Analostan Boat Club and other respectable ladies were spectators at her events.[41] Some businesses, however, profited by satirizing her efforts. Von Hillern was the focus of burlesque shows in Philadelphia and Washington, D.C.[42] Despite her popularity, the pedestrienne is said to have quit the walking track for a more respectable life in Boston high society.[43] A woman in Britain, however, was ready to fill her shoes.

Before Von Hillern retired, an outspoken and muscular middle-aged performer named Ada Anderson began making walking exhibitions. Madame Anderson, as she became known, claimed humble origins, born to a "Cockney Jew" father and English mother. The unconventional woman was single most of her life and worked as an actress, circus clown, singer, and theater proprietress before becoming a pedestrienne in 1877. In contrast to Von Hillern's walks that usually lasted a day, Anderson's efforts were much longer, matching or nearly matching men's all-time endurance records. Her typical walks spanned hundreds of miles and many weeks with minimal sleep. Anderson's training as a pedestrienne was important in gaining skill and conditioning. The pedestrienne took three months' instruction with William Gale, arguably the best endurance athlete of the era and the only man to attempt longer efforts. In addition to her athletic talent, Anderson was an exceptional entertainer who fascinated spectators with songs, comical pranks, and short speeches. Anderson's efforts profited the sporting entertainment business. Within the year the pedestrienne performed at least nine walks at seven different venues. She also gathered an entourage who depended on her success: a new husband, a manager, and a nurse.[44]

Unlike Von Hillern's image, Anderson's persona was in more direct conflict with Victorian standards. Von Hillern was modest and physically small, a single lady who regularly visited church. In contrast, Anderson was straightforward and muscular, a half-Jewish woman who was middle aged, twice married, and who performed on Sundays. In her behavior and speech, Anderson displayed outspoken confidence rather than humility. In her speeches she exposed cruelty toward working-class women and publicly fought for her own material success. According to the *Lynn News* dated August 17, 1878:

> Addressing herself to the ladies she assured them that she would never try to perform a task she was unable to accomplish, and for which she had not the strength. Some had said "'poor woman,' what she has to endure!" But she did not say so. She was a Londoner herself and had often seen the seamstresses . . . go to their daily toil and often sit up all night with a small piece of candle and only bread and butter to eat. Though she had to stay up all night, she was only too thankful that she was well fed and well taken care of. She then alluded to the present management in uncomplimentary terms and intimated that next week she would perform under new management altogether.[45]

In October 1878, convinced that she could gain greater fame and fortune in America, the pedestrienne and her entourage boarded a steamship for New York. According to newspaper accounts, she hoped to secure a large arena, Gilmore's Garden in New York, for a 28-day walk. Unfortunately for Anderson, arena owner and railroad baron William Vanderbilt was unwilling to rent her the venue. Madame Anderson was forced to occupy a smaller and less respectable site at Mozart Garden in Brooklyn.[46]

Despite her assertive nature Anderson considered herself a moral woman. In an interview given later in the year, she gave her impression of Vanderbilt's rejection and the inauspicious beginnings of the event:

> As a consequence I was forced to make my first appearance in this country at a summer garden in Brooklyn, and never shall I forget my feelings on that first night, for with the rough men below me drinking beer and lewd women congregated in the building where I was to walk, it seemed as though I should sink from the thoughts of contamination, and that it would ruin me. I knew, however, that it was my only chance to get before the public, and determined that I should make these people feel I was a lady and not of their stripe, that they would make the locality and give way for good people. They did. In forty-eight hours not one of them looked in. The better class of Brooklyn soon learned this through the kindness of the members of the press, and it was not long before I had crowds of them watching my progress.[47]

Anderson hoped to gain respectability for her event, and her management made several moves to ensure success. The *Brooklyn Daily Eagle* noted, "The management intend that the strictest decorum shall be preserved and that ladies and children shall have a good opportunity of viewing this exhibition of human pluck and endurance." Anderson encouraged gentlemen to bring their families, and a special entrance for families allowed respectable people to avoid unsavory characters. The management also enlisted newspaper personnel as judges to ensure that the contest was fair and honest. The track was certified by the city surveyor as exactly seven laps for a quarter-mile, and a railing was built to prevent spectators from impeding her path. The management even offered a $100 reward to anyone who would find Anderson off the track during her appointed times. Mozart Garden was remodeled with a three-foot-wide tan bark walking oval in the center of the building, allowing for a seating capacity of 800 spectators. Admission prices were twenty-five cents for adults, fifteen cents for children, and five dollars for a season ticket.[48]

Madame Anderson's efforts were newsworthy, and the coverage was generally positive from the start. Newspaper accounts of her month-long walk began December 16, 1878, in the *Brooklyn Daily Eagle* (daily circulation, 20,000 copies). Coverage by the *New York Sun* (with circulation more than 100,000 daily) and *New York Times* (daily circulation, 25,000) started December 17. Headlines from the *Sun* and *Times* described Anderson as "a woman of wonderful endurance," while the *Times* noted that "many ladies were present, and the best of order was maintained." The newspapers described her as a determined but dignified, muscular woman, noting her previous accomplishments in England. Nearly every day, the newspapers reported her condition: whether she had fatigue or blisters, her temperament, who accompanied her on her laps, each recorded lap time, what she ate and drank, how her nurse woke her, and what musical numbers she sang. News reports noted that doctors visited Anderson. One doctor publicly referred to her as "the finest specimen of physical womanhood he ever saw."[49]

Prominent people visited Anderson, including local government officials and their wives, opera singers, and other entertainment celebrities. By late December the hall was filled every night with an estimated 4,000 people.[50] Lists of prominent spectators made the performance more newsworthy. The *Brooklyn Daily Eagle* reported that "among the gentlemen who were present during the evening were Dr. Swaim, Justice Vorhiss, District Attorney Catlin, General Slocum, Alderman Dwyer, Rev. Mr. Parker of the Sands Street M.E. Church, Assistant District Attorney Jyre Wernberg, ex-judge Morris, William A. Fowler and wife, Dr. Waters and family, . . . Alderman McIntyre, . . . Dr. Rosalind, Counselor Barrett and many others."[51]

Anderson's comments were sought and recorded by newspaper reporters, and her ability to speak eloquently as well as walk were vital for her continued popularity. The *New York Times* and *New York Sun* illustrated the performer's confident and engaging demeanor:

> Ladies and Gentlemen: I have on two or three occasions before thanked you for your personal and cheerful encouragement. I could not go on without your assistance. You have done your part, and I thank God I have been enabled to do mine. In every twenty-four hours I have tits of sleepiness which are very severe. While I sleep I suffer. Sometimes I wish I could never sleep, it is so painful to wake up. When I first began my walk I asked the ladies for their presence. I think from the number of ladies that they are satisfied. It is good for women to see how much a woman can endure. When I came to this country I heard that American ladies would sometimes walk two blocks. I did not know how much two blocks meant, but supposed that it must be two miles. Now I don't think it good for a lady to ride two blocks when she can walk. As a lady experienced in walking, allow me to say that it is beneficial to walk.[52]

Anderson publicly and perhaps shrewdly deflected moral derision when she thanked God for her abilities. As a proponent of physical culture, she also gained support from ladies by repeatedly expressing that her effort would show women their true capabilities. The *Brooklyn Daily Eagle* and other newspapers promptly wrote articles regarding women's health, stating that women should walk more, though not to Anderson's extraordinary or excessive levels.[53]

Anderson's popularity continued to rise. By early January more New York papers and out-of-town newspapers began to cover Madame Anderson's exploits. General ticket prices were doubled to 50 cents, then raised to $1, with special tickets on the stage for ladies and gentlemen raised to $2. Yet customers continued to till Mozart Garden to suffocation levels. The *New York Sun* and *Brooklyn Daily Eagle* continued to list many notable and respectable spectators. Women were her most loyal supporters. According to the *New York Times*, the women were "so fascinated by the spectacle of a woman on the track performing a feat of which the majority of men would be incapable, that they watch her for hours at a time, day after day, with unflagging interest."[54] Noting that many churchgoers attended Anderson's walk, even on Sundays, the editor of the *New York Sun* remarked, "What will Brooklynites do next Sunday for an *entr'acte* between services? The past four weeks it has been just the thing to stroll in to see Mrs. ANDERSON walk, before or after church. But next Sunday this resource will be gone. TALMAGE [referring to evangelist Thomas DeWitt Talmage] is about the only athletic exhibition left for Sundays."[55]

The *New York Tribune* and the Brooklyn Women's Christian Temperance Union (WCTU), however, opposed Anderson. The newspaper first cast doubts about the authenticity of the walk, then published a political order by temperance officials.[56] The *Tribune* rumored that an Anderson double might be taking her place on the track at night, but the claims were never substantiated. Temperance officials were outraged that Anderson exhibited herself in a smoke-filed, drinking atmosphere, and that their fellow church members were attending the show on Sundays. As a result, the *Tribune* published a public denouncement by the Brooklyn WCTU. The article presented a signed petition by the Brooklyn temperance officials to the Board of Alderman, calling for enforcement of the Sunday laws:

> We claim that the opening on the Sabbath of all stores, exhibitions, etc., to which an admission fee is charged, is illegal, and in this particular instance the illegality is heightened by the amount of Sunday liquor-selling which is an inevitable accompaniment, and also we, as women, enter our protest against this pitiful display of womanhood as alike contrary to the dictates of humanity and God.[57]

Despite the WCTU protest, Anderson's performance was allowed to continue with great success. Her exhibition ended with more than 2,000 people filling the hall and hundreds of people lining the area for three blocks along Fulton Street waiting for news updates from inside. Newspapers noted that many in the audience "represented the best classes of city life—society queens who nestled in sealskin sacques and rustling silks." As Anderson made her last laps she draped herself in an American flag and again publicly thanked God for her success. News of her triumph was telegraphed to papers from London to San Francisco, and press reports stated that the woman had received approximately $7,000 in earnings, a substantial portion of the $32,000 in total revenues. Anderson was showered with gifts, from flower bouquets to silverware, and some newspapers hailed her performance as a symbol of women's great capabilities.[58] The editor of the *Brooklyn Daily Eagle* stated that "her success, it is not hard to prophecy, will revolutionize the opinions held by many of her sex on the subject of physical exercise, and particularly will it educate women in the direction of outdoor exercise. . . . The idea, as general as it is venerable, that a woman cannot, by reason of her sex, endure as much as a man, is exploded, and to Madame Anderson is due the overthrow of the mistaken notion."[59] District Attorney Catlin made a testimonial speech to Anderson, claiming:

> Her modest demeanor and a grace of movement unparalleled has captured the city of Brooklyn. Her victory is Brooklyn's victory. She has won the esteem and admiration of both sexes. The best women of Brooklyn have shown their sympathy by their patronage and applause and have been rewarded a hundred fold. She has taught women they are not the weak vessels they have been said to be. I hope that women of Brooklyn will imitate her example in taking exercise.[60]

Anderson's success prompted a pedestrian craze that profited women and businesses. Ladies in Brooklyn began to walk for better health and appearance while dozens of working class women across the country were inspired to walk for money. In an article "The Best of Health," the author remarked that "the interesting pedestrian feat which Madame Anderson brought to so successful a conclusion last week has given an impetus to walking, especially among the ladies who so much admired the grace and elegance of her motion and the perfect healthfulness of her appearance."[61] Working-class women throughout the United States were attempting to rival or surpass Anderson and profit from her celebrity status. Theater owners and entertainment managers were willing to oblige their new business for a percentage of the revenues, and doctors were willing to provide medical services. The *Washington Post* remarked that "Madame Anderson's success has served a powerful stimulus to the leg industry. From all parts of the country there are reports springing up like mushrooms, doctors certifying to pulses and temperatures and people paying out their hard earnings."[62] The *Spirit of the Times* added, "Imitators of Mme. Anderson are becoming so numerous that we have hardly room to catalogue them." During 1879, more than 100 women were walking for money, Hundreds of newspaper articles chronicled the endurance efforts of May Marshall in Washington, D.C.; Madame Andrews, ex-boxer Madame Franklin, and Annie Bartell in New York, French Canadian Exilda La Chapelle in Chicago; Fannie Edwards in San Francisco; ex-trapeze performer Lulu Loomer in Boston; Ida Vernon in Philadelphia; Millie Rose in Cincinnati; and Kitty Sherman in Wheeling, who were all attempting month-long walks. All of these efforts were promoted as attempts to break Anderson's record of 2,700 quarter miles in 2,700 quarter hours. At the same time dozens of others were involved in shorter events as part of the Madame Anderson craze. William Vanderbilt even agreed to a six-day women's walking contest for Gilmore's Garden, but the celebrity was already scheduled for other exhibitions.[63]

Ancillary businesses also profited from Anderson's success. Given that her performances were presented daily in large metropolitan newspapers, it would be logical to assume that articles about her increased newspaper circulation. Anderson's face and physique also appeared on the front page of two illustrated newspapers, the *New York Illustrated Times,* and *Frank Leslie's Illustrated Newspaper*. Other products were similarly affected by the Madame Anderson craze, as evidenced by newspaper advertisements. As advertised, women could buy pedometers for $5 at Tiffany & Company to monitor their daily walks, and retailers could buy mail-order illustrations of women pedestrians sold by the Metropolitan Job Printing Company for $20 per hundred.[64]

Yet, after Anderson's success, some newspapers and religious officials questioned the purpose of such exhibitions, and government officials intervened to prohibit further performances. A *New York Times* editorial acknowledged Anderson's "conspicuous pluck and wonderful powers of endurance," but suggested that such performances should not be repeated. Sporting newspapers trivialized her record. The *New York Clipper* stated that Anderson was "wonderfully plucky" but could not give her the record. The editor argued that although the woman had completed her task, she may have gained assistance by people accompanying her on the track. America's *Spirit of the Times* and England's *Bell's Life* remarked that "the performance has little merit as a purely pedestrian feat" and that women had already been acknowledged by medical authorities to be "superior" in "living with little or no sleep."[65] It is not surprising that this medical fact was accepted; undoubtedly this form of superior endurance supported women's oppression at home and in factories. Popular evangelist Thomas De Witt Talmage acknowledged Anderson's walk, but lamented that women doing traditional work were not given credit for their devotion.[66] A sermon by Reverend W. C. Steele titled "The Evils of Pedestrianism" in the *New York Herald* expressed the outrage that morally righteous people felt about such events.[67] In March 1879, police Captain Williams invoked a seldom used blue law to prohibit women's Sunday walks in New York City, making efforts such as Anderson's illegal in that locale.[68]

In contrast to her detractors, one suffragist acknowledged Anderson's success as a public service for women while criticizing temperance officials. "E.B." wrote in the *Woman's Journal* that Madame Anderson's performance was an important symbol of woman's capabilities and need for healthful exercise:

> I went to see Madame Anderson on her walk . . . and was completely fascinated by her gracefulness, her modest and businesslike deportment, and dignity, She carried her head worthy a queen. Every firm, elastic and graceful step was a lesson to dawdling women floundering in pullbacks and mincing on heels. A lesson worth a hundred simpering Sunday Schools, notwithstanding the Christian Temperance Women's protest. I believe Madame Anderson has done a good thing in demonstrating the ability and endurance of one woman, at least, beyond what a man is capable of. She has made speeches occasionally in her periods of rest, in which she has given utterance to her belief that women are committing daily suicide in not using more freely their powers of locomotion . . . . She has gained the respect of all who have witnessed her performance.[69]

Anderson continued her performances in six cities amid popularity and controversy. In Pittsburgh, the crowds were large despite competition from dramatic actress Mary Anderson and Buffalo Bill's Wild West Show. She initially received favorable reviews from the *Pittsburgh Post* and the *Pittsburgh Commercial Gazette*, each having a daily circulation of 5,000 copies. Madame Anderson encountered trouble, however, when powerful industrialist and church elder William Park, Jr., and officials of the First Presbyterian Church pressured the mayor to stop her Sunday performances. At least two other churches considered similar actions. With her business in jeopardy, the pedestrienne publicly countered Park's effort by noting that several of his employees were toiling on Sundays. In her speech reported by one newspaper, Anderson added:

> Let him employ his time in some other way than trying to hunt down a woman, both night and day to attain a position in society, in short let him go into his closet and study his Bible. There are a certain class of people who weave for

themselves a cloak of righteousness, and certainly to their liking, and anyone who lifts the hem of that garment, or has not one made in the very same style is nothing short of the devil. Such a man is Mr. Park.[70]

The *Pittsburgh Commercial Gazette* promptly rebuked her, and in succeeding issues criticized her performance in general. Anderson and her management continued to perform on Sunday, cleverly advertising the exhibition as a "sacred concert."[71] Though Anderson was allowed to continue her walk, she was fined by the mayor, and her husband and manager were arrested for violating Sunday laws. Business continued to be good, however, and Anderson performed for 2,000 customers on her last day of contested walking. Consistent with their Victorian beliefs, the *United Presbyterian* reported Anderson's irreverent defiance of authority and her continued popularity as a sign of world decline.[72]

Anderson and other pedestriennes continued to attract crowds and increasing controversy. In Chicago, Anderson's exhibition reportedly sold 24,000 tickets in the first two weeks. However, the *Chicago Tribune* (circulation 25,000) published several lengthy letters, editorials, and articles complaining about the cruelty and immorality of women's pedestrianism. Anderson's walk was called a brutal exhibition, and newspaper accounts described Anderson as walking in agony. Nationally, newspapers referred to the walking phenomenon as an unhealthy enterprise, a virulent epidemic, a madness or mania. Competition brought greater records and intense competition as Victorian standards of decorum were increasingly ignored.[73] Yet thousands of customers continued to pay to see such contests. Editors somewhat correctly described women's endurance efforts as cruel torture brought on by profit-hungry managers. Further, they invoked medical authorities such as Dr. Benjamin Lee to substantiate the abuse claims and force government officials to stop women's sports for their own protection.[74] The morality of the pedestriennes remained an underlying reason for trying to stop the contests, however. A *Chicago Tribune* letter to the editor titled "Public Brutality" stated, "Our modern female pedestrians are a disgrace to themselves and dishonor to society, and an outrageous insult to every virtue which adorns true womanhood. Preaching and exhorting can have little effect in its attempt at moral reformation so long as such sinful spectacles are witnessed by respectable citizens."[75] Another letter entitled "Indignant About Mme. Anderson" called for government officials to arrest her managers for cruelty. Subsequently, police "benevolently" arrested her husband and one of her managers for cruelty. Although an impartial doctor cleared her to continue, Anderson reportedly slept through a few scheduled laps, and the contest was labeled a failure. The exhibition gained another scandal when the pedestrienne's managers accused a *Chicago Tribune* reporter of attempted blackmail. Confident in herself, Anderson publicly fired one manager for what she wrote was "incompetent and neglectful management and gross conduct."[76] In April she attracted large audiences in Cincinnati. Unfortunately, the pedestrienne's performance was marred by a lawsuit against two of her managers. According to the *Cincinnati Enquirer*, "had she one responsible manager, with none of the miserable hangers-on such as her husband, Wood, and some of the others, she would make both fame and money, As it is, she is in a fair way to lose both."[77]

Irresponsible and sometimes corrupt management and disreputable audiences were to lead pedestrianism in general into further criticism. Newspapers reported that at least two male pedestrians had died. In New York City, several pedestriennes were carried off the track, one of whom was rumored to have died. Editors and reporters noted that many women were untrained for endurance events but walked in desperation to improve their lot in life.[78] In Louisville, Anderson quit due to poor attendance, but she was well received in Detroit with an average daily attendance of 1,000 spectators. According to the *Detroit Free Press*, "her behavior is entirely free from the slightest tinge of boldness or immodesty." In Buffalo, Anderson's detractors stood to profit if Anderson quit, but the bold woman continued. When a glass shard was found on the track, evidently placed there to stop her, "she informed the audience that a cut foot would not make her leave the track, and she would complete her task despite the efforts of those who wished to injure her."[79] The intrepid pedestrienne continued to walk despite poor attendance and an ulcerated mouth that required a tooth extraction between laps.[80]

Anderson's newsworthiness declined as pedestrianism fell into further disrepute. Her next walk in New York City was barely covered by the newspapers, except when the *National Police Gazette* reported that "roughs" had broken up the race and police had made arrests. In December 1879, Anderson eventually competed in William Vanderbilt's building, now known as Madison Square Garden. The veteran of thousands of miles completed a respectable 351 miles in six days, but she was surpassed by competitors half her age. Although audiences for the New York contest were numbered in the thousands, the pedestriennes' livelihoods were threatened as pressure to eliminate women's contests gained momentum. Citing acts of cruelty to pedestriennes in Baltimore, Milwaukee, Indianapolis, Cleveland, and St. Louis, the *New York Times* called for an end to such contests. Whether news stories of brutality and immorality were true or not, they undoubtedly affected public opinion. Women's pedestrianism appeared to serve no great purpose. With dozens of events held in dozens of cities, the events could no longer be substantiated as educational for women, or even supported as novelties. Pedestrianism had now become associated with excess and brutality, as well as immorality. Doctors and suffragists who supported pedestrianism fell silent, and newspapers reduced reports on women's sporting entertainment, In New York, the local Council of Aldermen agreed to make women's contests illegal in the name of protecting women. Men's contests were not affected by these restrictions until several years later.[81]

In early 1880, Anderson returned to her singing career as women's pedestrianism became less popular. It is known, however, that she gave at least one more walking performance, a solo effort at Central Theatre in Baltimore in 1880. Anderson's faded status was bolstered by a front-page advertisement that electric lights would illuminate her effort, and $500 would be paid to anyone who detected her missing a single lap. Anderson's walk was closed to the public on Sundays to avoid conflict. At the end of her exhibition, she "made a speech from the front of the stage in which she returned her thanks to the throng and hoped to meet them all again." It is not readily apparent what happened to Madame Anderson, although she had stated a year earlier that she hoped to retire by 1880. Women's records continued to improve in the early 1880s, but their performances were considered less newsworthy.[82]

Several factors may be considered in the decline of women's pedestrianism. Organized social pressure by temperance officials, religious conservatives, and doctors against women's sporting entertainment appears to be a major factor in its marginalization. Government actions ranging from arrests to legislation against the events are also factors. Managers and theater owners who exploited women performers and created a dangerous atmosphere also contributed to discouraging spectators. Apparently, it was not simply public disapproval of the women's morality, but also efforts to protect women that led to a reduction in vigorous sporting efforts. As events were represented as cruel torture against women, it would have been difficult for suffragists or doctors to continue supporting the performances. Bloody sports such as cockfighting and dogfighting had already been reduced because of their cruelty to animals.[83] Certainly women deserved at least the same protection. The impression that such events were abusive toward women as well as immoral seemed to tip the scales toward greater marginalization. It should be noted that men's professional events also fell into disrepute for their excesses and abuses as amateur sports became more legitimate and newsworthy.[84]

Still, women continued endurance efforts in pedestrianism, bicycling, and transcontinental walks for more than a decade. Women entertainer-athletes received some newspaper attention, though not at the levels of the Madame Anderson craze. Pedestriennes Millie Rose, Sarah Tobias, Bella Kilbury, and Indian Princess, who began their careers during the craze of 1879, appeared in six-day matches in Baltimore and Washington, D.C., in 1889. The *Washington Post* published daily articles about the matches.[85] Three other pedestriennes, Louise Armaindo, May Stanley, and Elsa Von Blumen, became professional bicyclists. To safeguard their health, pedestriennes and female bicyclists were usually limited to performing twelve hours per day.[86] Presently, it is difficult to assess when women's professional sporting entertainment stopped, if it stopped at all. At least one pedestrienne, Spanish immigrant Zoe Gayton, was walking in 1896.[87]

For most of the twentieth century, images of women professional sporting entertainers faded as the idea of female frailty lingered. The most vivid memories of these women were that they were brazen and immoral burlesque entertainers. The myth of female frailty in sport, particularly in distance running, continued into the 1960s. Physical educators and doctors perpetuated this myth by restricting girls and women from vigorous sports and exercise. Several bold women did compete, but often against the rules and with the threat of being labeled as deviants. Women were not allowed to participate in most marathons until the 1960s, and the first official Olympics women's marathon was not held until 1984.[88]

It is not coincidental that stories about the pedestriennes resurfaced in the late 1960s and 1970s, during the rise of feminist ideology in popular culture. As women gained power and as histories of working women's lives became legitimate, popular and favorable short stories about the pedestriennes were written.[89] One feminist writer Barbara Walder, even referred to the pedestriennes as "foremothers," giving them a status of legitimacy. Although the issue of gender inequality in sport gained scholarly attention, the pedestriennes did not receive serious mention. In the 1990s, historians identified the phenomenon, but did not see the historical relevance in conducting critical research. Unfortunately, popular articles about the pedestriennes written in the 1960s and 1970s have been neglected, and the status of these women in sport history is marginal at best. Feminists in sport sociology note that women athletes are portrayed as sex symbols or given less press coverage than male athletes in the male-dominated sports realm.[90] The example of the pedestriennes points out that such trivialization and marginalization can result in historical amnesia.

In the 1990s, women have become increasingly newsworthy but controversial participants in global sporting entertainment. Women entertainer-athletes have gained ground, but powerful interest groups and ideologies continue to determine how the athletes are portrayed. According to *Sports Illustrated*, Algerian world champion 1,500-meter runner Hassiba Boulmerka was symbolized both as a hero and an antihero in her country. Although some citizens were proud of her achievement, Boulmerka offended many fundamentalist Muslims by appearing in public without being covered. With rising conflict between Muslims groups in Algeria, Boulmerka became "a symbol of antifundamentalists."[91] In China, world-record holders Wang Junxia and Qu Yunxia were portrayed as poor rural girls who were willing to train in harsh conditions for their future material betterment. In their own country, these women were heroes. In other countries, newspapers and magazines reported rumors of their use of illegal performance-enhancing drugs. In *Runner's World*, "independent sports scientists" were quoted to discredit their performances.[92] In Ethiopia, Derartu Tulu's victory in the Olympic 10,000-meter run "symbolized the possibilities of an emerging Africa and the potential for African women." According to the *New York Times*, "her success, however, has not come without criticism."[93] The newsworthy but controversial nature of these women has striking parallels with the pedestriennes. Although it would appear that women have gained a stronger foothold in sporting entertainment, the pedestrienne story may illustrate how powerful interest groups and ideologies continue to influence how women athletes are perceived and symbolized.

Endnotes

1. John Krout, *Annals of America Sport: The Pageant of America* (New Haven: Yale University Press, 1929), 200; Robert B. Weaver, *Amusements and Sports in American Life* (Chicago: University of Chicago Press, 1939; New York: Greenwood Press, 1968), 63.

2. Guy M. Lewis, "The Ladies Walked and Walked," *Sports Illustrated*, no. 27 (1967): R34; Barbara Walder, "Walking Mania," *Women Sports*, June 1976, 16–17; Anonymous, "Pedestrianism in Perry Hall," *Branching Out*, July/August 1976, 34–35; George Gipe, "Mary Marshall Was Strides Ahead of the Times When She Beat a Man," *Sports Illustrated*, October 24, 1977, ES.

3. Benjamin G. Rader, *American Sports: From the Age of Folk Games to the Age of Televised Sports* (Englewood Cliffs, NJ: Prentice Hall, 1996), 36–38; John A. Lucas, "Pedestrianism and the Struggle for the Astley Belt, 1878–1879" *Research Quarterly*, 39 (1968): 587–594; John A. Lucas and Ronald A. Smith, *Saga of American Sport* (Philadelphia: Lea & Febiger, 1978), 342–372, Nina Kuscsik, "The History of Women's Participation in the Marathon," *Annals of the New York Academy of Sciences*, 301 (1977), 862–876; Allen Guttmann, *From Ritual to Record: The Nature of Modern Sports* (New York: Columbia University Press, 1978), 33–36; Patricia Vertinsky, "Women, Sport and Exercise in the Nineteenth Century," in *Women and Sport: Interdisciplinary Perspectives*, D. Margaret Costa and Sharon R. Guthrie, eds. (Champaign, IL: Human Kinetics, 1994), 63–82.

4. John Cumming, *Runners & Walkers: A Nineteenth Century Sports Chronicle* (Chicago: Regnery Gateway, 1981), 102-105; Dale A. Somers, *The Rise of Sport in New Orleans: 1850–1900* (Baton Rouge, LA: Louisiana State University Press, 1972), 62.

5. Douglas A. Noverr and Lawrence E. Ziwecz, *The Games They Played: Sports in American History, 1865–1980* (Chicago: Nelson-Hall, 1983), 37; Mary A. Boutilier and Lucinda SanGiovanni, *The Sporting Woman* (Champaign, IL: Human Kinetics, 1983), 33.

6. Jennifer Hargreaves, *Sporting Females: Critical Issues in the History and Sociology of Women's Sports* (London: Routledge, 1994), 143–144; Karen Kenney, "The Realm of Sports and the Athletic Woman, 1850–1900," in Reet Howell, ed., *Her Story in Sport*, (West Point, NY: Leisure Press, 1982), 124–126. Joan S. Huh, "The Female American Runner: A Modern Quest for Visibility," in Barbara L. Drinkwater, ed., *Female Endurance Athletes* (Champaign, IL: Human Kinetics, 1986), 6.

7. Peter F. Radford, "Women's Footraces in the Eighteenth and Nineteenth Centuries: A Popular and Widespread Practice," *Canadian Journal of History of Sport* 25 (1994): 50–61; Allen Guttmann, *Women's Sports* (New York Columbia University Press, 1991), 48–49, 64, 71–73.

8. Gerald R. Gems, "Working Class Women and Sport: An Untold Story," *Women in Sport and Physical Activity Journal*, 2 (1993): 17–30; Susan K. Cahn, *Coming on Strong: Gender and Sexuality in Twentieth Century Women's Sport* (New York Free Press, 1994), 14.

9. For a description of women's endurance from a critical postmodern perspective, see Dahn Shaulis, "Women of Endurance: Pedestriennes, Marathoners, Ultramarathoners, and Other—Two Hundred Years of Women and Endurance," *Women in Sport and Physical Activity Journal*, 5 (Winter 1996): 127.

10. See George H. Sage, *Power and Ideology in American Sport* (Champaign, IL: Human Kinetics); Robert Goldman and David R. Dickens, "Leisure and Legitimation," *Society and Leisure,* 7 (1984): 293–323.

11. This work depends heavily on newspapers as original sources for historical interpretation. Nevertheless, it is difficult to consider newspapers as a monolithic source. Democrat, independent, religious, Republican, sporting entertainment, and suffragist newspapers presented varying perspectives on news, editorials, and advertisements.

12. Victorian beliefs reflected some conservative religious ideas such as Puritanism that predated the Victorian era. See Ellen W. Gerber et al., *The American Woman in Sport* (Reading, MA: Addison Wesley Publishing Company, 1974), 347; Jennifer A. Hargreaves, "Victorian Familialism and the Formative Years of Female Sport," in James A. Mangan and Roberta J. Park, eds., *From Fair Sex to Feminism: Sport and Socialization of Women in the Industrial and Post-Industrial Eras* (London: Frank Cass and Co., Ltd., 1987), 130–143; Kathleen McCrone, "Class, Gender, and English Women's Sport, c. 1890–1914," *Journal of Sport History,* 18 (1991): 159–182.

13. For various perspectives regarding female sport and medical regulation see Patricia Vertinsky, "Women, Sport, and Exercise in the Nineteenth Century in Costa and Guthrie, eds., *Women in Sport: Interdisciplinary Perspectives* (Champaign, IL: Human Kinetics, 1994), 63–82; Roberta J. Park, "Physiology and Anatomy are Destiny!? Brains, Bodies, and Exercise in Nineteenth Century American Thought," *Journal of Sport History,* 18 (1991) 31–63, Allen Guttmann, *Women's Sports: A History* (New York Columbia University Press, 1991), 84–105.

14. On, for example, the moral illegitimacy of the *National Police Gazette,* see Elliott J. Gorn, "The Wicked World," *Media Studies Journal,* 6 (Winter 1992): 115.

15. For conditions of American working-class women, see Gerda Lerner, *The Female Experience: An American Documentary* (New York: Oxford University Press, 1992), 273–316.

16. For interpretations of nineteenth-century physical culture, see Harvey Green, *Fit for America* (New York: Pantheon Books, 1986); and James C. Wharton, *Crusaders for Fitness* (Princeton: Princeton University Press, 1982).

17. Bureau of the Census. 1975. *Historical Statistics of the United States, Colonial Times to 1970, Bicentennial Edition, Part 1* (Washington, D.C.), 138.

18. For descriptions of the intermingling between classes, see Kathy Peiss, *Cheap Amusements: Working Women and Leisure in Turn-of-the-Century New York* (Philadelphia: Temple University Press, 1986), 37, 97–114; William L. Slout, ed., *Broadway Below the Sidewalk. Concert Saloons of Old New York* (San Bernadino, CA: The Borgo Press, 1994), 99–104; and *Popular Amusements in Horse and Buggy America* (San Bernadino, CA: Borgo Press, 1995), 178–184. For descriptions of gentlemen's amateur sport and working-class professional sport, see Richard Gruneau, *Class, Sport, and Social Development* (Amherst, MA: University of Massachusetts Press, 1983); John A. Lucas and Ronald A. Smith, *Saga of American Sport* (Philadelphia: Lea & Febiger, 1978), 135–37.

19. Newspapers promoted actress Mary Anderson, pedestrians Edward Weston and Daniel O'Leary, swimmer Paul Boynton, rower Edward Hanlan, entertainers Tom Thumb and Buffalo Bill Cody, religious lecturers Thomas Dewitt Talmage and Henry Ward Beecher, and author/performers Mark Twain and Anna Dickinson. For statistics regarding entertainment establishments, see Department of the Interior, *Report on the Social Statistics of Cities,* George E. Waring, ed. (Washington, DC: Government Printing Office, 1883): 533–568. For circulation records, see the *American Newspaper Directory* (New York, George P. Rowell, 1879). For the role of newspapers, particularly sporting newspapers, in promoting sport, see Melvin L. Adelman, *A Sporting Time: New York City and the Rise of Modern Athletics* (Urbana, IL: University of Illinois Press, 1986), 268–286; and Lucas and Smith, *Saga of American Sport,* 80.

20. For details of social stratification, and the distinction between "legitimate" and "illegitimate" in the English theater, see Tracy C. Davis, *Actresses as Working Women: Their Social Identity in Victorian Culture* (London: Routledge, 1991). See also Peter Bailey, ed., *Music Hall: The Business of Pleasure* (Milton Keynes: Open University Press, 1986); and Michael R. Booth, *Theatre in the Victorian Age* (Cambridge: Cambridge University Press, 1991).

21. Guttmann, *Women's Sports*, 48–49, 64, 71–73.

22. Shaulis, "Women of Endurance," 3. According to *Telegraph and Argus,* September 17, 1964, 336–339, more than 100,000 people witnessed Emma Sharp walk 1,000 miles in 1,000 hours from September 17, 1864, to October 29, 1864.

23. Charles M. Andrews, *Colonial Folkways* (New Haven: Yale University Press, 1919), 121; John Cumming, *Runners & Walkers: A Nineteenth Century Sports Chronicle* (Chicago: Regnery Gateway, 1981); *Spirit of the Times,* November 1, 1851, 438 and *Saint Louis Intelligencer,* November 1, 1851, 3.

24. *New York Times,* March 29, 1875, 9; and March 30, 1875, 7.

25. Ibid., September 18, 1875, 10; and September 20, 1875, 2; *Spirit of the Times,* October 9, 1875, 219. Beckwith continued swimming in England and the United States. See the *New York Times,* May 22, 1880, 2; and June 9, 1883, 2.

26. *Chicago Field,* January 23, 1876, 372.

27. Ibid., February 7, 1876, 393.

28. *Chicago Times,* February 1, 1876, 1; and February 6, 1876, 3. *New York Times,* February 5, 1876, 1; November 10, 1876, 5; and November 12, 1876, 7. *New York Sun,* November 9, 1876, 1.

29. *New York Times,* November 18, 1876, 4.

30. Marshall's matches against male pedestrian Peter Van Ness were reported in the *New York Times,* November 19, 1876, 2; November 23, 1876, 1. *Spirit of the Times,* February 19, 1876, 42; February 26, 1876, 68; *Cincinnati Daily Enquirer,* February 19, 1876, 4; *London Times,* December 5, 1877, 5; *New York Clipper,* April 7, 1877, 11.

31. *Woman's Journal,* December 23, 1876, 412; and January 7, 1877, 26–27. For Dr. Clarke's role in supporting female frailty, see Park, "Physiology and Anatomy are Destiny!?," 36–39.

32. *Woman's Journal,* December 30, 1876, 421.

33. *Boston Post,* January 21, 1877, 2; January 22, 1877, 3. *Worchester Daily Spy,* May 12, 1877, 3.

34. *Worchester Evening Gazette,* May 15, 1877, 2.

35. Ibid., June 2, 1877, 2.

36. *Washington Post,* January 28, 1878, 4, advertised Von Hillern's exhibition as an effort of "physical culture" and an "exemplification of her theory of health."

37. *Washington Star,* January 19, 1878, 1.

38. *Washington Post,* January 14, 1878, 4.

39. Ibid., January 21, 1878, 4.

40. Ibid., January 29, 1878, 2.

41. Ibid., January 30, 1878, 4.

42. *Washington Star,* February 8, 1878, reported Von Hillern's performance favorably, but ridiculed women's baseball efforts, June 7, 1878, 6. *Detroit Free Press,* August 17, 1879, 6, reported weak and inept female baseball players despite an attendance estimated at 2,000. For advertisements of burlesque satires of Von Hillern, see the *Philadelphia Public Ledger,* November 20, 1877, 1; and *Washington Evening Star,* February 8, 1878, 4.

43. *New York Clipper,* February 15, 1879, 370; *National Police Gazette,* April 17, 1880, 14.

44. *Brooklyn Daily Eagle,* January 14, 1879, 3; *Louisville, Courier-Journal,* June 7, 1879, 4; *New York Sun,* December 17, 1878, 3; *London Times,* August 26, 1878, 8; *Bell's Life,* February 9, 1878, 9; *New York Sun,* January 14, 1879; *Brooklyn Daily Eagle,* December 16, 1878, 2; *New York Times,* December 17, 1878, 2.

45. Peter Lovesey, *"Nineteenth Century Women Walkers,"* unpublished manuscript, 16–17.

46. For a description of William Vanderbilt and other industrialists, see Matthew Josephson, *The Robber Barons* (New York: Harcourt Brace and Company, 1934).

47. *Buffalo Courier,* August 23, 1879, 2.

48. *Brooklyn Daily Eagle,* December 16, 1878, 2.

49. *New York Sun,* December 17, 1878, 1; December 23, 1878, 1; and December 25, 1878, 1. *New York Times,* December 17, 1878, 2; *Brooklyn Daily Eagle,* December 18, 1878, 4; December 22, 1878, 4; and December 28, 1878, 4.

50. *New York Sun,* December 26, 1878, 1; *Brooklyn Daily Eagle,* December 30, 1878, 4; January 13, 1879, 4.

51. Ibid., January 11, 1879, 4.

52. *New York Sun,* December 31, 1878, 3.

53. *Brooklyn Daily Eagle,* December 29, 1878, 2, compared Anderson's contribution to women's health with the walking of Queen Victoria's daughter, Princess Louise, in Canada. For favorable reviews of Anderson's endurance capacity, see the *New York Sun,* December 31, 1878, 3; *Brooklyn Daily Eagle,* January 13, 1879, 2; January 14, 1879, 2; January 17, 1879, 3; and January 19, 1879, 3.

54. *New York Times,* January 13, 1879, 5.

55. *New York Sun,* January 14, 1879, 12.

56. The *New York Tribune,* January 7, 1879, 8, suggested fraud was possible. The *New York Evening Post,* January 10, 1879, 4, and *New York Times,* January 9, 1879, 5, refitted claims of fraud.

57. *New York Tribune,* January 14, 1879, 5.

58. *Brooklyn Daily Eagle,* January 12, 1879, 2; January 14, 1879, 2; January 17, 1879, 3. *Washington Post,* beginning January 2, 1879, 1; *Rocky Mountain News,* January 10, 1879, 1; *San Francisco Chronicle,* January 13, 1879, 3; *Chicago Tribune,* January 17, 1879, 12. The *Salt Lake Tribune,* January 15, 1879, carried news of the WCTU protest with no mention of her success.

59. *Brooklyn Daily Eagle,* January 14, 1879, 2.

60. Ibid., January 14, 1879, 3.

61. *Brooklyn Daily Eagle,* January 19, 1879, 3.

62. *Washington Post,* January 22, 1879, 2.

63. *New York Times,* January 14, 1879, 4, 5; *Spirit of the Times,* January 18, 1879, 633; and February 8, 1879, 12; *New York Clipper,* February 8, 1879, 363; and March 1, 1879, 387. Minority women included Dianna de Cristoral, "The Great Egyptian Pedestrienne," and Tek Sek, "the Indian girl." See the *Philadelphia Inquirer,* April 2, 1879, 2; National *Police Gazette,* January 31, 1880, 15.

64. Tiffany pedometers were advertised in the *New York Evening Post,* January 30, 1879, 3. Advertisements for illustrations appeared in the *New York Herald,* March 24, 1879, 1. The *New York Illustrated Times,* January 4, 1879, 195, and Frank *Leslie's Illustrated Newspaper,* February 1, 1879, 1, presented front-page action pictures and stories of Anderson.

65. *Bell's Life,* February 1, 1879, 12; and *New York Clipper,* January 18, 1879, 338. John M. Hoberman, *Mortal Engines* (New York The Free Press, 1992), 33–61, suggested that gentlemen's interests in male physical prowess were ambiguous compared to their interest in promoting white male intel-

lectual prowess. The acknowledged ability of Blacks and women to withstand pain were considered indicators of intellectual inferiority.

66. *Brooklyn Daily Eagle*, January 18, 1878, 2.

67. *New York Herald*, March 17, 1879, 3.

68. *New York Times*, March 24, 1879, 8.

69. *Woman's Journal*, 1 February 1879, 37.

70. *Pittsburgh Commercial Gazette*, February 10, 1879, 4; *New York Clipper*, February 22, 1879, 378.

71. *Pittsburgh Commercial Gazette*, February 6, 1879, 2.

72. Ibid., February 13, 1879, 4.

73. *New York Times*, February 2, 1879, 7; February 14, 1879, 5; and May 4, 1879, 6; *Washington Post*, February 14, 1879, 2; *Chicago Tribune*, March 5, 1879, 9; March 9, 1879, 12; *New York Clipper*, March 8, 1879, 396; and March 29, 1879, 4.

74. For the Philadelphia Medical Society's protest of women's matches, see the *New York Herald*, March 29, 1879, 4.

75. *Chicago Tribune*, March 11, 1879, 9.

76. *Chicago Inter-Ocean*, March 14, 1879, 8; and March 24, 1879, 3.

77. *Cincinnati Inquirer*, April 21, 1879, 4; May 8, 1879, 8; and May 12, 1879, 4.

78. *National Police Gazette*, April 12, 1879, 11.

79. *Louisville Courier-Journal*, June 7, 1879, 4; and June 21, 1879, 4; *Detroit Free Press*, July 22, 6; and August 14, 1879, 6; *Detroit Evening News*, August 12, 1879, 4.

80. *Buffalo Courier*, August 28, 1879, 2; and September 14, 1879, 2.

81. *New York Times*, December 14, 1879, 6; *Chicago Tribune*, March 5, 1879, 9; *National Police Gazette*, November 1, 1879, 12, 16; January 3, 1880, 2. According to the *New York Clipper*, April 26, 1879, 34, a bill to prosecute anyone for holding professional walking contests was presented to the New York State Legislature in April 1879. It did not pass.

82. *Baltimore American and Commercial Advertiser*, May 16, 1880, 4. Madame Anderson's reported performances included:

September 1877, Newport, Wales 1,000 half-miles in as many half-hours
November 1877, Plymouth, England 1,250 miles in 1,000 hours
December 1877, Plymouth, England 96 miles in 24 hours
January 1878, Plymouth, England 1,344 quarter-miles in as many quarter-hours
February 1878, Boston, England 1,008 miles in 672 hours
April 1878, Leeds, England 1,500 miles in 1,000 hours
June 1878, Skegness, England 1,008 miles in 672 hours
July 1878, King's Lynn, England 864 quarter-miles in as many 5 minute periods
August 1878, Peterborough, England 1,344 quarter-miles in as many quarter-hours
December 1878, Brooklyn, U.S.A. 2,700 quarter-miles in as many quarter-hours
January 1879, Pittsburgh, U.S.A. 1,350 quarter-miles in as many quarter-hours
May 1879, Chicago, U.S.A. 2,068 quarter-miles in as many quarter-hours*
April 1879, Cincinnati, U.S.A. 804 miles in 500 hours
June 1879, Louisville, U.S.A. Starts 1,100 quarter-miles in 1,100 quarter-hours**
July 1879, Detroit, U.S.A. 2,028 quarter-miles in as many quarter-hours
August 1879, Buffalo, U.S.A. 2,052 quarter-miles in as many quarter-hours***
November 1879, New York, U.S.A. Attempts 4,236 quarter-miles ****

December 1879, New York, U.S.A. 351 miles in 6 days
May 1880, Baltimore, U.S.A. 1,559 quarter-miles in as many 12 minute periods
*Reportedly missed a few laps;
**Quit early, due to poor attendance;
***Completed walk despite having tooth removed;
****Roughs attempted to stop race to win a bet.

83. For the protest against bloody animal sports, see Adelman, *A Sporting Time*, 240–243.

84. For interpretations of the downfall of pedestrianism, see Lucas, "Pedestrianism," 593–594. For information on the attack on professional sports and the legitimation of amateur sports through the ideology of nationalism, see S.W. Pope, *Patriotic Games: Sporting Traditions in the American Imagination, 1876–1926* (New York: Oxford University Press, 1997), 22–34.

85. *Washington Post*, May 19, 1889, 1; and June 2, 1889, 6.

86. Ibid., May 21, 1889, 1; *Chicago Inter-Ocean*, March 19, 1879, 8.

87. Transcontinental walks by Zoe Gayton and Mrs. Clara Estby were reported in the *New York Times*, March 28, 1891, 3; and December 24, 1896, 9; *The Virginia* [Nevada] *Evening Chronicle*, May 8, 1896, 3.

88. For a portrayal of pedestriennes as superannuated prostitutes see Edward Van Every, *Sins of New York* (1930, reprint, New York: Benjamin Blom, Inc., 1972), 294. George C. O'Dell, listed but trivialized pedestrienne performances in *Annals of the New York Stage*, volume 11 (New York: AMS Press, 1963), 120, 142, 193. Images of women pedestrians were reformed in Hult, "The Female American Runner: A Modern Quest for Visibility," 6; and Kuscsik, "The History of Women's Participation in the Marathon," 862–876.

89. Guy M. Lewis, "Madame Will You Walk," in *Yesterday in Sport* (New York: Time-Life Books, 1968), 147–150; Lewis, "The Ladies Walked and Walked," R3-4; Walder, "Walking Mania," 16–17. Anonymous, "Pedestrianism in Perry Hall," 34–35; Gipe, "Mary Marshall was Strides Ahead," ES.

90. See M. Ann Hall, *Feminism and Sporting Bodies* (Champaign, IL: Human Kinetics, 1996). See also Margaret C. Duncan and Cynthia A. Hasbrook, "Denial of Power in Televised Women's Sports," *Sociology of Sport Journal*, 5 (1988), 121; Margaret C. Duncan, "Beyond Analyses of Media Texts: An Argument for Formal Analyses of Institutional Structures," *Sociology of Sport Journal*, 10 (1993), 353–372.

91. "Veiled Threat," *Sports Illustrated*, January 27, 1992, 12.

92. Amby Burfoot, "Can of Worms; That's What a Group of Chinese Women Opened Last Summer with Their Amazing Performances, " *Runner's World*, December 1993, 60–69.

93 Jere Longman, "Tulu is Running for Herself and Millions of Sisters," *New York Times*, B9, B12.

Further Reading

Park, R. J. (1978). 'Embodied Selves': The Rise and Development of Concern for Physical Education, Active Games and Recreation for American Women, 1776–1865. *Journal of Sport History* 5(2).

Struna, N. (1991). Gender and Sporting Practices in Early America, 1750–1810. *Journal of Sport History* 18(1), 10–30.

Verbrugge, M. H. (1988). *Able-Bodied Womanhood: Personal Health and Social Change in Nineteenth Century Boston*. New York: Oxford University Press.

Vertinsky, P. (1994). *The Eternally Wounded Woman: Women, Exercise and Doctors in the Late 19th Century*. Manchester, U.K.: Manchester University Press.

Discussion Questions

1. What factors contributed to the growth of opportunities for female pedestriennes in the late nineteenth century?

2. Describe the athletic careers of Bertha Von Hillern and Ada Anderson.

3. What led to the decline in the popularity of women's pedestrianism?

2

"Look Out for the Ladies"

The Definition and Control of 'Appropriate' Athletics for Women in the United States in the 1920s

Alison M. Wrynn

© Corbis

A husky strong athlete was the rabid Roxanna,
Who in Idora High School had won a felt banner,
She went out for sports with a bang and a rush,
Her spirit of fight not a player could crush.
But now a sad light on the soul of our Roxie,
She was gossipy, selfish, and always quite foxy,
She'd win by subterfuge, where was her honor?
Not much like the rest of them—curses upon her!
On any committee she was never a worker,
But tried to gain glory—the base little shirker!
The meaning of service to Rox was a mystery,
Oh, she had an unspeakable, tragical history!

But enough for the failures, so sorry and sad,
Who were none to the good, but all to the bad.
There are none of them here, for they all have expired,
They fell by the wayside, or else they were fired.
And the girls who belong to the W.A.A
Have the spirit that wins—here's to you—I say![1] (1925)

Introduction

'Rabid Roxanna', with her overzealous competitive urges, was but one of the characters in the poem *Are You One of These?* 'Serious Susie', 'Nanette', 'Carrie the Co-ed', 'Maisie the Moron', and 'Rabid Roxanna', each illustrated on the presumably dire consequences for failing to follow the new rules for women's collegiate athletics in 1925. Receiving bad grades, breaking training, having poor posture, or playing no sports at all, made young women such as these "failures" in the eyes of the author, Violet Marshall, the head of the Department of Physical Education for Women at the University of California, Berkeley.

In contrast to these negative sentiments in regards to women's athletics, were the feelings of the student President of the University of California Women's Athletic Association (W.A.A.). The year prior to the publication of *Are You One of These?*, the W.A.A. President expressed her deep regret that the interclass-intercollegiate competition, between Stanford University, Mills College and the University of California, would have to cease. The contests, ". . . [were] in no way harmful physically and they [tended] toward a friendly feeling between the institutions."[2] What had transpired at the University of California, and other institutions of higher learning, to create such a sharp split in the philosophy supported by female physical educators, who were also the athletic coaches, and the beliefs of student participants in regards to what was appropriate versus inappropriate athletic competition for women? And what events occurred that caused a further shift in beliefs so that by 1930 the faculty advisor of the W.A.A. claimed, "[The students in the W.A.A.] can't bear the thought of any compromise that involves whole teams from one college competing against whole teams from any other..."?[3] The control that female physical educators exhibited over the philosophy of appropriate athletic competition for women was most influential in colleges and universities, and at times in high schools, during the 1920s. Who then was influencing the definition and development of women's athletics outside of this small area?

Donald Mrozek, in "The 'Amazon' and the American 'Lady': Sexual Fears of Women as Athletes," proposed the theory that the development of women's athletics in the late nineteenth and early twentieth centuries was restricted by several influences, but underlying nearly all of them was the element of fear. According to Mrozek, men were afraid that they could possibly lose their place in the social order if the lines between separate male and female spheres were allowed to fade. Women athletes, especially at the elite level, were perceived as a threat to the social order by men, since they sometimes blurred the distinctions between men and women.[4]

The first part of this paper will examine some of the consequences of men's fear in regards to elite women's athletics. If what Mrozek says is true, and men did feel threatened by elite female athletes and their ability to blur gender distinctions, then did their fear cause men to restrict women's athletics? Moreover, in "The 'Amazon' and the American 'Lady'," Mrozek only examined the fears of men in regards to athletic women. Thus, the second part of this paper will explore the anxieties of female physical educators and administrators in regards to athletic competition by women. Did they share with men the fear that Mrozek claims underlay all the others, ". . . the fear of losing identity and purpose?"[5] The final part of the paper will look at the outcome of the implementation of the new philosophy of athletic competition for women on the college campuses. Did all the female students support the new programs and their underlying ideology?

Although the 1920s were not the first decade of the twentieth century, they can be viewed as the first truly "modern" decade. Values, attitudes and activities that developed in the 1920s pointed towards the future rather than the past.[6] By 1920, women increasingly stepped outside the strictly defined sexual spheres of the nineteenth century and moved into the public arena. Women attended colleges, and worked in retail or in industry in increasing numbers in the first two decades of the twentieth century. In addition, women, like men, took to sport with increasing intensity and desire for enjoyment in the 1920s. Sport, like other aspects of the new mass culture, became not only a form of entertainment, but also a venue for personal improvement. Improving the individual, and through them the whole society, was an important premise of sport in the first part of the twentieth century.[7]

Women's athletic competition increasingly entered the public sphere in the 1920s. Women had competed in sports such as basketball, golf and tennis since the late nineteenth century, but they had rarely performed in front of crowds. When they did the spectators were usually limited to women. Following World War I, women's athletic contests became a greater focus of public attention. Girls competed in state-wide interscholastic basketball championships, young women played on basketball teams representing industrial or business concerns, women represented their college or university in intercollegiate competition, and women began to represent the United States in international competition. The audience for these contests now included men. Additionally, men could follow the exploits of these new women athletes in the sport's pages of their daily newspapers. Men began to enter more personally into women's athletics by coaching girl's and women's teams and also by sponsoring athletic events for women at previously all-male competitions such as the National (AAU) Track and Field Championships and the Olympics.[8]

Is There a Weaker Sex?

Pierre de Coubertin revived the Olympic Games at Athens in 1896 as a forum for young men from around the world to demonstrate their all around athletic ability in friendly international competition. He did not plan to add women to the Games, did not want them included, and fought against their inclusion throughout his life time.[9] As de Coubertin grew older, and wielded less control over the Games, however, women were allowed to participate. In 1900, the first women competed in the modern Olympics. The only event that women were allowed to compete in during the 1912 Games was swimming. A practical reason for the choice of swimming as the exclusive competitive milieu for women was the fact that swimming was organized on a national level in several countries.

However, this could not have been the only reason as many women were also competing basketball, tennis, and track and field. Perhaps an underlying reason was that the men of the International Olympic Committee felt less threatened by women who were confined to definite boundaries (a swimming pool) for their competitive events. Additionally, women who were clad only in bathing, even the somewhat unflattering suits of the 1920s, would look unmistakably like women, thus reinforcing the differences between men and women. Reaction in newspapers such as the New York Times favored the participation of American women in the Olympics. At the same time, however, the athletic accomplishments of the competitors were presented as flawed. Ethelda Bleibtrey, an Olympic swimming star, performed in a manner that was described as:

> . . . impressive, [but] the least bit marred by some erratic swimming on her part. In her energetic efforts to lower the world's mark she veered from her course on two occasions, the most conspicuous victim being Miss Helen Moses of Honolulu who at the 50 yard mark was forced out of the race because of a collision with Miss Bleibtrey. The latter also swam out of her course into that of Miss Boyle.[10]

The male sportswriters of the New York Times tempered their description of Bleibtrey's accomplishments by including a description of her wayward swimming. Women's athletic competition may have been encouraged to a degree, but it still was not taken seriously.

Tennis was added to the 1924 Olympic program for women and, along with the expanding program, debate increased about the suitability of Olympic competition for women. The debate was in part prompted by the exploits of elite female athletes, a few of whom were beginning to approach some of the standards of athletic excellence that had been established by male athletes. In 1924, Sybil Bauer swam the quarter-mile backstroke five seconds faster than any man previously had.[11] The New York Times reported than an effort would be made to convince Olympic officials to allow Bauer to compete against the men at the 1924 Games. The reports stated that she would be more competitive at the longer distance races that the men swam. However, at the Olympic Trials, and the Games themselves, Bauer was not allowed to swim against the men. Her time in the women's 100 meter backstroke, although fast enough for victory in the women's competition, would not have bettered that of the male winner in the same event.[12] In a longer race there was the possibility that she could challenge some of the men thus Bauer was limited to the shorter sprint race in which men had a distinct physiological advantage.

Some men, however, believed that it was a positive step that women were beginning to compete on closer terms with men in athletics. When Gertrude Ederle conquered the English Channel, in a time that was a record for both men and women, her achievement was acclaimed as not only a personal victory, but also as a victory for American womanhood:

> . . . the Channel has [become] the means of giving to women new physical dignity. . . . It often happens in the world of achievement, no matter what the field of her success, is set down as unique. If she manages a business, people will say that she has a man's knack of administration. If she attains a new athletic record those on the sidelines declare that she is strong or skillful—for a girl. Very reluctantly do the males, lords of creation admit that the females of their species are anything better than second raters. . . . Much benefit to American womanhood will result from the worldwide fame earned by Gertrude [Ederle]. Athletic sports will be made more popular and new champions will appear. The development of physical grace, strength and health will be most useful to the race.[13]

This was not, however, a completely positive compliment for women as athletes. The benefits that would accrue from Ederle's triumph would be improved physical grace, strength and the health of women, something that would be useful to the "race." Studies had been undertaken in the 1920s and before to examine the effects of athletics on the reproductive organs; and women's capacity to improve their reproductive ability and the health of their offspring was seen by the author of this article as being at least as important as any other benefit that might result from her victory.[14]

In addition to the question surrounding the effect of competitive athletics on women's reproductive health, the debate about women's athletic ability, as compared to men's, was a popular topic in many magazines during the 1920s. The *Woman Citizen, Literary Digest, Canada Magazine* and others, each included at least one article in the 1920s or early 1930s that compared women's athletics with men's.[15] It is more than likely that this increased discussion and debate about elite female athletes is evidence that some people were uncomfortable about women's expanding athletic ability, especially on the elite level. *Colliers* was one magazine that contained several articles that explored the athletic exploits of women versus men during the 1920s. In "Look Out for the Ladies!" Grantland Rice, a well-known sportswriter of the era, claimed that female athletes would rival the records of their male counterparts within a few generations.[16]

By 1928 the novelty of women challenging men in athletic competition began to fade and some articles appeared in popular magazines that were critical of the "new" athletic woman. Popular sportswomen like Helen Wills and Gertrude Ederle were faulted for their inability to compete on the same level as elite males in their sport.[17] The most intense criticism, however, was reserved for female track and field athletes who some writers labeled as an "Amazon race of women." Grantland Rice expressed the belief that: "Golf, tennis, swimming, diving, the shorter sprint, and other forms of competition are fine things, but women are not yet ready for marathons, football, boxing and wrestling."[18]

The concern that was expressed with respect to women's ability to compete in the longer track events was exacerbated by the results of the recently concluded track and field competition at the 1928 Olympics. This was the first time that women were allowed to compete in track and field in the Olympic Games. The event which evoked the most emotional response among Olympic officials, sportswriters, and the general public, was the 800 meter race. The addition of the 800 meter race to the Olympic program could be seen as an attempt to set the female athletes up for failure. Although many women participated in races that were longer than 800 meters by 1928, women's competition was generally limited to 400 meters (or 440 yards). American women had not been allowed to run the 800 meter race in competition until the 1928 indoor track season, and some concerns were expressed about the women's ability to complete the distance.[19] At the conclusion of the women's Olympic 800 meter final, several of the competitors were so exhausted that they needed to be carried from the track. Following the race, the *New York Times* claimed that the results " . . . demonstrate that even this distance makes too great a call on feminine strength."[20] Olympic officials apparently agreed with this sentiment as they decided in the future to limit running races for women to 200 meters.[21]

The reports of the 100 meter race in the 1928 Olympics exemplified the lack of respect that some members of the popular press accorded elite female track and field competitors. According to the New York Times the most interesting part of the 100 meters was not the race itself but rather:

> . . . scenes entirely unfeminine and never before witnessed in any Olympic Stadium. When the starter [disqualified a runner for a false start] she seemed not to comprehend for a moment and then burst into tears. She soon had company on the sidelines when Fraulein Schmidt, a buxom German blonde, also made a [false start]. But instead of tears, the German girl shook her fist under the starter's nose and the spectators for a moment thought she might stage a face scratching and hair pulling act. The harassed official backed away, waving the irate sprinter off the track...[and] turned to comfort [the other competitor] who had sat down too near the starting line and was sobbing lustily.[22]

The results of the race were not important, only the emotions of women under the stress of competition were of consequence. The description of the German competitor as "buxom" was not a unique phenomenon. Female athletes were often judged on their appearance, no matter what their ability.

In 1930 an attempt was made by the International Olympic Committee (IOC) to restrict the participation of women in future Olympics to fencing, lawn tennis and gymnastics, sports which some people felt were more appropriate for women. Very few members of the all-male IOC supported the proposal, however. Gustavus Kirby, one of the members of the American contingent to the International Amateur Athletic Federation, the international controlling body of track and field, threatened to boycott the men's track and field events at the 1932 Olympics if women were not allowed to compete in track as well; the IOC quickly defeated the proposal and voted to allow the women to compete in track and field.[23] This decision, however, did not end the debate concerning female athletes in the Olympics. Although the IOC voted to approve the participation of women in track and field, individual members of different athletic organizations were still allowed to express their own opinions.

One of those in the middle of the debate was Avery Brundage, who was to become the most influential person in regards to amateur athletics, male or female, in the world. In 1932 he was the head of the Amateur Athletic Union; over the next four decades he would go on to head the American Olympic Committee and then the International Olympic Committee. From these positions he was able to directly influence the competitive opportunities available to women for several decades. Brundage allied himself with women who were opposed to competitive athletics for girls and women. Responding to a letter written by Edith Gates, Director of Health Education of the YWCA, Brundage stated that he was ". . . in considerable sympathy with [her] ideas." Gates believed that:

> . . . championship events such as the AAU organizes are quite out of the usual realm of interest to the normal girl . . . I consider the spectacle of the Olympic Games one of the sorriest sights I have ever seen. There are so very, very few girls like Babe Didrikson, and an equal proportion of girls who would ever want to be like her. I hope that the American Committee on the Olympics and the AAU will see fit to omit the events for girls in the next Olympics.[24]

Brundage also communicated with Lou Henry Hoover and the Women's Division of the National Amateur Athletic Federation (NAAF) and he expressed support for their goal of eliminating women's athletic competition. In 1932 he expressed the opinion that perhaps the Greeks had the right idea when they barred women from the ancient Olympics.[25] Ernest Lee Jahncke, one of the American members to the IOC, opposed the participation of girls and women in the Olympic Games as well.[26] As an alternative to the women's athletic events at the 1932 Olympics in Los Angeles, he supported the proposed program of the Women's Division of the NAAF who offered to assist in entertaining the female participants by putting on a festival, which might include dancing, singing, music, mass sports and games, banquets and conferences.[27] Despite the increasing calls for the exclusion of women from the 1932 Games, they competed in a limited manner at Los Angeles.

The woman who is best remembered as a competitor from the 1932 Olympics is Mildred (Babe) Didrikson. Didrikson, who was a versatile athlete, is an example of a woman who stepped outside the boundaries that had been established for women's athletic competition in the 1920s. Babe was said to be equally proficient in swimming, boxing, tennis, baseball, basketball and track and field.[28] In one of the few interviews that she gave before she became a public figure following the 1932 Games, the reporter included an intimate discussion of her physical appearance:

> . . . her lines and features are almost wholly masculine. She isn't pretty in the usually accepted sense of the term, yet she is certainly far from unattractive. A husky voice, a direct manner of speech that often drops into the sporting argot, and an almost complete absence of feminine frills heighten the impression of masculinity. It is, however, a misleading impression. The Babe is thoroughly feminine. "I know I'm not pretty," she says, "but I do try to be graceful." She doesn't care much for boys but she has a few close girlfriends. She has no definite program of diet or training. She doesn't drink, of course, and doesn't smoke . . . "Are you trying to ask me," said Babe, in her husky, straight-to-the-point fashion, "if I wear girdles, brassieres and the rest of that junk?" . . . "The answer is no," she snapped. "What do you think I am, a sissy?[29]

Although the article claimed that Didrikson was "thoroughly feminine" there was little evidence within it to support the claim. The article enhanced the belief that successful female athletes, especially those in track and field, tended to be somewhat masculine in both their appearance and behavior.

The example of 'Babe' Didrikson in the decades following the 1920s also illustrates the consequences for stepping outside the boundaries that were drawn to define appropriate competition for women. At the 1932 Olympics, Didrikson won the 80 meter hurdles and the javelin throw and in 1943 she was acclaimed as the ". . . greatest woman athlete of all time. . . . "[30] From 1932 until 1943, however, she was rarely mentioned in the popular press. Other elite women athletes, such as tennis stars Helen Wills and Helen Jacobs, continued to be the subject of articles written during those years.[31] Didrikson spent the ten years following the Olympics of 1932 improving her golf game. Her public appearances during the 1930s included playing in professional women's basketball contests, appearing in celebrity golf tournaments and pitching against the Brooklyn Dodgers during spring training. In 1947, when she became a champion in women's professional golf, 'Babe' once again became a prominent example of the competitive woman athlete. In the late 1940s, however, she was complimented not only on her outstanding athletic ability, but on her transformation from tomboy athlete to ". . . pleasant, mannerly companion . . ." for her husband George Zaharias.[32] "Babe is a Lady Now," an article in *Life* magazine detailed her new feminine ways:

> Today Mildred Zaharias likes to perch a silly hat on her head, dress up in nylon stockings she once scorned, patronize the hair dresser and wear satins....A few years ago a sportswriter who had known the old Babe Didrikson stood on a golf course grinning at the new Mildred Zaharias. She was applying lipstick and rouge from a dainty compact. She grinned right back at him and said, 'Yeah, and Ah got silk on underneath and Ah like it.[33]

'Babe' had now completed the transformation from tomboy athlete in the early 1930s, who competed in track and field, baseball and basketball, and scorned "sissy" female undergarments, to the truly feminine athlete who was a competitive golfer and who loved her makeup and "silk." Although 'Babe' Didrikson Zaharias did not complete her transformation until the 1940s, she was a product of a philosophy that began in the late 1920s and early 1930s. Didrikson Zaharias no longer blurred the lines between male and female, thus she had become an acceptable example of a female athlete, not an object of fear or ridicule.

A Sport for Every Girl and A Girl for Every Sport

The area of women's athletic competition that women were most able to control was the programs in the colleges and universities. Although the female physical educators had been expanding their influence over women's athletics at the collegiate level since their inception in the late 19th century, it was in the 1920s that they began to exert maximum control, both at the local and the national level. The 1920s were a transitional decade for women's collegiate athletics. As the decade began, inter-school competition, although not universally accepted, was available to many of them. By 1924, young women who wanted to compete were discouraged by their physical education instructors who exerted tremendous influence over them. Even if they had wanted to continue competing intercollegiately after 1924 they would have been unable to do so as the competitive structure no longer existed at most colleges and universities in the United States.

By the early 1920s, several groups sought to control the organization and administration of women's athletics. In 1899, the National Women's Basketball Committee had formed and in 1917, the Committee on Women's Athletics (CWA) of the American Physical Education Association (APEA) was established to oversee the expanding athletic opportunities for girls and women.[34] Another group, which began administering national competitions in Track and

Field for women in 1922, was the Amateur Athletic Union (AAU). Martin A. Klein, the Chairman of the Metropolitan (N.Y.) Women's Committee on Activities of the AAU appealed to the male athletic clubs that were sponsoring indoor track meets to include events for women on their programs:

> Only through the co-operation of the organizations holding athletic meets can we hope to stimulate interest in women's athletics...the AAU has decided to conduct and supervise women's track and field competitions for the purpose of encouraging the women in beneficial competition. [By including women on the program] we expect to furnish plenty of activity for the women competitors and an abundance of interesting competition for admirers of this new branch of sport.[35]

Following the AAU's announcement that they would begin offering women's championships, the American Physical Education Association's (APEA) Committee on Women's Athletics, which was composed of prominent male and female physical educators, met to ". . . consider questions which may arise regarding athletics for girls and women."[36] When the Committee met in early 1923, they were confronted with the problem of deciding whether or not to cooperate with the AAU in its quest to control women's track and field. The AAU had asked several leading female physical educators to serve as members of an AAU advisory committee on women's athletics. One of the male members of the APEA Committee on Women's Athletics (CWA), George T. Hepbron of Spaulding Brother's Athletic Supply, suggested that the members of the CWA accept positions on the AAU's committee. Several of the women on the APEA-CWA, including Blanche Trilling, Ethel Perrin and Elizabeth Burchenal, felt that they could best demonstrate their disapproval of the AAU's attempts to control women's athletics by refusing to serve on their committee.[37] One reason that the women did not want to serve on the AAU's committee was that they would have been a minority of only a few women among a large organization of men. On the CWA of the APEA, they constituted more than half the membership and they would soon set up a controlling section of their own consisting entirely of women.

In April 1923, the Women's Division of the National Amateur Athletic Federation (NAAF) was organized to look into the ". . . special athletic and physical problems of girls and women." The defining statement of this organization, when compared to that of the CWA of the APEA is of special interest. Several women were on both committees, but while the CWA of the APEA had male members, the Women's Division of the NAAF consisted only of women. The APEA-CWA wanted to "consider question" in regards to girls and women's athletics. The NAAF's Women's Division, however, was interested in "special athletic and physical problems" of girls and women. The women of the NAAF's attempts to define women's athletics as unique ("special") was crucial to the definition of the appropriate types of girls and women's athletics. The term "problem" as opposed to "questions" in regards to athletics is of significance as well. The NAAF Women's Division continually sought to correct what they felt were problems with the current state of girls and women's athletics. The Committee on Women's Athletics of the APEA, meanwhile, sought to ". . . assemble practical information and prepare reports . . ." on the state of athletics for girls and women.[38]

Lou Henry Hoover, the wife of Herbert Hoover, was one of those selected to head the Women's Division of the NAAF. Mrs. Hoover was also involved with other girl's organizations as President of the Girl Scouts of America. Additionally, she actively supported Prohibition through her work on the Women's Committee for Law Enforcement (of the Prohibition

Laws).[39] Her involvement with these groups illustrated her interest in establishing and maintaining separate organizations for girls and women. As one of the chairpersons of the NAAF Women's Division organizing committee, she helped to give legitimacy to the question of defining appropriate athletic competition for girls and women. Mrs. Hoover also donated money to keep the Women's Division of the NAAF viable, and, after the demise of the Men's Division of the NAAF in 1924, she assisted in the direction of the NAAF to keep it a vital organization for women's athletics.[40] At the initial meeting of the Women's Division of the NAAF, the committee proclaimed:

> . . . We believe that we are in the early stages of a great advancement in athletics for girls and women which is destined to be of incalculable value for the vigor, health, and character training of girls and women as citizens and future mothers, or of greater possibilities for harm . . .[41]

This statement included several elements of the philosophy which the female physical educators hoped to instill in girls and women's athletic programs. The great advancement in athletics to which they referred was the expansion in the number of opportunities for women to compete. It is important that they were calling it the "early stages" because this left open the possibility of defining the issues to be addressed. The ability of sport, on the male model, as a useful tool in "character training" had begun to be disputed by physical educators, especially the women. They claimed that to avoid the problems that had developed in men's sports, they needed to design their own separate model. Character training to make women better citizens was of increased importance in the 1920s since women had just received the right to vote. Including a discussion of women as "future mothers" helped to establish another reason for a separate type of athletics for women. As discussed in the previous section on elite women athletes, concerns about women's reproductive health were a common theme in discussions of appropriate athletics for women.

One of the central objectives of the Women's Division of the NAAF was to create a clear distinction between women's competitive athletics and men's. The women claimed that they sought this separation because they feared male coaches would take over women's jobs. Additionally, they expressed the concern that male coaches did not properly understand the possible danger to women who competed during their menstrual period. They also believed that while men were interested only in *coaching* athletics, women were teachers who wished to *educate* their teams. Men who were interested in assisting female athletes were increasingly ostracized by female physical educators in the early 1920s. The experiences of Dr. Harry Stewart, of the New Have Normal School of Gymnastics, illustrate the wall that female physical educators wished to put between men and women's athletic competition.

In a 1922 article on women's track and field in the *American Physical Education Review*, the professional journal of the American Physical Education Association (APEA), Stewart outlined the objectives and standards of athletic competition for girls and women:

> Athletics properly supervised, with preliminary medical examinations and well constructed equipment, have been of immense benefit to participants in the development of self-control, vigorous health and sportsmanship. They do not tend to make a girl less womanly. I am frankly one of those who believe most sincerely in inter-school competition for girls within reasonable limits. . . . Marked benefit follows moderate exercise in normal girls during menstruation and there is growing tendency to avoid complete inactivity at this time. It must

be made a rule to take as much time and care to get girls into condition for strenuous sport as is used in developing the boy's teams.[42]

Stewart addressed some of the key issues in the building debate about appropriate forms of competition for girls and women. Inter-school competition was one of the central points in the debate. Female physical educators believed that eliminating inter-school varsity competition would be a visible sight that women had reasserted their control over girls and women's athletics. Stewart also believed that girls and women should train for athletic competition in the same manner as boys and men. This was a point that was strongly disputed by female physical educators who were interested in creating a unique type of program for girls and women. When the Committee on Women's Athletics of the APEA had formed in 1917, Stewart was not placed on the track and field committee; instead he was a member of the basketball committee. Even in 1923, when the CWA expanded, Stewart remained a member of the basketball committee.

This was significant because Stewart had recently become involved in the organization of women's track and field on an international scale through the International Federation for Women's Sport (IFWS). Stewart, who was the vice-president of the IFWS, agreed in August 1922, to take a team of female track athletes to the first International Women's Track and Field Meet in Paris. Stewart hoped that through their involvement in this international competition, women's track and field would gain a place on the Olympic program in 1924.[43] When the CWA of the APEA found out about Stewart's decision to take a team to the Paris meet, they contacted him and told him they disagreed with his decision. Stewart responded that he was obligated to bring a team to compete, but he promised on his return from Paris to cooperate with the APEA in the organization of women's track and field. However, when Stewart returned he established the National Women's Track Athletic Association (NWTAA) to guide and direct women's track athletics. The organizing committee of the NWTAA consisted of four men and eight women; none of the women were involved in the APEA or the NAAF's attempts to control women's athletics. Stewart had stepped completely outside the organizational structure that women physical educators were constructing to control women's athletics in the 1920s.

Stewart and his newly established committee represented some of the female physical educator's greatest fears. They were concerned that their organizations, such as the Women's Division of the NAAF and the Committee on Women's Athletics of the APEA, would become obsolete if groups such as Stewart's and the AAU continued to organize women's competitions. Although the female physical educators wished to control all segments of women's athletic competition, they were forced to initially focus on women's athletic competition at the colleges and universities of which they were a part. From programs instituted at this level they would begin to influence the development of girl's athletic programs in the high schools. Their effect over the competitive programs for women outside of the school and university setting would remain limited, especially during the 1920s, but by the 1930s, they increasingly influenced the debate over appropriate competition for women at the national and international level.

Female physical educators had sought to develop unique types of sport for women in the decades prior to 1920. Soon after James Naismith developed the game of basketball at Springfield College in 1891, Senda Berensen, of nearby Smith College, and others adapted the rules of the game for girls and women. The women's game divided the court into segments to reduce the amount of running that each girl had to do and also included rules to limit fouls and overexertion. By 1920, some female physical educators were calling for a re-evaluation of women's rules. One physical educator, Helen Kirk, of Philadelphia, declared in the APER in 1920:

> The time has come when basketball for women ought to be changed in the schools and colleges. In the last decade women have increased tremendously in their strength, energy and coordination of mind and body; while the game has not changed in its science in proportion to this increase. Women today are more ready to play a quick, skillful game and a game more filled to show these superior qualities...today we have a new type of athlete in our schools and colleges; we have a more robust, active, a more daring type which is eager for a game which will meet this added strength.[44]

Women like Kirk believed that it was acceptable for women to compete with the men's rules. Additionally, she encouraged women to display their increased skills in public competition. Kirk's belief that the rules of women's basketball needed to be changed to reflect the increasingly competitive nature of women's athletics was shared by few female physical educators. One woman who did not agree with Kirk was Elizabeth Richards of Smith College. Richards felt that if women competed too strenuously in basketball, many problems would result. Some of her arguments against inter-school competition based on men's rules included:

1. the fact that they allowed for participation by too few people;
2. they took too much time and energy;
3. they tended toward the professional rather than the recreational spirit;
4. they were apt to make girls play for the fighting spirit and to get before the public rather than for fun;
5. they were apt to cause too great tension and nervous strain;
6. they were apt to lead to mental and physical strain.[45]

The significance of these arguments should not be overlooked as they were to become the core of the philosophy of appropriate athletics for women that developed in the 1920s.

Many women were involved in the development of women's athletics in the 1920s. Several of the women who influenced the definition of appropriate athletic competition for women were graduates of the Boston Normal School of Gymnastics (BNSG). These women were trained as physical educators. Unlike most male coaches, female coaches were members of Physical Education departments. For some men, by the 1920s, coaching at the collegiate level had become a career. There were no such opportunities for women. Amy Morris Homans, the director of the BNSG from 1889–1918, strongly influenced each woman who graduated from the BNSG. Homan's philosophy incorporated the belief that "...each girl graduate not only as a trained physical educator, but a lady of fine character."[46]

Blanche Trilling, a graduate of the BNSG and chair of the Department of Physical Education for Women at the University of Wisconsin, was the chair of both the Committee on Women's Athletics of the APEA and the organizing committee of the Women's Division of the NAAF. These were the two organizations which had the greatest impact on the development of appropriate competition for women. At the 1922 meeting of the CWA of the APEA, Trilling discussed the present state of women's athletics. She said that women realized that their programs were behind those of men, but, to avoid the problems associated with the men's athletic programs, women had chosen to proceed slowly. The primary concerns of female physical educators, according to Trilling, were the educational aspects of athletics and the importance of mass participation rather than individual glory.[47] Trilling also expressed concern that some girl's and women's basketball teams continued to play under boy's rules and were coached by men. Responding to women such as Helen Kirk, Trilling said that the committee needed to continue to work to modify the game of basketball for women to make it ". . . safe and sane for the majority."[48]

Another influential physical educator, Ethel Perrin, also expressed interest in the present state of girls and women's athletics. Perrin, a graduate and former faculty member of the BNSG, supported limited athletic competition for girls and women. However, she sought to discourage the girls and women's athletic teams which were traveling unchaperoned from town to town to play basketball games, many still coached by men. Additionally, she disagreed with women who were competing on the international level at events such as the Olympics.[49]

Mabel Lee, the first woman president of the American Physical Education Association, was another prominent graduate of the BNSG. In an influential article in 1924 she set forth the case for and against women's intercollegiate athletics based on a survey she had conducted of fifty college and university athletic programs. In what she referred to as a "thorough" study, Lee listed the effects of athletics upon girls who made athletic teams and girls who didn't. She also included the effect that athletics had upon the teaching staff of the colleges and universities. At the end of the article she included her suggestions for improving the athletic programs for girls and women. These centered on the elimination of interscholastic and intercollegiate competition:

> . . . intercollegiate athletics for women do not exist at the leading colleges of the United States, except in limited numbers, varsity competition was found only in a few eastern schools, interclass-intercollegiate competition was found only in the far west and the telegraphic meet was favored in the Midwest. Of those women physical educators who had experience in intercollegiate athletics for women, 93% opposed it.[50]

Although these seemed to be significant results, the survey was limited in scope as it was based on only fifty colleges and universities. In addition, most of the schools that had responded to the survey already belonged to the NAAF and supported its philosophy and program.

As stated by Mabel Lee, many of the female physical educators had competed in inter-school athletics while they were students. Now that they were in positions of authority, however, they were renouncing inter-school competition for a new generation of girls and women. Lillian Schoedler, the Executive Secretary of the Women's Division of the NAAF, although not a trained physical educator, was a self-described former "star" athlete. She believed that she could only describe her competitive past as a negative experience:

> We certainly were a selfish, unconstructive lot of college students . . . Our athletic association was merely a means of making possible the activities which a few of us wanted . . . It is with shame that I realize the part which . . . I played . . . We were doing the best we could with the light we had—and our fault was not a lack of willingness, but of guidance.[51]

Schoedler faulted the generation of female teachers and coaches who had influenced her. With proper guidance, she believed that the Women's Division of the NAAF could correct the mistakes of the past. Other women, who were professional physical educators, expressed similar feelings in regards to women's athletic competition.

In 1931 Mabel Lee presented the results of her survey once again in the *Research Quarterly* of the American Physical Education Association. She included anecdotal descriptions of the feelings of female physical educators at the college and university level in regards to the benefits and harms—physically, mentally and socially—of intercollegiate athletics for women. One woman observed:

> The competitive element is already greatly overemphasized in all phases of our society. With the comparatively recent background which we have for women's athletics, a country wide acceptance of the 'varsity' idea must necessarily be based on the poor standards of men. I do not believe we are in the stage of development which warrants a belief that this type of activity can be promoted to the extent that it will be beneficial.[52]

Another female physical educator was even more dramatic in her argument against women's intercollegiate competition:

> Let us fight if necessary to keep our young women free to play healthfully and wholesomely. As a student I was captain of our varsity hockey team that played matches with two different colleges as "curtain raisers" to football games. As a young teacher I refereed many a shameful interscholastic basketball match. Any one, who has had such experiences and is interested in educational ideals and in creating in this world a spirit of friendliness towards others, knows that there is positively nothing of value to gain in an intercollegiate program, but that there is much of value to lose.[53]

Most of the women who responded to Lee's survey had competed in intercollegiate sports. Additionally, they had either coached or refereed interscholastic sports for girls and women. Why, if they had been so adverse to women's competition, had they previously been such active promoters and participants? Now that a new type of athletics for girls and women was being proposed, female physical educators were eager to become part of it. They quickly realized that if they wished to remain as physical educators, they had to fit into the framework that was being developed. Moving outside of the boundaries meant that a female physical educator would most likely lose her job. Additionally, she risked losing the acceptance and approval of her colleagues. Once these women decided to become part of the "new" model for women's athletic competition, they denounced their competitive past and supported the new programs as vigorously as possible.

Promoting this new philosophy of appropriate types of competition for girls and women was one of the primary goals of the female physical educators. To achieve this goal, soon after the establishment of the Women's Division of the NAAF, plans were made to transition from a national organization to a broader local organization.[54] This transition would allow the NAAF to acquire greater influence over girls and women's high school and recreational sports, in addition to those in colleges and universities. Promotional speeches were given at recreation meetings, state educational conferences, and physical education meetings; where ever a group interested in girls and women's athletics gathered. The speeches tended to follow a similar format. They began by informing the organization they were addressing that women's athletics was at a critical stage in its development. Programs of the past, with inter-school competition, male coaches and win at all cost methods, needed to be discarded and the NAAF's program of the future adopted. They would then relate to the audience one of the "horror stories" of the state of girls and women's athletics before the "rational" intervention of the Women's Division of the NAAF:

> I wonder how many individuals who watch a girl's basketball game and think what a wonderful thing it is to see these girls playing an active game, and how much it does for the school, etc., have ever gone behind the scenes at the close of a game and seen that same group in a state of hysteria, their nervous systems completely broken, and all thoughts of sportsmanship, loyalty and health thrown to the four winds in the winning or losing of that game.[55]

Another woman recalled a high school basketball tournament where "The team was utterly exhausted by playing six games in two days and three girls were removed from the floor in fainting and hysterical condition..."[56]

The speaker would then conclude with a glowing summary of the current state of women's athletics at the collegiate level since the end of intercollegiate competition and the start of play days and field days.[57] Finally, the group would be encouraged to adopt this new form of competition for their programs, whether they were high schools, colleges or recreation departments. Even with an extensive promotional campaign, the central focus of the female physical educator's program remained the reform of the women's athletic programs in the colleges and universities. It was there that they exerted the most control, and they would also influence the next generation of young women through their teaching.

Playing By the Rules

The 1934 volume *Recent Social Trends* claimed that one of the distinguishing characteristics of American education was the fact that girls and women had the opportunity to secure an education beyond the elementary level. In 1920, 128,677 women were enrolled in colleges. By 1930, that number had more than doubled to 311,842.[58] Women received their post-secondary education at public and private coeducational universities, normal schools and teacher's colleges, and at women's colleges.

Mills College, a small women's college located in Oakland, California, had an extensive activity program which included interclass and intercollegiate athletics by 1920. According to reports in the *Mills College Weekly*, intense competition and school spirit were integral parts of the athletic program from 1920-22. Victory in competition was one of the primary goals of the athletic program:

> . . . If we expect to show Stanford and California a few things in hockey and handball it is time we were taking matters more seriously. Last year [handball] was the only sport in which Mills was not victorious, . . . shall we make the interest this year insure our winning . . . in an intercollegiate game? A defeat like that of last year must not be repeated. . . . Mills College has a remarkable player in the person of Dorothy Holland, who played on Saturday a spectacular game.[59]

These quotes from the Mills College Weekly demonstrate that the athletic program at Mills included many of the competitive aspects that the female physical educators sought to eliminate from women's athletics. Women at Mills were encouraged to compete not only for fun but for victory as well. Additionally, individual stars were lauded and the college newspaper claimed it was "fortunate" to have outstanding individual players.[60] The female physical educators in charge of the athletic programs at Mills expressed support for the intercollegiate competitions in many ways. They would hold extra practices in the mornings and on weekends and they also helped the students to organize the intercollegiate contests with Stanford and California.[61]

At the nearby co-educational University of California, sports for women were an important part of the activity program. Intercollegiate athletic competition began in 1896 with a basketball game against Stanford University. By 1920, dozens of athletic teams were organized for women at the class, organization and varsity level. Several hundred spectators would attend the different types of contests which were held throughout the semester.[62] Additionally, in 1922, more than 2,000 women attended an athletic rally for women's sports. Athletics for women, the student yearbook claimed, held a high place in campus interest.[63]

At the University of California, unlike Mills College, men sometimes entered the debate on the definition of appropriate athletics for women. Men expressed interest in women who were participating in athletics. Although the women's Physical Education department was separate from the Men's, male instructors did at times influence the female students. Frank Kleeberger, the head of the men's department of Physical Education, was the coordinator of the department's summer school program which admitted both men and women, thus his beliefs in regards to appropriate competition for women were significant. In 1920 Kleeberger expressed his concern that athletic competition could possibly make women less feminine:

> The physical education of girls should aim at practical objectives and at the same time seek to make women more feminine, avoiding the development of masculine traits of mind and body . . . dancing, swimming, athletic games and gymnasium exercises based upon natural rather than artificial coordination should constitute the basis for physical education for girls . . . physical training for women should occupy itself with the elimination of undesirable mannerisms, with the development of grace in carriage and the promotion of good taste in dress and conduct.[64]

Kleeberger supported an entirely separate type of Physical Education for girls and women, one that would consciously seek to make them "more feminine." Although Kleeberger did not state which undesirable mannerisms he would like to see eliminated, the fact that posture improvement was an extremely important part of physical training for women in the early 20th century, would lead one to believe he was interested in improving women's "carriage."

The student newspaper at California occasionally provided a forum for debates concerning issues related to women's physical activity. In one "Letter to the Editor," a male student argued that: women did not play tennis for the benefit of a stimulated blood circulation or excessive perspiration or to reduce their increasing girth. He claimed that women were more concerned with their skirts than their tennis.[65] The writer could possibly have been upset about the limited availability of the University tennis courts, which at times were reserved exclusively for women. A group of women responded to the letter by arguing that they were required by the University to wear their skirts during tennis, although not during other sport activities. The women raised the question as to whether tennis was to be considered an "athletic" contest or an "aesthetic" one. They would rather wear their "bloomer" costumes for the greater mobility that was possible in the less restrictive garments.[66]

From 1920–22, intercollegiate contests with Stanford and Mills were the culmination of nearly every women's sport activity at California. The Women's Athletic Association (WAA) of each of the schools organized the competitions. Additionally, some non-competitive activities such as hiking were under the direction of the WAA.[67] By 1923, the recreationally oriented "Outing Club" (Crop and Saddle, hiking, riflery) of the University of California, had increased substantially in popularity and the number of intercollegiate contests was reduced. However, more than 1,000 girls still competed in athletics of some type in 1923. The WAA eagerly encourage competition and provided the opportunity for elite competition for selected young women.[68]

One reason for the decrease in intercollegiate competition at California in 1923 was the decision the previous year by Mills College to reduce the number of intercollegiate competitions in which they participated. Women at Mills College began to express concerns about intercollegiate competition even before the Women's Division of the NAAF had organized to define and control women's athletics. The student body was asked to vote on the withdrawal of Mills from the intercollegiate triangle "league" of California, Stanford and Mills. According to the Mills College Weekly:

> The principle reason for bringing this debated issue to a crisis, was a letter received from Stanford stating since Mills had defaulted four games within the past two and one half years, Stanford considered it her duty to warn Mills that if another game was defaulted some 'drastic action would be taken.'. . . Mills feels that because of the seemingly unavoidable, petty differences between the contestants, the real spirit of the sport is lost, and therefore there is nothing to be gained from intercollegiate athletics.[69]

The article continued by suggesting "those who knew the details of intercollegiate competition," most likely referring to the female physical educators, had wanted for some time to restrict competition to the interclass variety. Mills College students believed that the debate surrounding the issue of competition for women to be at a crisis point. Their reaction was to reduce the schedule, not abandon it completely. Without the influence of a national organization to discourage them from competing, the students and physical educators at Mills College still supported intercollegiate athletics, but on a somewhat more limited scale. Not everyone at Mills was united behind the decision to de-emphasize intercollegiate competition. In the same issue of the newspaper that denounces intercollegiate athletics, students were urged to come out and root for Mills at the upcoming intercollegiate basketball game with California, so that Mill's athletic reputation would not be "diminished."[70] The following fall, however, the intercollegiate program was reduced to four contests. The students still supported the athletic teams and students were encouraged to participate in athletics as well as attend contests as spectators.

Throughout the rest of 1923 and the fall of 1924, Mills continued to compete in a limited number of intercollegiate field hockey, handball, basketball and tennis contests with California and Stanford. This limited program of competition would not last very long, however, as the impact of the Women's Division of the NAAF began to be felt at Mills, California and Stanford in the Spring of 1924. The Western Athletic Conference of the Athletic Conference of American College Women (ACACW) was held at the University of California in April 1924 and the three schools were among the delegates to the conference. After much debate, the delegates decided that they were "definitely opposed" to all forms of intercollegiate competition in which the teams actually met.[71] Their justification for supporting this decision was that intercollegiate athletics were harmful to women and caused too great a strain on the individual players. They also felt that intense rivalries caused rough, strenuous play, and women's athletics had the potential of becoming as commercialized as the men's programs. The solution, according to the delegates, was interclass play days. They believed that this was the only way to further the true aim of athletics for girls and women.[72] All of the "new" beliefs that the delegates to the conference set forth were based on the philosophy of the recently formed NAAF Women's Division.

Just prior to the Western Athletic Conference in 1924, the Women's 'C' Society, a group of the top female athletes on the University of California campus, gathered to discuss Mabel Lee's article which set forth the case for and against women's intercollegiate athletics. This group of women would be most affected by the decision to withdraw from intercollegiate competition since they were mostly the first team 'varsity' athletes. It is significant that there was almost no mention of their beliefs in regards to intercollegiate competition in the minutes of their meetings. The minutes from the Spring of 1924, when competition ceased, did not in any way reflect their feelings about this decision. If these women disagreed with the decision to limit athletics to interclass competitions, they did not express themselves very vehemently. The following September, some suggestions were made by the Women's 'C' Society to "improve" sports for women at California:

> More attention should be put on interclass and second teams so that the people who do not make the teams may be kept interested. . . . Hockey practices [should] be more informal, less serious, and the girls should not be discouraged early in the semester by rating tests. . . . Emphasize the social side of sports, . . . do not overemphasize efficiency and rules and lose the spirit of fun.[73]

The emphasis of the athletic program had obviously been on the first team intercollegiate squad prior to this time. But, following the policies of the Women's Division of the NAAF, women's athletics now aimed to provide opportunities for more women to participate. It was also to become a more social and less serious activity.

The Women's Athletic Association (WAA), the student group responsible for organizing women's athletics at the University of California, soon realized that they too would have to react to the new philosophy on competition. The policy committee of the WAA met in February 1925 to discuss interclass-intercollegiate competition and decided that they were "definitely opposed" to intercollegiate athletics; California favored a Triangle play day with Mills and Stanford if it could be arranged.[74] On the California campus in the Spring of 1925 some women still favored competition and were upset by the lack of intercollegiate contests. According to the Women's 'C' Society, the number of women involved in the interclass athletic program that Spring had dropped to 708. The previous Spring, nearly 1,900 women had participated in the interclass-intercollegiate competitions. The WAA had a somewhat smaller number of participants listed in their report for Spring 1924 (1,130), and there was no report for 1925.[75] Even with this incomplete date, it would seem that many women who had previously competed intercollegiately chose not to participate in the exclusively interclass program.[76]

In 1925, Lillian Schoedler, the executive secretary of the Women's Division of the National Amateur Athletic Federation, explained the ideas of the new type of competition to a group of students and faculty on the University of California campus. According to Schoedler, men and women needed to work independently and unhampered in their own fields, thus the need for a separate Women's Division of the NAAF to be responsible for girls and women's athletics. Women's athletics now strived to adapt athletics for girls, and reduce the strain possible in athletics.[77] Schoedler's speech was part of the promotional campaign that the NAAF had embarked upon to bring their philosophy to the local level. A group of physical educators attending summer school was the perfect audience to receive their message. The Women's Division of the NAAF, along with the Committee on Women's Athletics of the APEA, actively sought to change the rules of the different sports in order to make them more acceptable for girls and women.[78]

In the Fall of 1925, Mills and California were ready to renew athletic event with play days, which the NAAF recommended as an alternative to the old intercollegiate forms of competition.[79] Stanford University, however, was reluctant to denounce the old ideal of intercollegiate competition. In 1925, Stanford refused to participate in the Triangle play day that Mills and California organized. Then, in 1928, at the Western Athletic Conference, Stanford requested that the colleges return to the interclass-intercollegiate form of competition. Stanford claimed that interest in sport, especially on their campus, had waned considerably since intercollegiate sports programs had changed to play days. Although this pattern had occurred at other colleges and universities (including, for a short time, the University of California) the delegates stated that they were "absolutely opposed" to returning to any form of intercollegiate competition. Stanford had no choice but to rescind their request and accept the programs of the Women's Division of the NAAF and the Committee on Women's Athletics of the APEA, if they did not want to be isolated from the other colleges and universities.[80] Elaborate interclass field weeks continued throughout the end of the decade at Mills and California. The yearly triangle sports/field day with Stanford, Mills and California was no longer a forum for intercollegiate competition, but rather a time for fun and play among the women of all three institutions.

By the end of the decade, the number of women involved in sports rose as they adapted to the new forms of competition that were offered. The 1928 interclass basketball tournament at California included twenty-four teams.[81] Additionally, intercollegiate competition resumed in the form of "telegraphic meets" which did not require the competitors to actually meet face to face.[82] Other post-secondary institutions in the Bay Area became interested in the Triangle play day and requested admittance to the activity. San Jose and San Francisco State Normal Schools and Dominican College were all possible members of an expanded play day "league." As long as the women from the various institutions utilized this form of "competition," they were strongly encouraged by the Women's Division of the NAAF and the Committee on Women's Athletics of the APEA. They believed that the more schools that were involved in play days the better, as that provided evidence that they were reaching their goal of wider control of women's athletics.[83]

Conclusion

Although it appeared that men were assisting in the expansion of women's elite athletic, a closer examination revealed the attempts by some men to restrict women's competition. When the Amateur Athletic Union made a decision to invite women to compete in their track and field championships, they were responding to not only the increase in the number of women who were participating in track and field, but, additionally, to the other organizations that were attempting to organize women's athletics. Harry Stewart's National Women's Track Athletic Association would have intruded upon the AAU's territory so they could not allow him to continue to organize track and field for women. By sponsoring championships for women in track and field, they solidified their position as the representative of all amateur athletics outside of the colleges and universities.

The International Olympic Committee (IOC) provided another forum for elite women's athletics in the 1920s. The addition of women's events to the Olympic program was a slow and deliberate process, however, and this gave the IOC some control over women's athletics. Many influential members of the IOC sought to restrict the events available to women according to values and beliefs that the members supported. The increasing influence of the Olympic movement throughout the 20th century made it a compelling force for defining appropriate versus inappropriate athletics for women. Some individual men did seek to expand athletic opportunities for elite women athletes. Harry Stewart and Gustavus Kirby each went out of their way to expand the programs and competitions that were available to women. However, predominantly male organizations such as the AAU and the IOC, although they presented some new opportunities for elite women athletes, oftentimes put restrictions on the type of competition that would be designated as official.

Elite women athletes were encouraged to compete in two sports in the 1920s, golf and tennis. Class considerations made these sports more acceptable to men and women who were interested in elite women's athletics. The upper class, country club set were the supporters of both sports and the fact that the female participants were not required to exhibit visible strain made them even more suitable. Even if a tennis player such as Helen Wills exerted herself on the court, in her skirt and rolled stocking she was definitely feminine.

Women's control over women's athletics was restricted in the 1920s to the colleges and universities. In these institutions, with an increasing number of female students as the decade progressed, they sought to create their own unique programs for girls and women. Mrozek has stated that for men the impetus behind the desire to control women's athletics was an underlying fear of loss of identity and purpose. For women as well, fear was a powerful fundamental motivation in their attempts to define and control women's athletics. The female physical educators believed very strongly in the need to keep women's athletics separate from men's. They continually expressed the fear that without the cessation of intercollegiate competition for women, the women's programs were in danger of becoming duplicates of the men's programs. The women also established modified rules for sports so that it would take a distinct type of knowledge to coach and officiate them as compared with male sports.

The female physical educators defined what the athletic program was to be for girls and women. (Play days and telegraphic meets) In the realm where they exerted the most control and influence—the colleges and universities—they implemented their programs on as wide a scale as possible. However, restricted forms of competition were never unanimously supported by female physical educators. Those who did disagree, however, were shut out of the organizational structure of women's college athletics.

The female physical educators were concerned that their programs be established in as many schools, colleges and organizations as possible. They sought the acceptance of national organizations such as the Women's Division of the NAAF and the Committee on Women's Athletics of the APEA, and, although they did not achieve their instrumental goal of stopping all women from competing, the symbolic acceptance of their programs as the norm for women's competitive athletics for the next fifty years was of great significance.[84]

Carroll Smith-Rosenberg has claimed that the generation of women of the 1920s sought to be autonomous through the use of androgynous language and behavior. In this way they endeavored to affirm their validity and centrality, but they only verified their intensifying marginality—to both women and men.[85] Independent activities, such as elite athletic competition or intercollegiate competition, were increasingly defined as inappropriate in the 1920s; and female physical educators quickly organized to establish organizations to control athletics for girls and women in colleges and universities. Because young women who participated in athletics on college campuses in the 1920s sought the acceptance of both their peers and their instructors, they were quick to support the philosophy of the "new" athletics for girls and women.

Endnotes

1. Violet B. Marshall, "Are You One of These?" *Newsletter of the Athletic Conference of American College Women*, Department of Physical Education Archives, University of California, Berkeley (hereafter cited as DPEA), 1925, 7.

2. "Annual Report of the President of the W.A.A.," DPEA, May 1924.

3. "W.A.A. Advisor's Report—Review of W.A.A.," DPEA, Spring 1930.

4. Donald A. Mrozek, "The 'Amazon' and the American 'Lady': Sexual Fears of Women as Athletes," in J.A. Mangan and R.J. Park, eds., *From "Fair Sex" to Feminism: Sport and the Socialization of Women in the Industrial and Post-Industrial Eras* (London: Frank Cass and Co., Ltd., 1987): 283-284.

5. Mrozek, "The 'Amazon' and the American 'Lady'," 283. For a more comprehensive examination of the fears and concerns of men and women in the late nineteenth and early twentieth centuries over the oftentimes dislocating changes that were occuring see, Robert H. Wiebe, *The Search for Order, 1877–1920* (New York: Hill and Wang, 1967).

6. John D'Emilio and Estelle Freedman, *Intimate Matters: A History of Sexuality in America* (New York: Harper and Row Publishers, 1988): 233.

7. Donald Mrozek, "Sport in American Life," in Kathryn Grover, ed., *Fitness in American Culture: Images of Health, Sport and the Body, 1830–1940* (Amherst: University of Massachusetts Press, 1989): 42. In *Recent Social Trends in the United States: Report of the President's Research Committee on Social Trends* (New York: McGraw-Hill Book Company, Inc., 1934) one chapter is devoted to recreation and leisure. Additionally, the chapter on education includes a discussion of the 1929 Carnegie Foundation report *American College Athletics*. The report stated that the administration of athletics in schools and colleges was out of control. No mention was made of women athletes in the entire volume.

8. For an overview of women's athletic participation see, E. Gerber, J. Felshin, P. Berlin and W. Wyrick, eds., *The American Woman in Sport* (Reading, MA: Addison-Wesley, 1974); Reet Howell, ed., *Her Story in Sport: An Historical Anthology of Women in Sports* (West Point, NY: Leisure Press, 1982); Stephanie Twin, ed., *Out of the Bleachers* (New York: The Feminist Press, 1979); Mary A. Boutillier and Lucinda SanGiovanni, *The Sporting Woman* (Champaign: Human Kinetics, 1983).

9. Allen Guttman, *The Games Must Go On: Avery Brundage and the Olympic Movement* (New York: Columbia University Press, 1984): 56. For more on de Coubertin, his ideology and its influence on the development of the modern Olympic movement, see John J. MacCaloon, *This Great Symbol: Pierre de Coubertin and the Origins of the Modern Olympic Games* (Chicago: University of Chicago Press, 1981).

10. "Miss Ethelda Bleibtrey Twice Betters World's Record for 100 Meter Swim," *New York Times* 11 July 1920.

11. "Greeks, Girls and 1944," *The Nation* 27 February 1924.

12. "Girl May Race Men Olympians," *New York Times* 9 March 1924.

13. "How a Girl Beat Leander at the Hero Game," *Literary Digest* 21 August 1926, 54.

14. "Athletics for Women," *School Life* April 1924. Several articles claimed that sports would cause serious damage to women's reproductive health. "Strenuous athletics can cause bruises on the breast and abdomen which are likely to be serious. Jumping and falling sometimes result in displacements which require an operation to prevent sterility." Mary B. Ryan, "A College Training in Health," *Hygeia* October 1926.

15. "Frailty Thy Name is Not Woman," *Woman Citizen* June 1927; "Girl Who Fanned Babe Ruth," "Will American Girls Decide the 1924 Olympics," "Man's Athletic Crown in Danger," *Literary Digest* 18 April 1931, 19 April 1924, 28 July 1923; "Illusion of Masculine Supremacy," *Canada Magazine* May 1935.

16. Grantland Rice, "Look Out for the Ladies!" *Colliers* 21 February 1925, 18.

17. Ederle's record for the English Channel crossing was surpassed by a male swimmer within a few months.

18. Grantland Rice, "Slightly Weaker Sex," *Colliers,* 29 September 1928, 12.

19. "Olympic Tryouts for Women, July 4," *New York Times,* 1 April 1928.

20. "Americans Beaten in Four Olympic Tests," *New York Times,* 3 August 1928.

21. The 800 meter race for women was not included in the Olympic Games again until 1960, in 1968 the 1500 meter race was added and in 1984 the marathon. Questions about the appropriateness of distance events for women were once again raised when Swiss runner, Gabriele Andersen-Scheiss struggled, in obvious physical distress, to complete the 1984 marathon.

22. "Americans Capture Two Olympic Events," *New York Times,* 1 August 1928.

23. "Olympic Officials Face New Problems," *New York Times,* 22 May 1930.

24. Edith M. Gates, "Personal Communication to Daniel J. Ferris," 3 March 1933, Box 111, Avery Brundage Collection, California State University, Long Beach.

25. "Greeks Were Right, Brundage Believes," *New York Times,* 25 December 1932. For more on Brundage and his influence on the Olympics see Allen Guttmann, *The Games Must Go On: Avery Brundage and the Olympic Movement* (New York: Columbia University Press, 1984).

26. "Wants Women Barred," *New York Times,* 8 June 1930.

27. "Fifth Annual Meeting, Women's Division, National Amateur Athletic Federation," *American Physical Education Review,* 1929.

28. Arthur J. Daley, "World Mark Set by Miss Didrikson," *New York Times,* 26 July 1931.

29. "Texas Flash," *Colliers,* 6 August 1932.

30. "Whatever Became Of . . .," *Saturday Evening Post,* 20 November 1943, 91.

31. In the *Reader's Guide to Periodical Literature,* from 1932–1943, there were twenty-three articles by or about Wills, twenty by or about Jacobs and eight about Didrikson.

32. Gene Farmer, "Babe is a Lady Now," *Life,* 23 June 1947, 90.

33. Ibid.

34. Joan S. Hult, "The Governance of Athletics for Girls and women: Leadership by Women Physical Educators, 1899-1949," *Research Quarterly for Exercise and Sport.* Centennial Issue. 1985. 64. Hult's article thoroughly describes the various groups that organized to administer women's collegiate athletics in the first half of the 20th century.

35. "Women's Program is Ready for Vote, *New York Times,* 13 December 1922.

36. "Committee on Women's Athletics," *American Physical Education Review,* 1922, 298.

37. Blanche Trilling, "Women's Athletic Committee Report," *American Physical Education Review,* 1923, 68–69.

38. Elmer D. Mitchell, "The American Physical Education Association," *Journal of Health and Physical Education,* January 1932, 46.

39. Dale C. Mayer, "An Uncommon Woman: The Quiet Leadership Style of Lou Henry Hoover," *Presidential Studies Quarterly* **20**, Fall 1990, 689.

40. ibid., 690.

41. "Report on the Committee on Organization of the Committee on Athletics and Physical Education for Women and Girls, April 6 and 7, 1923, at Washington, D.C.," *American Physical Education Review*, 1923, 284.

42. Harry E. Stewart, "Track Athletics for Women," *American Physical Education Review*, 1922, 207.

43. "Women's Athletic Tryout Arranged," *New York Times*, 16 April 1922.

44. Helen R. Kirk, "Discussion," *American Physical Education Review*, 1920, 411.

45. Elizabeth Richards, "Everyday Problems in Girl's Basketball," *American Physical Education Review*, 1920, 407.

46. Ellen Gerber, *Innovators and Institutions in Physical Education* (Philadelphia: Lea and Febiger, 1971). In 1909, the Boston Normal School of Gymnastics moved to Wellesley College. Homans remained in charge of the new department of physical education until her retirement in 1918.

47. Cynthia M. Wesson, "Purposes of the Committee on Women's Athletic of the American Physical Education Association and its Progress Up to the Present," *NEA Proceedings and Addresses*, 1922, 1095.

48. ibid., 1096.

49. Ethel Perrin, "Girl's Athletics-Abstract," *NEA Proceedings and Addresses*, 1924, 643.

50 Mabel Lee, "The Case For and Against Intercollegiate Athletics for Women and the Situation as it Stands To-day," *American Physical Education Review*, 1924, 13, 19.

51. Lillian Schoedler, "Inter-relationship of ACACW and NAAF," *Newsletter of the Athletic Conference of American College Women*, DPEA, 1925.

52. Mabel Lee, "The Case For and Against Women's Athletics," *Research Quarterly*, 1931.

53. ibid.

54. Lillian Schoedler, "Report of Progress, Women's Division, National Amateur Athletic Federation of America," *American Physical Education Review*, 1924, 305.

55. Helen N. Smith, "Athletic Education," *American Physical Education Review*, 1927.

56. Helen L. Coops, "Sports for Women," *American Physical Education Review*, 1926.

57. A play day was a form of competition during which athletes from two or more schools would come together to form new teams. None of the newly formed teams would represent the participating institutions. In this way the girls could experience the benefits of inter-school athletics without the "harmful" side effects of school spirit and excessive competition.

58. *Recent Social Trends in the United States*, 342. The percentage of women in colleges in 1920 was 37.7% and in 1930 41.4%. Additionally, nearly 300,000 students who attended teacher's colleges and normal schools were not included in the survey's totals.

59. "Athletic Notes," *Mills College Weekly*, 30 September 1920; "Hockey and Handball," *Mills College Weekly*, 21 October 1920; "Who Wins," *Mills College Weekly*, 28 October 1920, 4.

60. "Mills-UC Games Close," *Mills College Weekly*, 3 Novemeber 1921, 1.

61. "Hockey," *Mills College Junior Yearbook*, 1922, 132.

62. "Women's Athletics," *Blue and Gold*, 1921, 282.

63. "Sports and Pastimes," *Blue and Gold*, 1922, 294.

64. "Women Taught the Art of Self-defense," *The Intersession Bulletin*, 19 May 1920, 1.

65. "Women and Exercise," *The Summer Session Californian*, 16 July 1920, 4.

66. "From the Bloomin' Ladies," *The Summer Session Californian*, 20 July 1920, 4.

67. "Hiking," *Blue and Gold*, 1924, 285.

68. *Minutes of the Women's Athletic Council*, DPEA, 27 February 1923.

69. "Athletics to Be Limited," *Mills College Weekly*, 16 March 1922, 1.

70. "Intercollegiate Basketball," *Mills College Weekly*, 16 March 1922, 3.

71. *Report of the Athletic Conference of American College Women*, DPEA, 10–12 April 1924, 19–20.

72. "Athletic Conference Held," *Mills College Weekly*, 17 April 1924, 1.

73. *Minutes of the Women's 'C' Society*, DPEA, 2 April 1924; 3 September 1924; 17 November 1924.

74. *Minutes of the Women's Athletic Council*, DPEA, 10 February 1925.

75. *Annual Report of the President of the WAA*, DPEA, May 1924. The only report that was missing from the 1920-1930 file was the 1925 report.

76. *Minutes of the Women's 'C' Society*, DPEA, 19 March 1925.

77. "Athletic Ideals Explained in Talk," *The Daily Californian*, 24 July 1925, 7.

78. Hult, "Governance," The CWA of the APEA exerted tremendous control over the rules by editing their own rule books for the various sports and designating them as the only "official" rules available.

79. "Intercollegiate Athletics to be Stopped," *Mills College Weekly*, 18 April 1924, 1.

80. "University of Arizona Scene of 6th Annual Western Athletic Conference," *Mills College Weekly*, 3 May 1928, 3.

81. *Minutes of the Women's Athletic Council*, DPEA, 25 January 1927.

82. "Telegraphic Rifle Meet Completed," *The Daily Californian*, 3 April 1928, 2.

83. "Interclass Games to Start Today," *The Daily Californian*, 6 March 1928, 3.

84. This successful adoption of symbolic rather than instrumental goals is similar to that noted by Gussfield for Prohibition and temperance. Joseph Gussfield, *Symbolic Crusade: Status Politics and the Temperance Movement* (Urbana: University of Illinois Press, 1963, 1986), 166.

85. Carroll Smith-Rosenberg, *Disorderly Conduct: Visions of Gender in Victorian America* (Oxford: Oxford University Press, 1985), 295–296.

Further Reading

Bouchier, N. (1998). Let Us Take Care of Our Field: The National Association for Physical Education of College Women and World War II. *Journal of Sport History* 25(1): 65–86.

Gerber, E. W. (1971). *Innovators and Institutions in Physical Education*. Philadelphia: Lea and Febiger

Discussion Questions

1. Why would women physical educators want to restrict the opportunities in sport for their female students?

2. What would happen today if female coaches and physical educators sought to restrict the opportunities of girls and women in sport?

3. What would you have done if you were a student at a college in the mid-1920s and you were told you could no longer play competitive, intercollegiate sports?

3

"The Tuskegee Flash" and "the Slender Harlem Stroker"

Black Women Athletes on the Margin

Jennifer H. Lansbury

Image © 2009 Kovalev Serguei. Used under license from Shutterstock, Inc.

The author would like to thank Professor Suzanne Smith and Professor David Wiggins, as well as the anonymous readers for the *Journal of Sport History*, for their insightful and helpful comments on earlier drafts.

In July 1948, as track and field athlete Alice Coachman was arriving in London to represent the United States in the Olympic high-jump competition, the *Chicago Defender* ran a story in its sports section featuring Coachman and the U.S. women's track and field team. Entitled "Rush Carver Peanut Oil to Olympic Team Gals," sportswriter Russ Cowans described how the prized peanut oil, long used by track and field powerhouse Tuskegee Institute as a rubbing liniment, had been left behind in the United States. "It was Miss Coachman who sent the coaches and trainers into a dither," wrote Cowans. 'A day out of New York, Miss Coachman discovered that the peanut rubbing oil was not in the luggage, although Coach Cleve Abbott of Tuskegee had promised to have some in New York for the gals to take to London." The article continued by reporting how Olympic Coach Harry Hainsworth wired Abbott to send the oil over as quickly as possible. "Miss Coachman and the girls from Tuskegee have talked so much about the benefits they've derived from the oil . . . that all the girls want to use it," commented Coach Hainsworth.[1]

Coachman went on to win the gold, the first African American woman to win the prized medal, and the *Defender* and other black weeklies celebrated her victory and achievement. However, despite what one scholar has labeled our own culture's "sports fixation," Coachman's achievement and those of many other female African American athletes are all but forgotten today.[2] Even a historical field full of vitality and growth has not helped rescue these women from general obscurity.[3] Why are female African American athletes neglected to the point that they and their achievements have been essentially forgotten? This study suggests that sources for news in the 1940s and 1950s contributed to the loss of at least two black women athletes from the public memory—1940s track star Alice Coachman and 1950s tennis great Althea Gibson. In short, by focusing primarily on race or gender rather than athletic talent, the white and black press constructed public identities for Coachman and Gibson that marginalized them as athletes.

It was not necessarily a lack of press coverage of black female athletes that led to their marginalization, although this was certainly a contributing factor in the case of Alice Coachman. Often more harmful was the type of coverage suggested by the aforementioned "peanut oil" article. The story suggests a certain vibrancy surrounding the coverage, but it also reveals a tendency to neglect the skills of the athletes and identify them in nonathletic terms. The lighthearted tone of the article and the reference to the athletes as "the gals" suggests that they were to be indulged but not taken too seriously. Indeed, contemporary sportswriters routinely constructed Coachman's and Gibson's identities along race or gender lines, leaving their athletic prowess to be inferred from their accomplishments.

While the white and black press differed in the ways they presented these two women, neither treatment proved beneficial in securing their athletic place in history. In the white press, gender became the essential element around which their careers were interpreted. This is not to say that race was never a factor, but it was generally secondary to gender. This construction worked to Alice Coachman's detriment. As a female track and field athlete, she received little coverage from the white press mainly because she participated in a male-gendered sport. Not usually isolated for being African American, she nonetheless existed on the margin in white news accounts for being a woman competing in a "man's sport." On the other hand, Althea Gibson excelled in a sport in which women's participation had long been sanctioned. As a result, she enjoyed considerably more coverage through the construction of her by the white press as a female athlete. However, she also suffered from this emphasis on gender when the public began to *perceive* her tennis playing as too masculine.

Whereas the presentation of Coachman and Gibson in the white press revolved primarily around gender, race became the focal point for constructing their identities in the black press. This latter construction led to more press for Alice Coachman than she received in white papers as black sportswriters highlighted her achievements in terms of her status as an African American. However, the black press was aware of the unpopularity of track and field for women in the 1940s and their efforts to introduce gender into news accounts with the purpose of feminizing Coachman often had the effect of trivializing her athletic talent. Althea Gibson suffered in more explicit ways from this racial construction of her identity and athletic career. Initially celebrated by the black press for her achievement in breaking down the color line in the elite world of tennis, black sportswriters eventually turned on her for her refusal to assume the role of a race hero in the vein of Jackie Robinson.

The choice of Alice Coachman and Althea Gibson grants important insights into not only change over time but also the gender and class distinctions associated with track and field versus tennis. During Coachman's career, the sport of track and field remained a decidedly masculine endeavor. While women first began competing in the 1920s and initially enjoyed popularity, physical education leaders soon began criticizing female participation in the sport, positing that the jarring movements required by track events put too much strain on the female anatomy. Furthermore, experts also expressed concern that the "masculinizing effects" of such activity would make women unfit for their feminine roles, particularly that of motherhood. As a result, participation by white women declined, and many talented African American female track athletes emerged to take advantage of the exodus. Some white women continued to flock to the sport in the 1930s and 1940s, such as Babe Didrickson, Helen Stephens, and Stella Walsh. However, their working class backgrounds and "mannish" appearances upset the middle-class sensibilities of physical education instructors, pushing women's track and field even further to the margins of white society.[4]

The arena of track and field did not necessarily carry with it the same set of unattractive qualities for black women as it did for most white women. On the contrary, the elements of survival, even victory, in the face of adversity and struggle fit nicely into the African American woman's concept of ideal womanhood. Generally barred from the exclusive role of full-time mother, black women out of necessity assumed the multiple roles of wage earner, mother, homemaker, and community activist. African American femininity, therefore, was not constructed through limited attributes set in opposition to masculinity. Rather, ideal black womanhood was imbued with the positive qualities of strength, morality, and family and community commitments that had been forged through difficult circumstances as well as through the respect accorded them in the successful assumption of these different roles.[5]

The prowess of African American women in track and field during the 1930s and 1940s could be a double-edged sword, however. Most of the athletes enjoyed personal opportunities beyond what many of their race and gender would otherwise experience, such as the excitement of competition and educational and travel opportunities. Furthermore, their achievements served as a symbol of pride for their African American community. However, the success came at a price. White America often neglected them or, perhaps worse, perpetuated the negative stereotype of the black "mannish" woman, naturally suited to the role of athlete.[6]

While Coachman excelled in a sport that was considered unladylike and inappropriate for women, Gibson's story was altogether different. Tennis, a sport more associated with feminine qualities, had long accepted women. Though more inclusive of women than track and field, it was not, however, more inclusive of race. Not until 1948 did the first African American play in a major United States Lawn Tennis Association (USLTA) tournament. Furthermore, the class issues associated with tennis were perhaps even more rigid than that of track and field. Developed as a sport of the elite, tennis did not openly welcome working class participants.[7]

The choice of Coachman and Gibson also introduces the contrast of individuals raised in different regions of the country. Coachman was born and educated in the Jim Crow society of the Deep South so that "separate but equal" was an entrenched way of life for this Albany, Georgia, native. Although Gibson was educated in North Carolina and Florida, she spent her formative years in Harlem. While New York was not immune to racism, Gibson noted the difference as she journeyed in the South at the age of nineteen. Confronting the "White in front, Colored in rear" sign on her first bus ride in downtown Wilmington, North Carolina, she remembered, "It disgusted me, and it made me feel ashamed in a way I'd never been ashamed back in New York."[8]

The sports in which they competed, the regions of the country in which they lived, and even the decades in which they forged their careers mark important differences in Coachman's and Gibson's lives. Despite these differences, the ways in which the press constructed the public identities of these athletes were remarkably similar. Choosing to emphasize either gender or race over athletic skill and hard work, both black and white sports journalists unknowingly contributed to confining these women to the historical margin.

"The Tuskegee Flash"

From 1937 to 1948, the women's track and field team of Tuskegee Institute dominated the Amateur Athletic Union (AAU) outdoor championships, winning every year but 1943, when they placed second to the Cleveland Olympic Club. While numerous talented African American women competed under their banner, Alice Coachman ranks among the top. Eventually referred to in the black press as the "Tuskegee flash" for her sprinting prowess, Coachman caught the attention of the Tuskegee Institute coaching staff during the late 1930s and first competed for them the summer before beginning high school classes there. During her nine years of competition, first at Tuskegee and later at Albany State College, she forged a career that stands unrivaled in the record books. From 1939 when she burst on the scene by winning the high jump at the AAU outdoor women's championship, she dominated her events by amassing twenty-six national championships, more than any other American woman with the exception of her Polish-American rival, Stella Walsh.[9]

Yet, within the white press, Coachman was seldom portrayed as a record-breaking track star. In fact, women track athletes in general suffered from the portrayal of them in the white press, which generally emphasized gender over either race or athletic prowess. In Coachman's nine-year career, the limited coverage granted female track and field athletes by white newspapers and magazines is startling. Rarely did photographs of the athletes accompany the short articles that reported the national AAU outdoor championships, whereas male track and field events routinely received one- and two-page spreads, complete with pictures.[10]

At no time does the neglect of women's track and field stand out more than during coverage of the 1948 Summer Olympic Games in London.[11] Indeed, track and field was synonymous with masculinity, and the men's events in this sport completely dominated the white press coverage. Regardless of whether male track and field athletes were white or African American, they received not only extensive article coverage with accompanying photographs but also analysis by contemporary sports journalists. However, not even the very complete Olympic coverage by the *New York Times* included any pictures of American female track and field ath-letes. This is replicated by the *Times's* counterparts in other U.S. cities such as the *Chicago Tribune*, the *Boston Globe*, and the *Atlanta Constitution*.[12]

In part, the lack of coverage of American women's track and field during the 1948 Olympics may have resulted from their disappointing performances. Most of the American women failed to make it to the finals, and only Coachman and sprinter Audrey Patterson placed in their events.[13] Furthermore, the performance of Dutch runner Fanny Blankers-Koen tended to dominate the games. Her four gold track medals earned her the honor of being pho-tographed by the American white press. However, in spite of Blankers-Koen's record-breaking Olympics, white sportswriters constructed her identity predominantly through gender. Journalists routinely referred to her as "the Dutch housewife" and "the blond, slender, 30-year-old mother of two," as opposed to confining their reports to her sprinting prowess. These descriptions served to feminize the Dutch athlete, necessary since she competed in a suppos-edly masculine sport.[14]

Although coverage of women track champions, regardless of race, paled in comparison to that of the men, the attention Coachman received was generally commensurate with her white female competitors. Indeed, one of the compelling things about Coachman's white press cov-erage is how remarkably like her white competitors' it is. As early in her career as 1942, when she began to take home multiple titles at the AAU Women's Outdoor Nationals, Coachman was mentioned by white papers, and the Tuskegee team even took the headline that year in the *Chicago Tribune*—"Tuskegee Wins 6th Women's AAU Title in Track." By 1945 and 1946, when Coachman was at the peak of her career, she began to make headlines when the *Boston Globe* reported "Tuskegee Girl Eclipses Stella in Title Meet," and the *New York Times* reported her being awarded three places on the All-American Track and Field Team with a headline in the sports section.[15] The white press routinely referred to Coachman as the "star sprinter," the "Tuskegee star," or the "Tuskegee flash" in ways not only similar to the black press but also quite similar to its own references to white female track and field athletes.[16]

To subordinate race to gender was not to ignore it, however. While Coachman was often depicted in terms similar to white women track athletes, race did at times play a factor. Indeed, the coverage by the *New York Times* illustrates the role of race. The *Times* not only pho-tographed Fanny Blankers-Koen but also gave her more article coverage than any member of the U.S. women's track team. Incredibly, from August 8 when Coachman won her gold to August 15 when the *Times* wrapped up its reporting, it granted Alice Coachman-the only American woman to win a gold in track and field, the first African American, and a new Olympic record holder—just one sentence. Its startling lack of coverage of Coachman's ath-letic achievement reveals that second to gender came race. Athletic competence was of little significance.[17]

Moreover, the Olympics were not the first time the white paper had slighted Coachman. When she became a triple winner at the 1945 AAU Women's Nationals, finally beating out Stella Walsh in the 100-meter dash after coming close the previous two years, the *Times* com-pletely ignored the Tuskegee star's achievement. The short three-paragraph article entitled "Miss Walsh Wins Easily" covered Walsh's single win in the 200-meter despite the fact that Coachman took the title in the 50-meter, the 100-meter, and the high jump. And in 1946, while Coachman dominated both the AAU Women's Nationals as well as the *Times's* coverage of it by retaining all three of her titles, the one photograph accompanying the article was of the white 80-meter hurdles champion, Nancy Cowperthwaite.[18]

Even when her home state overlooked gender in order to honor one of its own as a new Olympic record holder, Coachman's race came before her athletic achievement. "Albany Negress is Olympic Champ: Alice Coachman Wins High Jump," headlined the *Atlanta Constitution* in an article devoted entirely to the newest native Georgia champion. For a white paper in the Deep South in 1948, the article unexpectedly celebrates Coachman's achievement, reporting that there were over 70,000 on hand to watch Coachman set a new Olympic record, the "greatest [crowd] ever to witness a high jump exhibition." However, in addition to the several overt references to her race, the account also contains subtle messages of race and gender: "An all-around athlete, Alice is an outstanding forward on the basketball team at college, but her instructors say confidentially that she's 'just a fair student' in home economics."[19] The article hints at two negative stereotypes—that of the African American who excels athletically but not academically and of the woman who participates in a mannish sport because she is not "feminine" enough to do well in the female college course of home economics.

While the white press offered limited coverage of Alice Coachman's athletic prowess, the black press heralded her achievements, as well as those of other black female track stars. Constructing her identity primarily through race rather than gender, African American journalists overlooked the gender concerns of their white counterparts. Indeed, black weeklies often gave the Tuskegee team and Coachman headlines in the sports page, accompanied by team photos or individual shots of the athletes in action. As early as 1941, before she had become a dominant force in the sprints, the *Pittsburgh Courier* captures a photographic image of Coachman performing the high jump at the AAU Women's Nationals, noting how she "clears the bar with a spectacular leap." By 1942, three years before she bested Stella Walsh in the 100-meter sprint, the *Baltimore Afro-American* recognized that the Tuskegee team took their sixth straight championship title "paced by Alice Coachman, national indoor and outdoor jumping champion, who captured two titles in addition to running the anchor leg on the championship relay quartet." The spread featured several pictures, including a single of Coachman, the "Tuskegee flash," crossing the finish line in the 400-meter relay.[20] Moreover, in the prewar years African American sports journalists often discussed female track and field athletes in their regular columns. As early in Coachman's career as 1940, Charles Campbell of the *Baltimore Afro-American,* in his weekly column "Philly Points," predicted that she would eventually break the world record for the high jump.[21]

Although sports coverage in general fell off during the later war years, Coachman continued to be hailed by the black press for her dominance in women's track and field. Aided by descriptive monikers such as the "Tuskegee star," the "flying Miss Coachman," "Tuskegee's 21-year-old speed queen," and "Americas No. One woman track athlete," African American journalists continued to celebrate Coachman's achievements as she came to the pinnacle of her career in the United States.[22] Compared to the *New York Times's* and *Chicago Tribune's* lackluster coverage of women's track and field, black weeklies put Coachman front and center in 1945 as they celebrated her spectacular performance at the AAU Women's Nationals. "Alice Coachman Crowned National Sprint Queen," headlined the *Baltimore Afro-American* that year, noting how she had reached "the acme of her brilliant career" by dethroning Stella Walsh, who was "generally recognized as one of the all-time greats of feminine history." Indeed, recognizing Walsh's brilliance in the sport served to enhance Coachman's overall achievement when she finally outran her competitor in 1945 after having been nosed out by Walsh in the 100-meter for the two prior years. In an interview with Walsh in 1944, the renowned *Afro-American's* sportswriter, Sam Lacy, reported how the "Polish flyer" referred to Coachman as "the toughest opponent I have ever met," and "the finest runner I've ever raced against."[23]

In truth, the black press's extensive coverage of Coachman's achievements, along with other African Americans, was often necessary to balance the fact that white dailies overlooked or downplayed the contributions of African Americans. However, while black journalists constructed Coachman's public identity primarily in terms of race, they were aware of the gender concerns that accompanied her sport. As such, they sometimes used feature articles or weekly columns to "feminize" black women track and field athletes. In 1941 the *Baltimore Afro-American* ran a feature article on the Tuskegee women track stars' plans after graduation. Playing up the femininity of the athletes, Levi Jolley wrote: "These young women, while mixing athletics with studies, enjoy all the pleasures and indicated desires to become a nurse, ... teachers, and social workers." Alice Coachman's plans included teaching or social work, but Jolley also reported that she believed "being a good wife when she marries will probably be the fulfilment of her secret ambitions."[24] Celebrating her achievements as an African American female track athlete, the black press was still quick to realize the importance of projecting femininity onto Coachman's identity.

Efforts by the black press to feminize Coachman and other female track athletes resulted in trivializing the athlete's abilities in their sport. The peanut oil story, which originated years before the Olympics, best illustrates this tendency. In his 1940 article "Tigerettes Owe Success to Dr. Carver's Peanut Oil," Levi Jolley refused to accept Coach Christine Evans Petty's assertion that the team's success could be attributed to strict training and competing against male athletes during practice. Due to "the smooth velvet appearance of the girls' skin in addition to their rhythm in motion," the reporter repeatedly inquired about "what was used for rubbing the girls." Petty finally acknowledged that the exclusive use of Dr. George Washington Carver's peanut oil by the women's team, but also more broadly within the athletic department, helped prevent strained muscles and Charlie horses. This allowed coaches to concentrate more on form and speed during practice and not worry about muscle problems that developed from strenuous training. There was an added benefit for the women, noted Jolley: "The girls like to use it because of the smoothness it gives their skin."[25]

The images that the peanut oil story evokes are not only disturbing but also reveal how even the black press marginalized Coachman and her teammates. First, the story suggests that the athletic abilities of these women derived not from hard work but from a magic potion like peanut oil. The entire article, including its title, suggests a "scoop"—the sportswriter has discovered the secret to the Tuskegee women's years of dominance in track and field. Secondly, the story goes beyond imbuing these women with feminine traits to creating images full of sensuality. While the writer's words discuss the oil's benefits largely in the very feminine terms of smooth skin, the whole concept of rubbing oil on women's bodies also evokes a very sexualized view of these women.

These efforts to project feminine, even sensualized, qualities on black women track athletes reflect their ambiguous identity even within their own community of African American supporters. Celebrated by the black press for their achievements because they were African Americans, they nonetheless had trouble overcoming the stigma of being females trying to excel in a masculine sport and being represented in the press by an essentially male cadre of sportswriters.[26] Certainly the fact that most sports journalists were men dictated, in part, the type of coverage women athletes, in general, and African American women athletes, more specifically, would receive. Defining what would make it to sports pages, white and African American sportswriters unknowingly contributed to the loss of these women athletes from the public memory. Even as Alice Coachman retired from track and field competition, the white and black press were busy constructing the identity of another athlete coming on the scene. The creation of the public Althea Gibson would be as equally complicated.

"The Slender Harlem Stroker"

The same summer Alice Coachman won Olympic gold, Althea Gibson took the national American Tennis Association (ATA) championship for the second straight year. She would go on to win the ATA title, the African American tennis association that existed alongside the white United States Lawn Tennis Association, for eight more years. However, she was still two years away from entering the hallowed grounds of Forest Hills, the national USLTA championship that eventually became the U.S. Open.[27]

While Gibson was living a tomboyish existence on the streets of Harlem, the African American elite saw in her an exceptional talent and, hoping she would be the one to break the color barrier, groomed her to enter and excel in the high-class world of tennis.[28] After ascending to the pinnacle of the African American tennis community, and with the help of former tennis greats like Alice Marble, Gibson finally broke into the USLTA in 1950, culminating in her play at Forest Hills in September of that year. In 1951, she became the first African American to play at Wimbledon.

What followed was a series of disappointing years in which Gibson continued to dominate the ATA but struggled in the USLTA. Ready to give up the sport and join the WACS, the State Department asked her, along with three other players, to represent the United States on a goodwill tour of Southeast Asia during the winter and spring of 1956. It was this tour that turned her career around. She won sixteen out of eighteen tournaments, although she faltered at Wimbledon and Forest Hills, losing both in the final round. It was the last time that would happen, however. In 1957, Gibson became the first African American—man or woman—to take the Wimbledon singles title. She entered the record books again in the late summer when she finally won at Forest Hills. From there, she seemed unstoppable. In 1958 she certainly was. She retained both the Wimbledon and Forest Hills titles, again entering the record books alongside the few other tennis greats who had enjoyed back-to-back wins of both tournaments.

As with Alice Coachman, the construction of Althea Gibson's identity by the white press rested primarily on gender. While she was at times singled out for special attention due to the racial significance of her accomplishments, generally, the amount and tenor of the coverage she received was commensurate with her white female tennis competitors. Although women were more accepted in a sport less masculinized than track and field, they had to endure negative gender labels if their play became too powerful or aggressive.[29]

While the sport of tennis was not gendered in the same way as track and field, Gibson and her contemporaries, male and female, were routinely described in quite physical, gendered terms. Contemporary news accounts routinely commented especially on Gibson's size, referring to her as "the lithe and muscular Miss Gibson," a "lanky jumping jack of a girl," and "tall and leggy."[30] Furthermore, they often used such physical attributes to explain the masculine power with which she played the game. Gibson is "lean and her long arms are muscular.... When she hits the ball, it travels like a bolt out of a crossbow," wrote Kenneth Love of the *New York Times*. Following her win at Forest Hills in 1957, *Life* magazine showed a picture of Gibson in action and explained, "Althea's service gains power from her height."[31]

With her big service and powerful delivery, Gibson was often noticed in the white press for the "masculine" way in which she played the game. Yet this was a fate common of any woman who chose to play aggressive tennis, and many shied away from such displays of power to avoid being labeled masculine by the press.[32] In a bio-piece that appeared in conjunction with her 1957 Wimbledon win, the *New York Times* noted that Gibson, as early as her debut at Forest Hills, had been compared to another female tennis great, Alice Marble, for her "mannish style of play." Her teaming with Maria Bueno of Brazil to capture the 1958 Wimbledon doubles championship garnered the attention of sports journalists who noticed how the Gibson-Bueno team "crushed" their opponents, "hitting the ball with manlike power." Following her win at Forest Hills in 1957, *Life* magazine compared Gibson's tennis to that of the men's singles champion Malcolm Anderson, "The two winners, as these pictures show, also played remarkably alike. Their power proved again that it takes a big serve to win in modern tennis."[33] Unlike Coachman, Gibson received more coverage from the white press, probably due in large measure to the acceptability of women's participation in the sport of tennis. However, she did have to contend with the attention given her for the "unladylike" way in which she played the game.[34]

As evidenced by treatments from the white press, race played a more important part in Coachman's identity than in Gibson's. The hometown papers of these athletes are particularly illustrative of this difference. During the peak of Coachman's career from 1943 to 1948, the *New York Times* occasionally overlooked Coachman's achievement, highlighting instead that of white female track athletes. The *Atlanta Constitution*, however, celebrated this native Georgian's Olympic achievement, albeit with both explicit and implicit racial commentary.

The *Times* coverage of Gibson, however, was generally anything but racialized.[35] Certainly much of this could be attributed to the New York paper promoting an athlete from their city, which they did with gusto. There were likely two reasons for the differences in intensity of these athletes' home town coverage. First, Gibson was a Harlem girl, whereas Coachman's home was the smaller southwest Georgia town of Albany rather than the city of Atlanta. Second, the white press of the more segregated South would be less likely to publicize the ongoing achievements of a young African American female athlete outside of some spectacular feat, such as the capturing of an Olympic gold medal and a new world record. The Northern *New York Times*, however, quickly fashioned the tennis star as "our own Althea Gibson," and not only highlighted her tennis matches but also often mentioned her in their editorial section.[36]

The difference between Coachman's and Gibson's white press coverages in terms of race also reflected the changes that occurred in American society during the 1940s and 1950s. Although only a decade separated their achievements, the racial dynamics of the country had changed considerably. Even as Alice Coachman was capturing women's track titles year after year, America's participation in World War II became what is now recognized as a turning point in the African American struggle for civil rights.[37] Black soldiers returning from war began to question the inequity of defending a country that denied them full participation in white society. Toward the end of Coachman's career, advancement was already being made in the area of sports. In 1946 Jackie Robinson breached the color line in professional baseball when he made his debut with the Montreal Royals, the top farm team of the Brooklyn Dodgers. A year later, major league baseball saw its first African American player in the twentieth century when Robinson donned a Dodger uniform. Also in 1946, the Los Angeles Rams signed Kenny Washington and Woody Strode to break professional football's thirteen-year exclusion of black athletes.[38]

By the time Gibson won her first singles title at Wimbledon, the larger society reverberated with changes on race issues. In 1954, the Supreme Court handed down their verdict in *Brown v. Board of Education*, which declared unconstitutional the long-standing practice of "separate but equal" facilities for African Americans. Most of Gibson's advances in the world of tennis would be played, then, against the backdrop of the *Brown* decision working its way throughout the country as now well-known names in the civil rights struggle forged their way into history. Moreover, the postwar years and the onset of the Cold War further contributed to African American advances as external scrutiny of American race relations resulted in heightened internal sensitivity. Indeed, Althea Gibson benefitted from this changing America. Around the same time Rosa Parks was refusing to give her seat over to a white patron on a Montgomery, Alabama, bus, Althea Gibson's beleaguered tennis career received a second chance, thanks not only to the forward momentum of the African American civil rights movement but also to national concern with cold war enemies' criticism of racial problems within the United States.'"[39]

In December 1955, the State Department invited Gibson to join three other tennis players on a tour of Southeast Asian countries, playing exhibition matches and international tournaments along the way. By including a successful African American, they hoped to improve the image of race relations in the United States against attacks from its communist antagonists.[40] Looking back on the experience, Gibson herself recognized the racial significance of her participation:

> I've never been exactly sure why I was selected to make the tour in the first place. . . . I know it happened soon after the killing of Emmett Till in Georgia, and world opinion of the racial situation in the United States was at a low ebb, So I suppose that was the main reason why I, a colored girl, was invited to help represent our country in Southeast Asia. I certainly wasn't picked because I was a champion; at the time I was champion of nothing and unlikely ever to be.[41]

Certainly in light of the country's changing racial climate, Althea Gibson's significance as a race hero was important to a black press that viewed the achievement of black women athletes primarily in racial terms. Indeed, Gibson's first win at Forest Hills in 1957 was played against the backdrop of the events of the "Little Rock Nine," when the governor of Arkansas called out the National Guard to prevent nine African American children from entering a white public school.[42] During this heightened struggle for civil rights, the black press looked to Gibson to be visible and vocal concerning race issues. Unfortunately, these expectations proved to be ones under which Gibson would eventually suffer when, at the height of her career, the black press turned on her for refusing to assume a more outspoken role as race hero.

Gibson's relationship with the black press began in the late 1940s when she was regularly featured in sports sections for her consecutive victories at the ATA nationals. In 1950, however, she took on new prominence in black weeklies when she was invited to play at Forest Hills and in 1951 at Wimbledon, breaking the color barrier at both of these bastions of the white tennis world. "Althea Gibson will become the first Negro tennis star to crash the 'lily-white' citadel of this American sport," printed the *Pittsburgh Courier* following the news that Gibson would participate in the 1950 Forest Hills tournament. Most black papers were quick to identify the young and inexperienced star as a work in progress, however. "She plays a good attacking game, but it is erratic," noted one journalist. Nonetheless, Jackie Reemes of the *New York Amsterdam News* represented the common opinion of the day among African American writers when he reported that "there is little doubt that more will be heard from Althea in future competition."[43]

During the lean years of 1952-1955 when Gibson continued to dominate the African American ATA tournaments but was struggling in the white USLTA, the black press remained respectively silent on her struggles. However, from the time Gibson participated in the State Department's goodwill tour in 1956 to her eventual win at Wimbledon, her exploits in the "lily-white" world of tennis once again became common fare in sports columns of the black press. During this period of Gibson's career, African American journalists celebrated her achievements through their positive physical descriptions of her and their tendency to come to her defense when necessary.[44]

Similar to the white press, black sportswriters often described Gibson in physical terms. However, their descriptions highlighted both her statuesque femininity and her powerful game, constructions the black press did not see as contradictory. Historians Patricia Vertinsky and Gwendolyn Captain have posited that African American leaders, coaches, and journalists worked hard to dispel the myth of the black "Amazon" woman by cultivating instead a more feminine image of female athletes.[45] "The willowy Miss Gibson," "the slender Harlem stroker," and "the lean New Yorker" were common descriptions of Gibson during this period in her career. The *Baltimore Afro-American* also reported that she was "looking fresh and sporting an attractive hair-do" when she appeared on the Dave Garroway "This is New York" television show in 1956.[46]

At the same time, however, African American journalists did not shy away from referring to Gibson's power. Femininity and strength joined nicely in the female African American ideal, in contrast to white womanhood that shied away from physical strength as a masculine characteristic.[47] "Lithe and quick in action," reported the *Pittsburgh Courier* early in her career, Gibson "loves to slam the ball with exuberance." Describing her win at Wimbledon, Gibson's opponent Darlene Hard "was simply no match for the powerful all-court game of Miss Gibson." Later that year, *Ebony* highlighted her "extraordinary power and big service."[48]

The second characteristic of Gibson's coverage prior to her falling out with the black press was the tendency on the part of African American journalists to defend her, as necessary, against negative reports. Following news that she was somewhat aloof with other players at the 1956 Wimbledon tournament, a writer for the *Chicago Defender* commented, "She is one of the most dignified girls I've ever seen, with more poise and personality than all the rest of the tennis players put together." With all her positive attributes, he continued, it is no wonder that Gibson had "become the target for jealousy." The following week, after her loss at Wimbledon, Fay Young devoted his entire weekly column to the tennis star. Discussing how misunderstood she was and how he had attempted to mold her, Young wrote of how he had gently chided her at an ATA meet for not mixing more with other players. The sportswriter remembered how Gibson had graciously accepted his advice. He concluded with further support: "We are all with her—win or lose."[49]

The point at which the black press began to attack Gibson rather than revere and defend her came during the summer of 1957. Following her win at Wimbledon, she traveled to Chicago to play in the USLTA tournament at River Forest. On the surface, the black press was upset by Gibson's unwillingness to be more attentive to them at the Chicago tournament in July. Journalists for the *Chicago Defender* and the *Pittsburgh Courier* were particularly indignant. In a feature article, the *Defender's* Russ Cowans accused her of giving reporters "one of the best brush-offs most of them had ever had" and suggested that instead of the Wimbledon trophy, the Queen should have "given her a few words of advice on graciousness." Continuing the diatribe in his weekly column, Cowans again laid into Gibson for being "as ungracious as a stubborn jackass" and "the most arrogant athlete it has been my displeasure to meet." Wendell Smith of the Courier attacked Gibson for taking on the persona of a prima donna after her Wimbledon victory: "The lean girl from the streets of Harlem has become so obsessed with herself and her court skill that she apparently speaks with only kings and queens." Smith even resorted to attacking Gibson intellectually. Suggesting that she merely "skipped" through Florida A&M College with the help of her African American benefactors, he continued, "She clearly established the fact here last week that she is neither scholarly nor smart by her arrogant, despicable treatment of friendly sportswriters."[50]

Both papers also continued to attack Gibson in subtle ways. In 1958, rather than highlighting her repeat of the women's singles and doubles titles at Wimbledon, the Defender's coverage focused instead on her "failure" to also take the mixed doubles title. The Courier, though eventually somewhat more forgiving than the Chicago weekly, spoke of Gibson in masculinized terms, a description more common to the white press but unheard of by the black press prior to the Chicago affair. Their coverage of the now famed River Forest tournament in Chicago reported that "there was never any doubts that mannish-playing Miss Gibson would emerge victorious" [emphasis by author].[51]

However, the prima donna explanation was, in reality, a smoke screen. References to Gibson's "difficult" personality had long been a source of discussion by the black press. In 1956, Fay Young of the Chicago Defender noted how he had tried to help her along in this area, as another Defender journalist complained that "the Gibson gal is being accused of giving herself airs" because of her incredible success on the Southeast Asia tour. Baltimore APO-American sportswriter Sam Lacy's biographical sketch of Gibson published just before the 1957 Wimbledon play identified these tendencies as part of her personality: "It is her makeup to be moody, indifferent, sometimes arrogant." Chalking this up to her "tomboy" upbringing on the streets of Harlem, Lacy observed that "she has a way of going into her hard shell and refusing to come out of it." In a prescient conclusion, he offered the observation that "more often than not, it is the press that feels the brunt of the Gibson arrogance."[52]

Her problems with the black press, then, are best understood if considered in terms of how they constructed her public identity as an African American. To black journalists, her acceptance into the white, high-class world of tennis was imbued with deep racial significance. Sam Lacy called her win at Wimbledon "the greatest triumph a colored athlete has accomplished in my time" and "the biggest sports victory ever placed in the record books for a person of my race." He carved out Gibson's achievement in such heroic proportions, in part, because she did it alone with no others who had come before her to smooth the way. Given the integral part Lacy played in the Jackie Robinson saga, his compliment to Gibson during the Robinson era was high praise indeed.[53]

Yet Gibson's position as a race hero in the black press was fraught with ambiguity. Earlier in her career, while defending her from attackers who called her "tight-lipped and moody," a journalist for the Chicago Defender assured his readers that "she looks upon herself as an evangelist whose skill with the tennis racquet, and her sincerity, is breaking the colour barriers." Apparently, while she was accepting of the role in some measure, the press was accepting of her "quirks." During the Chicago fiasco, however, reports circulated that, when asked if she like being compared to Jackie Robinson, she responded, "No, I don't consider myself a representative of my people. I am thinking of me and nobody else."[54]

There were those of the black press who defended Gibson even after the Chicago incident. Lacy continued to suggest that her bad press was, in part, due to her personality: "She answers readily and honestly, with no thought of softening her opinion for the sake of sparing feelings or playing the diplomat." Calling her a "distaff Jackie Robinson," he compared the two, suggesting that reporters often became offended and were "set back on their heels when they learned that neither Althea nor Jackie could be patient with veneers." The *Pittsburgh Courier* even gave equal time to her supporters by printing a representative letter from a fan who attacked the black press for its treatment of Gibson. Reminding people that the State Department thought her a responsible and good representative of the country in 1956, the fan insisted that "she does not go on the tennis court to represent her race and any question put to her along this line can only be a subtle trap."[55]

Comments from the white press on this subject give insight into how much the issue centered around Gibson's position as a race hero. In the fall of 1957, the *Pittsburgh Courier* reprinted a series of biographical articles written by Ted Poston of the *New York Post*. Calling Gibson a community project, Poston suggested that she was a throwback to postslavery days when African Americans came together to promote the most talented ones of the community. Here, he concluded, "a Harlem urchin discovered by Negroes, nurtured by Negroes, trained by Negroes, educated by Negroes, was now the best in the world in 'the game for ladies and gentlemen.'" Against the backdrop of her racial significance, a *Time* magazine cover story may grant the best insight into the source of the problem. The feature story reported how Gibson came up against some Jim Crow problems in Chicago, being refused a room at the Oak Park Hotel and a reservation at a swanky Chicago restaurant. "Officials and newsmen burned with rage," the journalist wrote, "but Althea hardly noticed it."[56] The African American community had much invested in Althea Gibson and were disappointed when she did not live up to their expectations as a race figure.

Finally, Gibson herself attributed her problems with the black press to her hesitancy to be a trailblazer for her race. "I have never set myself up as a champion of the Negro race," she wrote in her autobiography. Taking her hat off to Jackie Robinson's achievements, Gibson nonetheless chose to handle her success in her own way, which was to shy away from any role as a race hero. However, she recognized that there were those in the African American community who disagreed with her position. The real reason that quite a few members of the black press had been uncomplimentary, she contended, was that they resented her refusal "to turn my tennis achievements into a rousing crusade for racial equality."[57]

How do we come to terms with the contemporary press treatment of these two athletes and their subsequent neglect by the historical community? Black and white sportswriters alike covered Coachman's and Gibson's athletic careers at least to some extent, and in Gibson's case, expansively. However, the sports stories about these women were more about gender or race rather than their prowess on the track field or the tennis court. Instead of attributing their athletic accomplishments to dedication and hard work, even the black press sometimes searched for the answer in magic potions like peanut oil.

It is no wonder then that Alice Coachman, Althea Gibson, and others like them have been lost to the public memory. While sources are available, contemporary press accounts trivialized them as athletes to the extent that they have been essentially forgotten for the very achievements that made them newsworthy in the first place. Yet the status of these women within the African American community, as well as their contributions toward breaking down racial barriers, make them important subjects of study. However, even as black women athletes are popular subjects for children's biographies, their absence from the genre of the historical biography is striking and begs for correction.[58] Moreover, more research into the ways in which the contemporary African American community viewed these athletes' achievements and their position in the African American public memory are other areas ripe for study.

In 1956, Kenneth Love of the *New York Times* related a comment from Gibson regarding her public identity. "I am just another tennis player, not a Negro tennis player," she insisted.[59] Yet even at the height of her career, neither the white or black press cast her as such. Rather, as the press constructed Alice Coachman and Althea Gibson primarily in terms of gender or race, their identities as athletes were relegated to a distant third. Fraught with ambiguity for both these athletes during their careers, such construction has also led to their current status as black women athletes on the margin.

Endnotes

1. *Chicago Defender,* 31 July 1948, p. 11.

2. See John Hoberman, *Darwin's Athletes: How Sport Has Damaged Black America and Preserved the Myth of Race* (Boston: Houghton Mifflin Company, 1997), xxi.

3. Scholarly work on the subject of race and sport, particularly the African American experience, has exploded in the last ten to fifteen years. Recent influential studies on some of the key issues involved in the subject are Hoberman, *Darwin's Athletes* and David K. Wiggins, *Glory Bound: Black Athletes in a White America* (Syracuse, N.Y.: Syracuse University Press, 1997). There are also excellent biographies on Jackie Robinson and Jesse Owens that provide valuable historical context and take up issues of athleticism and the cultural construction of race, such as Jules Tygiel, *Baseball's Great Experiment: Jackie Robinson and His Legacy,* expanded ed. (New York: Oxford University Press, 1997) and William J. Baker, *Jesse Owens: An American Life* (New York: Free Press, 1986). John Carroll has covered similar territory for football with a lesser known twentieth-century athlete in *Fritz Pollard: Pioneer in Racial Advancement* (Urbana: University of Illinois Press, 1998). Two valuable historiographical essays exist on the subject. Jeffrey T. Sammons, "'Race' and Sport: A Critical Historical Examination," *Journal of Sport History* 21 (Fall 1994): 203–278, although at this juncture somewhat dated, provides an important assessment of the scholarship, especially his summary on gender on pages 266–269. For a recent, extensive bibliography, see David K. Wiggins, "The African American Athletic Experience," in *The African American Experience: An Historiographical and Bibliographical Guide,* ed. Arvarh E. Strickland and Robert E. Weems, Jr. (Westport, Conn.: Greenwood Press, 2001), 255–277. While the field of African American women in sports has lagged somewhat behind that of men, the 1990s has witnessed substantial growth in this area as well. Some of the best include "'Cinderellas' of Sport: Black Women in Track and Field," in Susan K. Cahn, *Coming on Strong: Gender and Sexuality in Twentieth-Century Women? Sport* (New York: Free Press, 1994), 110–139; "Members Only: Class, Race, and Amateur Tennis for Women in the 1950s," in Mary Jo Festle, *Playing Nice: Politics and Apologies in Women's Sports* (New York: Columbia University Press, 1996), 53–71; Gwendolyn Captain, "Enter Ladies and Gentlemen of Color: Gender, Sport, and the Ideal of African American Manhood and Womanhood During the Late Nineteenth and Early Twentieth Centuries,", *Journal of Sport History* 18 (Spring 1991): 81–102; Patricia Vertinsky and Gwendolyn Captain, "More Myth than History: American Culture and Representations of the Black Female's Athletic Ability," *Journal of Sport History* 25 (Fall 1998): 532–561; Cindy Himes Gissendanner, "'African-American Women in Competitive Sport, 1920–1960," in *Women, Sport, and Culture,* ed. Susan Birrell and Cheryl L. Cole (Champaign, Ill.: Human Kinetics, 1994); Gissendanner, "African American Women Olympians: The Impact of Race, Gender, and Class Ideologies, 1932–1968," *Research Quarterly for Exercise and Sport* 67 (June 1996):

172–182; and Linda D. Williams, "Sportswomen in Black and White: Sports History From an Afro-American Perspective," in *Women, Media and Sport: Challenging Gender Values,* ed. Pamela J. Creedon (Thousand Oaks, California: Sage, 1994), 45–66. One interesting phenomenon that exists in the study of black women athletes is the absence of historical biographies of these women. While biographies of Jackie Robinson, Jesse Owens, Muhammad Ali, and other male black athletes abound, the stories of even better-known women athletes such as Althea Gibson and Wilma Rudolph have been relegated to children's books. Indeed, the question of why the stories of black women athletes are appropriate for children's books but not adult literature deserves further study. In addition to Gibson and Rudolph, Alice Coachman and her quest for the gold has also been created in juvenile literature. Furthermore, the trend continues into the present. Both Jackie Joyner-Kersee and Marion Jones, two recent African American female Olympic gold medal winners, have had their stories limited to this genre.

4. Cahn, *Coming on Strong,* 114–117.

5. Ibid., 117–118. For more on the influence of work on the identity of African American women, see Jacqueline Jones, *Labor of Love, Labor of Sorrow: Black Women, Work, and the Family from Slavery to the Present* (New York: Basic Books, 1985).

6. Cahn, *Coming on Strong,* 121, 125–128.

7. Festle, *Playing Nice,* 55, 58. Dr. Reginald Weir was the first African American to play in a USLTA tournament, the National Indoor Championships, also in New York. This is not to be confused with the famed Forest Hills tournament, which was the National Outdoor Championships, where Althea Gibson eventually broke the color barrier in 1950. Althea Gibson, *I Always Wanted To Be Somebody* (New York: Harper & Brothers, 1958), 55.

8. Gibson, *I Always Wanted To Be Somebody,* 46.

9. Michael D. Davis, *Black American Women in Olympic Track and Field* (Jefferson, N. C.: McFarland & Company, Inc., 1992), 40; Ed Decker, "Alice Coachman," in *Contemporary Black Biography: Profiles fiom the International Black Community,* 32 vols., ed. Shirelle Phelps (Detroit: Gale Research, Inc., 1992), 18: 29.

10. My references to the "white press" are inclusive of the following newspapers—*New York Times, Chicago Tribune, Boston Globe, Atlanta Constitution*—and *Time* and *Life* magazines. "Black press" references include the following black weeklies—*New York Age, New York Amsterdam News, Chicago Defender, Baltimore Afro-American,* and *Pittsburgh Courier*—as well as *Ebony* magazine. Research into these publications' reporting of Alice Coachman's career covers 1939 through 1948, and 1950 through 1958 for Althea Gibson's. Although Gibson was featured regularly in the black press in the late 1940s as a dominant force in the black American Tennis Association (ATA), she did not emerge in the white press until 1950. In the white press, the New York and Atlanta papers were chosen in particular because they represent the closest to a "home town" paper available for Gibson and Coachman. The black weeklies were selected in general because of their prominence in the black community as well as the influence of sportswriters such as Sam Lacy (*Baltimore Afro-American*) and Wendell Smith (*Pittsburgh Courier*) in the black sporting world.

11. The extent to which the white press highlighted gender in their news accounts is further illustrated when the neglect of women's track and field is compared with the extensive treatment accorded American female swimmers during the Olympics. Women swimmers received considerably more coverage than women track athletes, including spreads in several newspapers complete with photographs. The difference is largely attributable to the fact that swimming was an acceptable sport for women. Swimming was not thought to be injurious to women's bodies, nor did it detract from their femininity Historian Susan Cahn argues that the acceptability of swimming over track also speaks to race and class distinctions since most swimmers were white, middle-class women. See Cahn, *Coming on Strong,* 130.

12. The *New York Times* did feature a picture of the women's track and field team marching in the opening ceremonies, although the caption did not identify them. However, none of the U.S. women's track and field team were photographed participating in their sport. See *New York Times,* 1 August 1948, sec. V, p. 3.

13. Audrey Patterson became the first African American woman to medal in the Olympic Games, taking a bronze in the 200-meter sprint.

14. 'American Athletes Sweep the Olympics," *Life,* 23 August 1948, p. 28; *New York Times,* 15 August 1948, sec. V, p. 1.

15. *Chicago Tribune,* 5 July 1942, sec. 2, p. 2; *Boston Globe,* 1 July 1945, sec. 2, p. 4; *New York Times,* 11 January 1946, p. 24.

16. *Chicago Tribune,* 1 July 1945, sec. 2, p. 4; *New York Times,* 9 July 1944, sec. III, p. 1; *New York Times,* 5 August 1946, p. 27.

17. *New York Times,* 15 August 1948, sec. V, p. 1.

18. *New York Times,* 1 July 1945, sec. III, p. 3; *New York Times,* 5 August 1946, p. 27.

19. *Atlanta Constitution,* 8 August 1948, sec. B, p. 11. The *Chicago Tribune* subordinated both gender and race in their Olympic coverage but not to highlight Coachman as an athlete. Rather, it portrayed her as a victorious American. The *Tribune* dramatized the high-jump competition, describing how darkness and drizzling rain descended upon the stadium, with Coachman in the end victorious. "Thus the track meet ended as begun eight days ago, with victory for an American and the Star Spangled Banner of the United States providing the closing music" (*Chicago Tribune,* 8 August 1948, sec. 2, p. 1.). By the 1950s, the victory would be not only for an American but also for America, as the United States and the Soviets discovered the world of international sports as another arena in which to wage their cold war. As a result, women's track and field would gain acceptability in the United States as part of the arsenal to assert American superiority over the Soviet system. For more on the Cold War status of the sport, see Cahn, *Coming on Strong,* 130–133.

20. *Pittsburgh Courier,* 9 July 1941, p. 16; *Baltimore Afro-American,* 11 July 1942, p. 23.

21. *Baltimore Afro-American,* 13 July 1940, p. 19. The *Chicago Defender's* Fay Young also discusses women's track and held in his weekly column, pointing to the white press's biased coverage of the 1941 AAU Indoor Nationals. See the *Chicago Defender,* 19 April 1941, p. 24.

22. *Chicago Defender,* 21 August 1943, p. 19; *Baltimore Afro-American,* 15 August 1944, p. 18; *Pittsburgh Courier,* 7 July 1945, p. 18.

23. *Baltimore Afro-American,* 7 July 1945, p. 18; *Baltimore Afro-American,* 15 July 1944, p. 18.

24. *Baltimore Afro-American,* 12 July 1941, p. 19. This effort to imbue Coachman with feminine qualities resurfaced during the Olympics. Although discussing in some detail that she was favored to win the high jump, the *Pittsburgh Courier* suggested that the two-year course in tailoring she completed at Tuskegee made her popular with her teammates when they needed help mending their uniforms. See the *Pittsburgh Courier,* 7 August 1948, p. 26.

25. *Baltimore Afro-American,* 13 July 1940, p. 19.

26. Coverage of the later war years and 1948 Olympic games likewise reflects Coachman's ambiguous status within the black press community. When newspapers began to scale back their press in support of the war effort, photographic coverage of the women all but disappeared while pictures of male track and field athletes continued. Even Coachman's Olympic coverage, although expansive compared to white papers, does not compare favorably with the extensive press she received in the early years of her career.

27. Biographical information for Althea Gibson is extracted from her autobiography, Gibson, *I Always Wanted to Be Somebody* and a bio-piece written for the *New York Post,* reprinted in the magazine

section of the *Pittsburgh Courier* in installments, September 21, 28, and October 5, 12, 19, and 26, 1957.

28. Festle, *Playing Nice*, 60.

29. Festle has likewise explored the theme of women tennis players being criticized for playing too masculine a game. See Festle, *Playing Nice*, 67.

30. *New York Times*, 9 September 1957, p. 33; "That Gibson Girl," *Time*, 26 August 1957, p. 44; *Chicago Tribune*, 31 August 1950, sec. 4, p. 2; *Boston Globe*, 9 September 1957, p. 11.

31. *New York Times*, 24 June 1956, sec. V, p. 3; "A Cowpuncher and Negro Make Tennis History," *Life*, 23 September 1957, p. 56.

32. Festle, *Playing Nice*, 67.

33. *New York Times*, 7 July 1957, sec. V, p. 4; *Atlanta Constitution*, 5 July 1958, p. 10; "Cowpuncher and Negro," p. 56.

34. Also at issue for Gibson that had not been a concern for Coachman was the standard of propriety and class demanded by the tennis elite. When such standards were breached, the white press could be brutal. During the 1957 Wimbledon contest, the *Boston Globe* reported that, after receiving their trophies from Queen Elizabeth II, "Althea backed away in the prescribed fashion but the irrepressible Miss Hard turned her back and blithely skipped toward the dressing room." As a result, Gibson's opponent became referred to as "California's chunky Darlene Hard" and the "chirpy blonde waitress." See the *Boston Globe*, 7 July 1957, p. 57; "The Power Game," *Time*, 15 July 1957, p. 61; *Chicago Tribune*, 7 July 1957, sec. 2, p. 1.

35. This is not to say that race was absent from the *Times* coverage of Gibson. Kenneth Love likened her to a "panther on an Arizona mesa" when he described how at home she was on the tennis court. "As she waits, half crouching for a serve," he wrote, "the comparison comes naturally to mind" (*New York Times*, 24 June 1956, sec. V, p. 3.). Even in describing her play at the 1957 Wimbledon win, another *Times* journalist could not resist the animal comparison: "Behind her serves and her severe ground shots, Althea moved tigerishly to the net to cut away her volleys" (*New York Times*, 7 July 1957, sec. V, p. 1.).

36. For example, see *New York Times*, 11 September 1956, p. 34; 8 July 1957, p. 20; 10 September 1957, p. 32; and 9 September 1958, p. 34. The reference to "our own Althea Gibson" is from 8 July 1957, p. 22.

37. C. Vann Woodward, *The Strange Career of Jim Crow*, 3rd rev. ed. (New York: Oxford University Press, 1974), 130–131.

38. For an excellent study of the integration of major league baseball, see Tygiel, *Baseball's Great Experiment*. For football see Thomas G. Smith, "Outside the Pale: The Exclusion of Blacks from the National Football League, 1934–1946," *Journal of Sport History* 15 (Winter 1988): 277.

39. For a good overview of the importance of the Cold War to the African American civil rights movement, see especially the introduction in Mary L. Dudziak, *Cold War, Civil Rights: Race and the Image of American Democracy* (Princeton, N.J.: Princeton University Press, 2000), 3–17.

40. Festle, *Playing Nice*, 62.

41. Gibson, *I Always Wanted To Be Somebody*, 101. Emmett Till was a 14-year-old African American teenager from Chicago who was beaten and lynched for "flirting" with a white woman in 1955. Gibson was mistaken about the location, however. The crime occurred in Mississippi, while Till was visiting his uncle. The two men arrested for the crime were acquitted by an all-white jury in September of the same year. Bruce Adelson, *Brushing Back Jim Crow: The Integration of Minor-League Baseball in the American South* (Charlotresville: University Press of Virginia, 1999), 160–161.

42. Dudziak, *Cold War*, 115–118.

43. *Pittsburgh Courier,* 12 August 1950, p. 23; *New York Amsterdam News,* 9 September 1950, p. 27.

44. In particular, see sports sections in the *Baltimore Afro-American,* the *Pittsburgh Courier,* and the *Chicago Defender* for the period 1952–1955, which all featured Gibson and her victories in the black ATA tournaments but stayed conspicuously silent as she struggled to regain her foothold in the white USLTA tournaments.

45. Vertinsky and Captain, "More Myth than History," 545.

46. *Chicago Defender,* 21 July 1956, p. 17; *Baltimore Afro-American,* 22 June 1957, p. 16; *Baltimore Afro-American,* 30 June 1956, p. 14; *Baltimore Afro-American,* 21 July 1956, p. 7.

47. Cahn, *Coming on Strong,* 117–118.

48. *Pittsburgh Courier,* 2 September 1950, p. 1; *Pittsburgh Courier,* 13 July 1957, p. 24; "Tennis Queen From Harlem," *Ebony,* October 1957, p. 91.

49. *Chicago Defender,* 7 July 1956, p. 17; *Chicago Defender,* 14 July 1956, p. 17.

50. *Chicago Defender,* 27 July 1957, p. 1; *Chicago Defender,* 2 July 1957, p. 24; *Pittsburgh Courier,* 27 July 1957, p. 24.

51. *Chicago Defender,* 12 July 1958, p. 1; *Pittsburgh Courier,* 3 August 1957, p. 27.

52. *Chicago Defender,* 14 July 1956, p. 17; *Chicago Defender,* 7 July 1956, p. 17; *Baltimore Afro-American,* 29 June 1957, magazine section, pp. 2, 6.

53. *Baltimore Afro-American,* 13 July 1957, p. 14. For Lacy's contribution to the Jackie Robinson crusade, see Tygiel, *Baseball's Great Experiment,* 42–43, 63–64.

54. *Chicago Defender,* 7 July 1956, p. 17; *Pittsburgh Courier,* 27 July 1957, p. 24.

55. *Baltimore Afro-American,* 20 September 1958, p. 13; *Pittsburgh Courier,* 10 August 1957, p. 24.

56. *Pittsburgh Courier,* 21 September 1957, p. 24; *Pittsburgh Courier,* 26 October 1957, magazine section, p. 3; "That Gibson Girl," *Time,* 26 August 1957, p. 48.

57. Gibson, *I Always Wanted To Be Somebody,* 158–159.

58. See conclusion of note 3.

59. *New York Times,* 24 June 1956, sec. V, p. 3.

Further Reading

Grundy, P. (2001). *Learning to Win: Sports, Education and Social Change in Twentieth Century North Carolina.* Chapel Hill: University of North Carolina Press.

Hult, J. S., & Trekell, M. (Eds.) (1991). A Century of Women's Basketball: From Frailty to Final Four. Reston, VA: American Alliance for Health, Physical Education, Recreation and Dance.

Discussion Questions

1. How do the issues of class, race, and gender intersect in the athletic careers of Alice Coachman and Althea Gibson?

2. How does the African-American press write about Alice Coachman and Althea Gibson?

3. How does the White press write about Alice Coachman and Althea Gibson?

4

A Sense of Community: Japanese-American Girl's and Women's Softball in Los Angeles, 1930–1950

Alison M. Wrynn

© Corbis

In recent years the sporting experiences of people of color have become the focus of an increasing number of studies. In spite of this increase, the study of Asian-American sport, including Japanese-American sport, has been virtually neglected.[1] This study examines a Japanese-American sporting institution which was popular from the 1930s through World War II, women's softball. In the greater Los Angeles area a number of leagues were formed by Japanese-American women who wanted to participate within their own communities. Moreover, they were forced to establish their own organizations because of prevailing views which excluded them from the leagues of the surrounding white community.

Prelude to the Nisei Softball Leagues

Although softball came to be an extremely popular recreational sport in twentieth century America it has been studied by few historians. The game's popularity began to grow during the Depression stimulated in part by the increased amount of leisure time which was available to many Americans. Additionally, costs for equipment were very small and almost any vacant lot could easily become a softball field. Many softball parks were built under the auspices of the Works Progress Administration and leagues were organized to fill them. It was a game that attracted many females, claimed *Recreation* magazine in 1936, and was popular because women were capable of playing it.[2] Many *nisei* girls also took an interest in the game.[3] Viewing it as a popular American past time, they began by playing somewhat informally and later established softball leagues in the greater Los Angeles area.

Roger Daniels has argued that during the Depression years the Japanese-Americans didn't look outside their own community for support, but rather relied on their own resources and what their own community could provide for support, and to fill their leisure time.[4] During the 1932 Olympic Games that were held in their own community of Los Angeles, the leading Japanese-American newspaper in Los Angeles, *Rafu Shimpo*, carried many stories about the success of Japanese Olympians, including women.[5] Most of these stories were in the Japanese section of the newspaper and were obviously a source of pride for the *issei*. By the mid 1930s the Japanese community in Los Angeles was in a state of transition to a greater focus on the *nisei*. One area in which this was increasingly evident was Japanese-American girl's and women's softball. There is some limited evidence that *nisei* girls enjoyed softball on an informal basis during the 1930s and 1940s. This paper, however, will focus on the formal softball leagues that were organized for Japanese-American girls and women from 1930–1950. These leagues, formed by the Japanese-American community for their own people, gave the *nisei* girls and women an opportunity to participate in a sport that was a popular form of recreation in the United States during the Depression and World War II.

Softball for women enjoyed considerable popularity in the 1930s and 1940s as evidenced in community papers in the Los Angeles area such as the *Long Beach Press Telegram*. However, the general circulation press gave little attention to ethnic group activities; to obtain information about Japanese-American events one must consult the *Rafu Shimpo* which was the leading Japanese-American newspaper in Los Angeles. The *Rafu Shimpo* included a Japanese section for the convenience of the *issei*, many of whom did not read English, and an English section for the *nisei*, most of whom read no Japanese. According to the *Rafu Shimpo* the pre war softball programs for Japanese-American girls and women were as large or larger than those of neighboring "white" communities against whom they competed only in exhibition or "all-star" contests. According to the *Long Beach Press Telegram* the women's recreational softball league in Long Beach reached a peak in 1940 when twelve teams competed. Comparatively, the highest level of participation for Japanese-American women was in 1938 when there were twenty teams in their league.[6] Given the small number of Japanese-American girls and women residing in the greater Los Angeles geographic area, twenty teams would seem to represent a substantial number.

From 1939–1945, the number of women's softball teams in the Los Angeles area expanded substantially as a consequence of the influx of service women and women to work in war related industries. The number of Japanese-American teams was reduced to zero as a result of Executive Order 9066, which relocated the Japanese-Americans away from the west coast of the United States. However, these young *nisei* women did not abandon their interest in the game. They continued their participation in new locations, such as "assembly centers" and "internment camps", in which the Japanese-Americans were placed in the spring of 1942.

Following their release from these camps, which began in late 1944 and early 1945, many Japanese-Americans were not permitted to relocate to "sensitive" areas. Because Los Angeles was considered to be one of these, they were forced to relocate elsewhere. When these restrictions were subsequently lifted many did return to the Los Angeles area and re-established softball programs, on a much more limited scale than prior to World War II. The breakup of the secure Japanese-American community due to internment in 1942 and the relocation which dispersed families must be seen as a major reason for the smaller leagues. Another factor which was undoubtedly a contributing reason was the desire to not be too closely identified with anything Japanese following the war.

Pre-War Softball

The first report of a Japanese girl playing softball in the Los Angeles area occurred in 1931. The Rafu Shimpo recorded "Kim" Okizaki as a member of Alhambra High School's playday team and the only Japanese representative. The article encouraged other Japanese girls to participate in playdays in order to "make new friends" and to "keep well and healthy."[7] The following week, the paper included a report of a series of ball games played between two neighborhood gakuen. One of the games was played by a team of girls.[8] Softball continued to be reported throughout 1932. Additionally, an "inter-racial" game against the Chinese Mei Wah girls from little Cathay was played.[9] Activities such as these were organized by the issei who wished to encourage their children to participate in the language school (gakuen) and the other Japanese-oriented organizations. Such endeavors were a catalyst for the establishment of competitive softball leagues for nisei girls.

Although coverage of girls and women's softball in *Rafu Shimpo* from 1933–1935 was extremely limited, beginning in 1936 it came to enjoy considerable attention. This coincided with the establishment of an all Japanese softball league under the sponsorship of the Women's Athletic Union (WAU). The WAU sponsored volleyball and basketball leagues for girls in the winter, as well as the softball league in the spring. The popularity of girl's softball was acknowledged in May of that year in the sport's pages of the *Rafu Shimpo*. Under the heading titled "SUCCESSFUL" sportswriter Frank Sugiyama noted:

> Softball is popular in Lil' Tokio. When the WAU innovated [sic] the softball league as another of the fads of local athletic circles, it had the fans pondering whether the league would be a success or not. From the standpoint of baseball turnouts, the girl's league appears to have won an overwhelming victory. Last week, at least 200 Angelenos sat in the bleachers out at Hazard playground and saw two well played games. And those spectators were very much interested too.[10]

It is interesting to note that the girls' softball league was organized even before a program had been started for the boys. Although a successful baseball league for boys and men existed under the auspices of the Japanese Athletic Union (JAU), with 16 teams participating in 1936, a softball league for males had not yet been formed, although the JAU was contemplating one.[11] By the mid 1930s, the *gakuens* were no longer the only sponsors of softball teams for girls and women. Interest had become so extensive that the Young Women's Buddhist Association (YWBA), social/service clubs and Christian churches located in Japanese-American communities also sponsored teams that were entered in the Japanese WAU.[12] There were thirteen teams in the WAU league in 1936 most of which were coached by men.[13]

The softball contests were reported in detail every week by the *Rafu Shimpo*. These reports included discussions of the athletic skill of the girls and commented upon the games in a style similar to that given to the boy's and men's games. The starting pitcher of a team called the "All-Arounds" was called a "big gun". The Queen Esthers, the paper reported, would ". . . pound out hit after hit . . ." against opponents. The shortstop of the L.A. Bussei's for example was credited with a ". . . sensational catch."[14] Members of boy's teams such as the Gakusei-kai Bees were said to have "pounded out" hits and utilized "stellar hurling" to win games.[15] The girls' softball contests were described in a manner similar to and given the same prominence as the boys' baseball leagues in the sport's pages or on the first page of the daily English section of the *Rafu Shimpo*. It should be noted that sports coverage in the *Rafu Shimpo* was extensive throughout the last half of the 1930s. Although boy's and men's sports were covered more often, the girl's and women's contests did not go unnoticed. When the season ended in June, the championship game of the WAU league was one of the headline stories in the daily English section of the newspaper.[16]

The growing interest and popularity which resulted in the formation of a girl's and women's league in 1936, also led to an all-star game at the close of the season. An "all-star" girl's softball team was to compete against what the *Rafu Shimpo* called an "American" team; by which they meant women's softball teams from the greater Los Angeles area. Commenting upon the forthcoming contest a reporter from the *Rafu Shimpo* felt that the *nisei* team would not be able to compete at the same level as the "white" team, primarily because of the disorganized play of the *nisei* girls.[17] It is interesting and probably not insignificant to note that at this time the only formal competitive contact between teams from the Women's Athletic Union and players from the larger community was through an all-star or exhibition game.

In 1937 the number of teams in the WAU softball league declined somewhat from thirteen to eleven, but no less attention was given to them in the sport's section of the *Rafu Shimpo*. Readers were urged to watch what one reporter called two "croocial" games which could possibly decide the league championship.[18] The following week a poem dedicated to the girls in the WAU league appeared on the sport's page. Although the poem was light-hearted in tone, it contained some telling imagery about the writer's perceptions of girls involved in sport. The girls were described as:

> "Full of vim and vigorous,
> forthright and not timorous,
> With muscles sinewy and hard as steel . . ."

The final stanza was a tongue-in-cheek compliment to the girls' athletic ability (tempered with a certain ambivalence in regard to what the writer perceived as the role for young Japanese-American women):

"The way you play this game, baseball,
has made me slightly cynical
Re: masculine superiority;
It would; perhaps, be fitting
If boys should take up knitting
Or learn to crochet with authority!"[19]

The WAU softball league again expanded in 1938 to eighteen teams divided into two divisions.[20] In the six weeks of league competition, more than fourteen articles were dedicated to the girls' league. This growth in the number of teams, and an altered tenor of reporting the contests, suggest that girl's and women's softball may have become more fully accepted within the Japanese-American community. In comparison with former years, the articles describing the contests were more factually straight forward and the sport's section described the results of WAU contests in the same manner as they described boy's and men's baseball.

In 1936 the *Rafu Shimpo* had implied that the players were not particularly skillful. By 1938 there were reports about teams such as the Queen Esthers, with a batting order described as a "murderers' row", who completed a sweep of all three WAU titles: volleyball, basketball and softball.[21] Marty Fiedler, whom a writer for the *Rafu Shimpo* described as a softball "impressario" in Hollywood, may have had teams like the Queen Esthers in mind when he sought to organize two all-star softball teams to send to Japan in the fall of 1938. One team was to be composed of "American" girls; the other team was described as being composed of *nisei* girls and girls of other races. This paper referred to the proposed tour as a "goodwill girls' baseball mission". Its avowed purpose was to bring goodwill messages from the President of the United States and the Governor of California to the people of Japan.[22] As no mention of this tour was to be found in the fall 1938 newspapers it is quite probable that the teams were never organized.

Interest in Japanese-American girl's and women's softball remained constant through the end of the decade with the eighteen teams divided into three divisions. Once again the championship was awarded to the undefeated Queen Esthers.[23] The increasing participation of young *nisei* women in softball did not mean, however, that the community did not still believe that females had gender related activities. Two examples may be cited: the WAU softball games for Mother's Day 1939 were cancelled although boys and men's baseball were not. Additionally, in late May, the WAU games were cancelled so the girls could help out at a community picnic; again boy's and men's contests were held.[24]

Although the reasons are not clear, there was a slight decline in the number of teams which comprised the WAU in 1940 and 1941. It is possible the original enthusiasm and novelty of the league began to wane. The Queen Esthers, who had won the softball title the three previous years, were not represented in 1940/41.[25] It seems likely that many of the young women who had been original members of the league in 1936 had by this time gone off to college, started careers or married.

The demise of the Queen Esthers, who had been strong participants in the WAU league, may have contributed to the slight downturn in participation and interest. So too would events which happened on 7 December 1941. The backlash which followed upon the Japanese Imperial Air Force's attack on Pearl Harbor resulted in dislocating and in some instances devastating consequences for Japanese-Americans in general and girl's and women's softball in the greater Los Angeles area. Executive Order 9066 called for the removal of Japanese-Americans from the western United States. People who had lived in the United States their whole life, and were citizens, were transported to assembly centers and internment camps and forced to reconstruct their community. Recreational activities, including softball, were an important part of the reconstruction of life in the camps.

Softball in the Assembly Centers and Internment Camps

The bombing of Pearl Harbor was the catalyst used by anti-Japanese organizations to finally remove the Japanese-Americans from their midst. The bombing focused and intensified anti-Japanese sentiment that had been building for decades. In the first three months of 1942, Los Angeles Mayor Fletcher Bowron received 305 letters in favor of evacuating the Japanese-Americans from the west coast; only twenty-two supported the position that Japanese-Americans be permitted to remain.[26] Groups which included the Los Angeles Junior Chamber of Commerce, the Los Angeles Industrial Union Council-CIO, and the International Fishermen and Allied Workers of America all sent letters encouraging the removal of the Japanese from the area as soon as possible.[27] Mayor Bowron supported these views. In a July 1943 interview he stated that he did not feel that the American born Japanese were citizens.[28] Local attitudes were soon reflected in national policy when in February 1942 President Franklin Delano Roosevelt signed Executive Order 9066 which directed the Secretary of War to remove any person from areas deemed "sensitive" to the war effort.[29]

When in March 1942 the United States government issued an order which called for the removal of Japanese-Americans from the western United States, this removed all possibility that the WAU softball leagues in the greater Los Angeles area could continue. The internment of all persons of Japanese ancestry, whether or not they were American citizens, began in the late spring of 1942. Men, women and children were first removed to hastily built assembly centers, which were constructed at converted fairgrounds and racetracks.[30] For most this was the first step in a relocation process that would end with 110,000 Japanese-Americans in one of ten internment camps located in various parts of the United States. Internees remained in the assembly centers until the fall of 1942; during these few months they tried to establish some sense of normalcy in their lives to help replace the community structures from which they had been uprooted. They quickly organized schools to complete the academic semester, and recreational activities to fill the enforced leisure time. They also printed a newspaper to keep everyone informed of the daily news.[31]

From the assembly centers, Japanese-Americans were transported to "internment" camps far from their west coast homes. The camps were located in California (Manzanar, Tule Lake), Arizona (Poston, Gila River), Arkansas (Rohwer, Jerome), Utah (Topaz), Colorado (Granada), Wyoming (Heart Mountain), and Idaho (Minidoka).[32] The Wartime Civil Control Administration (WCCA) was the initial government agency responsible for organizing and administering the assembly centers. It soon became apparent that to the greatest extent possible the camps would have to be run by the evacuees. There were several reasons, but two were paramount: (1) to maximize the internee's sense of control over their situation and (2) to minimize the cost of the internment to the Federal government.[33] The War Relocation Authority (WRA) was the agency that was ultimately organized to work with the Japanese-Americans in the camps. At an early point, both the government and the internees recognized the importance of an efficiently organized recreation program. From the standpoint of the federal government the main objective of the recreation program in the camps was to keep people busy and eradicate "discontent and social friction" within the camp which could result from increased free time and boredom.[34]

A wide range of recreational activities were organized which included things of interest for both *issei* and *nisei*. The programs included such things as arts and crafts classes, language and citizenship classes, libraries, and athletics. Softball, both for men and women, was to be an important part of the recreation program in many of the assembly centers and internment camps. A preliminary report issued by the WCCA in 1942 outlined the recreational needs of the camps and noted that softball diamonds could be placed on any level piece of ground. In addition, bleachers could be constructed so the people could watch the softball games. The report concluded that: "The Japanese, as a rule—even the older people—are very interested spectators of all types of athletic contests."[35]

Santa Anita, a large racetrack in southern California that was converted into an assembly center for more than 10,000 Japanese-Americans, had several softball teams competing by April 1942. One internee wrote to a former teacher informing him that since school was no longer in session an extensive program of recreation was needed to keep the *nisei* occupied. Softball was the sport of choice at Santa Anita that summer, and girls' as well as boys' teams were formed.[36] By May 1942, eight teams were competing in the junior girls' softball league and seven teams in the senior girls' league at the Santa Anita center.[37] The formation of an additional league was announced shortly thereafter. This was called the twilight league and would allow the older girls to play in the evening after work.[38] With the limited facilities and the lack of extensive sports equipment, softball was one of the few sports activities in which the internees could participate. Since teams did not have the former community based organizations to sponsor them (these having been broken up as a consequence of relocation) softball teams tended to be organized around the concept of former hometowns. This arrangement was facilitated by the government who had evacuated virtually intact communities from Japanese-American neighborhoods. Additionally, other girls, from apparently different areas, joined to form teams such as: Seabiscuits, Stablemates, Eligibles, many of the names were obviously an acknowledgment that they were located in a former race track.[39]

At the Pomona assembly center that spring and summer of 1942, softball was also a main part of the recreation program. At the Pomona center, which had a much smaller population then did Santa Anita, softball appears to have been particularly popular; approximately one in six of the girls and women between the ages of 15-25 participated.[40] The main attractions of their league that summer were the much anticipated contests between the Dimonettes and the Malinettes. These two teams were named after their "sponsors", the head of the recreation program Eugene Dimon (who would later head the recreation program at the Tule Lake internment camp) and the housing Director Douglas Malin. Although the softball programs in the assembly centers had been organized quickly, they provided recreation and diversion for many of the residents. Therefore, the leagues were considered a success by the camp administrators as they distracted the internee's attention from the conditions of camp life. The internees, on the other hand, appreciated the diversion that the games offered.

It had been somewhat easy to maintain interest in the programs during the short stays in the assembly centers. As the internees began to move on to more permanent internment camps, however, the challenge would be whether or not a similar interest in recreational activities, such as softball, could be sustained over a period of two or three years. By fall 1942, internment camps in various parts of the nation had been readied to receive Japanese-Americans. A great deal of work was necessary to make these camps achieve any semblance of hospitable or even acceptable living conditions. Most of the internees from the Pomona assembly center were sent to Heart Mountain in Cody, Wyoming. Having arrived in fall of 1942, they immediately organized schools for the children. They also organized leisure and recreation programs which included movies, crafts classes, dances, shows, language classes, and athletics. Here, too, softball occupied a prominent place in the recreation program. The first season six girl's teams participated even though residents were busy with the relocation and did not yet have extensive amounts of leisure time.[41] The number of teams remained small in part because by late October the weather in Wyoming was very cold, something that the Southern Californians were not used to. Many girls did not want to be outside playing softball; and the boys had by then switched to the more vigorous games of football and basketball.

In spring 1943, however, twelve girls' softball teams had been organized into two leagues.[42] The following year the number had risen to more than seventeen.[43] This increase is noteworthy because over the two year period the number of girls in their late teens who remained in the camps declined as many relocated to jobs in the Midwest or East, or to colleges and universities throughout the country. Those who remained in the camps played on teams organized around their "block" (the camp's living areas were divided into blocks for organizational purposes), youth groups or work organizations (e.g. clerks from the camp Co-op or recreation program assistants).[44]

The Manzanar internment camp had originally been an assembly center and was located in the desert of Southern California. Recreational programs began shortly after the first residents arrived in March 1942; by April a softball league for girls had been organized. The first teams that were organized tended to center around the former home towns of their members (e.g. Bainbridge Island [Washington] Girls and Los Angeles Girls). Each of the seasons from 1942–1945 the Manzanar girls' softball league consisted of eleven teams. These teams followed the Los Angeles WAU softball league rules, possibly due to the fact that many of the girls were from the Los Angeles area.[45] The Colorado River Relocation Center, generally known as Poston, attained a peak population of 17,833 in September of 1942. An older girls' softball league was formed shortly after the camp opened in the summer of that year. This was conducted under the supervision of the leader of women's sports.[46] The stated purpose of the Poston Women's Athletic Union (PWAU) was to organize the physical, social and recreational activities among the young women of the center.[47]

From these and similar experiences reported at other camps, it is reasonable to conclude that recreation was an important aspect of daily life in the assembly centers and internment camps for *nisei* girls during World War II. Not only did it occupy their time; it also gave them opportunities to socialize with their peers. To the extent that it was possible to have fun while imprisoned behind barbed wire, the softball leagues gave the Japanese-American girls an opportunity to have fun in an otherwise demoralizing situation and allowed them to temporarily forget the circumstances of their internment. It is highly probable that the pre-war WAU softball programs in Los Angeles were the basis for the interest in softball programs in Pomona, Santa Anita, Heart Mountain and Manzanar. Indeed, several girls who were mentioned in *Rafu Shimpo* before the war in Los Angeles were also referred to during the war in the *Pomona Center News* and the *Heart Mountain Sentinel*, two representative publications initiated by the internees at these camps.

POST WAR SOFTBALL PROGRAMS

Although the signing of the Japanese surrender aboard the battleship *Missouri* had not yet occurred, by late 1944 and into early 1945 most of the internees had been released from the camps, in part due to the realization by the United States government that the internment was too unwieldy and expensive. Many had been relocated to the interior of the country after the government had segregated what it referred to as the "loyal from the disloyal". To classify evacuees who would be eligible to relocate throughout the United States, the government utilized several criteria. The more significant were: (1) *nisei*, who were eligible if they had no family in Japan, had not visited Japan just prior to the war, had never worked for the Japanese government, etc. (2) eligible *issei* included those who had served in the United States armed services or had sons in the United States armed services or daughters in the United States auxiliary services. In addition, these individuals would still be subject to the same criteria as outlined above for the *nisei*.[48] A large proportion of those evacuees who had been relocated to the interior of the United States wanted to move back to California and the west coast when the war ended. They would face numerous difficulties caused by continuing racist sentiments. Moreover, many of their homes had been taken over during the war due to severe housing shortages that had occurred as a result of the large influx of war industry workers to the Los Angeles area.[49] The new occupants were not willing to relinquish the homes and the government would not assist the Japanese-Americans in re-acquiring their property.

The War Relocation Authority was anxious for the post war safety of the Japanese-Americans. As they released them from the camps, the agency recommended that the *issei* and *nisei* not come together with large groups of Japanese and that they not utilize the Japanese language.[50] Although this created certain dilemmas for the *nisei*, this was a particular burden for the *issei* who as first generation still retained the culture and language of their homeland. The formerly tightly structured Japanese-American communities were loosened somewhat by the dislocations that had occurred during the war. It was further influenced by the fact that many of the *nisei* were able to take advantage of somewhat less restrictive housing covenants following the war and move out into the suburbs. This opportunity for them to disperse more widely throughout the Los Angeles area may have influenced the post war softball program for girls. Because their geographical distribution was more disparate, there were not the same opportunities or tendencies to re-establish softball programs for girls and women in the ways that had occurred in the 1930s.

The *nisei* who returned to the Los Angeles area following World War II did try, however, to reorganize some of the social and cultural groups that had been so important to the community in the pre war era. These efforts included athletic teams that were formed for many sports and age groups.[51] Softball for girls was one of these. In the summer of 1946, the *Rafu Shimpo* contained no reports of girl's softball. One reason may have been the newspaper's decreased size from the pre war era and the overall limited coverage of sports. A more important reason perhaps was the uncertainty over the transition and return to Los Angeles. A contributory factor may have been the widely dispersed community which would have made it difficult to reorganize teams. In the spring of 1947 an announcement appeared in *Rafu Shimpo* asking girls who were interested in playing softball to attend a meeting of the newly formed Women's Athletic Association (WAA).[52] In the week preceding this announcement, basketball leagues sponsored by the WAA had completed a successful season of play and it was hoped that interest in girl's sports could be continued with a softball league that summer.[53] By early June, however, there was evidence that there was not enough interest and plans for the softball league were cancelled.[54]

In 1948 the Japanese-American girl's softball program was reinstituted in Los Angeles. Seven teams entered the league and began competition for a championship trophy offered by a neighborhood store.[55] Within a few weeks the league was reduced to five teams, two teams having dropped out due to insufficient participation. In spite of the reduced involvement there is some evidence that the community wished to support the girls' softball league. For example a sportsmanship trophy was sponsored by a local sporting goods store.[56] In spite of such efforts the season could not be considered a success as it ended in August with the championship awarded by a forfeit. In fact, nearly one-third of the WAA league contests during 1948 had ended in forfeits.[57] In one of the few bright notes that summer an all-star WAA team traveled to Riverside and defeated the local *nisei* team 20–0.[58]

Only five teams competed in the Women's Athletic Association league in 1949 and the season lasted only a month. Once again there were several forfeits and the season ended with one dominant team.[59] No all-star game or championship trophy highlighted the 1949 season. The softball leagues which had once attracted between eighteen and twenty teams of active and interested participants now could barely field five teams on a regular basis. Among the factors which contributed to this decline were: the loss of established ethnic institutions such as *gakuen* and Buddhist temples, which had before the war given focus to Japanese culture as a part of the *nisei's* lives; an overall decrease in the Japanese population throughout California; the wider dispersal of Japanese throughout the nation and throughout the Los Angeles area; the greater opportunities for Japanese-American girls and women to participate in other activities, such as basketball which became a very popular sport in the post war era; and the desire not to be identified as belonging to a Japanese organization.[60]

Conclusion

The pre war programs were prompted by the desire on the part of *issei* to perpetuate Japanese culture and heritage among their children. They recognized that the *nisei* were interested in many activities of the larger society, one of which was softball, so they offered recreational programs in the *gakuen* and Buddhist temples in order to make these institutions more appealing to the *nisei*. Softball for girls in Los Angeles started on a small scale in the *gakuen* and expanded into a separate league as interest and participation grew. The parents of the girls would watch the games and, if newspaper accounts are accurate, apparently enjoyed the novelty of the sport. Even when the number of teams declined somewhat in the late 1930s, the community continued to encourage the girls in their athletic pursuits.

The relocations imposed upon the Japanese-Americans during World War II created extreme disruptions within their communities. During the years of forced internment, recreational pursuits, including softball, performed an important role. George Eisen has shown a similar circumstance for another group which was forcibly imprisoned during World War II. His *Children and Play in the Holocaust* argues that play remained central to the lives of many Jewish children while they were in ghettos and concentration camps. Although the experiences of the two groups were certainly not identical, they both shared the facts of extreme dislocation and lengthy internment. Recreational activity continued to be of great importance to the Japanese-American community in the assembly centers and internment camps as they tried to recreate a sense of community within the camps. In addition to school and work, recreation was the most important aspect of the internee's lives. Since they couldn't leave the camps they had limited outlets for recreation. Recreation served the interests of the United States' government because it occupied the internee's free time and it was relatively inexpensive and easy to organize. The internees appreciated the diversion that the recreational programs provided as well as the opportunity to reconstruct their pre war community in some small way. Many activities other than softball were organized in the camps, but softball remained a major focus for much of the recreational activity. One of the possible reasons was the strong pre war base that had been established in leagues such as the Women's Athletic Union in Los Angeles.

As citizens, the *nisei* were denied their civil rights and removed from their homes, schools, jobs, and communities. The vast majority of the *issei*, although not citizens, were loyal to the United States and not to the Imperial government of Japan. All were incarcerated, however, for their own safety they were told, in reality because of growing negative public sentiment. In the "camps" they could either accept the situation or take up the fight with more vigor. Most of those who were vocal in their opposition to the internment were sent to segregated facilities, many others were against the internment, but for the sake of their families did not publicly condemn it.

The Japanese-Americans could not go on with their lives as before, but they could do their best to survive the internment and reconstruct their communities. When they were released from the internment camps, they had little hope of returning to their pre war lives. Some had lost their homes and property at the beginning of the war and had not been adequately compensated for their losses; some went elsewhere to live in the United States; of the many *issei* and *nisei* who did return to Los Angeles they were so busy trying to put their lives back together they had little time for fun and recreation; those who did return were dispersed more widely which contributed to the breakdown of the formerly stable communities. When the *nisei* girls did begin playing softball again, the leagues were much smaller than they had been before the war.

Endnotes

1. Ronald T. Takaki, ed. *From Different Shores: Perspectives on Race and Ethnicity in America* (New York: Oxford University Press, 1987), 161. Recently, historians have begun to examine the sporting experiences of Japanese American women. For example: Sam Regaldo's examination of the recreational experiences of *nisei* women in the World War II internment camps.

2. Arthur T. Noren, "Softball—The Game for All," *Recreation*, April 1936, 508.

3. The emigration of Japanese from their homeland did not begin in significant numbers until 1868. Prior to that, immigration was forbidden by the feudal rulers of the *Tokugawa Shogunate*. The Japanese who first arrived in the United States during the late 1800s and early 1900s had been strongly influenced by the policies and practices of the *Meiji* (1868–1912) government and the Confucian ethics which were adopted as the basis of society by the *Meiji*. Traditionally, Confucian ethics emphasized such things as duty and obedience, and codes of appropriate behavior according to role-status, age and sex.[3] In Japan the family, or *ie*, adopted these principles as a framework for their behavior. In America, the typical Japanese family consisted of *issei*, the Japanese immigrant who could not become a United States citizen, and *nisei*, children of the *issei* who were born in the United States and thus were automatically granted citizenship. When the *issei* came to the United States, the *ken*, or larger Japanese community, took over the functions of the *ie* and perpetuated many of the same Confucian ethics

4. Roger Daniels, "Japanese America, 1930–1941: An Ethnic Community in the Great Depression," *Journal of the West* , 35.

5. "Japan's Swim Aces To Open Bid Tomorrow," *Rafu Shimpo,* 5 May 1932.

6. Alison M. Wrynn, "Women's Industrial and Recreation League Softball in Southern California, 1930-1950," (M.A. thesis, California State University, Long Beach, 1989), 63.

7. "Lone Japanese Girl Captains Ball Team," *Rafu Shimpo* 22 May 1931.

8. "Gardena-Hawthorne Split Ball Games," *Rafu Shimpo* 29 May 1931.

9. "Oliver Girls Win Baseball from Chinese," *Rafu Shimpo* 13 June 1932.

10. Frank Sugiyama, "Sportdom's What-nots," *Rafu Shimpo* 3 May 1936.

11. Ibid.

12. "Close Battle Anticipated in WAU Loop," *Rafu Shimpo* 10 May 1936.

13. Sugiyama; "Close Battle".

14. "One Upset Staged as JAU and WAU Games Played," *Rafu Shimpo* 25 May 1936.

15. "Hollywood Victors in Pitching Duel," *Rafu Shimpo* 11 May 1936; "Midget Nine Upsets Hollywood Seinens," *Rafu Shimpo* 25 May 1936 .

16. "Queen Esthers Take '37 WAU Title; Cougars, Stars Play in JAU Tilt," *Rafu Shimpo* 7 June 1937.

17. "Softball Teams Practice Monday," *Rafu Shimpo* 14 June 1936; WAU All-Stars," *Rafu Shimpo* 28 June 1936. A careful search of ensuing issues of *Rafu Shimpo* did not elicit any mention of the game

18. "Two 'Croocial' Games on Tap for WAU Fans," *Rafu Shimpo* 9 May 1937.

19. De Numa, "Oh Girls!," *Rafu Shimpo* 16 May 1937.

20. "Girls Teams Continue Tilts," *Rafu Shimpo* 8 May 1938.

21. "Hollywood Queen Esthers Take Third WAU Crown," *Rafu Shimpo* 27 June 1938.

22. Tony Gomez, "From the Bleachers," *Rafu Shimpo* 26 June 1938.

23. "Dis' n Dat," *Rafu Shimpo* 11 June 1939.

24. "Mothers Day Postpones WAU Games," *Rafu Shimpo* 14 May 1939; "WAU Teams Take Day Off Today," *Rafu Shimpo* 28 May 1939.

25. "Standings," *Rafu Shimpo* 19 May 1940; "Royalettes Take on Marienettes," *Rafu Shimpo* 1 June 1941.

26. "Mayor Fletcher Bowron, Los Angeles, Correspondence," A15.15, Japanese Evacuation and Relocation Collection, the Bancroft Library, University of California, Berkeley (hereafter cited as JERS).

27. Ibid.

28. Ibid.

29. Takaki, *Strangers From a Different Shore*, 391.

30. Ibid., 394.

31. "Girls' Sports," *Pomona Center News* 23 May 1942.

32. Daniels, *Asian America*, 216.

33. Daniels, *Asian America*, 234.

34. "Recommended Recreation Programs," B1.15, JERS.

35. Ibid.

36. "Santa Anita Correspondence," **B12.49, JERS.

37. "Girl's Start Softball Loops," *Santa Anita Pacemaker* 1 May 1942.

38. "Fem Leagues to be Formed," *Santa Anita Pacemaker* 8 May 1942.

39. "Twilight Softball Standings," *Santa Anita Pacemaker* 27 June 1942.

40. "Numbers in Camp," *Pomona Center News* 2 June 1942.

41. "Two Unbeaten Girls Teams Meet Sunday," *Heart Mountain Sentinel* 24 October 1942.

42. "Jinx-Coms Split Softball Contests," *Heart Mountain Sentinel* 19 June 1943.

43. "Three Loops Open Play Next Week," *Heart Mountain Sentinel* 10 June 1944.

44. Ibid.

45. "Girls to Follow WAU Softball Rules," *Manzanar Free Press* 2 June 1942.

46. "Report on Various Activities," J2.85, JERS.

47. Ibid.

48. "Proposed Segregation of Loyal from Disloyal," D2.050, JERS.

49. Modell, 188.

50. Daniels, *Asian Americans*, 294.

51. Ichiro Mike Murase, *Little Tokyo: One Hundred Years in Pictures* (Los Angeles: Visual Communications Asian American Studies Central, Inc., 1983), 11.

52. "Women's Softball," *Rafu Shimpo* 10 May 1947.

53. "WAU Softball Leagues Formulated," *Rafu Shimpo* 17 May 1947.

54. "No Girls Softball," *Rafu Shimpo* 7 June 1947.

55. "WAA Releases Softball Dates," *Rafu Shimpo* 13 May 1948.

56. "WAA Releases Revised Sked," *Rafu Shimpo* 1 June 1948.

57. "Miyatake Jugs Take WAA Title," *Rafu Shimpo* 16 August 1948.

58. "Butchers Riverside," *Rafu Shimpo* 16 August 1948.

59. "Pennant Within Wla Girls' Grasp," *Rafu Shimpo* 13 June 1949.

60. Daniels, *Asian Americans*, 282.

Further Reading

Hargreaves, J. (1994). *Sporting Females: Critical Issues in the History and Sociology of Women's Sports.* London and New York: Routledge.

Regalado, S. (1992). Sport and Community in California's Japanese American "Yamato Colony," 1930–1945. *Journal of Sport History*, 19:130–143.

Wrynn, A. (1994). The Recreation and Leisure Pursuits of Japanese Americans in World War II Internment Camps. In *Ethnicity and Sport in North American History and Culture*, G. Eisen & D. K. Wiggins. (Ed.) Westport: Greenwood Publishing Group, Inc.

Discussion Questions

1. Describe the importance of the family and community to Japanese American women and the impact that had on their sport participation.

2. What was the impact of World War II on the opportunities for Japanese American women in sport?

3. What happened to Japanese American women's softball in the years following the Second World War?

5

A Brief Legal History of Women in Sport

Sarah K. Fields, J.D., Ph. D.

© Shutterstock

Introduction

The year 1972 was transcendent for women's participation in sport in the United States (U.S.). Sport in America was largely considered a masculine preserve, a place to teach boys how to be men in the absence of women.[1] Although girls and women had participated in sports throughout history, they had done so in much smaller numbers than their male counterparts.[2] In 1971 just fewer than 300,000 girls participated in organized high school sports, which meant that girls comprised about 5 percent of all high school athletes.[3] A confluence of laws and a change in social attitudes in 1972 would transform the gender of sport in America dramatically. The women's movement culminated in shifting courts' interpretation of the Equal Protection Clause of the 14th Amendment of the U.S. Constitution and getting Congress to enact new laws, the Equal Rights Amendment and Title IX. As a result of these social and legal movements, the numbers of women and girls in sport rose dramatically and quickly: by 1978 almost two million girls, constituting 32 percent of all high school athletes, competed in organized sport at the high school level.[4] The laws would allow women and girls the opportunity to play sport and would also require a certain level of equity in their playing experience.

A Watershed Year

In 1972, the women's movement reached the apex of its demands for gender equality under the law. Prior to that year, women's rights activists had succeeded in changing some laws to include gender equity. The first step occurred in 1920 when women in the U.S. received the right to vote. In 1963, Congress enacted the Equal Pay Act which required that men and women receive the same pay for the same work; however, the law exempted many major job categories including executives, professionals, and administrative employees which meant that employers and the courts could justify paying women less based on job descriptions.[5] The 1964 Civil Rights Act included a prohibition of gender discrimination in the section called Title VII which banned discrimination in employment and employment promotions.

In 1972, women's rights activists were able to broaden the gender equity laws even further. First, Congress passed and President Richard M. Nixon signed the Equal Rights Amendment (ERA) to the U.S. Constitution; the ERA stated that "equality of rights under the law shall not be denied or abridged by the United States or by any state on account of sex."[6] The ERA could not become part of the Constitution, however, until three-fourths of the states ratified it. In 1972, this seemed quite likely.[7] Proponents of the ERA recognized that passage of the amendment would take years and so, in what at the time seemed like almost a stop-gap measure, Congress enacted Title IX. Title IX read "no person in the United States shall, on the basis of sex, be excluded from participation in, be denied the benefits of, or be subjected to discrimination under any education program or activity receiving Federal financial assistance."[8] Title IX proved to be vastly more influential for women and sport than the ERA because the ERA was never ratified by enough states to become an amendment to the U.S. Constitution, although a number of individual states incorporated the ERA into their state constitutions.[9]

Preexisting all of these laws was the Equal Protection Clause of the 14th Amendment of the U.S. Constitution which read "no state shall . . . deny to any person within its jurisdiction the equal protection of the laws."[10] Although originally enacted in 1868 after the Civil War, the courts had never applied it literally, especially to women, which is why many women's rights activists viewed the ERA as critical. The limitations of the Equal Protection Clause were particularly apparent in one of the few legal decisions involving gender and sport prior to 1972. In 1971 a high school girl in Connecticut wanted to run cross country but her school only had a boys' team and the league prohibited co-educational sports teams. She filed suit claiming that her rights under the Equal Protection Clause had been violated, but the judge rejected her argument. He concluded that "with boys vying with girls . . . the challenge to win, and the glory of achievement, at least for many boys, would lose incentive and become nullified. Athletic competition builds character in our boys. We do not need that kind of character in our girls, the women of tomorrow." The court added that girls should compete only against each other and only when boys were not using the equipment or the facilities.[11] The overt discrimination against this high school girl clearly proved that prior to 1972, the courts were not willing to apply the Equal Protection Clause literally with regard to girls and sport.

The changes in the law, the enactment of Title IX and the passage through Congress of the ERA, however, suggested that the courts' interpretation of the Equal Protection Clause might change with the times. Although the remainder of this article will focus on the legal history and impact of Title IX, the ERA, and the Equal Protection Clause, the significance of the social movements of the preceding decades cannot be overstated. Without a strong social push from women's rights activists, Congress would not have spontaneously enacted legislation protecting women's rights after centuries of marginalizing women. The change in law stemmed from the change in society.

Access to Sport

Title IX

The first challenge for women and girls was simply getting an opportunity to try out for existing teams and to get the support to create new teams and leagues for girls. Although Title IX was originally enacted without much thought about how it would apply to sport because the initial focus on the law had simply been on ending discrimination in the classroom, American legislators and leaders in sport quickly realized that the law could have a strong impact on sport. Therefore, a number of opponents to the law tried to minimize that impact before it could really occur. First, in 1974 Senator John Tower from Texas introduced a bill which would have exempted revenue producing sports from Title IX. His bill failed to define revenue producing and would have allowed a school or conference to determine what sports fit the definition; at the time, the assumption was that men's college football and basketball would be considered revenue producing and thus exempt. The amendment was not passed. Instead Congress passed the Javits Amendment that year which maintained that because different sports carried different expenses nothing in the law should be read as requiring equal spending for different collegiate sports.[12]

The real battle over Title IX and how it would apply to sport, however, occurred over the enforcement regulations promulgated by the Department of Housing, Education, and Welfare.[13] First came the debate over what those regulations would actually say. After extensive public debate, the enforcement regulations were sent to Congress in 1975. Once approved by Congress, the enforcement regulations had the force of law and took effect in 1978. The enforcement regulations, however, vastly limited Title IX's impact on sport by exempting contact sport from the law. The regulations stated that if a school offered a team for boys but not girls, girls had to be allowed to try out for that team "unless the sport involved is a contact sport." Contact sport was defined as "boxing, wrestling, rugby, ice hockey, football, basketball and other sports the purpose or major activity of which involved bodily contact."[14] For all legal purposes, girls could not use Title IX to gain access to contact sports; they could only use the law to gain access to non-contact sports. Based on the increase in the number of girls participating in high school sports between 1971 and 1978, girls did use the law and did participate in sport in greater numbers than ever before.

Even though Congress approved the enforcement regulations with its contact sport exemption, the struggle over Title IX and what the law entailed continued in the courts. Various lawsuits were filed challenging the power of the law, with some decisions increasing its power and others decreasing it. In 1979, the U.S. Supreme Court concluded that the law included a private right of action; this meant that individuals who had been discriminated against under Title IX could file a lawsuit directly instead of being required to go through any governmental agency.[15] Having a private right of action gave Title IX considerably more power because individuals could sue for change more quickly and more directly.

In 1984, however, the Supreme Court essentially exempted all sport from Title IX. In deciding *Grove City College v. Bell*, the Court ruled that Title IX only applied to the portion of an institution which received federal funding directly.[16] Previously the assumption had been that if an institution received any federal funding, the law applied to the whole institution. For example, if the students at a college received federal financial aid or the biology department had grant money from the National Institutes of Health, then every part of the college, including the athletic department had to comply with the law. After *Grove City*, only the financial aid office or the biology department had to comply with the law. Because no federal funding went directly to any athletic department, athletics thus became exempt from the law until 1988 when Congress enacted the Civil Rights Restoration Act which specifically stated that if any part of an institution received any federal money, then the entire institution needed to comply with the law. Thus on a practical level, Title IX did not clearly and unequivocally apply to sporting programs until 1988.

In 1992, however, the U.S. Supreme Court concluded that a person who had been discriminated against under Title IX could be awarded monetary damages.[17] This was a significant decision on several levels. First, it gave a more pragmatic incentive for plaintiffs to file suit; if all the individual who sued under Title IX could hope for was an injunction ordering her the opportunity to try out for a team, a woman or girl might be less likely to invest the time and energy into suing, but if she was likely to be awarded monetary damages, her motivation could increase. Second, monetary damages were a greater deterrent against discrimination. If a school stood to lose thousands or millions of dollars, that school might be more reluctant to violate Title IX than it would be if the only deterrent was losing a lawsuit that forced the school to let the girl try out. Third, the possibility of monetary damages made lawyers more likely to take the case on a contingency basis which made it financially more plausible for a greater number of plaintiffs to file lawsuits. Lawyers are primarily paid in one of two ways or in combination of those two. One way is the plaintiff pays the lawyer an hourly fee, which can ultimately be very expensive, and the lawyer gets paid regardless of the outcome of the case which means that the plaintiff needs to have enough money to pay for the lawsuit. The other way is the lawyer gets a percentage of the jury verdict and gets paid little or nothing if the case is lost. This allows the cash-strapped plaintiff as well as the wealthy one to file a lawsuit. On a practical level, this Court decision was very important in making Title IX more powerful.

Equal Protection Clause and State ERAs

Title IX was socially significant. The law seems to have inspired women and girls to demand their rights to participate in sport even when Title IX did not clearly apply to them. For example, in a number of lawsuits filed in which girls asked the courts for the right to try out for contact sports teams, Title IX was listed as a cause of action even though contact sports were exempt from Title IX.[18] Regardless of its power in the social imagination, in the courtroom Title IX could do nothing to get girls into contact sport. The Equal Protection Clause and various state ERAs, though, closed Title IX's contact sport exemption.

Title IX was enacted in 1972, and almost immediately girls and women began filing lawsuits under the Equal Protection Clause and (when applicable) their state ERA to gain access to contact sports teams. The first lawsuit published involved a girl who wanted to play in a community baseball league in Pennsylvania in 1973.[19] This would be one of the few cases published after 1972 to conclude that girls could be excluded from try-outs for contact sports teams on the grounds of safety. Under the Equal Protection Clause, females can be treated differently than males if the organization which wants to discriminate can establish that the state has a legitimate reason for doing so and that reason is rationally related to the gender classification.[20] In the 1973 baseball case, the federal district court judge concluded that ten-year-old girls were at risk physically if they played baseball with boys and that safety was a legitimate state interest. The judge presumed that the difference between the genders at that age was rationally related to the safety issue.

That baseball case was, however, very much in the minority of gender and contact sport cases. In 1974 courts in Ohio and New Jersey concluded that school aged girls should be allowed to try out for football and baseball respectively under the Equal Protection Clause.[21] In each case the courts concluded that no evidence established that contact sports for girls was any more dangerous than it was for boys, thus they dismissed the safety argument because even though the safety of youth was a legitimate and important interest for the state, gender was not even rationally related to promoting safety. The courts noted that some boys were bigger and stronger than some girls but that the converse was also true. In 1977 a federal district court judge in Colorado would reach the same conclusion for soccer.[22] This judge added that courts needed to remember that the gap in size and strength within a gender was often greater than the gap in size and strength between the genders. Further, this court told schools that when it came to sports, the Equal Protection Clause offered three options: schools could allow girls to try out for boys' teams, schools could offer comparable teams for girls in comparable sports, or schools could drop the sport entirely. The only option schools could not exercise was to refuse to allow girls to try out for boys' teams when no comparable team existed for girls. In 1988 and 1996, federal district courts in Nebraska and Kansas confirmed that girls had the right under the Equal Protection Clause to try out for wrestling even though the sport required touching and grappling.[23] Again the courts dismissed the safety concerns and this time they also dismissed concerns that girls would accuse coaches and other wrestlers of sexual harassment after being touched. The courts expressed confidence that wrestlers of both genders understood the difference between wrestling and sexual harassment.

Although the Equal Protection Clause pushed the door shut on Title IX's contact sport exemption, those states with Equal Rights Amendments locked the door. In 1975 two sisters used the Washington state ERA to earn the right to try out for their high school football team. The state had argued that girls should be excluded from football because it was a dangerous sport and because the entire system of girls' sport would collapse if a few girls were allowed to play on boys' teams. The Washington Supreme Court rejected both of these arguments.[24] Court decisions in Pennsylvania and Massachusetts reached essentially the same conclusion: state ERAs prohibited preventing girls from trying out for boys' teams if no comparable girls' team existed. The same also held for boys trying out for girls' teams in those states.[25]

Together, the three laws—Title IX, the Equal Protection Clause, and state ERAs—clearly allowed women and girls the right to try out for sports teams which received any federal funding or were otherwise somehow tied to the government. This meant that the public schools, community leagues, and almost every college and university in the U.S. must allow females the opportunity to try out for the male's team if no comparable team exists for females. Purely private organizations which receive no federal funding and have no connection to the state may have gender exclusive teams; for example a church ice hockey league which played only in private facilities could exclude women if it liked. Similarly professional leagues could choose to exclude one gender or the other. Further, note that the laws only gave girls and women the right to try out for the team: none of these laws guaranteed a female a spot on the team or any playing time. One court has ruled, however, that under Title IX, no gender discrimination can occur during the try-outs regardless of whether the sport is contact or non-contact. That is to say, a coach of a college football team may cut a woman because of her attitude or her skill level just like he would a man; however, the woman cannot be cut or treated differently because of her gender.[26]

Opportunities in Sport

Title IX has been the key law for keeping opportunities relatively equitable in sport. Once girls and women have access to sport, Title IX has three areas of concentration in which women and girls must be treated similarly to men and boys: financial assistance; benefits, opportunities, and treatment; and effective accommodation of interests.

Financial Assistance

Section 106.37 of the enforcement regulations explains what the law requires of those schools that offer athletic scholarships. The law simply says institutions cannot provide different amounts or types of scholarships for one gender and not the other. Nor can the criteria for male athletes be different than for female athletes.[27] In 1998 the Office of Civil Rights (OCR), which is charged with enforcing Title IX, offered some guidance for schools attempting to comply with this section of the law. Beginning in 1979, the understanding had been that total amounts of scholarship aid to male and female athletes should be "substantially proportionate" to the participation rates of male and female athletes. This meant that the number of scholarships for men and women did not have to be equal nor did individual scholarship values need to be equal. The clarification letter in 1998 specified that for Title IX's purposes, substantially proportionate meant total scholarships in the aggregate with a little room for variance. That is, if 55 percent of the athletes at a school were female, 55 percent of the total athletic scholarship dollars should have gone to female athletes, with a plus or minus one percent variance. Thus if this school offered 54 to 56 percent of its scholarship dollars to female athletes, the school would be in compliance.[28]

The other major issue of financial assistance had to do with restricted funding by private donors. The question that frequently arose in college sport was how to handle restricted donations that, for example, endowed scholarships for male athletes only. The enforcement regulations asserted that private funding could be accepted provided it did not affect overall funding proportions. If, for example, a booster club raised $1 million for funding for male athletic scholarships, the university could accept that money but only if the money was essentially matched for female scholarships. The school could do this by finding donors for female scholarships or they could do this by decreasing university funding of male scholarships by $1 million. No matter where the money came from, the Title IX enforcement regulations clearly stated that the overall proportion of funding must remain equitable for male and female athletes.[29] In 2003–2004, women constituted approximately 44 percent of all athletes at the Division I level of the National College Athletic Association and they received approximately 45 percent of all athletic scholarship money, thus generally complying with the enforcement regulations on this point.[30]

Benefits, Opportunities, Treatment

The enforcement regulations emphasize that the athletic experience for girls and women should be comparable, although not necessarily equal, to that of boys and men. Between the original enforcement regulations and subsequent policy interpretations, thirteen areas have been highlighted as points to examine whether the experiences are comparable. They are:

1. Whether the selection of sports and the level of competition effectively accommodates the interests and abilities of the students
2. Provision of equipment and supplies
3. Scheduling of games and practice times
4. Travel and per diem allowance
5. Opportunity to receive coaching and academic tutoring
6. Assignment and compensation of coaches and tutors
7. Provision of locker rooms, practice, and competitive facilities
8. Provision of medical and training facilities and services
9. Provision of housing and dining facilities and services
10. Publicity
11. Recruitment
12. Support services
13. Financial assistance[31]

Except for financial assistance, these areas have been evaluated based on whether or not the experience was comparable and not necessarily equal. For example, the equipment for football is very expensive, but the equipment for women's swimming is not; therefore a school is permitted to spend more on football equipment than it spends on equipment for the women's swim team. What the school is not permitted to do is to buy new uniforms for the men's soccer team annually and then give the women's soccer team the men's old uniforms. The 1979 Policy Interpretations specifically noted that compliance for this area was based on an overall evaluation of the male and female sports programs. Therefore, spending for boys' lacrosse might exceed that of the spending for girls' lacrosse at the same institution provided the overall spending in the programs was roughly equivalent. The policy specifically stated that compliance would be obtained when "the compared program components [were] equivalent, that is, equal or equal in effect. Under this standard, identical benefits, opportunities, or treatments are not required, provided the overall effects of any differences is negligible."[32] Further the policy added that even if the genders were treated differently, the school could still be in compliance provided the differences were the result of "nondiscriminatory factors," which included the inherent expense of football. Similarly, this law did not require that the coach of the men's and women's basketball teams be paid the same, but rather it required that if the men's team had a full-time paid, competent coach then the women's team must as well. The law left open the opportunity to pay coaches based on their experience and their qualifications, noting specifically that some individual might have an "outstanding record of achievement as to justify an abnormally high salary."[33]

The dollar amount spent on these areas varies dramatically by gender despite the policy requirements for roughly equal spending. For example in 2003–2004 at the NCAA Division I level, schools spent 30 percent of their recruiting budget on women's sport compared to the 70 percent they spent on men's sport.[34] Similarly, schools at that level spent about 38 percent of their travel budget on women's sport.[35] On average, Division I schools spent more money on men's programs in every single area except fundraising and marketing. The average total expenses for men's teams were $7,285,500 compared to $4,194,800 for women's teams, meaning that women's teams received on average just under 37 percent of the athletic budget at Division I schools.[36] Despite Title IX's requirements and the vast increases in funding over the last thirty years, women's programs at the Division I level in the NCAA have remained underfunded compared to men's programs.

The trends have been similar but not identical for Division III of the NCAA (programs that offer no athletic scholarships). Men's teams received more funding on average in every area except administrative salaries and benefits and fundraising and marketing. Although women's head coaches received more compensation from third parties than men's head coaches did, the overall salaries for men's head coaches were higher.[37] Overall women received just over 42 percent of the average Division III athletic budget and they constituted about 42 percent of the athletes.[38] While this suggests that Division III schools were more likely in compliance with the law, note that 55 percent of the undergraduate population was female making it likely that these schools would have problems meeting the requirements of compliance under the third area as discussed in the next section.[39]

Effective Accommodation of Interest

The third component of the comparable benefits component of Title IX has been divisive. The 1979 policy interpretation specifically noted that both male and female athletes had to have the opportunity to compete in intercollegiate athletics and then offered three methods to comply with this area.

1. Provide participation opportunities which are substantially proportional to the undergraduate enrollments (e.g., if women are forty percent of the undergraduate population, they should be forty percent of the athletes), or
2. Show a history and continuing practice of expanding athletic opportunities for women, or
3. Demonstrate that the interests and abilities of the students have been "fully and effectively accommodated."[40]

The key to this "three prong test" was that a school could meet any single prong and be in compliance; schools did not have to meet all three prongs.

In 1996 the Office of Civil Rights offered a policy clarification letter elaborating on the three prong test. First it defined athletes as those who received institutional support and who participated in organized practices and other team events. Those who were injured counted as athletes only if they still received athletic scholarships. Dual sport athletes could count twice, and all athletes on a team counted even if they were not on scholarship or did not travel with the team. The OCR also acknowledged that the enrollment proportions of the total undergraduate population varied from year to year and allowed schools to still be in compliance once those variations were factored in.[41]

With regard to the history prong, the 1996 Clarification Letter said that the OCR would review the "entire history of the athletic program" and noted that there was "no fixed interval of time" for which schools needed to added women's teams. The goal was to look at the program and the history in total. The letter also noted that cutting women's sports was unacceptable if the school was not in compliance with Title IX.[42] The Clarification Letter gave a number of specific examples of what would and would not constitute compliance under the history prong, but the bottom line seemed to be that the OCR would examine each case individually and look at the larger picture of history of expansion and of interest.[43]

Just months after the 1996 Clarification Letter was released, the First Circuit Court of Appeals released a decision in *Cohen v. Brown* concluding that Title IX and the associated regulations and policies were not quotas and that the three prong test was an appropriate way to evaluate interests and abilities. The court rejected Brown's claim that women were inherently less interested in sport and that they could cut women's sports because the women were not interested. The court noted that "interests and abilities rarely develop in a vacuum; they evolve as a function of opportunity and experience" and concluded that Brown University must fully meet the interests and abilities of its female students. The court was skeptical of a survey approach to satisfy the third prong of the test but noted that a survey approach was irrelevant in this case because Brown University was demoting women's teams that were filled with eligible, qualified and clearly interested athletes.[44]

The third prong of the test, meeting interests and abilities, was the most nebulous of the prongs. The 1996 Clarification Letter said it would look at a variety of factors including requests by students to add a sport, requests that an existing club sport be elevated to varsity status, and participation in club and intramural sports. Interviews and surveys could also be used as evidence. The OCR would also look at participation rates at the youth level in the area to ascertain interest and ability at the local level. Ability to be competitive would not be a determining factor. The OCR insisted that ability simply meant the ability to play and not the ability to win.[45]

In 2005 the OCR issued another Clarification Letter elaborating on how to comply with the interest prong. For the first time in Title IX's history the OCR suggested that a simple survey could be used to determine interest and indicated that unless the survey showed "direct and very persuasive evidence of unmet interest sufficient to sustain a varsity team," compliance would be presumed.[46] Opponents to the new survey policy argued that methodologically the survey was flawed because the response rate to internet surveys has been notoriously low, and the OCR had determined that non-responses indicated no interest.[47] Further, the survey method ignores the statement of the *Cohen v. Brown* court which noted that interest does not develop in a vacuum meaning that asking people about their interest about something they have no access to often results in a people saying they have no interest in that topic. Even the NCAA opposed the survey.[48] Despite this opposition, the 2005 Compliance Letter remains in force.

Conclusion

Although women and girls have long participated in sports in relatively small numbers, the women's movement of the 1970s and the laws which were enacted and enforced because of those social changes vastly increased the numbers of females involved in sport. In 2006–2007 just over 3 million girls participated in organized high school sports,[49] and 172,534 women participated in NCAA sport.[50] Both are all time highs and remarkable compared to the number of girls who competed in 1971 (less than 300,000 in high school sports and almost none in NCAA sports).

Although the levels of girls' and women's participation rates in sport have dramatically increased over the years, the female experience in sport still differs from the male experience. After their playing days are over, fewer women are hired as sport administrators and as coaches compared to men. In 2008 only 20.6 percent of all teams (male and female) at the college level were coached by women and only 42.8 percent of women's teams were coached by women. Just over 21 percent of athletic directors were female and just over twenty-seven percent of head athletic trainers were female.[51] Title IX does nothing to promote women's involvement in sport beyond playing the game and the Equal Protection Clause and Equal Rights Amendments only prohibit overt discrimination. Sport remains predominantly male.

Although Title IX has often been blamed for cuts in men's sport, the law itself does not require that men's sport be limited in order to grow women's sport. In fact in 2006–2007, record numbers of boys (over 4.3 million) competed in high school sports[52] and record numbers of men (230,259) competed in the NCAA.[53] Despite these record high numbers, some groups still argue that men's opportunity in sport is diminishing.[54] The work of sports economist Andrew Zimbalist, however, refutes these arguments. Although the average number of male athletes at an NCAA DI school did drop from 323 to 322 from 1991–1992 to 2003–2004, this is hardly a huge decline.[55] Some social opposition and mythic discourse, though, still lead some to erroneously argue that Title IX has been responsible when schools have chosen to cut men's sport.[56]

The conviction of some that Title IX and other gender laws hurt men and men's sport has resulted in opposition which has continued into the twenty-first century. In 2002 the National Wrestling Coaches Association (NWCA) filed a lawsuit arguing that Title IX enforced a quota system which was harming men's wrestling programs. Two years later the case was dismissed prior to trial because the court concluded that even if everything the NWCA alleged was true, they could not prove that the law itself hurt wrestlers.[57] In 2003, after a year of nationwide hearings the Secretary of Education's Commission on Opportunity in Athletics released its report. Despite fears that the Commission would change Title IX, the Commission could not reach any unanimous suggestions for change and the Secretary of Education declined to make changes at that time.[58]

Despite these challenges, Title IX has continued to exist and has grown only stronger since its enactment in 1972. Furthermore, the Equal Protection Clause of the 14th Amendment of the United States Constitution has given women increasingly greater protection over the last fifty years. Although female participation in sport as administrators and coaches could still be increased, women's legal rights in sport and their participation in the games themselves have grown remarkably in the last three plus decades.

Endnotes

1. See Lois Bryson "Sport and the Maintenance of Masculine Hegemony" and Michael A. Messner "Sports and Male Domination: The Female Athlete as Contested Ideological Terrain" in *Women, Sport, and Culture* ed. Susan Birrell and Cheryl L. Cole (Champaign, IL: Human Kinetics, 1994).

2. See Allen Guttmann, *Women's Sport: A History* (New York, Columbia University Press, 1991).

3. Linda Jean Carpenter and C. Vivian Acosta, *Title IX* (Champaign, IL: Human Kinetics, 2005), 168.

4. Ibid.

5. The wage gap still exists in the twenty-first century: women on average earn 77% of the salary that men in comparable positions earn. Stephen J. Rose and Heidi I. Hartmann, "Still a Man's Labor Market: The Long-Term Wage Gap," Washington, D.C.: Institute for Women's Policy Research, 2004 (IWPR: C355), *http://www.iwpr.org/pdf/C355.pdf* (accessed 4 July 2008).

6. "The Equal Rights Amendment," *http://www.equalrightsamendment.org/* (accessed 23 July 2008).

7. See Walter LaFeber, Richard Polenberg, and Nancy Woloch, *The American Centruy: A History of the United States since the 1890s*, 4th ed. (New York: McGraw Hill, 1992), 477–80 for a discussion of the ERA. In fact the ERA was not ratified by enough states and thus ultimately was never added as an amendment to the Constitution.

8. Education Amendments of 1972, Publ. L. No. 92-318, §§ 901-9, 86 Stat. 235, codified at 20 U.S.C. §§ 1681–88 (1990) [hereinafter Title IX].

9. Twenty-one of the fifty states have a state ERA. League of Women's Voters of the Fairfax Area Education Fund, "Ratification Status in the States and State ERAs," March 2004 *http://www.lwv-fairfax.org/pdf_folder/era_ratifications.pdf* (accessed 4 July 2008).

10. U.S. Constitution, amend. 14, sec I (1868).

11. Hollander v. Connecticut Interscholastic Athletic Conference No. 12447 (Conn. Super. Ct., New Haven County, 1971) quoted in Bil Gilbert and Nancy Richardson, "Sport is Unfair to Women," *Sports Illustrated* 28 May 1973, 88–98, reprinted in *Equal Play: Title IX and Social Change*, ed. Nancy Hogshead-Maker and Andrew Zimbalist (Philadelphia: Temple University Press, 2007), 41.

12. Nicole Mitchell and Lisa A. Ennis, *Encyclopedia of Title IX and Sports* (Westwood, CT: Greenwood Press, 2007).

13. After Congress passes a law and the president signs it, the administrative branch of the government is charged with enforcing the law. Usually the enforcement arm is one of the many administrative departments.

14. C.F.R. § 106.41(b) (1991).

15. Cannon v. University of Chicago, 441 U.S. 677 (1979).

16. Grove City College v. Bell, 465 U.S. 555 (1984).

17. Franklin v. Gwinnett County Public Schools, 503 U.S. 60 (1992).

18. See Sarah K. Fields, *Female Gladiators: Gender, Law, and Contact Sport in America* (Urbana: University of Illinois Press, 2005).

19. Magill v. Avonworth Baseball Conference, 364 F.Supp. 1212 (W.D. Pa. 1973). Note that this is the first published decision regarding girls and contact sport; it was probably not the first case filed or even heard. Not every lawsuit filed goes to trial—most are settled or dismissed before the full case is heard. At the state trial court level, decisions are rarely published because there are so many of them and because if a jury heard the case, all they render is the verdict. Supreme Court decisions (both state and federal) are always published as are almost all appellate court decisions (especially federal ones). Federal district court decisions are published at the discretion of the judge.

20. The courts have long concluded that different groups can be treated differently provided that the discrimination passes a test. The level of test depends on the categorization. Prior to 1971, gender as a classification was one of the easiest grounds for discrimination; all the state needed to prove was that they had a legitimate reason for discriminating against women and that the discrimination was rationally related to that reason. See Goessaert v. Cleary, 335 U.S. 464 (1948) and Reed v. Reed, 404 U.S. 71 1971). After 1971, the Supreme Court began to make it more difficult to discriminate on the basis of gender and in 1976 the Court created a more difficult test, saying that to discriminate on the basis of gender the state needed to establish that the reason for gender discrimination was substantially related to an important governmental interest. Craig v. Boren, 429 U.S. 190 (1976). In 1996 the Court ratcheted up the test even more saying that the test remained the same but that the state's justification for discrimination must be "exceedingly persuasive." U.S. v. Virginia, 518 U.S. 515 (1996). For a more complete discussion of gender and the Equal Protection Clause see William A. Devan, "Note: Towards a New Standard in Gender Discrimination: The Case of Virginia Military Institute," *William and Mary Law Review* 33 (1992): 489–542.

21. Clinton v. Nagy, 411 F. Supp. 1396 (N.D. Ohio 1974) and National Organization for Women v. Little League Baseball, Inc., 318 A.2d 33 (N.J. Super. Ct. App. Div. 1974).

22. Hoover v. Meiklejohn, 430 F. Supp. 164 (D. Colo. 1977). For a more complete description of the case and its social and legal history see Sarah K. Fields, "*Hoover v. Meiklejohn*: The Equal Protection Clause, Girls, and Soccer," *Journal of Sport History* 30 (Fall 2003): 201–214.

23. Saint v. Nebraska School Activities Association, 684 F. Supp. 626 (D. Neb. 1988) and Adams v. Baker, 919 F. Supp. 1496 (D. Kan. 1996).

24. Darrin v. Gould, 540 P.2d 882 (Wash. 1975).

25. Commonwealth ex rel. Packel v. Pennsylvania Interscholastic Athletic Association, 334 A.2d 839 (Pa. 1975) and Opinion of the Justices to the House of Representatives, 371 N.E. 2d 426 (Mass, 1977).

26. Mercer v. Duke University, 190 F. 3d 643 (4th Cir. 1999), *overruling* 32 F Supp. 2d 836 (M.D. N.C. 1998).

27. C.F.R. § 106.37 (1991).

28. "Letter from the U.S. Department of Education to Bowling Green State University," in *Equal Play: Title IX and Social Change*, eds. Nancy Hogshead-Maker and Andrew Zimbalist (Philadelphia: Temple University Press, 2007).

29. C.F.R. § 106.37 (1991).

30. Numbers were available at "2003–2004 Gender Equity Report" available at *http://www.ncaapublications.com/Uploads/PDF/2003-04_gender_equity_report4e63345f-94e2-4c23-8f7c-7c47fa1a1b0d.pdf* (accessed 7 July 2008). Calculations by author. Note, however, that in that same school year, females constituted almost fifty-four percent of the total undergraduate student body.

31. Carpenter and Acosta, 78.

32. 44 Fed. Reg. 71,413, 71,423 (1979) quoted in Hogshead-Maker and Zimbalist, 73.

33. Ibid., 76.

34. "2003–2004 Equity Report," 13.

35. Ibid, 21 (calculations by author).

36. Ibid.

37. Ibid., 91 and 98.

38. Ibid., 14.

39. Ibid.

40. 44 Fed. Reg. 71,413, 71,423 (1979) quoted in Hogshead-Maker and Zimbalist, 80.

41. 1996 Clarification of Intercollegiate Athletics Policy Guidance: The Three-Part Test reprinted in Hogshead-Maker and Zimbalist, 152–162 [hereinafter 1996 Clarification].

42. The Third Circuit Court of Appeals had already rejected schools' attempts to cut women's sports for budget reasons when not in compliance with Title IX. Cutting men's sports as well did not protect the school unless the cuts brought the school into compliance. Favia v. Indiana University of Pennsylvania, 812 F.Supp.578 (W.D.Pa. 1992), motion to modify order denied, 7 F.3d 332 (3d Cir. 1993). The 1996 letter simply expanded the Third Circuit's ruling to the entire country.

43. 1996 Clarification, 156–159.

44. Cohen v. Brown University, 101 F.3d 155, 179 (1st Cir. 1996).

45. Ibid. 160–2.

46. Additional Clarification of Intercollegiate Athletics Policy: Three-Part-Test—Part Three, 17 Mar. 2005, *http://www.ed.gov/about/offices/list/ocr/docs/title9guidanceadditional.html* accessed 16 July 2008.

47. Don Sabo and Christine Grant, "Limitations of the Department of Education's On-Line Survey Method for Measuring Athletic Interest and Ability on U.S.A. Campuses," in *Equal Play*.

48. "In Honor of Title IX Anniversary, NCAA Urges Department of Education to Rescind Additional Clarification of Federal Law," 22 June 2005, *http://www2.ncaa.org/portal/media_and_events/press_room/2005/june/20050622_titleixanniv.html* accessed 16 July 2008 and

49. "NFHS Participation Figures Search," *http://www.nfhs.org/custom/participation_figures/default.aspx* accessed 16 July 2008.

50. Gary Brown, "Student-Athlete Court Tops 400,000," *http://www.ncaachampionmagazine.org/Championship%20Magazine/ChampionMagazineStory/ArticleListings/tabid/61/articleType/ArticleView/articleId/102/Default.aspx* accessed 16 July 2008.

51. Linda J. Carpenter and C. Vivian Acosta, "Women in Intercollegiate Sport: A Longitudinal, National Study, Thirty-One Year Update, 1977–2008," *http://webpages.charter.net/womeninsport/2008%20Summary%20Final.pdf* accessed 16 July 2006.

52. "NFHS Participation Figures Search."

53. Brown, "Student-Athlete Court Tops 400,000."

54. Amy Fagen, "Men's College Sports Dwindling; Study Blames Title IX for Cuts in Team Sports," *Washington Times*, 30 Mar. 2007, A06.

55. Andrew Zimbalist, "Title IX by the Numbers," in *Equal Play*, 303.

56. Bill Pennington, "At James Madison, Title IX is Satisfied but Students Are Not," *New York Times*, 7 Oct. 2006, D1. See Theresa Walton, "Pinned by Gender Construction?: Media Representations of Girls' Wrestling," *Women in Sport and Physical Activity Journal* 14 (2005): 52–69 and her discussion of how Title IX was blamed for the decline in wresting programs.

57. National Wrestling Coaches Association v. Department of Education, 366 F.3d 930 (D.C. Cir. 2004).

58. For a complete copy of the report and the minority report see Simon, Rita J. Simon, ed. *Sporting Equality: Title IX Thirty Years Later* (New Brunswick, NJ: Transaction Publishers, 2005).

Further Reading

Carpenter, L. J., & Acosta, R. V. (2004). *Title IX*. Champaign, IL: Human Kinetics.

Fields, S. K. (2005). *Female Gladiators: Gender, Law, and Contact Sport in America*. Urbana: University of Illinois Press.

Hogshead-Maker, N., & Zimbalist, A. (2007). *Equal Play: Title IX and Social Change*. Philadelphia: Temple University Press.

Simon, R. (Ed.) (2005). *Sporting Equality: Title IX Thirty Years Later*. New Brunswick, NJ: Transaction Publishers.

Suggs, W. (2006). *A Place on the Team: The Triumph and Tragedy of Title IX*. Princeton, NJ: Princeton University Press.

Discussion Questions

1. Would women's sports have changed as much as they have since 1972 if Title IX had not been enacted?

2. Which of the laws surrounding women's access to sport was most significant? Which had the least impact on the face of sport?

3. If you were an athletic director at a university which part of the three prong test would you focus on in complying with Title IX?

4. Should any of these laws be changed?

Worksheet 1

My Personal Sport History

Name _____ Date _____

To get you ready to write your essay, take some time to first write down some of your earliest memories of your participation in sport and physical activity.

_____

_____

_____

_____

_____

Who influenced you to begin participating in sport and physical activity? How did they do so?

_____

_____

_____

_____

_____

Describe the impact of your gender on opportunities to participate in sport and physical activity.

_____

_____

_____

_____

_____

List some challenges you have faced while participating in sport and physical activity.

_____

_____

_____

_____

_____

_____

List some triumphs you have had while participating in sport and physical activity.

_____

_____

_____

_____

_____

_____

Follow the specific instructions provided by your instructor for completing this assignment.

Worksheet 2

Oral Interview Project

Name _____ Date _____

Interview a woman over 60 years of age about her sport and physical activity background. This could be your mother, grandmother, aunt or any other woman that you know. Try to get the person you interview to tell you stories—if something they talk about sounds interesting, ask them about it and get them to expand on it. Don't prompt them too much at first—but if you are having trouble getting them to talk then you might need to ask them some more leading questions. (For example: "Did your brothers get to go out and play while you were asked to stay inside and do household chores? How did that make you feel?")

Begin by asking what her first memories of playing sports or physical activity are.

_____

_____

_____

_____

Did she ever play competitive sports?

_____

_____

_____

_____

Was her family supportive of her activities in sport and physical activity?

_____

_____

_____

_____

_____

Did she ever feel that other people were less than supportive of her attempts to be involved in sport and physical activity?

_____

_____

_____

_____

_____

What are the biggest changes she has seen in her lifetime in relation to women's sport and physical activity?

_____

_____

_____

_____

_____

_____

Other questions/information:

_____

_____

_____

_____

_____

Follow the specific instructions provided by your instructor for completing this assignment.

Worksheet 3

Comparing the Past with the Present

Name _____   Date _____

Select a sport or activity that you are interested in that women took part in prior to 1970. List a few potential topics below and discuss them with your classmates.

_____

_____

_____

_____

_____

Find a newspaper article about women's sport prior to 1970. Write out the citation for this article (and you should also find a couple others as backups) in proper APA format.

_____

_____

_____

_____

_____

_____

Find a newspaper article about the same sport/event in the last 5 years. Write out the citation for this article (and you should also find a couple others as backups) in proper APA format.

_____

_____

_____

_____

_____

Where should you go to locate these articles?

Your campus library should have access to newspapers. Over the past few years, several of these have become available over the Internet (through your campus library). The Historical *New York Times* and the Historical *Los Angeles Times* are available through many campus libraries. In addition, your library will have hard copies of local newspapers. The Historical *New York Times* and *Los Angeles Times* databases are easier to use than the hard copies because they are searchable by key words.

Describe and Analyze: What does each article tell you about the specific event? What happened, where, why, etc. Was anything else going on in the larger society that may have influenced the events described in your article?

_____

_____

_____

_____

_____

_____

_____

Compare and Contrast: What differences do you see between the two articles? How has this sport or event changed over the years? Why do you think this has happened? What has been the influence of Title IX on this sport—base this analysis on what you have learned in class so far as well as what you find in your research of the newspapers from the past and the present.

_____

_____

_____

_____

_____

_____

_____

Follow the specific instructions provided by your instructor for completing this assignment.

Worksheet 4

Athlete Matching

Name _____   Date _____

	Name			**Name**			**Sport**
1 _____	Aileen Riggin Soule		30 _____	Louise Suggs		a	Auto Racing
2 _____	Alice Coachman		31 _____	Lynette Woodard		b	Baseball
3 _____	Althea Gibson		32 _____	Lynn Hill		c	Basketball
4 _____	Anita DeFrantz		33 _____	Margo Oberg		d	Cycling
5 _____	Ann Meyers		34 _____	Marion Jones		e	Distance Running
6 _____	Babe Didridson Zaharias		35 _____	Martina Navaratilova		f	Diving
7 _____	Billie Jean King		36 _____	Mary Decker Slaney		g	Dogsledding
8 _____	Bonnie Blair		37 _____	Mary Lou Retton		h	Fencing
9 _____	Cammi Granato		38 _____	Mia Hamm		i	Figure Skating
10 _____	Carol Blazejowski		39 _____	Misty May		j	Golf
11 _____	Cheryl Miller		40 _____	Nadia Comaneci		k	Gymnastics
12 _____	Chris Evert		41 _____	Nancy Lieberman-Cline		l	Horse Racing
13 _____	Connie Carpenter		42 _____	Nancy Lopez		m	Ice Hockey
14 _____	Danica Patrick		43 _____	Pat McCormick		n	Mountain Biking
15 _____	Dorothy Hamill		44 _____	Paula Newby-Fraser		o	Rock Climbing
16 _____	Dorothy Kamenshek		45 _____	Peggy Fleming		p	Rowing
17 _____	Evonne Goolagong Cawley		46 _____	Picabo Street		q	Skiing
18 _____	Flo Hyman		47 _____	Sheila Young		r	Soccer
19 _____	Florence Griffith-Joyner		48 _____	Sheryl Swoopes		s	Softball
20 _____	Gertrude Ederle		49 _____	Shirley Muldowny		t	Speedskating
21 _____	Grete Waitz		50 _____	Sonja Henie		u	Surfing
22 _____	Helen Mayer		51 _____	Steffi Graf		v	Swimming
23 _____	Jackie Joyner-Kersee		52 _____	Susan Butcher		w	Tennis
24 _____	Jean Driscoll		53 _____	Suzanne Lenglen		x	Track and Field
25 _____	Joan Benoit Samuelson		54 _____	Teresa Edwards		y	Triathlete
26 _____	Juli Futado		55 _____	Tracy Caulkins		z	Volleyball
27 _____	Julie Krone		56 _____	Willye White		aa	Wheelchair Racing
28 _____	Kathy Whitworth		57 _____	Wyomia Tyus			
29 _____	Lisa Fernandez						

Select the correct sport from the list on the right and write the corresponding letter next to the name of the female athlete who participated in that sport.

The answer key is on the next page, but don't look!

Worksheet 4

Athlete Matching (Answer Key)

		Name				Name
1	v or f	Aileen Riggin Soule		30	j	Louise Suggs
2	x	Alice Coachman		31	c	Lynette Woodard
3	w	Althea Gibson		32	o	Lynn Hill
4	p	Anita DeFrantz		33	u	Margo Oberg
5	c	Ann Meyers		34	x	Marion Jones
6	x or j	Babe Didridson Zaharias		35	w	Martina Navaratilova
7	w	Billie Jean King		36	e	Mary Decker Slaney
8	t	Bonnie Blair		37	k	Mary Lou Retton
9	m	Cammi Granato		38	r	Mia Hamm
10	c	Carol Blazejowski		39	z	Misty May
11	c	Cheryl Miller		40	k	Nadia Comaneci
12	w	Chris Evert		41	c	Nancy Lieberman-Cline
13	t or d	Connie Carpenter		42	j	Nancy Lopez
14	a	Danica Patrick		43	f	Pat McCormick
15	i	Dorothy Hamill		44	y	Paula Newby-Fraser
16	b	Dorothy Kamenshek		45	h	Peggy Fleming
17	w	Evonne Goolagong Cawley		46	q	Picabo Street
18	z	Flo Hyman		47	t or d	Sheila Young
19	x	Florence Griffith-Joyner		48	c	Sheryl Swoopes
20	v	Gertrude Ederle		49	a	Shirley Muldowny
21	e	Grete Waitz		50	i	Sonja Henie
22	h	Helen Mayer		51	w	Steffi Graf
23	x	Jackie Joyner-Kersee		52	g	Susan Butcher
24	aa	Jean Driscoll		53	w	Suzanne Lenglen
25	e	Joan Benoit Samuelson		54	c	Teresa Edwards
26	n	Juli Futado		55	v	Tracy Caulkins
27	l	Julie Krone		56	x	Willye White
28	j	Kathy Whitworth		57	x	Wyomia Tyus
29	s	Lisa Fernandez				

SECTION 2

Sociological Perspectives on Women in Sport and Physical Activity

© Corbis

"I'm not sure the men would really know the women's game.
I mean, how do you know exactly how the women are
feeling certain times of the month?"

John McEnroe, on Men Announcing Women's Tennis

Section 2
Introduction

Sharon R. Guthrie

More than ever before, girls and women have access to sport and physical activity and receive encouragement to develop their athletic abilities. Thirty years ago, many of us could not have imagined the explosive increase in the number of females engaged in sport and exercise that we see today. Although women have had a long history of participation in sport, as you have learned in previous sections of this book, much of the somatic freedom we have gained since the early 1970s has been the direct result of feminist activity and changes in the way females view their abilities and opportunities. Actively involved in the examination and analysis of these sociopolitical changes have been sport sociologists.

In this section of the book, you will read a variety of essays written by scholars who adopt a sociological perspective. Sociologists study human social life in a wide variety of arenas. Those who call themselves sport sociologists focus primarily on the realm of sport and physical activity. Sport sociologists view sport as a very powerful social institution, partly because it is such a popular cultural practice, but also because it is instrumental in shaping and reinforcing the way we view ourselves and our bodies. They also see the connections between sport and other social institutions such as the political economy, media, education, and religion, and how these relationships influence our life experiences and opportunities.

Although sociologists analyze the social world from a variety of perspectives, their work often includes a critical examination of the social order and strategies for changing power relationships, such as those grounded in gender, race, ethnicity, class, ability, and sexual orientation. In the early 1970s, female sociologists (e.g., Dorothy Smith, Marcia Millman, Rosabeth Moss Kanter) and sport sociologists (e.g., Ann Hall) were among the first to write about the problems of gender bias in their respective fields. Since that time, numerous social scholars and practitioners have contributed to this important line of inquiry and analysis. The readings in this section provide a sampling of this important work.

We begin with Judith Lorber's article, entitled "The Social Construction of Gender." Lorber emphasizes the fact that gender is a social construct that is produced and reinforced through human interaction and social practice. Gender is also a process that fosters a differing social status for males and females, as well as different rights, responsibilities, and expectations.

Lorber points out that in a gender-stratified society, what men do is generally valued more highly than what women do. As a result, men typically have more access to what are considered the "goods" of society. Sport has historically been one of these "goods." Although exceptions to this rule exist, and certainly social change has occurred, the author makes clear that absolute gender equity in sport and elsewhere has yet to be achieved.

In the second essay, "Just Do . . . What? Sport, Bodies, Gender," Shari Dworkin and Michael Messner focus on sport as an important location for studying the social construction of gender. They claim that "sport, as a cultural and commercial production, constructs and markets gender; in fact, "besides making money, making gender may be sport's chief function." This provocative statement holds a great deal of merit. Think about the tremendous popularity of sport, both nationally and internationally, and the values that sport celebrates: hard work and hard bodies. While these values have their physical manifestations in both male and female athletes, only a modest level of "hardness," usually termed "toned," is considered acceptable for females. Indeed, it is this centrality of the body, as well as the touted physical differences between male and female athletes, that makes sport so perfect for studying the "making of gender" and gender relations.

Dworkin and Messner remind us that although recent changes have revolutionized perceptions of female physical capability and promoted greater equity for women in sport, women's and men's sports remain segregated, and male sports remain dominant in the media and capitalist marketplace. Moreover, the elite sporting arena still emphasizes traditional femininity, which counters, and ultimately softens, the accentuated markers of physical empowerment found among highly trained female athletes.

In "Disability Management among Women with Physical Impairments: The Contribution of Physical Activity," Sharon Guthrie and Shirley Castelnuovo describe how 34 women with physical mobility impairments manage their disabilities in our able-bodyist society. The researchers' findings demonstrate how three different strategies associated with physical activity are used with varying degrees of success to enhance self-perception among these women. These findings indicate that having a disability does not preclude positive physical and global self-perceptions; they also indicate that attention should be focused on increasing the participation of persons with disabilities not only in elite sport but also in recreational sporting contexts and non-competitive physical activities such as regular exercise.

In the fourth essay, Katherine Jamieson examines an often overlooked population of female athletes—Latinas. Using qualitative methodology and a Chicana feminist analysis, Jamieson examines the athletic experiences of 27 current and former collegiate softball players—specifically their athletic backgrounds and the sociocultural paths they took to participating in collegiate softball. Particular attention is paid to the influence of the family and educational systems on the sporting aspirations and expectations of this female sample. Jamieson's study demonstrates the complex interactions among gender, race/ethnicity, and social class, and that sport can be one of many cultural sites in which Latinas may empower themselves and foster positive social change.

In the fifth essay, Sharon Guthrie and Kerrie Kauer call the reader's attention to the phenomenon of homophobia in women's sport and its problematic consequences for female athletes, coaches, administrators, and physical educators, as well as its connection to sexism and heterosexism in American culture. Historically, sport and athleticism have been linked with men and masculinity; thus, girls and women who participate in athletics, particularly team and contact sports, have had their sexuality called into question. Guthrie and Kauer present the reader with a brief history of homophobia in women's sport, including the social changes that have occurred in the past few decades as a result of theoretical advancements, increased data-based research, and a generally more enlightened social climate.

Although contemporary female athletes, coaches, and athletic administrators may not experience the same breadth and intensity of homophobia as those who participated in the distant past, Guthrie and Kauer remind us that we still have a long way to go if we care about creating an environment in which female athletes, regardless of sexual orientation, are free to develop their mind-body powers without fear of negative social repercussion. As is it has been said, "it takes a team." We hope that each reader will join in our efforts to lessen and ultimately overcome homophobia, both in sport and the broader sociocultural environment. Although this is not an easy task, current and future female athletes have much to gain from your efforts in this regard.

As mentioned earlier, the feminist movement was instrumental in advancing opportunities and promoting the benefits of physical activity for girls and women. Interestingly, however, many women, particularly those who are young, have great concerns about becoming a feminist or even being labeled as such. The last reading in this section, "Fear of Feminism: Why Young Women Get the Willies," addresses this issue.

According to Hogeland, young women are gender-conscious—that is, they are aware of their differences from men and that they sometimes suffer as a result (e.g., receiving less pay for equal work, experiencing fewer leadership opportunities, being vulnerable to male aggression and violence). Although this gender-consciousness is a prerequisite for developing a feminist consciousness, many women choose not to go down this path.

This is unfortunate because feminist analysis enables a woman to understand systems of domination and privilege and how such systems impact her opportunities and life experiences. Such knowledge can be very empowering. However, feminism also calls for a dismantling of the ideology and practices that hinder female self-determination and actualization. This requires political work.

Women who are exposed to feminist thought, while often valuing their newfound knowledge and insights, do not always take the next step to become politically involved. Indeed, translating one's personal gender issues into feminist work can be a dangerous and frightening prospect, particularly for younger women who are attempting to build their professional identities and romantic relationships. Consequently, reticence about branding oneself a "feminist," which carries the risk of being labeled a man-hater or lesbian, and working to accomplish feminist goals is hardly surprising. Interestingly, however, many of these women, while not openly identifying themselves as feminists, are quietly supportive of feminist goals. It is quite possible that these passive seeds of support may blossom later into a desire to become more actively involved in promoting social change.

1

The Social Construction of Gender

Judith Lorber

© Adobe

You can bet your ass if you have women around—
and I've talked to psychiatrists about this—you aren't
going to be worth a damn ... Man has to dominate.

Woody Hayes, on Oberlin College Adopting a Women's Sports Program

Talking about gender for most people is the equivalent of fish talking about water. Gender is so much the routine ground of everyday activities that questioning its taken-for-granted assumptions and presuppositions is like thinking about whether the sun will come up.[1] Gender is so pervasive that in our society we assume it is bred into our genes. Most people find it hard to believe that gender is constantly created and re-created out of human interaction, out of social life, and is the texture and order of that social life. Yet gender, like culture, is a human production that depends on everyone constantly "doing gender" (West and Zimmerman 1987).

And everyone "does gender" without thinking about it. Today, on the subway, I saw a well-dressed man with a year-old child in a stroller. Yesterday, on a bus, I saw a man with a tiny baby in a carrier on his chest. Seeing men taking care of small children in public is increasingly common—at least in New York City. But both men were quite obviously stared at—and smiled at, approvingly. Everyone was doing gender—the men who were changing the role of fathers and the other passengers, who were applauding them silently. But there was more gendering going on that probably fewer people noticed. The baby was wearing a white crocheted cap and white clothes. You couldn't tell if it was a boy or a girl. The child in the stroller was wearing a dark blue T-shirt and dark print pants. As they started to leave the train, the father put a Yankee baseball cap on the child's head. Ah, a boy, I thought. Then I noticed the gleam of tiny earrings in the child's ears, and as they got off, I saw the little flowered sneakers and lace-trimmed socks. Not a boy after all. Gender done.

. . .

For the individual, gender construction starts with assignment to a sex category on the basis of what the genitalia look like at birth.[2] Then babies are dressed or adorned in a way that displays the category because parents don't want to be constantly asked whether their baby is a girl or a boy. A sex category becomes a gender status through naming, dress, and the use of other gender markers. Once a child's gender is evident, others treat those in one gender differently from those in the other, and the children respond to the different treatment by feeling different and behaving differently. As soon as they can talk, they start to refer to themselves as members of their gender. Sex doesn't come into play again until puberty, but by that time, sexual feelings and desires and practices have been shaped by gendered norms and expectations. Adolescent boys and girls approach and avoid each other in an elaborately scripted and gendered mating dance. Parenting is gendered, with different expectations for mothers and fathers, and people of different genders work at different kinds of jobs. The work adults do as mothers and fathers and as low-level workers and high-level bosses, shapes women's and men's life experiences, and these experiences produce different feelings, consciousness, relationships, skills—ways of being what we call feminine or masculine.[3] All of these processes constitute the social construction of gender.

. . .

To explain why gendering is done from birth, constantly and by everyone, we have to look not only at the way individuals experience gender but at gender as a social institution. As a social institution, gender is one of the major ways that human beings organize their lives. Human society depends on a predictable division of labor, a designated allocation of scarce goods, assigned responsibility for children and others who cannot care for themselves, common values and their systematic transmission to new members, legitimate leadership, music, art, stories, games, and other symbolic productions. One way of choosing people for the different tasks of society is on the basis of their talents, motivations, and competence—their demonstrated achievements. The other way is on the basis of gender, race, ethnicity—ascribed membership in a category of people. Although societies vary in the extent to which they use one or the other of these ways of allocating people to work and to carry out other responsibilities, every society uses gender and age grades. Every society classifies people as "girl and boy children," "girls and boys ready to be married," and "fully adult women and men," constructs similarities among them and differences between them, and assigns them to different roles and responsibilities. Personality characteristics, feelings, motivations, and ambitions flow from these different life experiences so that the members of these different groups become different kinds of people. The process of gendering and its outcome are legitimated by religion, law, science and the society's entire set of values.

Gender as Process, Stratification, and Structure

As a social institution, gender is a process of creating distinguishable social statuses for the assignment of rights and responsibilities. As part of a stratification system that ranks these statuses unequally, gender is a major building block in the social structures built on these unequal statuses.

As a *process*, gender creates the social differences that define "woman" and "man." In social interaction throughout their lives, individuals learn what is expected, see what is expected, act and react in expected ways, and thus simultaneously construct and maintain the gender order . . .

Gendered patterns of interaction acquire additional layers of gendered sexuality, parenting, and work behaviors in childhood, adolescence, and adulthood. Gendered norms and expectations are enforced through informal sanctions of gender-inappropriate behavior by peers and by formal punishment or threat of punishment by those in authority should behavior deviate too far from socially imposed standards for women and men.

. . .

As part of a *stratification* system, gender ranks men above women of the same race and class. Women and men could be different but equal. In practice, the process of creating difference depends to a great extent on differential evaluation. . . . The dominant categories are the hegemonic ideals, taken so for granted as the way things should be that white is not ordinarily thought of as a race, middle class as a class, or men as a gender. The characteristics of these categories define the Other as that which lacks the valuable qualities the dominants exhibit.

In a gender-stratified society, what men do is usually valued more highly than what women do because men do it, even when their activities are very similar or the same. In different regions of southern India, for example, harvesting rice is men's work, shared work, or women's work. "Wherever a task is done by women it is considered easy, and where it is done by [men] it is considered difficult" (Mencher 1988, 104). A gathering and hunting society's survival usually depends on the nuts, grubs, and small animals brought in by the women's foraging trips, but when the men's hunt is successful, it is the occasion for a celebration. Conversely, because they are the superior group, white men do not have to do the "dirty work," such as housework; the most inferior group does it, usually poor women of color (Palmer 1989).

. . .

When gender is a major component of structured inequality, the devalued genders have less power, prestige, and economic rewards than the valued genders. In countries that discourage gender discrimination, many major roles are still gendered; women still do most of the domestic labor and child rearing, even while doing full-time paid work; women and men are segregated on the job and each does work considered "appropriate"; women's work is usually paid less than men's work. Men dominate the positions of authority and leadership in government, the military, and the law; cultural productions, religions, and sports reflect men's interests.

In societies that create the greatest gender difference, such as Saudi Arabia, women are kept out of sight behind walls or veils, have no civil rights, and often create a cultural and emotional world of their own (Bernard 1981). But even in societies with less rigid gender boundaries, women and men spend much of their time with people of their own gender because of the way work and family are organized. This spatial separation of women and men reinforces gendered differences, identity, and ways of thinking and behaving (Coser 1986).

Gender inequality—the devaluation of "women" and the social domination of "men"—has social functions and social history. It is not the result of sex, procreation, physiology, anatomy, hormones, or genetic predispositions. It is produced and maintained by identifiable social processes and built into the general social structure and individual identities deliberately and purposefully. The social order as we know it in Western societies is organized around racial, ethnic, class, and gender inequality. I contend, therefore, that the continuing purpose of gender as a modern social institution is to construct women as a group to be the subordinates of men as a group.

The Paradox of Human Nature

To say that sex, sexuality, and gender are all socially constructed is not to minimize their social power. These categorical imperatives govern our lives in the most profound and pervasive ways, through the social experiences and social practices of what Dorothy Smith calls the "everday/everynight world" (1990, 31–57). The paradox of human nature is that it is *always* a manifestation of cultural meanings, social relationships, and power politics; "not biology, but culture, becomes destiny" (J. Butler 1990, 8). Gendered people emerge not from physiology or sexual orientations but from the exigencies of the social order, mostly, from the need for a reliable division of the work of food production and the social (not physical) reproduction of new members. The moral imperatives of religion and cultural representations guard the boundary lines among genders and ensure that what is demanded, what is permitted, and what is tabooed for the people in each gender is well known and followed by most (C. Davies 1982). Political power, control of scarce resources, and, if necessary, violence uphold the gendered social order in the face of resistance and rebellion. Most people, however, voluntarily go along with their society's prescriptions for those of their gender status, because the norms and expectations get built into their sense of worth and identity as [the way we] think, the way we see and hear and speak, the way we fantasy, and the way we feel.

There is no core or bedrock in human nature below these endlessly looping processes of the social production of sex and gender, self and other, identity and psyche, each of which is a "complex cultural construction" (J. Butler 1990, 36). *For humans, the social is the natural....*

Endnotes

1. Gender is, in Erving Goffman's words, an aspect of *Felicity's Condition:* "any arrangement which leads us to judge an individual's . . . acts not to be a manifestation of strangeness. Behind Felicity's Condition is our sense of what it is to be sane" (1983:27). Also see Bem 1993; Frye 1983, 17–40; Goffman 1977.

2. In cases of ambiguity in countries with modern medicine, surgery is usually performed to make the genitalia more clearly male or female.

3. See J. Butler 1990 for an analysis of how doing gender is gender identity.

References

Bem, Sandara Lipsitz. (1993). *The Lenses of Gender: Transforming the Debate on Sexual Inequality.* New Haven: Yale University Press.

Bernard, Jessie. (1981). *The Female World.* New York: Free Press.

Butler, Judith. (1990). *Gender Trouble: Feminism and the Subversion of Identity.* New York and London: Routledge.

Coser, Rose Laub. (1986). "Cognitive structure and the use of social space," *Sociological Forum,* 1:1–26.

Davies, Christie. (1982). "Sexual taboos and social boundaries," *American Journal of Sociology,* 87:1032–1063.

Dwyer, Daisy & Bruce Judith (Eds.). (1988). *A Home Divided: Women and Income in the Third World.* Palo Alto, Calif.: Stanford University Press.

Frye, Marilyn. (1983). *The Politics of Reality: Essays in Feminist Theory.* Trumansburg, N.Y.: Crossing Press.

Goffman, Erving. (1977). "The arrangement between the sexes," *Theory and Society,* 4:301–333.

Mencher, Joan. (1988). "Women's work and poverty: Women's contribution to household maintenance in South India." In *Dwyer and Bruce.*

Palmer, Phyllis. (1989). *Domesticity and Dirt: Housewives and Domestic Servants in the United States, 1920–1945.* Philadelphia: Temple University Press.

Smith, Dorothy. (1990). *The Conceptual Practices of Power: A Feminist Sociology of Knowledge.* Toronto: University of Toronto Press.

West, Candace, & Don Zimmerman. (1987). "Doing gender." *Gender & Society* 1:125–151.

Discussion Questions

1. What does the author mean when she says that gender is a social construct? Give an example of the social construction of gender in women's sport.

2. Why is gender stratification problematic and for whom?

3. From your perspective and that of the author, how have the obstacles to achieving gender equity changed over time? What are your predictions for the future?

4. What is the paradox of human nature, as defined by the author?

2

Just Do . . . What? Sport, Bodies and Gender

Shari L. Dworkin and Michael A. Messner

© Adobe

> Every day I struggle with my femininity. Boxing is such a boy's club—I'm
> constantly on guard. It's taken a lot of work, but I finally feel that what
> makes me a woman is what gives me power.
>
> *Lucia Ruker, Boxer*

"Just Do . . . What? Sport, bodies, gender" by Shari L. Dworkin and Michael A. Messner abridged from
Revisioning Gender, M. Ferree, J. Lorber and B. Hess, 1999. Reprinted by permission of AltaMira Press/Rowman
and Littlefield.

Sport has proven to be one of the key institutional sites for the study of the social construction of gender. Organized sport, as we now know it, was created in the late nineteenth and early twentieth centuries by and for White middle class men to bolster a sagging ideology of "natural superiority" over women and over race- and class-subordinated groups of men (Crosset 1990; Kimmel 1990; McKay 1991; Messner 1988; Whitson 1990). Thus, although sport was seemingly based in natural physical endowments, it was socially constructed out of the gender, race, and class-based stratification systems of Europe and the United States. [. . .]

It took a gender analysis of sports ideologies and commercialization to unravel the ways sport is organized to sell masculinity to men. Today, that same gender analysis is being applied to the deconstruction of the selling of a shifting imagery of physical femininity in women athletes. Note, however, the persistence of the gender segregation so evident in organized sport from the beginning—in nearly all cases, men's and women's sports are carefully segregated, and men's sports are still assumed to be mostly for male spectators. Women's sports, however, to be successful, have to be attractive to men as well as women viewers. As a result, notions of conventional masculinity and femininity persist. Sport, as a cultural and commercial production, constructs and markets gender; besides making money, making gender may be sport's chief function.

It may appear ironic that an institution that has continued to contribute to the reconstitution of hegemonic masculinity throughout the twentieth century has become a key site for the development of a critical feminist scholarship on gender (e.g., Birrell 1988; Birrell and Cole 1994; Bryson 1987; Hall 1988, 1996; Hargreaves 1994; Messner and Sabo 1990; Theberge 1981). In fact, it is the very centrality of the body in sport practice and ideology that provides an opportunity to examine critically and illuminate the social construction of gender (Connell 1987; Lorber 1994). [. . .]

[. . .] Sport has become a fascinating subfield in which to revisit perennial feminist questions of structure and agency, as well as to explore more recent debates over embodiment, identity, and power. We begin this chapter with an examination of recent research on men and sport to reflect on the limitations of employing an analytic gender lens that ignores or marginalizes the centrality of race and class. Then we discuss the extent to which bodily agency by athletic women represents resistance to oppression by exploring three contexts: the Title IX struggle for sex equity in high school and college sports, the recent championing of women's athletic participation by corporate liberals such as Nike and the contradictory meanings surrounding muscular female bodies.

Athletic Men: Paying the Price

When we disentangle the historical and contemporary relationship between sport and men's power, we must recognize the distinction between sport as a cultural practice that constructs dominant belief systems and the individual experience of sport as an athletic career. Clearly, for at least the past 100 years, the dominant cultural meanings surrounding athletic masculinity have served mostly to stabilize hegemonic masculinity in the face of challenges by women, working-class men, men of color, and immigrants (Crosset 1990; Kimmel 1990). However, the experience of male athletes is often fraught with contradiction and paradox. Although many male athletes may dream of being the next Michael Jordan, very few ever actually make a living playing sports (Messner 1992). Even for extremely successful male athletes, the rigor of attaining and maintaining athletic stardom often comes at the cost of emotional and interpersonal development (Connell 1990). And although athletic masculinity symbolizes an image of physical health and sexual virility, athletes commonly develop alienated relationships with their bodies, learning to relate to them like machines, tools, or even weapons to be "used up" to get a job done. As a result, many athletes and former athletes suffer from permanent injuries, poor health, and low life expectancy (Sabo 1994; White, Young, and McTeer 1995). In particular, it is disproportionately young men from poor socioeconomic and racial/ethnic backgrounds who pay these costs.

To put it simply, young men from race- or class-subordinated backgrounds disproportionately seek status, respect, empowerment, and upward mobility through athletic careers. Most of them do not make it to the mythical "top," but this majority is mostly invisible to the general public. Instead, those very few who do make it into the limelight—especially those in sports like football or boxing, that reward the most extreme possibilities of large, powerful, and violent male bodies—serve as public symbols of exemplary masculinity, with whom all men can identify *as men*, as separate and superior to women (Messner 1988, 1992). While serving to differentiate "men" from "women" symbolically, top male athletes—especially African American men in violent sports—are simultaneously available to be used by men as cultural symbols of differences among them. African American male athletes—for instance, boxer Mike Tyson—have become icons of an atavistic masculinity, in comparison to whom White middle-class men can construct themselves as kinder, gentler "new men" (Messner 1993a). This imagery of Black men includes a package of sexual potency and muscular power wrapped in danger. Just as African American males have been used in the past to symbolize fears of a "primitive" sexuality unleashed (Hoch 1979; Davis 1981), Americans are increasingly obsessed with documenting the sexual misbehaviors of Black male athletes (Messner 1993b).

Men's sport, then, constructs masculinities in complex and contradictory ways. At a time in history when physical strength is of less and less practical significance in workplaces, especially in the professional and managerial jobs of most White, college-educated men, African American, poor, and working-class men have increasingly "taken over" the sports to which they have access. But having played sports is of little or no practical use to most of these young men once their athletic careers have ended. Athletic skills rarely transfer over into nonsports careers. The significance of successful African American male athletes in the current gender order is *not* that they challenge dominant social meanings or power relations. To the contrary, they serve to stabilize ideas of natural difference and hierarchy between women and men and among men of different social classes and races.

We can draw two conclusions from this brief discussion of men's sports. First, although we can see African American men's struggles to achieve success and respect through sport as a collective response to class and racial constraints, this agency operates largely to *reproduce*—rather than to resist or challenge—current race, class, and gender relations of power. [. . .] Second, we can see by looking at men's sports that *simply* employing a "gender lens" to analyze sport critically is limiting, even dangerous. The current literature supports the claim that men's sport does continue to empower "men," but for the most part, it is not the men who are doing the playing who are being empowered. Clearly, when we speak of "sport and empowerment" for men, we need to ask, Which men? These two points—that "agency" is not necessarily synonymous with "resistance," and that we need to be very cautious about employing a simplistic gender lens to speak categorically about "men and sport"—will inform our examination of women's current movement into sports.

Sex Equity for "Women in Sport"

Since the passage of Title IX of the Education Act Amendments, adopted by Congress in 1972, girls' and women's sports in the United States have changed in dramatic, but paradoxical, ways. On the one hand, there is no denying the rapid movement toward equity in the number of female participants and programs for women and girls (Calm 1994; Carpenter 1993). [. . .] These numerical increases in opportunities to participate in such a masculine-structured institution as school sports prove the effectiveness of organizing politically and legally around the concept "woman." Indeed, the relative success of this post-Title IX liberal strategy of gender equity in sport was premised on the deployment of separate "male" and "female" sports.

On the one hand, at least within the confines of liberalism, a "strategic essentialism" that successfully deploys the category "woman" can result in moves toward greater distributive justice. [. . .]

[. . .] Yet, Title IX has not yet yielded anything close to equity for girls and women within sports—more boys and men still play sports; they still have far more opportunities, from the peewee level through professional sports; and girls and women often have to struggle for access to uniforms, travel money, practice facilities, and scholarships that boys and men routinely take for granted (Lopiano 1993; Women's Sports Foundation 1997). But the dramatic movement of girls and women into sport—and the continued legal basis for challenges to inequities that are provided by Title IX precedents—makes sport an impressive example of a previously almost entirely masculine terrain that is now gender contested. The very existence of skilled and strong women athletes demanding recognition and equal access to resources is a destabilizing tendency in the current gender order.

On the other hand, there are obvious limits in the liberal quest for gender equity in sport. [. . .] First, as the popularity, opportunities, and funding for women's sports have risen, the leadership positions have markedly shifted away from women to men. Radical critics of sport have argued that this shift toward men's control of girl and women athletes is but one indicator of the limits and dangers of a gender-blind model of equity that uncritically adopts the men's "military model" of sport (Nelson 1991). To be sure, this shift to men coaches was heroically resisted throughout the 1970s by many women coaches and athletic administrators behind the banner of the Association for Intercollegiate Athletics for Women (AIAW). [. . .] Locally, most women's athletic departments were folded into male athletic departments, and the hiring of coaches for women's sports was placed in the hands of male athletic directors.

As women's sports has become controlled by men, it increasingly reflects the most valued characteristics of men's sports: "hierarchy, competitiveness and aggression" (Hall 1996: 91). In the most "feminine" sports, men coaches are simultaneously demanding the aggressiveness of adult men athletes and the submissiveness of little girls—a most complex gender message! A poignant example of these dangers can be seen in women's gymnastics and ice-skating, where very young girls, typically coached mostly by men coaches who are often abusive, learn to practice with painful injuries and often develop severe eating disorders in order to keep their bodies "small, thin and prepubescent" (Ryan 1995: 103). [. . .]

As girls and women push for equity in sport, they are moving—often uncritically—into a hierarchical system that has as its main goal to produce winners, champions, and profits. Although increased participation for girls and women apparently has its benefits at the lower levels, as the incentives mount for girl and women athletes to professionalize, they increasingly face many of the same limitations and dangers (in addition to some others, such as sexual harassment and rape) as those experienced by highly competitive men.

"If You Let Me Play . . ."

In recent years, corporate America has begun to awaken to the vast and lucrative potential markets that might be developed within and subsidiary to women's sports.

[. . .] In recent years, athletic footwear advertisements by Reebok and Nike have exemplified the ways that corporations have made themselves champions of women's athletic participation. In the early 1990s, Reebok was first to seize the lion's share of the female athletic shoe market. But by the mid-1990s, Nike had made great gains with a highly successful advertising campaign that positioned the corporation as the champion of girls' and women's rights inside and outside of sports. One influential TV spot included images of athletically active girls and women, with the voice-over saying things like, "If you let me play, I'll be less likely to drop out of school," and "If you let me play, I'll be better able to say no to unwanted sexual activity." These ads made use of the research findings from such organizations as the Women's Sports Foundation, documenting the positive, healthy, and empowering aspects of athletic participation for girls. Couching this information in the language of individual empowerment, Nike sold it to girls and women in the form of athletic shoes.

To be sure, the power of these commercials lies partly in the fact that they almost never mentioned shoes or even the Nike name. The message is that individual girls will be happier, healthier, and more in charge of their lives if we "let them play." The Nike "swoosh" logo is subtly displayed in the corner of the ads so that the viewer knows who is the source of these liberating ideas. It is through this kind of campaign that Nike has positioned itself as what Cole and Hribar (1995) call a "celebrity feminist," a corporate liberal entity that has successfully appropriated and co-opted the language of individual empowerment underlying the dominant discourse of opportunity for girls and women in sports. Aspiring athletes are then encouraged by slick advertising campaigns to identify their own individual empowerment—in essence, *their relationship to feminism*—with that of the corporate entity that acts as a celebrity feminist. If "feminist identity" can be displayed most readily through the wearing of the Nike logo on shoes and other athletic apparel, then displaying the Nike "swoosh" on one's body becomes a statement to the world that one is an independent, empowered individual—a successful young woman of the nineties.

There are fundamental limitations to this kind of "empowerment." If radical feminists are correct in claiming that patriarchy reproduces itself largely through men's ability to dominate and exploit women's bodies, we might suggest a corollary: Corporations have found peace and profit with liberal feminism by co-opting a genuine quest by women for bodily agency and empowerment and channeling it toward a goal of physical achievement severely limited by its consumerist context. The kind of collective women's agency that emphasizes the building of institutions such as rape crisis centers, domestic violence shelters, and community women's athletic leagues is a *resistant agency* through which women have empowered themselves to fight against and change the institutions that oppress them. In contrast, individual women's agency expressed as identification with corporate consumerism is a *reproductive agency* that firmly situates women's actions and bodies within the structural gender order that oppresses them.

In addition, Nike's commitment to women's liberation is contradicted by its own corporate practices. In 1996, when it posted its largest profits, and its CEO Phillip Knight's stock was estimated to be worth $5 billion, the mostly women Indonesian workers who manufactured the shoes were paid about $2.25 a day. Workers who attempted to organize for higher pay and better working conditions were fired (Take Action for Girls 1996). Meanwhile, U.S. women's eager consumption of corporate celebrity feminism makes it almost impossible for them to see, much less to act upon, the exploitation of women workers halfway around the globe.

[. . .]

Liberal feminism in sport has come full circle: a universalized concept of "women" was strategically deployed to push—with some impressive but limited success—for equal opportunities for women in sport. As these successes mounted, a key ideological support for hegemonic masculinity—the naturalized equation of male bodies with athletic ability and physical strength—was destabilized. But corporations have recently seized upon the individualist impulse of female empowerment that underlies liberal feminism, and have sold it back to women as an ideology and bodily practice that largely precludes any actual mobilizing around the collective concept of "women." Individual women are now implored by Nike to "Just do it"—just like the men "do it." Undoubtedly, many women strongly approve of, and feel good about, the Nike ads. But Nike's individualized and depoliticized "feminism" ignores how individuals who "do it" with Nike are implicated in an international system of racial, g
ender, and class exploitation of women workers in less developed nations.

Just as we argued in our discussion of the limits of sports for raising the status of working-class and African American men, here, too, gender analysis alone is not enough. It is not just muscular, or athletic, or "fit" bodies that must be considered in women's liberation—it is also laboring bodies as well. In fact, as we will argue next, a danger in contemporary reductionist understandings of empowerment as being synonymous with the development of one's body is that concentrating on toning muscles can easily transfer energies—especially those of women privileged by class and race—away from collective organizing to change institutions that disadvantage all women, but especially those who are poor, working-class, and racially disadvantaged.

Women and Muscles

In addition to the ever-increasing numbers of women who compete in high school and college sport, more and more women today engage in fitness activities, lift weights, and enjoy the power of carrying musculature. [. . .] New bodily ideals can be said to have broadened from thin and slim to tight and toned, with an "allowance" for "substantial weight and bulk" (Bordo 1993: 191). By some standards, today's more muscular woman can be viewed as embodying agency, power, and independence in a way that exemplifies resistance to patriarchal ideals. However, just as within sport, women's bodily agency in fitness activities can be contradictory. Is this bodily agency resistant and/or empowering, or is the fit, muscled ideal simply the latest bodily requirement for women, a form of "self-surveillance and obedience" in service to patriarchal capitalism (Bartky 1988)?

Some feminists argue that when women exercise their agency to develop bodily mobility and muscular power, these activities are self-affirming for women and antithetical to patriarchal definitions of women as passive, docile, and weak (MacKinnon 1987; Nelson 1991; Young 1990). By fighting for access to participation in sport and fitness, women have created an empowering arena where the meaning of gender is being contested and renegotiated, and where active rejections of dominant notions of femininity may be forged (e.g., Bolin 1992; Gilroy 1989; Guthrie and Castelnuovo 1992; Kane and Lenskyj 1998; Lenskyj 1987; McDermott 1996; Theberge 1987). Other feminists, however, offer compelling counterarguments. First, there is the question as to whether bodily "empowerment" is merely a modern version of the "docile body," the intensely limiting and oppressive bodily management and scrutiny with which women learn to be complicit (Bordo 1993). For some women (especially those who are White, middle-class, and married heterosexuals) this complicit agency might result in more work on top of their already stifling "second shift" (Hochschild 1989)—a "third shift" that consists of long doses of effort invested in conforming to the latest touted bodily "requirement." It is these women, whose daily lives in families and careers might leave them feeling less than empowered, who would then respond to advertisements that encourage them to participate in sport and fitness in order to feel a sense of empowerment through their bodies. Couched in the logic of individualism and the Protestant work ethic, it seems that a woman needs only enact her free will and "just do it" in order to "have it all." But "doing it" the corporate individualist way involves a radical turning inward of agency toward the goal of transformation of one's own body, in contrast to a turning outward to mobilize for collective political purposes, with the goal of transforming social institutions. Clearly, despite its uplifting tone and seemingly patriotic commitment to American women, corporate slogans such as Nike's beg several questions, such as: Just do *what* And *for whom?*

Just as the cult of true womanhood excluded numerous women from its "ideal" in the early nineteenth century, a similar conceptual vacuum arises here. After all, the dominant fitness industry message very likely "has no relevance to the majority of working-class women, or to Black women, or those from other ethnic minorities" (Hargreaves 1994: 161). [. . .]

Just as images of physically powerful and financially successful African American men ultimately did not challenge, but instead continued to construct a stratified race, class, and gender order, current images of athletic women appear to represent a broadening of the definitional boundaries of what Connell (1987) calls "emphasized femininity" to include more muscular development. But the resis-tant possibilities in images of athletic women are largely contained by the continued strong assertion of (and commercial rewards for) retaining a link between heterosexual attractiveness and body image. For instance, many lauded Olympic track star Florence Griffith-Joyner's muscularity as a challenge to the dominant image of femininity and to images of men as physically superior. However, Griffith-Joyner's muscularity existed alongside "rapier-like" nails, flowing hair, and spectacular outfits, which ultimately situated her body and its markings firmly within a commercialized modernization of heterosexual femininity (Messner forthcoming). Now more than ever, the commodification of women's bodies may mean that when women "just do it," they are "just doing" 1990s "heterosexy" femininity. In the media, these bodies are not unambiguously resistant images of powerful women, but rather an ambivalent framing or subtle trivialization or sexualization of women's bodies that undermines their muscles and their athletic accomplishments (Duncan and Hasbrook 1988; Messner, Duncan, and Wachs 1996; Kane 1995; Kane and Lenskyj 1998). Female bodybuilders in particular illustrate these gender ambiguities. Research demonstrates that women can and do press and contest the limits of emphasized femininity. However, their agency is contained by the structure, rules, and ideologies of women's bodybuilding. [. . .]

Researchers who study women's participation in fitness activities find the same tendency to adhere to emphasized femininity as is shown by women athletes and bodybuilders. They tend to avoid lifting weights "too much" for fear of being "too big." Instead, they engage in long doses of cardiovascular work, which is thought to emphasize tone and leanness (Dworkin forthcoming; Markula 1996). Just as women in male-dominated occupations often hit a glass ceiling that halts their professional advancement, there appears to be a glass ceiling on women's musculature that constrains the development of women's muscular strength. Defined according to the latest commodified eroticization of heterosexual femininity, most women (with differences by race, class, sexuality, age) remain acutely aware of how much muscle is "allowed," how much is "still" attractive.

Conclusion

Through an examination of gender, bodies, and sport, we have made three main points in this chapter that may illuminate more general attempts to understand and change the current gender order. First, although sport has been an arena for contesting the status quo by men of color and by White women and women of color, the positive results have been individual rather than collective. A few star athletes have become celebrities, but their popularity has not raised the overall status of disadvantaged men and women (although it may have upgraded the physical potentiality of middle-class White women). Second, whatever sport has accomplished in terms of equity, women's and men's sports are still segregated, and men's sports are still dominant in commercial value and in the media. Third, rather than breaking down conventional concepts of masculinity and femininity, organized sport has overblown the cultural hegemony of heterosexualized, aggressive, violent, heavily muscled male athletes and heterosexualized, flirtatious, moderately muscled female athletes who are accomplished and competitive but expected to be submissive to the control of men coaches and managers.

The link in all these outcomes is that organized sport is a commercial activity first and foremost. Organized sport is financially underwritten by corporations that sell shoes and clothing to a public looking for vicarious thrills and personal "fitness." The corporations capitalize on the celebrity of star athletes, who use individual achievements to make more money, rather than to help upgrade the communities from which they have come. Their endorsements sell individual achievement and conventional beauty and sexuality as well as Nikes and Reeboks. A further negative consequence to the upbeat message of "Just do it" is that many of the appurtenances of sport and fitness are produced by the labor of poorly paid, malnourished, and probably physically unfit women workers.

Does this mean that women's agency in sports and other physical activities is a dead end that should be abandoned by feminist activists? Absolutely not. We think that sport is like any other institution: We cannot abandon it, nor can we escape from it. Instead, we must struggle within it. [. . .] We think feminists need to fight on two fronts in the battle for equity in sports. On the one hand, we must continue to push for equal opportunities for girls and women in sports. On the other hand, although the research points to benefits for girls and women who play sports at the lower levels, many of the girls and women who are professionalized into corporate sports can expect—just as most of their men counterparts in corporate sports can—to pay emotional and physical costs.

But in challenging women's uncritical adoption of the dominant values of corporate sport, we must be cautious not to fall into the same trap as have past activists for girls' and women's sports. In the 1920s and 1930s, in the wake of two decades of burgeoning athleticism by girls and women, medical leaders and physical educators responded with what now appear to be hysterical fears that vigorous physical activity for girls and women carried enormous physical and psychological dangers (Cahn 1994). The result of these fears was the institutionalization of an "adapted model" (i.e., "tamed down" sports for women) that served to ghettoize women's sports, leaving the hegemonic masculinity of men's sport virtually unchallenged for the next 40 years. Given this history, today's advocates of women's sports walk a perilous tightrope. They must assert the positive value of vigorous physical activity and muscular strength for girls and women while simultaneously criticizing the unhealthy aspects of men's sports. A key to the accomplishment of this task must involve the development of a critical analysis of the dominant assumptions, beliefs, and practices of *men's* sports (Thompson 1988; Messner and Sabo 1994). In addition, we need to continue to explore feminist alternatives, for women and for men, to the "military model," with its emphasis on heroism, "playing through pain," and winning at all costs (Birrell and Richter 1987; Nelson 1991; Theberge 1985).

The activist fight for women and girls as a group will not be helped by simplistic scholarship that acts as a cheering section for numerical increases in women's athletic participation, or for the increasing visibility of women's athletics in televised ads. Nor will a simple "gender lens" that views sport uncritically in terms of undifferentiated and falsely universalized categories of "men" and "women" take us very far in framing questions and analyzing data. Different groups of men and of women disproportionately benefit from and pay the costs of the current social organization of sports. We need an analytic framework that appreciates the importance of class, racial, and sexual differences among both men and women while retaining the feminist impulse that places the need to empower the disadvantaged in the foreground.

Data from empirical observation of sport demonstrate the absence of absolute categorical differences between "men" and "women"—instead, there is a "continuum of performance" that, when acknowledged, can radically deconstruct dichotomous sex categories (Kane 1995). Obscuring this continuum are the social processes through which sport constructs and naturalizes differences and inequality between "men" and "women." Does this observation lead us down the path of radical deconstruction? We think the discussion in this chapter demonstrates just the opposite. The current post-structuralist preoccupation with deconstructing binary categories like "men and women" (e.g., Butler 1990; Sedgewick 1990) has produced new discourses and practices that disrupt and fracture these binaries (Lorber 1996). Yet simply deconstructing our *discourse* about binary categories does not necessarily challenge the material basis of master categories to which subordinate categories of people stand in binary opposition: the capitalist class, men, heterosexuals, Whites. In fact, quite the contrary may be true (Stein and Plummer 1994). As many feminists have pointed out, although it is certainly true that every woman is somewhat uniquely situated, a radical deconstruction of the concept "woman" could lead to an individualism that denies similarity of experience, thus leading to depoliticized subjects. We would argue that it is currently corporations such as Nike that are in the forefront of the widespread development of this sort of depoliticized individualist "empowerment" among women. Radical deconstruction, therefore, is very much in the interests of the most powerful institutions in our world, as it leaves us feeling (at best) individually "empowered," so long as we are able to continue to consume the right products, while making it unlikely we will identify common interests with others in challenging institutions.

Rather than a shift toward radical deconstruction, the research on gender, bodies, and sport suggests that it is essential to retain and build upon the concept of social structure, with its attendant emphasis on the importance of people's shared positions within social institutions (Duncan 1993; Messner 1992). Such a materialist analysis reveals how differential access to resources and opportunities and the varieties of structured constraints shape the contexts in which people think, interact, and construct political practices and discourse. A critical analysis of gender within a materialist, structural analysis of institutions entails a reassertion of the crucial importance (though not necessarily the primacy) of social class. Interestingly, as recent intellectual trends have taken many scholars away from the study of institutions toward a preoccupation with individuals, bodies, and difference, the literature has highlighted race, gender, and sexual identities in new and important ways, but social class has too often dropped out of the analysis. As we have demonstrated, discussions of the possibilities and limits of women's agency in gender equity struggles in sport, the co-optation of feminism by Nike's "celebrity feminism," and the current encouragement of physical fitness for middle-class women all need to be examined within the context of distributive justice. We also need a clear analysis of the position of women and men as workers in organized sport; as marketable celebrities; as workers in sweatshops making sport shoes, clothing, and equipment; and as consumers of these products and symbols. This analysis must be informed by feminist theories of the intersections of race, class, and gender (e.g., Baca Zinn and Dill 1996). Politically, this work can inform an alliance politics that is grounded simultaneously in a structural analysis of power and a recognition of differences and inequalities between and among women and men.

References

Baca Zinn, Maxine, & Dill Bonnie Thornton. (1996). "Theorizing difference from Multiracial Feminism." Feminism Studies 22: 321–331.

Bartky, Sandra L. (1988). "Foucault, Femininity, and the Modernization of Patriarchal Power." In I. Diamond & L. Quinby (Eds.), *Feminism and Foucault: Reflections on Resistance.* Boston: Northeastern University Press.

Birrell, Susan. (1988). "Discourses on the Gender/Sport Relationship: From Women in Sport to Gender Relations." *Exercise and Sport Sciences Review* 16: 59–200.

Birrell, Susan & Cole, Cheryl L. (1990). "Double Fault: Rence Richards and the Construction and Naturalization of Difference." *Sociology of Sport Journal* 7: 1–21.

———. (Eds.) (1994). *Women, Sport, and Culture.* Champaign, IL: Human Kinetics.

Birrell, Susan & Richter, Diana M. (1987). "Is a Diamond Forever? Feminist Transformations of Sport." *Women's Studies International Forum* 10: 395–409.

Bolin, A. (1992). "Vandalized Vanity: Feminine Physique Betrayed and Portrayed." In F. E. Mascia-Lees & P. Sharpe (Eds.), *Tattoo, Torture, Mutilation, and Adornment: The Denaturalization of the Body in Culture and Text* (pp. 79–90). Albany: State University of New York Press.

Bordo, Susan. (1993). *Unbearable Weight: Feminism, Western Culture, and the Body.* Berkeley: University of California Press.

Bryson, Lois. (1987). "Sport and the Maintenance of Masculine Hegemony." *Women's Studies International Forum* 10: 349–360.

Butler, Judith. (1990). *Gender Trouble: Feminism and the Subversion of Identity.* New York: Routledge.

Cahn, Susan K. (1994). *Coming on Strong: Gender and Sexuality in Twentieth Century Women's Sport.* New York: Free Press.

Carpenter, Linda Jean. 1993. "Letters Home: My Life with Title IX." In G. L. Cohen (Ed.), *Women in Sport: Issues and Controversies* (pp. 79–94). Newbury Park, CA: Sage.

Cole, Cheryl L. & Hribar, Amy (1995). "Celebrity Feminism: Nike Style Post-Fordism Transcendence, and Consumer Power." *Sociology of Sport Journal* 12: 347–369.

Connell, R. W. (1987). *Gender and Power*. Stanford, CA: Stanford University Press.

———. (1990). "An Iron Man: The Body and Some Contradictions of Hegemonic Masculinity." In M. A. Messner & D. F. Sabo (Eds.), *Sport, Men and the Gender Order: Critical Feminist Perspectives* (pp. 83–95). Champaign, IL: Human Kinetics.

Crosset, Todd W. (1990). "Masculinity, Sexuality and the Development of Early Modern Sport." In M. A. Messner & D. F. Sabo (Eds.), *Sport, Men and the Gender Order: Critical Feminist Perspectives* (pp. 45–54). Champaign, IL: Human Kinetics.

Davis, Angela Y. (1981). *Women, Race, and Class*. New York: Random House.

Duncan, Margaret Carlisle. (1993). "Beyond Analyses of Sport Media Texts: An Argument for Formal Analyses of Institutional Structures." *Sociology of Sport Journal* 10: 353–72.

Duncan, Margaret Carlisle & Hasbrook, Cynthia A. (1988). "Denial of Power in Televised Women's Sports." *Sociology of Sport Journal* 5: 1–21.

Dworkin, Shari L. Forthcoming. "A Woman's Place Is in the . . . Cardiovascular Room? Gender Relations, the Body, and the Gym." In A, Bolin & J. Granskog (Eds.), *Athletic Intruders*. Albany: State University of New York Press.

Gilroy, S. (1989). "The Embody-ment of Power: Gender and Physical Activity." *Leisure Studies* 8: 163–171.

Guthrie, Sharon R. & Castelnuovo, Shirley (1992). "Elite Women Bodybuilders: Model of Resistance or Compliance?" *Play and Culture* 5: 378–400.

Hall, M. Ann. (1988). 'The Discourse of Gender and Sport: From Femininity to Feminism." *Sociology of Sport Journal* 5: 330–340.

———. (1996). *Feminism and Sporting Bodies: Essays on Theory and Practice*. Champaign, IL: Human Kinetics.

Hargreaves, Jennifer. (1994). *Sporting Females: Critical Issues in the History and Sociology of Women's Sport*. New York: Routledge.

Hoch, Paul. (1979). *White Hero Black Beast: Racism, Sexism and the Mask of Masculinity*. London: Pluto.

Hochschild, Arlie R. (1989). *The Second Shift*. New York: Avon.

Kane, Mary Jo. (1995). "Resistance/Transformation of the Oppositional Binary: Exposing Sport as a Continuum." *Journal of Sport and Social Issues* 19: 191–218.

Kane, Mary Jo & Lennskyj, Helen (1998). "Media Treatment of Female Athletes: Issues of Gender and Sexualities." In L. A. Wenner (Ed.), *MediaSport: Cultural Sensibilities and Sport in the Media Age*. London: Routledge.

Kimmel, Michael S. (1990). "Baseball and the Reconstitution of American Masculinity, 1880–1920." Pp. 55–66. In M. A. Messner & D. F. Sabo (Eds.), *Sport, Men and the Gender Order: Critical Feminist Perspectives* (pp. 55–66). Champaign, IL: Human Kinetics.

Lenskyj, Helen. (1987). "Female Sexuality and Women's Sport." *Women's Studies International Forum* 4: 381–386.

Lopiano, Donna A. 1993. "Political Analysis: Gender Equity Strategies for the Future." In G. L. Cohen (Ed.), *Women in Sport: Issues and Controversies* (pp. 104–216). Newbury Park, CA: Sage.

Lorber, Judith. (1994). *Paradoxes of Gender*. New Haven, CT: Yale University Press.

——. (1996). "Beyond the Binaries: Depolarizing the Categories of Sex, Sexuality, and Gender." *Sociological Inquiry* 66: 143–159.

MacKinnon, Catharine A. (1987). *Feminism Unmodified: Discourses on Life and Law.* Cambridge, MA: Harvard University Press.

Markula, Pirkko. (1996). "Firm but Shapely, Fit but Sexy, Strong but Thin: The Postmodern Aerobicizing Female Bodies." *Sociology of Sport Journal* 12: 424–453.

McDermott, Lisa. (1996). "Towards a Feminist Understanding of Physicality within the Context of Women's Physically Active and Sporting Lives." *Sociology of Sport Journal* 13: 12–30.

McKay, Jim. (1991). *No Pain, No Gain? Sport and Australian Culture.* Englewood Cliffs, NJ: Prentice Hall.

Messner, Michael A. & Sabo, Donald F. Champaign. IL: Human Kinetics.

Messner, Michael A. (1988). "Sports and Male Domination: The Female Athlete as Contested . . . Ideological Terrain." *Sociology of Sport Journal* 5: 197–211.

Messner, Michael A. (1992). *Power at Play: Sports and the Problem of Masculinity.* Boston: Beacon.

——. (1993a). "Changing Men and Feminist Politics in the United States." *Theory and Society* 22: 723–37.

——. (1993b). "White Men Misbehaving: Feminism, Afrocentrism, and the Promise of a Critical Standpoint." *Journal of Sport and Social Issues* 16: 136–144.

Messner, Michael A. Forthcoming. Theorizing Gendered Bodies: Beyond the Subject/Object Dichotomy." In C. L. Cole, J. Loy, & M. A. Messner (Eds.), *Exercising Power: The Making and Remaking of the Body.* Albany: State University of New York Press.

Messner, Michael A., Margaret Carlisle Duncan, & Wachs, Faye Linda (1996). "The Gender of Audience-Building: Televised Coverage of Men's and Women's NCAA Basketball." *Sociological Inquiry* 66: 422–439.

Messner, Michael A. & Sabo, Donald F. (1990). "Towards a Critical Feminist Reappraisal of Sport, Men and the Gender Order." In M. A. Messner & D. F. Sabo (Eds.), *Sport, Men and the Gender Order: Critical Feminist Perspectives.* Champaign, IL: Human Kinetics.

——. (1994). *Sex, Violence and Power in Sports: Rethinking Masculinity.* Freedom, CA: Crossing Press.

Nelson, Mariah Burton. (1991). *Are We Winning Yet? How Women Are Changing Sports and Sports Are Changing Women.* New York: Random House.

Ryan, Joan. (1995). *Little Girls in Pretty Boxes: The Making and Breaking of Elite Gymnasts and Figure Skaters.* New York: Warner.

Sabo, Donald F. (1994). "Pigskin, Patriarchy, and Pain." Pp. 82–88 in *Sex, Violence and Power in Sports: Rethinking Masculinity,* by Michael A. Messner and Donald F. Sabo. Freedom, CA: Crossing Press.

Sedgewick, Eve K. (1990). *Epistemology of the Closet.* Berkeley: University of California Press.

Stein, Arlene and Ken Plummer. (1994). "I Can't Even Think Straight': Queer Theory and the Missing Sexual Revolution in Sociology." *Sociological Theory* 12: 178–187.

Take Action for Girls. (1996). "The Two Faces of Nike." *Take Action for Girls Newsletter 1* (November): 2.

Theberge, Nancy. (1981). "A Critique of Critiques: Radical and Feminist Writings on Sport." *Social Forces* 60: 341–353.

——. (1985). "Toward a Feminist Alternative to Sport as a Male Preserve." *Quest* 37: 193–202.

——. (1987). "Sport and Women's Empowerment." *Women's Studies International Forum* 10: 387–393.

Thompson, Shona M. (1988). "Challenging the Hegemony: New Zealand Women's Opposition to Rugby and the Reproduction of Capitalist Patriarchy." *International Review of the Sociology of Sport,* 23: 205–212.

White, Philip G., Young, Kevin & McTeer, William G. (1995). "Sport, Masculinity, and the Injured Body." In D. F. Sabo & F. Gordon (Eds.), *Men's Health and Illness: Gender, Power, and the Body* (pp. 158–182). Thousand Oaks, CA: Sage.

Whitson, David. (1990). "Sport in the Social Construction of Masculinity." In M. A. Messner & D. F. Sabo (Eds.), *Sport, Men and the Gender Order: Critical Feminist Perspectives* (pp. 19–31). Champaign, IL: Human Kinetics.

Women's Sports Foundation. (1997). *The Women's Sports Foundation Gender Equity Report Card: A Survey of Athletic Opportunity in American Higher Education.* East Meadow, NY: Women's Sports Foundation.

Young, Iris M. (1990). *Throwing Like a Girl and Other Essays in Feminist Philosophy and Social Theory.* Bloomington: Indiana University Press.

Further Reading

Messner, M. A. (2002). *Taking the Field.* The University of Minnesota Press: Minneapolis, MN.

Discussion Questions

1. Why do the authors believe sport is an important site for studying the social construction of gender?

2. How does the institution of sport work together with other institutions (e.g., media, the family, political-economy, education, religion) to support and maintain the patriarchal status quo?

3. What are Dworkin and Messner's arguments against adopting only a gender analytical "lens," and what do they advocate instead?

4. Critically assess Nike's contribution to the empowerment of women.

5. How does sport as a social, political, and economic institution contribute to shaping current notions of *gender, race, disability, and sexuality?*

6. After reading this article, what do you believe sporting and physical activity participation will be like for girls and women in 2025? In 2050?

3

Disability Management Among Women with Physical Impairments

The Contribution of Physical Activity

Sharon R. Guthrie and Shirley Castelnuovo

Three times a week during the early afternoon hours, when few people are around, we lift weights at a local health club. Rita, a woman with paraplegia, does the same. She knows that at this time of day there will be fewer people exercising, thus less traffic to negotiate in her motorized wheelchair and more chance that the few machines she is capable of accessing will be available.

Rita begins each exercise by carefully positioning her chair as close to the machine as possible and at a particular angle. Then, after slowly and methodically transferring her weight from the seat of the chair to that of the machine, she prepares herself for lifting. This arrangement of her body takes Rita at least as much time as the routines she executes. Moreover, her facial expressions suggest that the process, from beginning to end, is difficult and sometimes painful. Yet Rita persists, asking for no one's help, until her workout is completed. Watching and admiring the tenacity and focus of this woman, we have often wondered what motivates her to lift weights amid myriad physical and social obstacles, and how her bodily experience differs from those of persons without disabilities.

It is clear that when Rita works out, she pays attention to her body and the exercise environment in ways that persons without disabilities typically do not. For example, Rita does not take for granted her movement from machine to machine or her ability to get in and out of the machines as able-bodied weightlifters are prone to do. What takes relatively little attentional space for persons without disabilities, she has to seriously contemplate. Thus, Rita's body does not fade as easily from focal awareness.

This tendency of the "able" body to disappear from consciousness until some form of distress or dysfunction (e.g., pain, fatigue, hunger) is experienced encourages support for mind-body dualism, which has dominated much of Western thought for centuries (Leder, 1990).

From *Sociology of Sport Journal,* Volume 19, 2001 by Sharon R. Guthrie and Shirley Castelnuovo. Reprinted by permissions of the authors.

One of the central reasons dualistic thought has maintained its influential power, despite an ongoing critique, is because it is confirmed by everyday experience. That is, when our bodies function without problems, they are hardly noticeable, yet when we are sick or feel aches and pains, they become the focus of attention. It is at times such as these that we are most likely to experience the body as divorced from the mind and incapable of being fully determined or controlled by the will.

Our weightlifting experience and that of Rita reminds us, however, that the body is more than a complex physico-chemical object, subject to inclinations of the immaterial mind. Rather, it is the medium through which our perceptions and experiences of the world emerge. When we interact physically with the world, in this case with the weight-lifting equipment, we are engaging in the process of self-definition or what Merleau-Ponty (1962) referred to as "motility." That is, human identity and consciousness are embodied experiences, which can be enhanced by moving the body in skillful and intentional ways.

It does seem true that when we lift weights and thus improve our muscular strength and endurance, we experience improvements in the more global, less physical dimensions of self as well. We also gain greater clarity of mind-body unity and interdependence rather than separation and opposition. Rita most likely shares this experience. In fact, she may feel this sense of empowerment even more profoundly than we because she is engaged in a process that challenges stereotypes associated with physical disability, in addition to developing her own mind-body capabilities.

Unfortunately, however, Rita's empowerment emerges in a sociocultural context in which able-bodied norms are firmly entrenched. Most every aspect of this context, from the society at large to the structuring and placement of weight machines in this particular gym, reflect such norms. Being a person with a disability, Rita confronts the physical reality of her impairment, as well as social indicators that her body is "abnormal" and "lesser than" those of able-bodied persons. As a woman, she receives messages that her body should be a particular size and shape. Living in a society that fosters dualistic thinking and individual responsibility, she is told that because her mind can control her body, she is accountable for her own health and normalization. She may also be informed, in subtle and not so subtle ways, that she is incapable of developing abstract, rational thought because her disability makes transcending the physical realm difficult.

It therefore appears that Rita and other women with disabilities encounter at least four social forces, which we refer to as discourses of embodiment, that can influence their identity formation: (a) the discourse of disability (i.e., able-bodyism), (b) the discourse of feminine body-beauty, (c) the discourse of dualism, and (d) the discourse of personal responsibility.[1] Moreover, if they are women of color, lesbian, bisexual, or financially disadvantaged, they must contend with additional discourses. Given these physical and social constraints, how do women like Rita manage to develop a healthy sense of self?

Foucauldian analysis helps to explain how this is possible. According to Foucault (1990), although discourses, particularly those associated with sexual identity, have a profound impact on the way people constitute themselves, resistance to these discourses also occurs. Rita exemplifies such resistance. Indeed, one day she told us that her identity as a sexually attractive, professional woman was demolished the day she was forced to use a wheelchair and that, against her will, "disabled woman" became her master status, particularly in able-bodied circles. She confessed that such restrictive notions of who she is are deeply disturbing; however, she finds that the focus weight training requires helps her to cope with the discrimination she experiences, as well as to destabilize stereotypes associated with physical limitation. Rita's reactions to the discourse associated with disability (i.e., able-bodyism) confirm Foucault's relational understanding of power: where power exists, there will also be resistance.

Foucault (1985, 1988, 1989) posited two types of resistance, however: "reverse resistance," which involves continued support of a power-knowledge discourse, and "resistance as freedom," which requires developing a self that is not grounded in the limiting aspects of the discourse. For example, if Rita engages in weight training as a way to normalize or beautify herself—attempting to minimize her disability in the eyes of others—her actions reinforce the discourse associated with able-bodied norms. In contrast, if she uses weight training to develop herself physically and mentally in ways that transcend the discourse, she is engaging in resistance as freedom.

While the Foucauldian distinction between reverse resistance and resistance as freedom is useful in deciphering Rita's experiences, his notion of resistance as an intellectual enterprise is less so. For example, Rita's disability and weight training are not solely mental experiences, they are also physical processes. Therefore, her acts of resistance and self-transformation have a physical dimension as well. Moreover, Foucault claimed that resistance as freedom must remain an individual act because if the potentially liberating practice becomes part of a group dynamic, the possibility of a new, yet equally confining, discourse is created; thus, he did not allow for collective resistance.

Because Foucauldian logic does not fully elucidate Rita's physical activity experiences or those of the other women we studied, we found it necessary to meld Foucault's ideas with those of Merleau-Ponty, who provides another, yet complementary, theoretical framework to fill the explanatory gap. The strength of Merleau-Ponty's philosophy is his belief that human subjectivity is located in the body rather than the mind and that movement, what he called "motility," is the critical factor in the construction of human identity. Motility, he claimed, which involves moving one's body in space, always results in a new embodied reality. Therefore, it is through the process of movement, as opposed to sheer mental activity, that one's consciousness develops. Merleau-Ponty also argued, in contrast to Foucault, that resis-tance, and ultimately social transformation, can never be a solitary activity, but rather must involve the interaction of multiple individuals who are collectively engaged in resistant activities.

Grounding our work in this combined phenomenological Foucauldian perspective, we thus set out to answer the following questions: (a) how do women like Rita shape their identities and manage their physical disabilities while living in an able-bodyist culture and (b) what function does physical activity serve in the management process, if any?[2]

Method

Participants

Thirty-four physically active adult female volunteers, ranging in age from 20–72 (M = 29.2), participated in this study.[3] All of the participants had physical mobility disabilities, including spinal cord injury ($n = 12$), congenital limb deficiency ($n = 9$), amputation ($n = 5$), acquired brain injury ($n = 1$), post-polio syndrome ($n = 2$), multiple sclerosis ($n = 2$), amyotrophic lateral sclerosis ($n = 1$), spina bifida ($n = 1$), and dwarfism ($n = 1$). Twenty-two of the women had acquired disabilities while 12 had congenital disabilities. The disability ages (i.e., the amount of time one has had a disability or disabilities) ranged from 6 months to 42 years: 18 had disability ages of less than 5 years (defined in this study as a short disability age) while 16 had lived with their disabilities for 5 years or more (defined as a long disability age).

The racial/ethnic composition of this sample included 22 Caucasians, 4 African-Americans, 1 Asian American, 2 Hispanics, and 5 multiracial individuals (i.e., those identifying with more than one racial/ethnic category). The majority ($n = 26$) had at least some college education ($n = 12$), or already possessed a bachelor's degree ($n = 12$), master's degree ($n = 1$), or doctoral degree ($n = 1$). Although the sample was comprised primarily of heterosexuals ($n = 25$), seven women identified themselves as lesbian and two as bisexual.

Ten of the participants were competing in various types of organized sports (i.e., basketball, tennis, marathon racing). The majority ($n = 24$) were not involved in sport but were exercising on a regular basis in non-competitive settings, that is, at least three times a week for at least 30 minutes. Of these regular exercisers, 10 had competed in sport in the past, most before they had acquired their disability ($n = 6$).

Procedures

The participants were recruited from various disability organizations (both sport and non-sport-related), the student populations at four universities, and by word of mouth. To be a participant in this study, a woman had to meet two criteria: (a) she had to have a physical mobility disability, and (b) she had to be participating in some form of regular physical activity (e.g., sport or exercise).

Instrumentation

An interview guide was developed specifically for the purposes of this study. The researchers drew upon their previous work with women with disabilities in constructing the interview questions and pilot-tested the guide with two women with physical disabilities—one with a physical mobility impairment and the other with congenital limb deficiency—to determine the appropriateness and clarity of the questions. As a result of these interviews, the questions were deemed appropriate and clear.

Interviews, all of which were conducted by the same person, consisted primarily of open-ended questions and were standardized to maximize consistency. Each question was read exactly as worded, only non-directive probes were used for clarification and elaboration (i. e., those that do not influence the content of the resulting answers), all responses were tape-recorded and transcribed without interviewer discretion, and the interviewer attempted to communicate a neutral, non-judgmental perspective with regard to the respondents' answers. These procedures are accepted among qualitative researchers (Fowler & Mangione, 1990).

Each woman was interviewed privately in her home, by phone, or in the researcher's office for approximately 90 minutes. The interview began by asking general questions about the nature of one's disability and physical activity history. It then became more focused by asking questions directly associated with the goal of the study.

All participants were made aware that they could refuse answering any question and terminate the interview at any time. At the end of the interview, they were allowed to add anything they believed to be important, and later, after the interviews were transcribed, participants also had the opportunity to review the transcripts and make corrections or additions.

Inductive Content Analysis

Each interview was transcribed verbatim in preparation for data analysis. After the transcripts were completed, each interview was read, question by question, and salient themes and illustrating quotes were recorded. The purpose of the inductive analysis was to synthesize specific perceptions reported by the participants into meaningful themes. To accomplish this, the data were first sorted into raw data themes associated with each of the research goals. Each of the raw data themes was then recorded on a separate sheet of paper. Quotations illustrating the theme were also written on the paper, in addition to a comment summarizing the quote. One reliability check was performed by having two other individuals trained in qualitative methods—one who was associated with the research investigation and another who was not— read all of the quotes and summary comments to determine if the summaries accurately reflected the quotes. The reviewers found the summaries to be accurate reflections of the quotes.

After the list of raw data themes was compiled, an inductive analysis of the data was undertaken in order to generate lower order and higher order themes (i.e., merging similar raw data themes together into broader concepts). A second reliability check was performed by a fourth person, not associated with the investigation, who independently read the transcripts and subsequently categorized raw data themes into more general themes. These categories were compared to those established by the researchers and found to be 100% consistent at both the lower and higher order levels. The trustworthiness and credibility of qualitative analyses may be established through the use of such techniques (Lincoln & Guba, 1985; Patton, 1990).

Results

The primary purpose of this study was to determine how women with physical mobility disabilities manage their disabilities while living in an able-bodyist culture, and in particular, how physical activity was used in the process. A total of 47 lower order themes were extracted relative to this goal. Inductive analysis revealed that these lower order themes coalesced into three general dimensions; that is, three distinct approaches to managing disability were identified, each of which was characterized by a different way of perceiving and valuing physical activity (see Table 1).

Management by Minimizing Bodily Significance

The first group (*n* = 10, 29%), comprised primarily of women with acquired disabilities (*n* = 7) and an equal number of long and short disability ages, have managed their disabilities by minimizing, as much as possible, their focus on the body and the physical dimension of living. For most of these women, the body was viewed as an encumbrance, quite separate from the mind. Although they used physical activity to manage their disabilities to some extent (e.g., preventing further disability and disability-related complications), it was not a significant aspect of their lives, and for most of them, it had never been. Instead, mental, social, and spiritual activities were more often used to facilitate the development of a positive identity and to cope with disability (e.g., being a competent student, worker, or professional; meditating; taking a religious perspective on disability and life; using the Internet to communicate and develop

TABLE 1 Disability Management Themes		
Lower Order Themes	**Higher Order Themes**	**General Dimensions**
Focus on: • Reading (i.e., fiction, autobiography, biography, poetry, religious/spiritual) • Artistic expression (i.e., painting, photography, sculpting, performing and composing music, writing) • Academic/job/professional aspirations	Mental strategies	All three groups ($N = 34$)
Focus on: • Involvement with religious/spiritual community • Religious/spiritual teachings • Trying to be a better, more moral person	Spiritual strategies	
Focus on: • Using the Internet to meet others • Social and professional support networks	Social strategies	
Physical activity (primarily exercise) used: • to control disease • to prevent further disability • to prevent disability-related complications • to avoid guilt, fear, worry, vacillation of negative emotions • to alleviate disability-related depression • to alleviate disability-related anger and frustration • to avoid self-pity	Physical activity for health and therapeutic purposes only	Minimalization of the body group ($n = 10, 29.5\%$)

support systems). Therefore, the discourse associated with dualism seemed to be very significant in shaping their attitudes and behaviors.

The most notable commonality among these women was that they viewed physical activity as unpleasant work and were active for physical health or therapeutic reasons only. Although two had been former athletes, the majority ($n = 8$) began their current exercise programs at the request of a doctor or physical therapist, mostly to avoid further physical disability. Moreover, none of these women reported physical activity to be helpful in coping with disability discrimination. The following comments made by one woman with an acquired spinal cord injury and another with multiple sclerosis (in response to the question, "what motivated you to become physically active?") illustrate the largely fear- and guilt-driven nature of this group's participation in physical activity:

TABLE I Cont. Disability Management Themes		
Lower Order Themes	Higher Order Themes	General Dimensions
Physical activity (primarily exercise) used: • to look and feel sexier • to lose weight • to look athletic • to look and feel fit • to avoid looking abnormal (either functionally or aesthetically) • to look and feel more womanly • to gain muscle tone • to be more popular with males	Physical activity to fit able-body ideals of beauty and mind-body function	Normalization/ beautification of the body group ($n = 14, 41\%$)
Physical activity (primarily sport) used: • to enhance self-efficacy • to enhance self-esteem • to enhance motor skill and control • to enhance perception of control (internal focus of control) • to enhance mind-body unity and awareness • to be stronger physically and mentally • to be great athlete • to be less vulnerable to psychosexual abuse in relationships, at work, and in social settings	Physical activity: • to enhance mind-body functioning • to challenge one's own internalized ableism • to enhance mind-body functioning • to challenge one's own and others' internalized ableism, as well as disability oppression in society	Optimizing mind-body functioning group ($n = 10, 29.5\%$) Non-collectives ($n = 6$) Collectives ($n = 4$)

I began exercising, mostly swimming, only because I was told by my doctor that it would be good for my health. Being in a wheelchair all the time isn't good for my circulation, heart, and overall health. I know I'm supposed to exercise, so I do. And it's true—exercise does help me deal with some of the physical aspects of my condition. Exercising does very little, however, for my overall self-esteem, nor has it helped me to be more accepting of my disability. Only my religious beliefs and focusing on my work helping others as a teacher help me to do that. I think the emphasis this society places on physical fitness is a bit obsessive. I have always been more interested in activities that are less physical in nature.

I started exercising regularly when I found out I have MS. The doctors told me it would be good for me. Even though I never cared much about exercising or other physical activities, it makes me feel like I am doing something for myself . . . that I am taking care of myself physically. I know a positive attitude helps. When I exercise I feel less fearful of my future.

Another commonality among this group was that they preferred exercise over sport. For those who did not consider themselves athletic, exercise was their activity of choice because they felt less uncoordinated and vulnerable to injury when exercising than when playing sport (*n* = 7). In contrast, the athletes, both of whom had competed before acquiring their disabilities, preferred exercise because sport reminded them of how their lives and physical capabilities had been altered forever. As one woman with a recently acquired spinal cord injury remarked,

> I used to pride myself on my physical prowess, particularly in team sports. After my accident, all I did was feel sorry for myself. Someone recommended that I join a wheelchair basketball league. "Go back to sports," they said, "you can shine again, maybe be even more successful because there will be less competition!" No way was I going to play wheelchair basketball. I still haven't fully come to terms with my disability and playing sport makes it worse. All I do is think about how it used to be. I lift weights though because I want to keep my upper body as fit as possible so I will be less dependent on others.

Management by Normalizing the Body

Women in the second group (*n* = 14, 41%), who had predominantly acquired disabilities (*n* = 11) and short disability ages (*n* = 11), managed disability by trying to normalize themselves, particularly their bodies, as much as possible; they used physical activity for the same purpose (e.g., to improve their physical appearance and sexual attractability; to lose weight, gain muscle tone, or maximize their body's functional status so that their bodies and motor function did not appear abnormal or aesthetically displeasing). In other words, their physical activity, which was primarily in exercise (*n* = 11) rather than sport (*n* = 3), was an attempt to align or, more often, realign themselves as much as possible with feminine body-beauty and other able-bodied ideals.

Although this group used a variety of non-physical strategies to manage disability (e.g., focusing on professional aspirations, non-physical hobbies, social networks, and religious beliefs), they placed far more importance on physical appearance and the physical dimension of living than the first group, who minimized the body's importance. Such emphasis is reflected in the comments of three women with acquired disabilities (i.e., post-polio syndrome, acquired brain injury, and amputation) when asked their reasons for engaging in physical activity:

> I have always been interested in keeping myself looking good and my body as sexually appealing as possible. Exercise helps me to feel better about my body and to feel more normal. This became particularly important after I got ill and realized that I am no longer able to have the life I took for granted. Feeling better about my body and my looks helps me feel OK about myself.
>
> I hate looking weird, but I don't have much choice. I walk with a stagger because of my accident. Exercising and keeping myself fit helps me to feel more normal. I also feel like it will keep me from regressing even further physically. Who knows, maybe someday they [the doctors] will come up with something to make me normal again.
>
> Before the accident, I was always known for my good body. Although I had to watch my weight, which I did with diet and exercise, I was considered very

> attractive. When I lost my leg and arm in the accident, I was really scared about whether anyone would find me attractive again. My boyfriend bagged out, almost immediately. I still have a lot of anger, and I hate the stares in the gym; I go there mostly to keep what body I've got left looking good so that I don't withdraw completely from the public life I used to have.

Thus, in comparison to the first group. these women had much more deeply internalized the discourse of feminine body-beauty. They also were much more influenced by the discourse of individual responsibility, which was reflected in their feeling pressure to "look like everyone else," at least as far as external appearance was concerned, and guilt when they felt they had failed (e.g., in their weight control). They were similar to the women in the first group in three ways, however: (a) they tended to view exercise as work and as a means to an end, in this case to normalize/beautify the body, (b) they were not participating in physical activity for political reasons (i.e., to challenge one's own or other's internalized ableism), and (c) they expressed little or no interest in being or becoming social change agents via any of their activities, physical or otherwise.

Management by Optimizing Mind-Body Functioning

The women in the third group ($n = 10$, 29%) had adopted what seemed to be a more balanced mind-body approach to living with disability than those in the first two groups. Rather than emphasizing the importance of either mental or physical strategies in managing disability, this group believed both to be important. They also seemed to be developing their identities, for the most part, according to their own criteria, as opposed to those considered acceptable by able-bodied society.

Although minimizing the negative influences of able-bodyism (i.e., the disability discourse) and the other discourses of embodiment was not an easy task for any of them, they had found ways of being in the world that challenged such constraints, thus allowing a more self-determined identity to emerge. As two participants (one with a spinal cord injury and another with congenital limb deficiency) remarked,

> When I became disabled I was freaked, literally and figuratively. It took about a year before I came around to realizing that although a precious part of me—the tall, forceful walker part—was gone, my true self was still very much present. I am trying to get in touch with that self in every way I can, and one of the ways I do that is by listening to my intuition and not so much to what society says I'm supposed to be like. Making yourself fit TAB [temporarily able-bodied individuals] standards is self-defeating for people like me. I tried that approach; it made me sick, mentally and physically. Now I'm listening to my own voice; as difficult as this can be at times, it has been my road to salvation.

> I was born without feet. By rights, I should feel sorry for myself or be angry at God, but I have never felt this to be healthy or productive. Most people who meet me seem surprised that I am confident and self-assured, that I expect to be loved for who I am and not necessarily how I look—even though I think I am attractive enough. When I was young, the doctors tried to get me to wear protheses so I would look more normal and probably because they felt bothered by my stumps. I refused because I felt they were cosmetic more than anything else and ultimately postponing the inevitable—me accepting my limitations.

This group used physical activity to optimize the functioning of their minds and bodies rather than to normalize or beautify themselves and tended to prefer competitive sport ($n = 7$) more than non-competitive exercise ($n = 3$) to achieve such goals. Also in contrast to the women in the other groups, they more often viewed physical activity as intrinsically rewarding, enjoyable, and a significant part of their lives and personal identities. As a result, most of those who were without disruptive health problems were trying to improve the quality or quantity of their motor performances (e.g., through increasing their training intensity or volume or taking advantage of advancements in prosthetic devices and sporting equipment for persons with disabilities) and to improve their physical fitness. For those with progressive medical conditions, physical exercise kept them in touch with their physical selves and satisfied their desire to do whatever movement was feasible. As a former elite athlete with advanced amyotrophic lateral sclerosis commented,

> I exercise because my physical self is a central part of the whole. It is the part of me that got the most fan-fare growing up. You can't just turn that off, in your dreams or awake. Although I am no longer at one with my body—I can't walk without help anymore and my body does and does not do many things I can't control—I still take walks around the house with my caregiver twice daily, and I still see myself as an athlete in my dreams. I plan on exercising my body until I am so weak it is impossible. It makes me feel like I am still engaged in living.

Although all of the women in the "optimizing mind-body functioning" group were constructing an identity at least partially rooted in their own criteria, the majority ($n = 6$) did not take this a step further by joining others in collective activities to contest ableism and disability oppression in society; rather, they focused primarily on their own self-development. Moreover, although they perceived, and even claimed to feel proud about, social change occurring as a result of their individual actions (e.g., being a role model for other disabled athletes or shattering negative stereotypes that women with disabilities are weak and helpless), they admitted that they did not, for the most part, consciously attempt to accomplish this goal.

In contrast, the remaining four, who were labeled "the collectives," were committed not only to managing their disability and achieving personal goals via physical and other forms of activity, but also to advancing social justice for all persons with disabilities. Not surprisingly, they were all involved in one or more civil rights movements (i.e., those associated with disability, sex, race, and sexual orientation). Also not surprisingly, the discourse of feminine body-beauty had a lesser influence in their lives than the women in the other groups. The collectives also raised questions about the discourse of individual responsibility believing that individuals with disabilities often require social and institutional programs to facilitate their independence.

Like the other members of their group, the collectives believed that liberating women with disabilities requires strategies designed to enhance both physical and psychological aspects of the self. They believed, however, that physical activity, particularly in organized sport, was more than just a tool to develop oneself; it also served the political purpose of deconstructing their own internalized ableism, as well as that of others with whom they come in contact (e.g., able-bodied persons who believe disabled women cannot perform successfully in sport or exercise settings).

The collectives also tended to take a more metaphysical approach to life than the other members of their group; that is, they believed there are reasons, beyond mere coincidence, that explained their circumstances and life experiences. Thus, the question, "why me?", often served as a stimulus for personal growth and fulfillment of a felt-mission rather than as a constant source of anger, frustration, and denial. For example, one woman with congenital limb deficiency felt that she had selected, while in a previous non-incarnate, non-temporal state of existence, to be disabled during this lifetime so that she could help others with disabilities accept themselves and teach able-bodied persons to be more humane:

> In the beginning when I became disabled, it was tough on me, just like it would be for anyone. I was fearful, angry, and feeling helpless. However, after a period of a few months, I said "that's it; get over it, get on with your life," and most importantly, I started moving and doing something, instead of moping around. Soon thereafter, I began to realize that I had a job to do—to help others with disabilities to realize or take back their power, to show the world that being disabled doesn't prevent you from being successful, or from experiencing joy and life satisfaction. This attitude came partially from my spiritual beliefs but also from being around others who see and believe the way I do.

Besides being a woman with a disability, all of the collectives were members of at least one additional marginalized group (e.g., lesbians, bisexuals, women of color or multiracial background). In this respect, they were different than the other members of their group, who were primarily Caucasian and heterosexual. As a whole, however, the "optimizing mind-body functioning" group was comprised of more women with congenital disabilities ($n = 6$ out of 10) and longer disability ages ($n = 8$ out of 10) than either of the other groups. Thus is particularly noteworthy in light of the fact that there were fewer women with congenital disabilities ($n = 12$), as opposed to acquired disabilities ($n = 22$) in this study.

Discussion

The findings of this study, which support our earlier work examining physical activity and disability management (Guthrie, 1999), indicate that this sample of women used a variety of strategies (i.e., mental, spiritual, social, and physical) in managing their disabilities and ultimately to enhance their overall identities. For most, participation in sport and/or exercise seemed valuable in this regard. There is no question that building a healthy sense of self is critical in confronting internalized ableism. If, however, oppressive notions and norms are to be seriously challenged at the societal level, individual resistance must eventually become collective and public in nature. That is, groups of women must commit themselves to work, collaboratively, to bring about social change. This requires extensive support and validation, which group activities often provide. Participation in sport may be more useful than individual exercise training in providing such affirmation.

This is not to deny the numerous health benefits women with physical disabilities can derive from regular exercise, nor the fact that physical and self-perceptions are often enhanced in exercise settings. Rita is a prime example, as are the many women in this study who found that exercise helped them manage both their disabilities and disability oppression. What makes sport different, however, is that it seems to provide a double benefit to its participants—personal and collective affirmation of the empowered self.

Contributing to this double sense of empowerment may be the fact that sporting participation allows more possibilities than individual exercise programs for public recognition of motor skill and efficiency because there is a greater likelihood of media coverage and spectators. When this occurs, the belief that women with disabilities are helpless and vulnerable and that physical activity, particularly sport, is an able-bodied domain can be more broadly challenged. This may help to explain why the collectives and the other women in their group, who were more often involved in sport than exercise, were using physical activity to extend their bodily capacities and were more likely than those in the other two groups to view their difference from able-bodied society as a source of pride.[4]

Did participation in sport play a critical role in fostering self-acceptance and esteem among the women who were optimizing mind-body functioning? It certainly could be argued that having congenital disabilities, and thus no "before and after" images with which to contend, and longer disability ages may have facilitated their ability to construct a healthy view of self apart from being physically active. The findings of this study provide compelling evidence, however, that sporting experience at least partially facilitated these positive self-perceptions; that is, all of the women who were using physical activity to maximize their mind-body powers believed sport, more than exercise alone, enhanced their sense of agency, as well as their pride in their bodies and themselves. Moreover, for the collectives whose physical activity was a form of political activism, sport was viewed as a site in which the discourses of embodiment and other restrictive notions of the body, ability, and physical performance could be effectively challenged.

It seems clear, then, that in order to produce the greatest good for the greatest number, more opportunities for women with disabilities in both sport and exercise must be made available, and those that do exist must be made more accessible and accommodating (Castelnuovo & Guthrie, 1998; DePauw, 1997; Guthrie, 1999, Henderson & Bedini, 1995, Sherill, 1997). Indeed, many of the participants in this study indicated that, despite disability legislation, persons with disabilities continue to have limited entrance to physical activity spaces. As long as such constraints continue, the ability of women with physical disabilities to transform themselves and able-bodyist notions of normality via physical activity is severely compromised. It is important to remember, however, that physical activity is not necessarily a remedy for problematic self- or societal perceptions of disability.

Indeed, there were women in this study who, while using physical activity to manage their disabilities on some level, found mental or spiritual activities to be far more helpful in this regard. There were also those who used their physical activity primarily to fit feminine body-beauty ideals. Although striving to normalize or beautify the body through physical activity (e.g., to appear sexier and thinner or more functionally normal) is certainly understandable considering the rigorous criteria to which all women are subjected, such actions ultimately reify ablebodied norms and images, and thus further the oppression of persons with disabilities. It is noteworthy, however, that the women with acquired disabilities and short disability ages were more likely than those with congenital disabilities and long disability ages to use physical activity for such purposes rather than for augmenting their mind-body capabilities. Such attitudes and behaviors can possibly be accounted for by the fact that those with recently acquired disabilities had a more vivid memory of their former able-bodied selves, as well as less time to come to terms with their disability; as a result, they were still trying to compensate for body image and self-esteem issues associated with their disabilities. The results of this study lend support for such an analysis.

They also suggest the complexity of identity formation among this sample of women, as well as the diverse ways disability is experienced in an able-bodyist culture. For example, although the four discourses of embodiment have been encountered by all of the participants, their responses (e.g., acceptance, resistance) to these discourses varied considerably. For the minimizing group, dualism was clearly evidenced in their devaluing of the body and physical activities; for the normalization group, feminine body-beauty ideals and individual responsibility for mainstreaming were particularly significant. Even the optimizing group was not immune to ideological forces. The women in the optimizing group did seem, however, to be more capable of resisting their negative potential.

Foucauldian discourse analysis was clearly helpful in identifying those discourses that most impact the lives of these women. Although the optimizing group was more actively involved in reconfiguring oppressive notions of disability on individual or societal levels, all of the women in this study challenge the postmodern notion that humans are merely products of the multiple discourses through which they are described and interpreted. That is, despite the restrictive notions and norms they regularly experience, these women have all found ways to successfully manage their disabilities, and thus enhance the quality of their lives.

Contesting the four discourses of embodiment, particularly that associated with disability, played an important role in this process, although oppositional strategies varied considerably. Foucault's distinction between reverse resistance and resistance as freedom was helpful here in differentiating the women who were reverse resistors, that is, those who were managing their disabilities via minimizing or beautifying the body, from those who were engaging in resistance as freedom (i.e., the optimizing group). Indeed, this latter group of women were striving to move beyond restrictive notions of embodiment by constructing identities grounded in their own criteria rather than those imposed by able-bodied norms. They also more often relied on a combination of mind-body strategies to manage their disabilities and more often used sport to achieve this goal. Such findings offer compelling evidence for Merleau-Ponty's conviction that we come to understand the world and ourselves through the lived-body and that our sense of identity is not simply the product of cognition.

The findings also support Merleau-Ponty's claim that group strategies facilitate the success of revolutionary acts. Although the "collectives" were most aware of the need for collaboration in combating oppressive structures and ideologies and the most involved in social activism, all of the women recognized that what is most disabling about their circumstances is not physical impairment per se, but a system of interlocking social forces that subjugates people with disabilities. They also realized that they cannot change the world, or their experience in the world, alone. Considering the magnitude of the social dictates with which women with disabilities must contend, this particular sample demonstrated a remarkable level of resiliency. Equally significant is the lesson they teach the rest of us: Living with disability does not preclude the development of a positive sense of self.

Endnotes

1. The term discourse is used in the Foucauldian sense of power-knowledge structures and language that shape social institutions and individual attitudes and behaviors.

2. This study is both a replication and extension of an earlier study (Guthrie, 1999).

3. Part of this data set was analyzed in another article (Guthrie, 1999).

4. It should be noted that the women with recently acquired disabilities had to put a good deal of energy into seeking rehabilitation, accommodations, and support networks and addressing immediate financial concerns, thus taking part in activities like sport is likely to have been of secondary importance.

References

Castelnuovo, S., & Guthrie, S. R. (1998). *Feminism and the female body: Liberating the Amazon within.* Boulder, CO: Lynne Rienner.

DePauw, K. P. (1997). The invisibility of disability: Cultural context and "sporting bodies." *Quest,* **49,** 416–430.

Foucault, M. (1985). *The use of pleasure: The history of sexuality, Volume 2.* New York: Pantheon Books.

Foucault, M. (1988). *The care of the self: The history of sexuality, Volume 3.* New York: Vintage Books.

Foucault, M. (1989). *The return of morality: Foucault life.* New York: Semniotexte.

Foucault, M. (1990). *The history of sexuality, Volume 1: An introduction.* New York: Vintage Books.

Fowler, F. J., & Mangione, T. W. (1990). *Standardized survey interviewing: Minimizing interviewer-related error.* Newbury Park, CA: Sage.

Guthrie, S. R. (1999). Managing imperfection in a perfectionistic culture: Physical activity and disability management among women with disabilities, *Quest,* **51**(4), 369–381.

Henderson, K. A., & Bedini, L. A. (1995). "I have a soul that dances like Tina Turner, but my body can't": Physical activity and women with mobility impairments. *Research Quarterly for Exercise and Sport,* **66**(2), 151–161.

Leder, D. (1990). *The absent body.* Chicago, IL: University of Chicago Press.

Lincoln, Y. S., & Guba, E. G. (1985). *Naturalistic inquiry.* Newbury Park, CA: Sage.

Merleau-Ponty, M. (1962). *Phenomenology of perception.* London: Routledgc & Kegan Paul Ltd.

Patton, M. Q. (1990). *Qualitative evaluation and research methods.* Newbury Park, CA: Sage.

Sherill, C. (1997). Disability, identity, and involvement in sport and exercise. In K. R. Fox (Ed.), *The physical self: From motivation to well-being* (pp. 257–286). Champaign, IL: Human Kinetics.

Discussion Questions

1.   How is physical activity used differently by the three groups of women with physical disabilities?

2.   According to the findings of this study and the authors' analysis, what are the pros and cons of women with disabilities participating in elite sport? Participating in regular exercise?

3.   Do you believe that males and females with physical disabilities experience their disability differently due to the social construction of gender in American society? Why or why not?

4.   What insights can be drawn from this study regarding the intersection of gender and disability in American society?

5.   According to the authors, what are the limitations of using Foucauldian theory to explain the experiences of this group of women? What have they done to counter this limitation?

4

"All My Hopes and Dreams"

Families, Schools, and Subjectivities in Collegiate Softball

Katherine M. Jamieson

It's almost like [parents] don't care if you go to college or not. There are two extremes. There's one that says "all my hopes and dreams . . . because we never went to college, now you have to do it for the family." Then there's the other extreme: "We never went to college. Get a job at J.C. Penney and be happy. You don't need college!"

Yolanda, a former division-one student athlete and division-one head coach, offered her insights about the mixed messages that some Latinas receive from parents about college attendance. Yolanda's words are not only biographical, but they also underscore the complicated and often contradictory nature of parents' "hopes and dreams" for their daughters. Structural realities facing many Latino families make it difficult for parents to hold expectations for their children to attend and graduate from college. For example, U.S. Latinos remain undereducated, unemployed, and underemployed at higher rates than their non–Latino peers (Ramirez & de la Cruz, 2002).[1] In spite of these enduring structural inequalities, early messages received by the women interviewed suggest that their success in both academics and athletics was important to parents and in some cases became a possible route to upward mobility.

In this analysis, interview data are presented to illustrate the interdependence of sport, families, and education, especially as they represent the intersections of historical projects of race, social class, and gender. Most importantly, these data illustrate how sport interconnects with family and school contexts to shape the lives of these particular women.

A Phenomenological Case Study

In the original study, 27 women were interviewed, of which 17 are represented in this analysis. My initial endeavor was guided by what I termed a phenomenological case study, or a case study focused on identifying the core components of paths to collegiate softball among Latinas

From *Journal of Sport and Social Issues,* Volume 29, No. 2, May 2005 by Katherine M. Jamieson. Reprinted by permission.

who had competed at any collegiate level. I began with three exploratory focus group interviews with a total of 10 former softball athletes, followed by individual interviews with 17 current collegiate softball athletes, all of whom had competed for at least one full season. Questions centered on the general topics of (a) initial involvement in sport and softball, (b) familial support for sport and softball, and (c) interpersonal interactions on and off the field related to their statuses as collegiate softball athletes. Interviews were transcribed verbatim and systematically reviewed for emergent themes across cases. In the phenomenological and interpretive process of identifying themes, I was most interested in what these women would articulate as the key issues in their own paths to collegiate softball.

As a group, these women were overwhelmingly of Mexican descent in their Latina ethnicity, but there were exceptions. Several of the women were of mixed racial and ethnic heritage, with a European-Latin mix being most prevalent (e.g., of Scottish and Puerto Rican parentage). Two of the women interviewed were of mixed African American and Mexican parentage, further complicating our understanding of Latina identities and experiences. The women ranged in age from 19 to 24 and were predominantly from working-class families. Within this group, 22% identified as gay, lesbian, or bisexual, and 70% identified as heterosexual, whereas 8% declined to self-identify with regard to sexuality. A majority (44%) of the women interviewed were at least in the third generation born in the United States, 19% were second generation, and 37% were first generation. Scholars have indicated that generational status has a unique influence on racial-ethnic and class identities (Valenzuela, 1999; Zavella, 1994); unfortunately a comprehensive analysis of generational status is beyond the scope of this article.

Families, Schools, and Sport

Since the passage of Title IX,[2] softball has been among the fastest growing sports for high school girls, and in 1998, softball ranked fourth among high school female student athletes in rate of participation (U.S. Bureau of the Census, 1998). Latinas remain largely underrepresented in the collegiate ranks, accounting for 7.3% of all National Collegiate Athletic Association (NCAA) female students and only 3.9% of all NCAA female student-athletes during the 2002–2003 academic year. In contrast, White women at NCAA institutions accounted for 68% of all female students and 70% of all female student-athletes (NCAA, 2003). Despite the presence of a few elite women of color in collegiate softball, the sport remains pervasively White and segregated across player positions (Jamieson, Reel, & Gill, 2002).

Contrary to popular belief, many young women in Latino families receive encouragement for involvement in sport, the labor force, and other social institutions, especially in ways that fit the family's particular social conditions (Acosta, 1999). Acosta (1999) conducted case studies of three Latinas who made their way to athletics and careers in physical education and concluded that Latinas face unique challenges because of the combination of (a) the absence of Latina role models, (b) limited financial resources, and (c) ambivalent attitudes of family members toward higher education and sport. Most importantly, previous findings reveal that despite some shared family traditions, Latinas often report receiving support in ways that are specific to the social location of the family. The women interviewed for this study articulated a complex blend of interactions in families, schools, and sport that greatly influence their chances to continue on their paths to collegiate softball.

Aspirations and Expectations

Scholarship and research focused on Latinas and educational achievement suggest that families play a critical role in the ability of students to navigate educational systems (Bettie, 2003; Cardoza, 1991; Gandara, 1995; Simoniello, 1981; Stanton-Salazar, 2001; Valenzuela, 1999). For example, although parents may aspire to support the educational goals of their daughters, they often may not expect to be able to do this because of financial limitations (Cardoza, 1991). Young women who receive messages about aspirations may then experience confusion when expectations and resources available do not match the aspirations at key developmental stages (Simoniello, 1981). Additionally, despite a legacy of educational dislocation and enduring inequalities in public schools, Latina and Latino students have found ways to achieve academic success and maintain ties to their home cultures (Bettie, 2003; Cardoza, 1991; Cuadraz, 1996; Florez-Gonzalez, 1999; Gandara, 1995; Simoniello, 1981; Stanton-Salazar, 2001; Valenzuela, 1999).

Thanks to the assistance of her older sister, Bugs was able to convince her father to enroll her in the local youth softball league, but when collegiate softball became an option, Bugs had to regain the support of her father.

> When I decided I was going to college and I showed my dad what tuition costs, he was finally enlightened to the fact that higher education had a price tag. All of us kids went to [k-12] school because it was free, and I really don't think he knew what college tuition was all about. So when I showed him what it cost to go to college, and then showed him that it was being paid for and on top of that I was gonna get financial aid because of my *background* (emphasis in original), he went out and bought me a car!

Similarly, after accepting a scholarship at a prestigious division-one institution away from home, Micaela learned that her father's indifference was because of failed attempts by her older brothers to attend and graduate from college. Micaela described his attitude in this way:

> My dad really didn't care if we went to college. He kind of expected us not to go. He didn't want to push us, I guess, but he's also very negative about it because he had been hurt by my two older brothers [who quit half way through college]. He didn't discourage me, but he told me I'd be just like my brothers. So it was hard to prove to him that "no. I'm not going to be like my brothers." He would always tell me that he had no money to send me to college. It hurt a lot.

Mickey also had to navigate ambivalence about collegiate softball from her mother, a single parent of two daughters:

> My first year at community college was a battle, and then, once my mom came down to the recruiting trip, she said "you know, you don't have to work next year." I've had a job for the last 6 years, and last year was the first year I didn't have a job. Now that my tuition's paid for, my books are paid for, and I get a little extra, she said "you don't have to work now!" So now she loves it that I play.

Although ambivalent about the value of softball, Mickey's mother was clear about her value for education and thus came to see softball as a viable route to a college degree. Family structural changes (e.g., divorce) certainly influence beliefs about the importance of collegiate athletic involvement, and in a reciprocal way, Mickey's athletic scholarship positively influenced her chances to achieve her educational goals. In no small way, softball became a family resource for achieving upward mobility. The experiences of both Bugs and Micaela point again to the difference between aspirations and expectations among parents. Although both Bugs and Micaela found ways to move through what seemed like indifference to higher education, they also learned about their father's particular experiences with higher education. For Bugs, it was a matter of putting her educational aspirations into a framework that reflected her father's concern for the family's financial stability. Micaela came to realize that the failure of her older brothers in college had forever jaded her father's perspective on the return of an investment in higher education. Mehan, Hubbard, and Villanueva (1994) reported similar findings, leading them to argue that Marxist explanations of working-class resistance to educational settings are limited and that actual causes of resistance to educational structures are much more complex. More specifically, they argue the following among working-class students in schools:

> Their willingness to participate comes from an assessment of the costs and benefits of playing the game. It is not that schooling will not propel them up the ladder of success: it is that chances are slim to warrant the attempt (p. 97).

This agency, coupled with lived experiences of exclusion and underachievement in educational settings, reveal compelling reasons for differential engagement among minority students and their families within school structures. In fact, not all of the women interviewed felt a need to convince parents of the benefits of higher education or sport involvement. Lucy tells a different story:

> Once I knew that I could play softball in college and continue on with education and get part of my education paid for, then I knew that I was probably gonna go. And if I didn't go to a 4-year, I was probably gonna go to a JC. I knew that for sure. That's the way my mom did it. My mom went to a 2-year. Then she went to UC Santa Cruz for a year. Both my parents were very focused on college, even though my dad didn't go to college; he finished high school.

Lucy perceived her parents to be proeducation, and her mom especially modeled a value for education, having attended community college and successfully transferred to a 4-year university. But still, she suggests that the opportunity to earn a scholarship to play softball in college was instrumental in her academic success. Thus, to move from aspiration to actual expectation, softball talent often became part of the family resources. This is not unlike Gandara's (1995) findings that when Latinos and Latinas have historically made inroads to higher education, it is largely because of resource availability, such as the American G.I. Bill.[3]

Softball as Family Resources

Not inconsequential to the educational and athletic paths of these women was their deep awareness of their family's economic conditions. Sometimes, softball represented a sort of contract between young women and their families, especially as precious family resources had been devoted to continued participation in elite forms of softball.[4] Several women alluded to desires to contribute to the family's economic stability and mobility. Ana seemed to have an especially poignant view of this family contract:

> Money is definitely an issue. My mom's a budget clerk. My dad's a teacher. That's not a lot of income. . . . I had a scholarship at the other school. They've only had to pay for one semester of school and now this year too. I tell my mom all the time, "I want to pay you back, 'cause I think its not fair that you are trying, and I'm not helping you out." The scholarship was supposed to be my part of the deal, you know?

I asked Nicole if she would be enrolled at the 4-year institution she was attending if she had not earned the athletic scholarship. She suggested the following:

> Would I come to school here? I think no, because the only way I would get to college is by a scholarship. I have a twin sister, and we graduated the same year and right now my parents couldn't afford it. . . . I might be able to go to junior-college or something, but I don't think so.

Connie also intimated a concern for her parents' well-being and articulated her desire to avoid placing extra financial and emotional burdens on them after their divorce:

> At the beginning of my college career, I could not depend—my mom pulled through for me financially—but I could not put more burdens on her because she was going through a divorce and a hard time in her life as well. But she was there, and my dad was there too.

Some women saw families as key resources in the pursuit of academic and athletic goals. In short, families were useable cultural resources on which these women were able to cultivate more resources. In some ways, the very static nature of families offered a complex blend of dependence and independence among members. The earning of scholarships often became an extension into a broader community and cultural context for the entire family, not only the athlete. Carmen expressed concern about not taking for granted the support of her parents but also trying to find balance in creating her own life that was taking shape away from her hometown and family:

> It's hard because I'm still so dependent on them, financially, and I want to keep them happy. I want to do things that can please everybody, but I also know that in order to do that, I've got to get *myself* going (emphasis in original). It's not that I don't want to come home, I would do anything to be able to be home and go to school, but I have stuff that I have to do, requirements to fill, and [my dad] doesn't understand that everything is here; all my schooling, all my connections within my program are here.

Ise expressed this push and pull in a different way and yet was also clear to suggest that for the Latinas that she had coached, success in softball was not centered on monetary reward but perhaps was more focused on the ability to turn athletic talent into cultural capital:

> If I was still coaching, I'd be pushing my girls to do something, and not just to get paid, but if you can use your athletic skills to go to school, take it, whatever it may be! A lot of girls are scared to go away, you know, go away to college, go to another state, and I'm like "just think about it. You'll only be gone 2 to 4 years. You can come home on the holidays. Your family is always going to be

here. You can always come back home."

It is clear from their own words that these women are simultaneously products of particular family environments and change agents within them. As Bettie (2003) argues in her ethnographic study of high school girls and social-class identities, families are crucial sites for the accumulation of cultural capital, and schools are sites for their display. Although economic conditions cannot and should not be ignored, analyses of class as culture unveil the many ways that one's experience of social class is more than work-identified income (Bettie, 2003; Ortner, 1998). In fact, class identities may also be expressed through familial relations and other "social relations unrelated to those of employment (like school and peer relations), and in leisure and consumption practices" (Bettie, 2003, p. 42). For the women interviewed here, social class is visible through sport identities as well as family and school identities.

Racialized Class Identities

Although it is enticing to see the conditions of these women's lives as simple reflections of social-class origins, many of them remind us of the inextricable link between race and social class. That is, class formation is always informed by race and gender (Bettie, 2003). Thus, although women are often left out of discourse on class and although race is often read as race-class, these women articulate a compelling understanding of the interworkings of their racial-ethnic, gender, and class subjectivities. Ortner (1998) argues that the "hidden life of class" operates on both a public culture level and an identity-subjecthood level. Ortner's critique calls for an unveiling of hidden racialized class identities (e.g., the middle class) and hidden class underpinnings of other naturalized identities (e.g., Mexican American). In concert with Bettie's (2003) call for seeing class as culture, Ortner argues that "it is precisely in the internalization and naturalization of public discourses about 'identities' that the fusion of class with race and ethnicity happens in American cultural practice" (p. 14).

For the women interviewed, it seems their academic and athletic endeavors represent refusals of preexisting race, class, and gender classifications. In fact, although none of the women interviewed here articulated a particular racial-ethnic location in talking about families, several alluded to the influence of racial-ethnic heritage on their current location as collegiate softball athletes. In all cases, social class is a mediating factor in the extent to which they articulate a particular kind of Latina identity. For example, Karin alludes to her privilege as the daughter of an Americanized father:

> My dad comes from a traditional Mexican family, you know, the wife does the cooking, the house, takes care of the kids, and the husband goes and works. But my dad does stuff too. He's a really good cook, so if he knows my mom's been doing a lot of running around, he does the cooking. But mom does the majority of it. I think she's the most amazing woman I know. She's always running around taking us to practices, working, then coming home. My dad helps her out—sometimes he forgets. I think that's the traditional side of him. But he's more Americanized than traditional, so that helps.

Ana, a biracial Latina (White and Mexican), who grew up with her extended Mexican family, speaks directly to the influence of her father's Whiteness in her academic and athletic choices. Ironically, in the same passage, she speaks very eloquently about the impact her achievements may have had on her Mexican family members and by extension, other young Mexican women:

> I'd say my biggest fans besides my parents are my grandma and my aunt, my mom's sister. They traveled to see me. I loved playing for them. They get a kick out seeing [sic] their granddaughter or niece play softball. None of my mom's sisters' or brothers' lives were like that at all. I think my life is different because my mom married a White guy. Really, he's the one that pushed me to get here. My mom, she's been a supporter. With all her daughters, whatever we want to do [is] fine with her, as long as we're doing better than they did, as long as I stay in school. If we didn't play softball, I don't think it would've been a big deal, but because she married a White guy, that's why my sisters and I play sports. But I think it's good. Not many Mexican girls get a chance to do that, just because of tradition and stuff like that.

Marisol, the daughter of Honduran parents who immigrated to the United States, also expressed a difference between her mother's perception of athletics and that of her American-born stepfather. She attributed the lack of interest in collegiate athletics to her mother's Honduran upbringing:

> All my friends were playing softball, and I wanted to play too, but it cost money. And my mom's like "no, you can't play sports." My [relatives], they'd rather see me just in school than involved in sports, 'cause sports isn't a big deal where my mom was raised. So [my step-dad said] "if you really want to play, I'll sign you up." And he signed me up. That's the first time I ever played an official sport.

It is interesting to note the clarity of understanding that these women possess in terms of economic relations and racial projects. As Bettie (2003) suggests about her own ethnographic participants, these women may not articulate this knowledge as a class analysis, but they clearly understand how race, class, and gender come together to contour their lives. Indeed, their assessment of the conditions of their lives demonstrates a complex understanding of the relations of privilege and penalty at the intersections of race, class, and gender. Moreover, they clearly articulate racial and gender projects that often masquerade as class differences (e.g., the power of White men in multiracial family structures).[5] Clearly, families are not the only social locations for engagement with such power relations; schools are also sites for engagement with projects of racial-ethnic, class, and gender inequality.

Subtractive Schooling

Valenzuela's (1999) concept of subtractive schooling precisely names the process of removing cultural values and linguistic skills from minority youth under the guise of promoting educational achievement in the current system. Sport studies scholars have paid little attention to the processes of schooling or subtractive schooling, however, related scholarship implicates U.S. school-based sport in the reproduction of dominant cultural values and behaviors (Bissinger, 1990; Foley, 1990; Grey, 1996; Thorne, 1993). Outside of sport, Segura (1993) examined the educational experiences of 20 adult Chicanas who had not graduated from high school and were later involved in an education and employment training program. Segura found that constraints to educational attainment included (a) reluctance of family members to interfere with the work of educational professionals, (b) channeling of Latina students into nonacademic programs offering a lower quality of instruction, (c) lack of encouragement or preparation from teachers and counselors for college attendance, and (d) lack of clearly safe, antiracist learning environments. Additionally, Segura argued that enhancement of educational attainment among Chicanas requires (a) consistent encouragement from parents for educational achievement, (b) teacher innovation, (c) multicultural curriculum, (d) teacher caring and involvement, and (e) formalized expectations for achievement. Others have found similar needs among Latino and Chicano youth (Gandara, 1995; Mehan et al., 1994).[6]

As the first in their families to compete in collegiate athletics, many of these women were disadvantaged throughout the recruitment process. Indeed, examples of educational dislocation were numerous among the women interviewed. Rosalia suggested that she had no idea what collegiate softball was all about, how it worked, how one accessed the most elite level. Her mother completed high school and works for a county library, and her father completed 8 years of formal education and works as a welder. Rosalia talked about her experience demanding a tryout for a division-one team:

> Even when I got into a division-one school, I didn't know anything about collegiate softball. A division-two school had been recruiting me, but I said "if I'm gonna' go on, I wanna go for the best." So I enrolled and walked on. I didn't know that no walk-ons actually made the team. I didn't know that wasn't the way you got into division one. I had no clue.

Monica reflected on the limited role of higher education in the lives of her parents as it influenced her knowledge of and strategies for gaining entry to collegiate softball. Additionally, having grown up in a small town with no organized sport programs for girls, Monica's vision for collegiate sport was somewhat limited, making her accomplishments as an Olympic-team alternate and big-time division-one head coach even more amazing:

> I played on my high school team, and I had no clue about college ball. I didn't know anything. My mom went to 2 years of business school, and my dad went to JC for a year or two. But no, they weren't familiar with the whole college thing, and I wasn't either. It was just friends that said "hey, there's a good coach at this JC." So I moved and played on the JC team for a year. That was my first experience with travel ball too. . . . That's when people started saying "you know, you're pretty good. Maybe you could get a scholarship." . . . My parents were real supportive, but they weren't familiar, and I wasn't familiar, so I did it on my own with the help of my coach.

Kim's parents each earned high school diplomas and completed 1 or 2 years of college. Kim talked about her lack of understanding and connection with colleges and universities:

> I never knew how to pursue. No one ever told me, and I never knew what I had to do. Luckily coach [helped out], or I don't know what would have happened. I probably would have never gone to university. [Coach] told me about the Educational Opportunity Program, or I never would have gotten into college. I did not score high on my SATs at all, so I had to go through the EOP for 1 year prior to softball. So I had to keep my C average 1 year in college. I could not have anything to do with the team until that year was over.

Connie, although heavily recruited and the daughter of college-educated parents, began her collegiate softball career as a walk-on:[7]

> Since my sophomore year, I received over a hundred letters from different schools across the country asking me to visit and offering scholarship money. But my parents didn't know how the system worked, they didn't know what was going on. And I guess that's where travel ball coaches came in. They would come over and help me. But still, my mom wasn't really on top of it and neither was my dad, but also they were going through a divorce. The letters would come in, and I would sometimes just throw 'em out. I wouldn't even open 'em. And now I look at it, and I go "what was I thinking?"

Micaela describes how she took care of the entire process of responding to recruitment letters, attending visits, and negotiating with coaches and academic personnel:

> My parents didn't know how this whole process worked, and so they kind of just stayed at home, they watched a few games, [but it was all me] getting my financial aid packet in and applying for schools. They never helped me at all, because they don't understand it, and they feel bad, and they told me they wished they could help me, but they don't understand the whole process. I had to talk to coaches myself. I had to find out the process on my own. Actually, nobody supported me for choosing a school for academics, you know, like, any university for them was academics.

Each of these women share a common experience of limited parental educational attainment or limited experience with the U.S. educational system. Still, they were able to achieve academic and athletic success, but in each case, they either had to enter the institutional setting on their own or with the aid of an institutional insider. In all cases, parents were unable to offer specific guidance in the process of athletic and academic recruitment. Even for Connie, whose parents had been collegiate athletes in Venezuela and had completed graduate degrees in the United States, her parents knew very little about how to pursue a collegiate athletic career in the United States.

Networking and Institutional Insiders

In her study of educationally successful Chicanos, Gandara (1995) found that two kinds of opportunity were significant to successful paths: (a) enrollment in a college preparatory curriculum and (b) availability of information and resources (e.g., the G.I. Bill) to make college a realizable goal. Moreover, Gandara found that this information most often came from older siblings, peers, and institutional insiders. Lucy describes how her schooling experience changed once she decided to stay in school, whereas many of her friends chose to leave high school. To add to her difficulty, it was mainly other Latinas who left during high school, leaving Lucy behind with an even more pervasively White student body:

> I liked high school. It was fun. It kind of got weird after awhile 'cause after my sophomore year, a lot of my friends who were Latina were (pause) in trouble. They stopped going to class. They just didn't want to, and I was the straight and narrow one, always telling them "come on, let's go. We gotta go to class." And

they just decided to do different. And so they went to the [alternative] high school. I don't know, maybe school just wasn't for them.

Unlike her friends, Lucy was able to stay in school despite experiencing what Cuadraz (1996) refers to as being "inside in an outside way." Although she does not mention a particular institutional insider that aided her along the way, as Stanton-Salazar (2001) points out, a key aspect of social capital is the ability to navigate institutional structures. Thus, Lucy may have been able to access enough social support outside of school that she was able to navigate what seemed like a hostile environment for her friends. For Marie, whose parents were born and raised in Honduras, it was her older sister's insider status that helped Marie get started at her community college:[8]

> My sister had a 4-year scholarship to a small college, and she gave that up after 2 years and came home. She was helping our coach, and that's how I got interested in City College. I also looked at going to a community college as a second option 'cause if you go to a community college, you get more time to prepare yourself to go on to a 4-year, and you possibly can get more offers when it comes to scholarships. So I look at going to community college as a benefit, rather than a negative thing.

Gloria's pregnancy during high school resulted in her falling short of the requirements to graduate with her class. She completed her general education degree and then was able to enroll in the local community college that her mother was attending:

> My [high school] counselors never once asked me if I wanted to go to college. They never once told me about college. I never knew about community college. My mom told me 'cause she took a class here. I didn't know anything about it. Nothing. They never mentioned anything. The counselor never asked me what I wanted to be, what I'm thinking of going into—never asked me anything.

Similar to Gloria, who was able to learn of community college through her mother, who had returned to college later in life, Micaela speaks of a chance connection with a soccer official who happened to work as an academic counselor:

> There were two counselors, and one of them happened to be Latino and was very involved in soccer. He's a referee, so he was encouraging me to play some kind of sport in college. As far as my own counselor, she was more of an academic counselor, and she knew how to pick up the extracurricular activity when you get to college. She was really encouraging me to keep going.

It is unclear what held these women in school: maybe softball, maybe parental support, maybe individual motivation. Indeed, not all Latinas experience school as a negative experience. In fact, despite challenges along the way, many Latinas are able to succeed in schools, but often, this requires a network of resources, whether they come from families, school personnel, or other community adults (Gandara, 1995; Stanton-Salazar, 2001). The women interviewed here suggest that they advocated for themselves but also mention various network resources, including parents, friends, siblings, coaches, referees, and extended family members.

Families, Schools, and Subjectivities—Toward a Less Hidden Life of Class

Previous sociological research and scholarship suggests that softball has potential as a site for contesting male privilege and hegemonic conceptions of femininity (Birrell & Richter, 1994; Lenskyj, 1994). In their interviews with feminist-identified participants in two women's softball leagues, Birrell and Richter (1994) revealed several different forms of feminist principles and opportunities for configuring sport as transformative, consciousness raising, and liberating for many women. Lenskyj's (1994) case study of the NotsoAmazon women's softball league in Toronto revealed softball as a site for rearticulating sport in a feminist and womanist framework. Similar to Lenskyj and Birrell and Richter above, I was most interested in how this group of women might reclaim softball as a site for their own projects, whatever those might be. Chicana feminist scholars have been writing about mobile subjectivities and strategies for resisting preexisting classifications (Anzaldua, 1987; Sandoval, 2000), and yet sport has not been a focus of Chicana feminist analyses.[9] Clearly, these women realize their potential to disrupt ongoing projects of race, social class, and gender, especially as they resist classification in the contexts of families, schools, and sport.

These abbreviated stories of women's lives provoke new thinking about the location of class identities, the "hidden life of class," as Ortner (1998) refers to it. It is clear that economic relations weigh heavily on these women and are experienced in interlocking ways with race and gender. Stanton-Salazar's (2001) employment of the concept of social capital would suggest that as a group, Latinas are situated differently than their White counterparts in terms of potential for exploiting the status of collegiate athlete in other meaningful spheres of life. Clearly, participation in collegiate softball is not the answer to social problems that most affect Latinas today, but it is one of many cultural spaces in which Latinas may enact subjectivities that refute essentialist identity categories. In fact, these data suggest that softball may be an integral part of a set of network relations that Latinas may engage as they craft their individual lives.

For example, among the women interviewed, part of the strategy for gaining entrée to higher education and collegiate athletics required separating from families and class origins but simultaneously finding ways to stay connected to these vital resources, what Zavella (1994) refers to as "culture in process" (pp. 206–207). Zavella's concept of culture in process refers to a simultaneous making and remaking of culture as Chicanas create lives of their own choosing. For some, sport may be a way to interact with college-track students or a way to untrack themselves within an institution that systematically guides them into a non-college-bound curriculum (Segura, 1993; Valenzuela, 1999). At the same time, sport in the lives of these women is part of the U.S. educational institution and as such, becomes a visible example of racialized and gendered class relations in U.S. schools (Bettie, 2003; Bissinger, 1990; Foley, 1990; Grey, 1996; Thorne, 1993).

Perhaps most instructive in the present analysis is the focus on the intermingling of cultural spaces of families, education, and sport. This legacy of educational exclusion, coupled with a legacy of determination, produces an almost inherently political experience of collegiate sport for Latinas. Though mostly the product of a White, middle-class imagination, the image of the passive, fatalistic, submissive Latina is annihilated when the diversity among Latinas responding to varied social conditions is affirmed (Zavella, 1994). Finally, the women interviewed here offer stories that beg for new analytic tools that more thoroughly articulate how projects of race, class, and gender operate in women's lives.

Endnotes

1. According to the March 2002 report on the Hispanic population in the United States, more than two in five Latinos ages 25 and older have not graduated from high school. More than 25% of Latinos had less than a ninth-grade education, compared with only 4% of non–Latino Whites. Only 11.1% of Latinos had a bachelor's degree or more, compared to 29.4% of non–Latino Whites. Also, in 2002, Latinos were much more likely to be unemployed than were Whites (8.1% vs.5.1%) and were more likely to work in service occupations as compared to Whites (22.1% vs. 11.6%). The census data also report that 26.3% of Latino full-time, year-round workers earned $35,000 or more, considerably less than the 53.8% of similar non–Latino White workers who earned $35,000 or more. More than 21% of Latinos lived in poverty in 2002, compared to 7.8% for non–Latino Whites. The poverty data are even more bleak for Latino children under 18 years of age, 28% of whom live below the poverty level, compared with 9.5% of non–Latino Whites (Ramirez & de la Cruz, 2002).

2. Title IX is the federal law passed in 1972 prohibiting sex-based discrimination in any educational institution receiving federal funds. Athletics has been the cultural space in which the law has been most widely tested.

3. The G.I. Bill is an educational assistance program for various military personnel. The program provides up to 36 months of education benefits for college, business, technical, or vocational courses; correspondence courses; apprenticeship and job training; and flight training. Currently, qualified veterans may earn up to $985.00 per monthor up to $35,000 total reimbursement for educational expenses. Its greatest impact for Latinos followed the Vietnam War. More information on the G.I. Bill may be found at http://www.gibill.va.gov/. Collegiate, athletic scholarships, and Equal Opportunity Program (EOP) funding may eventually demonstrate a similar influence on Latina access to higher education.

4. According to Amateur Softball Association (ASA) magazine, girls' fast-pitch tournaments were the most numerous and most profitable for host cities during 1998. Relying on the numbers reported by ASA, it is estimated that the cost per individual for a 2-day tournament was $250.00. This is a rough estimate that includes travel while in town, two-night stay in town, meals, and sightseeing (McCall, 1999). This estimate does not include costs for travel to the tournament site.

5. The U.S. Bureau of the Census reports that two in five Latinos are foreign born, with median earnings of foreign-born workers ($26,710) considerably less than those of native-born workers ($35,239), with Latinos fairing worse than all other categories of foreign-born workers ($21,538). Foreign-born U.S. residents are also more likely to be unemployed (6.9% vs. 6.1%) and to live below the poverty level (16.1% vs. 11.1%) as compared to native-born residents, and again, Latinos lag behind other racial-ethnic groups on these characteristics (7.9% and 20.6%, respectively).

6. Several scholars have identified multiple characteristics that make untracking possible for minority and working-class youths in school. Among these characteristics are the presence of (a) academically oriented peer groups, (b) strategies for academic identities at school and neighborhood identities at home, (c) affirmation of cultural identity (e.g., Movimiento Estudiantil Chicano de Aztlan), (d) acknowledgement of need for educational achievement for occupational success, (e) healthy disrespect for achievement ideology, (f) positive sibling influence, (g) parental encour-

agement (especially from mothers), and (h) parental preservation of child study time (Gandara, 1995; Mehan et al., 1994).

7. A *walk-on* is a student-athlete who goes through a tryout and earns a spot on a team roster but is typically not funded at all, or only minimally. Walk-on athletes typically have to earn their position on the team each year.

8. Nora and Rendòn (1994) found that approximately 75% of students who entera community college do so with the desire to transfer to a 4-year institution, but only about 25% of students execute this transfer successfully. Gandara (1995) found that one third of her respondents, who were Chicanos and had successfully graduated from college, had begun their academic careers at a community college. It is interesting that among the women I interviewed, 30% began their careers at community college and that 93% of these women were able to successfully transfer to a 4-year university.

9. Anzaldua (1987) and Sandoval (2001) are both widely known for their analytic work regarding mobile subjectivities and border consciousness.

References

Acosta, R. V. (1999). Hispanic women in sport. *Journal of Health, Physical Education, Recreation and Dance, 70*(4), 44–46.

Anzaldua, G. (1987). *Borderlands/La frontera: The new mestiza.* San Francisco: Spinsters/Aunt Lute.

Bettie, J. (2003). *Women without class: Girls, race, and identity.* Berkeley: University of California Press.

Birrell, S., & Richter, D. M. (1994). Is a diamond forever? Feminist transformations of sport. In S.Birrell & C. L. Cole (Eds.), *Women, sport, and culture* (pp. 221–244). Champaign, IL: Human Kinetics.

Bissinger, H. G. (1990). *Friday night lights.* Reading, MA: Addison-Wesley.

Cardoza, D. (1991). College attendance and persistence among Hispanic women: An examination of some contributing factors. *Sex Roles, 24*(3), 133–147.

Cuadraz, G. H. (1996). Experiences of multiple marginality: A case study of Chicana "scholarship women." In C. Turner, M. Garcia, A. Nora, & L. I. Rendon (Eds.), *Racial and ethnic diversity in higher education* (pp. 210–222). Needham Heights, MA: Simon & Schuster.

Flores-Gonzalez, N. (1999). Puerto Rican high achievers: An example of ethnic and academic identity compatibility. *Anthropology and Education Quarterly, 30*(3), 343–362.

Foley, D. E. (1990). The great American football ritual: Reproducing race, class, and gender inequality. *Sociology of Sport Journal, 7*(2), 111–135.

Gandara, P. (1995). *Over the ivy walls: The educational mobility of low-income Chicanos.* New York: State University of New York Press.

Grey, M. A. (1996). Sport and immigrant, minority, and Anglo relations in Garden City (Kansas) High School. In D. S. Eitzen (Ed.), *Sport in contemporary society: An anthology* (5th ed., pp. 295–312). New York: St. Martin's.

Jamieson, K. M., Reel, J. J., & Gill, D. L. (2002). Beyond the racial binary: Stacking in women's collegiate softball. *Women in Sport and Physical Activity Journal, 11*(1), 89–106.

Lenskyj, H. J. (1994). Sexuality and femininity in sport contexts: Issues and alternatives. *Journal of Sport and Social Issues, 18*(4), 356–376.

McCall, B. (1999). The economics of ASA softball. *Balls and Strikes Softball,* preseason, 32–33.

Mehan, H., Hubbard, L., & Villanueva, I. (1994). Forming academic identities: Accommodation without assimilation among involuntary minorities. *Anthropology and Education Quarterly, 25*(2), 91–117.

National Collegiate Athletic Association. (2003, August 1). *2003 graduation-rates report for division one schools*. Retrieved February 20, 2004, from *http://www.ncaa.org/ grad_rates/2003 /d1/d1_aggregate/DI.html*

Nora, A., & Rendon, L. (1994). Hispanic student retention in community colleges: Reconciling access with outcomes. In C. Turner, M. Garcia, A. Nora, & L. I. Rendon (Eds.), *Racial and ethnic diversity in higher education* (pp. 269–280). Needham Heights, MA: Simon & Schuster.

Ortner, S. B. (1998). Identities: The hidden life of class. *Journal of Anthropological Research, 54*(1), 1–17.

Ramirez, R. R., & de la Cruz, G. P. (2002). The Hispanic population in the United States: March, 2002. *Current Population Reports*, P20–545.

Sandoval, C. (2000). *Methodology of the oppressed*. Minneapolis: University of Minnesota Press.

Segura, D. A. (1993). Slipping through the cracks: Dilemmas in Chicana education. In A.de la Torre & B. M. Pesquera (Eds.), *Building with our hands: New directions in Chicana studies* (pp. 199–216). Berkeley: University of California Press.

Simoniello, K. (1981). On investigating the attitudes toward achievement and success in eight professional U.S. Mexican women. *Aztlan, 12*(1), 121–137.

Stanton-Salazar, R. (2001). *Manufacturing hope and despair: The school and kin support networks of U.S.–Mexican youth*. New York: Teachers College Press.

Thorne, B. (1993). *Gender play: Girls and boys in school.*New Brunswick, NJ: Rutgers University Press. U.S. Bureau of the Census. (1998). *Statistical abstract of the United States: 1998*. Washington, DC: U. S. Department of Commerce.

Valenzuela, A. (1999). *Subtractive schooling: U.S.–Mexican youth and the politics of caring*. New York: State University of New York Press.

Zavella, P. (1994). Reflections on diversity among Chicanas. In S. Gregory & R. Sanjek (Eds.), *Race* (pp. 199–212). New Brunswick, NJ: Rutgers University Press.

Discussion Questions

1. Describe how gender intersects with social class for young girls who aspire to play collegiate softball. Explain how social class is defined in this article.

2. Describe how both gender and social class intersect with race and ethnicity for Latina girls who are involved in softball.

3. How is softball used as a means of upward mobility in the Latino community for the girls in this particular study?

4. What might schools (e.g., public high schools) do structurally to engage differently with minority students and their families to help them succeed in higher education?

5. The author states, "Social class is visible through sport identities, as well as family and school identities." She argues that class is more than a work-related identity. In your own experience or through the information you gleaned from the article, in what other way(s) does social class become an identity for Latinas in sport?

5

The Ongoing Saga of Homophobia in Women's Sport

Sharon R. Guthrie and Kerrie Kauer

The claim that sport is a catalyst, or "breeding ground," for lesbian development has a very long and intractable history. Dating back as far as the early 20th century, medical doctors and other professionals warned that vigorous athletic participation would damage a woman's sexual identity by "masculinizing" her physically, psychologically, and behaviorally. Their thinking, of course, implied that with the "right" exposure and under certain conditions, females can become lesbians and that sport is a site where such socialization is likely to occur. Homophobia, classically defined as the irrational fear or intolerance of homosexuals and homosexuality, and the historical linkage of masculinity with athleticism, have fueled such perceptions.

Although homophobia is a term commonly used in the literature, some writers have preferred the term *homonegativity* because it implies negative attitudes and behaviors toward homosexuals rather than a deep-seated psychopathology in individuals (Krane, 1996). Others favor the expression *homonegating processes*, which emphasizes the external social context (sometimes called external homophobia) rather than the individual who has internalized society's pejorative attitudes about homosexuality (commonly called internalized homophobia). *Heterosexism*, another term emphasizing the external environment, refers to an ideological system that promotes heterosexuality as the only natural, "normal," and moral sexual orientation; hence, any non-normative form of sexual behavior, identity, relationship, or community is denigrated and stigmatized (Herek, 1992).

Regardless of these semantic debates over which terminology best describes the prejudice and discrimination experienced by non-heterosexuals, female athletes of all sexual orientations have endured the stigma of the lesbian label for over a century, particularly those who compete in sports most closely associated with masculinity (e.g., team and contact sports). Female physical educators also have experienced a long history of homophobic insinuations about their sexual orientation due to the longstanding perceived connection between sport participation and lesbianism.

Due to this onslaught of negative stereotyping, women who have chosen to compete in sport or attain careers in physical education, coaching, and sport administration have had to find ways to protect themselves, their sport and fan base and/or their profession. One of the most common stigma management strategies has been to exaggerate one's femininity through dress and mannerisms, or what has been called the "apologetic" defense. Another has been to participate in sports considered more socially acceptable for females, and therefore less vulnerable to lesbian labeling. Unfortunately, there have also been those girls or women who wanted to become elite athletes or physical educators, but felt that dropping out of sport or choosing an alternative career were the only ways to cope with challenges to their sexual identities.

Although it would be impossible to determine the exact number of girls and women who have felt the need to use such protective mechanisms, it is reasonable to conclude that internalized homophobia has limited the mind-body development of countless females, both lesbian and heterosexual, while also making advancements in professional women's sport (e.g., golf, softball, basketball) far more challenging.

Despite the long-term negative impact of homophobia on women in sport and physical education, it was not until the early 1980s that the phenomenon was examined from a controlled research perspective (Guthrie, 1982). Perhaps the main reason for this delay in scholarly investigation was that prospective researchers, who most likely would have been female faculty employed in college and university physical education departments, believed that their sexuality would be called into question or confirmed if they studied homophobia in their field. Indeed, for decades female physical educators had attempted to defend themselves and their profession from homophobic attack. They undoubtedly felt that conducting studies on homophobia or lesbianism in sport would cast further suspicion their way, and ultimately discourage generations of young girls and women from participating in sport. The fact that the author of a 1982 paper examining the lesbian presence in sport and physical education published her work under a pseudonym is indicative of this concern (Cobhan, 1982). For female physical educators during this time period, the choice must have seemed obvious—remain silent and, if questioned, deny any accusations of lesbianism in sport. Unfortunately, their silence (e.g., "don't ask, don't tell") and other protective strategies have perpetuated heteronormative ideologies in women's sport and the devaluing of lesbian experiences.

As the social climate has changed over time due to a series of human rights movements (i.e., Civil Rights, feminist, lesbian/gay/bisexual/transgender, disability movements), there has been increasing recognition that to effect change, open and honest communication, critical analysis, and liberatory action are required. Consequently, there is currently more dialogue about homophobia and the lesbian presence in sport. Scholarship emphasizing the critical role sexuality plays in constructing gender relations in sport and in constraining female sporting involvement has stimulated this discussion (Barber & Krane, 2005; Birrell & Cole, 1994; Blinde & Taub, 1992a, 1992b; Forbes & Lathrop, 2002; Griffin, 1992, 1993; Krane, 1996; 1997; Lenskyj, 1986, 1991, 1994, 1997; Messner & Sabo, 1990; Riemer, 1997; Vealey, 1997; Veri, 1999). Equally important in advancing social awareness has been research documenting the existence of a distinct lesbian sporting culture (Caudwell, 2007; Griffin, 1998; Krane, 1997; Pitts, 1997). Far more work is needed, however, to elucidate the ways in which heterosexism and homonegativity can be "uprooted" in the human psyche and the mechanisms by which individuals and groups become social change agents.

Historical Background of Homophobia in Women's Sport

Although sport has often been a site where gender relations have been contested, men's organized opposition to female athletes became more visible after voting rights for women had been achieved. Indeed, prior to the passage of the 19th amendment in 1920, women's sports in female-only colleges and universities were gaining acceptability and popularity. During the 1930s, however, the rosy-cheeked, healthy physical education major, as the prototype of the modern athletic female preparing for marriage and motherhood, was replaced by the negative image of a mannish social and sexual deviant.

Contributing to this shift in thinking were the works of Havelock Ellis and Sigmund Freud, which posited sexual identity as profoundly significant to personal identity. Equally important, doctors and psychologists incorporated this view into their research, categories of illness, and definitions of social deviance and sexual perversity. Susan Cahn (1994) describes this development in the following:

> In the 1930s, psychologists developed masculinity and femininity to define the masculine end of the women's scale. Early test results found that the only women who rated "more masculine" than lesbians were a group of 37 superior women college athletes. As the figure of the "mannish lesbian" entered popular awareness, within women's sports, pre-existing notions of mannishness and sexual release converged, providing a host culture for popular homophobic images (p. 331).

Women in physical education were singled out as particularly suspect. Physical educators responded by developing policies calling for a "separate sphere" for females because of their biological differences. Physical education courses became spaces to distance girls and women from the competition and aggressiveness of sport and were thought to provide a place for them to exercise without embarrassment or public disdain. Games were modified to reduce stress, and loose-fitting uniforms were adopted to preserve the modesty of the girls and young women who wore them.

Ultimately, such strategies, which were designed to combat homophobia, may have inadvertently advanced homophobia in women's sport. Female physical educators had criticized male-controlled sport because they felt it promoted unhealthy aspects of competition, athletic elitism, winning at any cost, and commercialism. Although their criticism certainly contributed to the backlash, it was the physical educators' separatist strategy that came under direct assault. The sense of community developed in these separate spaces was now viewed as a prime ingredient in fostering lesbianism.

To address this charge, female physical educators embraced an even more aggressive promotion of heterosexuality, which became the cornerstone of course offerings. Beauty and social charm were stressed, and rigorous exercise was deemphasized. Team sports were minimized and replaced by tennis, golf, bowling, and horseback riding because the latter were thought to possess more carryover value in heterosexual relationships with potential marriage partners. The trimness, grace, and beauty of the woman emerging from physical education courses were emphasized and accompanied by the claim that physical education and sport played an important role in supporting and advancing heterosexual development.

According to Cahn, the physical educators' response to the stigmatization of their profession unfortunately further solidified the linkage between lesbianism and women's sport. Thus, the images of physical education majors and teachers as "amazons, social misfits, prudes, or lesbians" became even more entrenched during the 1950s. In fact, Cahn has argued that the preexisting and ongoing association of sport with masculinity and the stereotype of the lesbian female physical educator may have actually generated a lesbian reality:

> The homophobic atmosphere, which is the historical legacy of physical educa-tion, functioned as a sort of sexual field-of-force. It repelled many heterosexual women who were uncomfortable with the P.E. image, while at the same time attracting many sportsminded lesbians. They surely also worried about the pro-fession's "queer aura," but may have been drawn by the sense of difference, the physical focus, and the female culture of physical education (p. 336).

Therefore, instead of dispelling associations of athletic women with deviant sexuality, physi-cal educators paradoxically (but unintentionally) reinforced heterosexism and lesbian oppres-sion. These female physical educators should not be blamed, however, for attempting to make sport and physical education an inviting environment for females of all ages and backgrounds or to diminish the negative stereotyping of their professional domain. They knew well the ben-efits, both physical and psychological, that could be attained from regular physical activity and wanted to share this information with others. In addition, some most likely understood not only the life-altering possibilities for individual girls and women, but also the social trans-formation that could result if a critical mass of females developed their physical and psychoe-motional powers via sport.

In a 1992 article entitled, "Homophobia and Women's Sport: The Disempowerment of Athletes," Elaine Blinde and Diane Taub concluded that the "L-word" will continue to disem-power women athletes "until the issues surrounding lesbianism in women's sport are redefined as a problem that rests with the homophobic and patriarchal society in which women's sport resides" (1992b, p. 165). Indeed, the L-word has been disempowering females for a disturbingly long time, even 17 years after this article was published. In an effort to solve the problem, Blinde and Taub, like so many others (Greendorfer & Rubinson, 1997; Griffin, 1998; Lenskyj, 1986; 1994; Krane, 1996, 1997; Sykes, 1996, 1998), have consistently called for changes in sporting ideology and practice, research emphasis, as well as the broader sociocultural arena.

Fortunately, some progress was made in the 1990s, and even more progress occurred after the turn of the 21st century. For one thing, homophobia, its etiological roots and intransigent nature, have undergone much critical analysis by scholars both within and outside of the dis-cipline of kinesiology/sport studies. Although data-based research examining homophobia and lesbianism in sport is still somewhat limited, it is no longer uncommon to find articles and books related to the topic. Alongside the research, there have also been theoretical advance-ments that have helped us to make sense of the ways in which heteronormativity, homopho-bia, and lesbians operate in sport. This surge in both empirical and theoretical scholarship provides evidence that the institution of sport is slowly changing and that the academic disci-plines producing this scholarship (e.g., kinesiology) are undertaking more progressive and social justice-oriented work. Additionally, the sociocultural context in which women's sport is embedded has become increasingly appreciative and supportive of female athleticism and physical prowess. Still, as most researchers and analysts have noted, homophobia (sometimes referred to as lesbophobia) in women's sport maintains a strong foothold, and will likely do so until the homonegating processes in society, out of which internalized homophobia takes root, are no longer socially acceptable to a critical mass of people. In this regard, we still have a long way to go.

Negative Consequences of Homophobia in Women's Sport

Homophobia in women's sport creates a climate in which all female athletes, coaches, and administrators, as well as other advocates of sport for women, often feel threatened, and thus the need to protect their sexual identities and the image of their sport in the public eye. This is particularly true for lesbians. Such defensive posturing, while understandable and rational, often results in negative consequences. In her 1998 book, *Strong Women, Deep Closets*, Pat Griffin comments on this dynamic in the following:

> As with most forms of social injustice, heterosexism and homophobia are not sustained merely by virulent "homophobes" who intentionally discriminate against lesbians. These injustices are also perpetuated by the larger number of well-intentioned people who do not understand how their fears about lesbians in sport form the basis for an acceptance of an athletic climate that forces a significant number of participants to live in fear of their colleagues' or teammates' prejudice and the institutional climate that supports that prejudice (p. 89).

Griffin also identifies some of the most common protective mechanisms used by women in sport. Silence and denial, that is, "I am not a lesbian, or there are no lesbians on our team" top the list. Other frequently used strategies include: a) promoting a heterosexual image via confirming romantic connections to males, b) emphasizing one's femininity and heterosexuality through hairstyle, dress, and behaviors, c) competing in sports considered more socially acceptable for females, d) downplaying the importance of one's sport participation, e) claiming a preference for male coaches, f) making negative or harassing comments about lesbians and homosexuality in public and/or private social circles, and g) distancing oneself as much as possible from perceived or actual lesbians on one's sport team. Although these strategies may become routinized over time, the energy that it takes to manage a false impression can be emotionally draining and lead to inauthentic personal and professional choices.

It is also not difficult to see that this felt need to guard oneself or one's sport can result in friction between lesbian and heterosexual athletes on the same team, which in turn can hinder athletic performance and prevent these women from working together to improve sociopolitical conditions in the athletic realm. Internalized homophobia is also associated with a variety of physical and mental health problems, among them depression, poor body image, and low self-esteem.

In American society, heterosexuality and a youthful, lean body are equated with feminine beauty and attractability, and thus can empower those who possess these qualities. Being a lesbian, or perceived as lesbian, which is often stereotyped as unattractive and stocky or overweight, typically diminishes this power. It is therefore not surprising that female athletes, particularly those who have the greatest anxiety about being stigmatized in this manner, are likely to fear fat and lesbian-baiting. The bodily objectification required to achieve athletic excellence, both in terms of function and form, and the pressures in some sports to maintain a very lean muscle mass and/or small body size magnify this likelihood.

Few individuals, regardless of sexual orientation, can resist the intense pressure to conform to these rigid athletic and sociocultural body-beauty ideals. Even fewer escape the constraints of heterosexism and homonegativity, which ultimately limit personal freedom and the development of a positive body image and sense of self. Indeed, in a recent study examining the relationship between lesbophobia and eating disorder symptomatology among lesbian athletes, those who expressed greater negativity about being perceived as lesbian, reported more body dissatisfaction, weight preoccupation, fat phobia, and other eating disordered attitudes and behaviors (Guthrie, 2005).

Theoretical Advancements: Making Sense of Homophobia in Women's Sport

As previously mentioned, the perceived connection between athleticism and masculinity, rooted in sexist ideology, has fueled much of the homophobia that exists in women's sport. Heterosexist social norms, which label non-normative sexualities as deviant, have contributed as well. Understanding how both sexism and heterosexism function in women's sport sheds light on how the athletic environment can be changed so that all females may participate fully and fairly.

Theories help us in this regard by providing the tools to make sense of particular phenomena. Three theoretical advancements, which developed in the last few decades of the 20th century, deepen our understanding of these complex processes and thereby sharpen our analytical lens. They are feminist theory, social identity theory, and queer theory.

Feminist Theory

Although there are several forms of feminist theory, a major tenet across theoretical approaches is that dominant values are socially constructed to perpetuate hegemony (i.e., a system of power and influence) in society. Within a patriarchal hegemonic system, females are systematically marginalized and oppressed, albeit to varying degrees (e.g., based on race/ethnicity, class, age, disability, age, sexual orientation), so that male supremacy and privilege are perpetuated. The gender inequity that results from such a system is glaringly evident in sport where men possess most of the power with regard to athletic administration, coaching, and control of the sport media.

Females who compete in sport pose a threat to these patriarchal structures and practices (Blinde & Taub, 1992a, 1992b; Veri, 1999). As female athletes gain muscularity, assertiveness, and tough-mindedness, these characteristics, which are closely associated with masculinity, are no longer unique to males, and male domination is thereby challenged (Griffin, 1998; Veri, 1999). Historically, there have always been men, both inside and outside of sport, who are disturbed by the fact that females can develop male-identified characteristics and excel physically and intellectually in male-dominated arenas (Messner, 2002). These individuals have preserved their power and privilege by developing strategies to control and contain the physical and mental powers of their female counterparts. Although individuals may not intentionally use these tactics to oppress females, or they are merely following what has become socially accepted practice for men and women in a culture, the result is still the same: female mind-body capabilities are diminished.

One of the ways female power is constricted is by emphasizing the importance of women maintaining "hegemonic femininity," a version of femininity that emphasizes passivity, weakness, frailty, thinness, and certain facial features and body shapes (Vigorito & Curry, 1998). Hegemonic femininity, or what has been called the "feminine body-beauty discourse," (Castelnuovo & Guthrie, 1998) is promoted by dominant groups because it is associated with characteristics and qualities that can be sharply contrasted to hegemonic masculinity. This rigid notion of femininity, which is touted as a critical way for women to heighten their sexual attractability to males, is also contrasted with non-dominant forms of femininity such as lesbianism. These contrasts support male hegemony, as do the negative stereotyping and denigration of persons who deviate from this way of being and self-presentation.

Many sport studies scholars have argued that the social construction of gender and hegemonic femininity are central to attempts to ostracize, denigrate, and exclude women from sport. Females who participate in sport, particularly high-involvement, elite forms of sport, develop characteristics perceived to be in opposition to hegemonic femininity; they therefore become targets of prejudice and discrimination. Moreover, as Vikki Krane has noted, "Female athletes must contend with an athletic body that is necessary to meet their sport goals, yet that also is contrary to society standards of the ideal female body" (2001, p. 118). This makes managing a positive image challenging for a large number of female athletes, particularly those whose bodies or presentational styles are least aligned with the feminine body-beauty discourse.

Social Identity Theory

Social identity theory (SIT) provides an analytical framework for understanding: (1) the psychological processes involved in developing a social identity and maintaining high self-esteem, and (2) how the sociocultural environment influences group identity (Hogg & Abrams, 1988; Worshel, 1998). The theory is therefore useful in examining the development of stereotypes, discrimination, and oppression that are experienced by marginalized groups (Cox & Gallois, 1996). SIT has been used to understand females in sport because of their devalued social identity in comparison to men and male athletes and their attempts to elevate their social status by developing a positive social identity (Krane & Barber, 2003).

According to SIT, certain groups of individuals, in this case female athletes, are stigmatized because they are viewed as conflicting with the values and ideals of the dominant social group (Leyens, Yzerbyt & Schadron, 1994). Stereotypes are a critical factor in this stigmatization process; therefore, the stereotypes directed at female athletes serve several social functions, among them *social causality, social justification, and social differentiation.*

An example of *social causality* is the following: Lesbian athletes are often blamed for a lack of fans in game attendance, a lack of sponsorship for women's sport teams, and the lack of gender equality in women's sport (Blinde & Taub, 1992a, 1992b; Griffin, 1998). That is, they become the *"scapegoat"* for many of the injustices that exist in women's athletics. This strategy has been successfully used by the members of dominant groups in sport to divert attention away from their own complicity in reinforcing gender inequity. An example of this scapegoating of lesbian athletes is when CBS golf commentator, Ben Wright, declared in 1996 that lesbian golfers were a "liability" for the Ladies Professional Golf Association. In essence, Wright was saying that lesbians are ruining the image of women's golf, and thus responsible for decreased fans, ticket sales, and media coverage (Griffin, 1998).

Labeling female athletes as lesbian serves the *social justification* function of stereotypes. Lesbian athletes and coaches are often seen as social deviants, justifying discriminatory actions toward them (Blinde & Taub, 1992a). For example, many coaches have reported knowing individuals who were not offered coaching positions or were fired from their current jobs due to their presumed lesbianism (Krane & Barber, 2003; Wellman & Blinde, 1997). Not hiring or firing a lesbian coach occurs when the persons making such decisions believe there is truth in the "lesbian as sexual predator" stereotype and thereby view their actions as protecting young female athletes from what Pat Griffin has called the "lesbian boogeywoman."

Athletes have suffered similar negative consequences in sport; for example, lesbian athletes often fear that they will be cut from a team or lose their athletic scholarships if their sexual orientation is presumed or disclosed (Krane, 1997). There are also cases of coaches mandating a "no lesbian" policy on their teams (Blinde, Taub & Han, 1994). Eliminating lesbian athletes from a team or preventing them from becoming members of the team in the first place are justified because lesbians are perceived as undesirable, immoral, and a bad influence on heterosexual team members.

"Negative recruiting" is another example of *social justification* because many coaches believe that young female athletes should not be exposed to lesbians. Negative recruiting occurs when coaches discourage athletes from attending a rival school by labeling the team or the coaches' at that school as lesbians. This practice has been reported frequently within the college coaching ranks and, in particular, has been used to intimidate and discriminate against college basketball coaches when they are recruiting athletes (Krane & Barber, 2003; Wellman & Blinde, 1997).

In women's sport, *social differentiation* occurs when female athletes distance themselves from women who are perceived as unfeminine or lesbian to enhance their social status (Barber & Krane, 2001). As discussed earlier, female athletes often go to great lengths to distinguish themselves from lesbian athletes by projecting a heterosexual image and performing hegemonic femininity (Baird, 2001; Krane, 2001).

As can be seen from the examples provided, stereotypes serve useful social functions, particularly for those in power. On the bright side, however, stereotypes may also mobilize social activism among groups who are devalued and/or denigrated in a particular setting or culture. These efforts to make social change are more likely to occur if a marginalized group's collective esteem (i.e., how the members feel about their social group as a whole) is generally positive. Recent studies employing SIT with female athletes have found that increasing numbers of female athletes are becoming social change agents via their attempts to enhance their sporting environments (Krane & Barber, 2003; Kauer & Krane, 2006).

Queer Theory

Queer theory builds on feminist challenges to the notion that gender is part of a person's essential (innate) self and to gay/lesbian studies scholars' investigation of the socially constructed nature of sexual acts and identities. Although queer theory is commonly used to understand lesbian, gay, bisexual, and/or transgendered individuals and experiences, it is far more comprehensive in its focus examining categories of gender, as well as sexual orientation.

Queer theoreticians and political activists contest the tenets of "heteronormativity," claiming that there is no one "natural" sexual orientation (i.e., heterosexuality) from which other sexualities deviate. They do this through a process called "deconstruction." Deconstruction is a form of criticism that questions traditional assumptions about truth and identity and seeks to expose the contradictions in a text or way of thinking by looking beneath its surface or commonly understood meaning. Deconstructing heterosexuality as the norm allows queer theoreticians to articulate the ways in which homophobia and heterosexism function in our culture as sources of power (Jagose, 1996; Walters, 1996). Thus, queer theoreticians and political activists examine the social and political spheres in which certain groups of people gain power and privilege via ideological discourses (i.e., written and verbal communications and texts, visual images) associated with sexuality and gender.

Queer theoreticians ask the question: "How does heterosexuality become normalized as a 'natural' sexual orientation?" (Britzman, 1995). They also question the naturalization of race and ethnicity, which is often excluded in gay and lesbian scholarship and attempt to transcend the notion of an "essentialized" lesbian or gay identity (i.e., one that is innate, essential to one's nature, and fixed) (Jargose, 1996). Instead, queer theorists advocate for a non-identity or anti-identity, claiming that conceptualizing and treating lesbians as a category of individuals who are distinct from non-lesbians reifies these binary sexual categories and ignores the fact that sexual identities are socially constructed and subject to change. Moreover, socially constructed categories such as gender, race, sexuality, and class most often become hierarchical. For example, White, heterosexual, male athletes are more privileged than Black, lesbian, female athletes in terms of resources, power, and privilege. Dismantling these categories helps to unravel the ways in which power and privilege are reproduced in sport and society.

Queer theory is useful in interrogating the boundaries of heteronormativity and sexual orientation in White, heterosexist, male-dominated institutions (Sykes, 1998). A queer theoretical analysis can therefore help us to understand the power relations associated with sexual orientation in the athletic culture. Queer theorists argue that the institution of sport must not be taken for granted, that is, it is a powerful sociopolitical domain that deeply impacts everyday thought and practices. As such, theoretical models emphasizing only the positive dimensions of sport (e.g., sport builds character, sport leads to physical fitness) are shortsighted because they do not adequately address the power, dominance, and oppressive elements upon which much of sport is grounded.

Queer theorists also argue that these socially constructed power and dominance aspects of sport must be contested and that female athletes are involved in this contestation, even if they do not realize or intend it. In fact, one sociologist has identified all women in sport, regardless of sexual orientation, as "queer" because they represent a disruption in the male hegemonic culture that sport attempts to reinforce (Broad, 2001). In this sense, all female athletes, albeit to varying extents, are transgressing and directly confronting sexual and gender power regimes in society and sport, and in this process, are normalizing lesbianism and other nontraditional forms of gender and sexual expression.

Social Change Efforts and Possibilities for the Future

Despite the difficulty of eradicating homophobia and heteronormativity in society and women's sport, there is reason to celebrate recent social change efforts and change. At the time of this writing (2008), the Supreme Court in the State of California has approved lesbian and gay marriage, and lesbian-positive images and roles are far more common in television and film than they were in the past. Moreover, recent Gallup polls indicate that an increasing number of Americans do not oppose the legalization of sexual relations between consenting adults of the same sex.

In the sporting context, there is also evidence of social change. Most notably, far more female athletes are comfortable and proud of their athletic identities and are actively contesting masculinist representations of sport and athleticism rather than relying on stigma management strategies to normalize themselves (Adams, Schmitke & Franklin, 2005). Additionally, more famous professional female athletes have publicly disclosed their lesbian identities, and there is a growing body of research documenting that on some athletic teams, lesbian and heterosexual athletes are supporting each other's right to live free of heterosexist oppression, both inside and outside of athletics (Griffin, 1998; Kauer & Krane, 2006, Krane, 2001).

Research Documenting Social Change in Women's Sport

Vikki Krane and her colleagues have examined the Gay Games as a site for social change (Krane, Barber & McClung, 2002). The Gay Games, established in 1984, have provided an inclusive atmosphere in which persons of diverse genders and sexualities and varying degrees of athletic skill can compete. There is, however, evidence of gay male privilege at the event, and several debates regarding the participation of transgendered athletes at the Games have transpired. Regardless, the Games emphasize the athleticism of lesbian, gay, bisexual, and transgendered (LGBT) athletes, which in turn enhances the status and recognition of these athletes while refuting negative stereotypes of LGBTs in sport and society at large (Krane & Waldron, 2000).

In another study, Shannon Baird (2001) found social change strategies employed by female rugby players who were making concerted efforts to redefine what it means to be feminine. According to these female ruggers, femininity was any act performed by a female, regardless of sexual orientation. Many claimed that playing rugby as a female is inherently a "feminine" act, and therefore refused to be stereotyped as masculine simply because of their participation in the sport. Additionally, many of the lesbians in Baird's study viewed their lesbian athlete identity as empowering and privileged in the sport of rugby, which in turn led to high levels of self- and collective esteem that transferred to non-sport contexts.

Jayne Caudwell (2006, 2007) found similar efforts to subvert traditional notions of femininity and sexuality when studying "out" lesbian football (i.e., soccer) athletes in the United Kingdom. She examined how feminine gender identities are (re)articulated in the space of women's football and how these femininities are detached from heterosexual relations. This "queer" athletic community provided a space where feminine, or what Caudwell calls "femme-inine," expressions of self were performed solely for the female gaze, and therefore could not be classified as hegemonic femininity (which is geared toward capturing male attention). This study illustrates the complexities of what is often perceived to be a simple and "natural" connection among biological sex, gender, and sexual desire and how feminine attitudes and behaviors have the potential to disrupt, rather than perpetuate, the heteronormative status quo.

Although there has been an explosion in scholarship examining sexuality in sport, more work exploring the intersections of sexuality, race, and social class is needed. Women of color often experience homophobia differently than White women, yet the vast majority of research to date has examined the experiences of White women only. Understanding how girls and women of diverse sociocultural groups experience homophobia is critical in the process of discovering strategies to destabilize heteronormativity in sport.

Organizations Working for Social Change in Women's Sport

In addition to the research documenting attempts to reduce homophobia in women's sport, several activist organizations have enhanced our knowledge of many of the issues discussed in this chapter. One of the most influential programs in this regard is the Women's Sports Foundation's, *It Takes a Team*. The director, Pat Griffin, has provided educational workshops on homophobia in sport to hundreds of high school and college athletes, coaches, and administrators. *It Takes a Team* offers an educational kit, including instructional and curriculum resources, action guides to help coaches, parents, athletes, and administrators address practical issues, administrative resources for addressing the athletic department climate, and legal resources (see Internet Resources at the end of this chapter).

Another organization working to diminish heterosexism and homophobia is the National Center for Lesbian Rights (NCLR). Since 2001, NCLR's Sports Project has taken on legal cases of lesbian athletes and coaches who have been fired or dismissed from their positions due to their sexual orientation, for example, the high profile case of basketball player, Jennifer Harris v. Rene Portland and Penn State. Coach Portland had a longstanding and well known "no lesbians" policy on her teams. Due to the courage of athletes and the litigation provided by the NCLR, Portland is no longer coaching at Penn State. Through this litigation, as well as advocacy and outreach, the NCLR is creating social change for all women in sport who are affected by homophobia.

Conclusion

Throughout this chapter, we have examined the history of homophobia in women's sport, the contemporary issues that females in sport continue to face due to homophobia, some theoretical frameworks to help understand these issues, and different types of social change taking place. Although we have seen progress in terms of the lessening of homophobia in women's sport, this chapter also highlights the problems still remaining.

One of these problems is that sport continues to perpetuate binary categories of gender, that is, male vs. female and masculinity vs. femininity, categories presumed by many to be interconnected with sexual categories. Although it is important to recognize that a relationship exists between gender and sexuality, the two phenomena should not be considered naturally linked. Once we broaden traditional notions of masculinity and femininity and stop equating binary gender categories with sexual categories (e.g., female athletes are lesbians because they exhibit "traditional" masculine characteristics), we can more successfully tackle larger issues associated with heterosexism and heteronormativity.

Sport holds a prominent place in American society and around the globe. As a result, many social change movements have occurred through and because of sport, and many people have received the benefits that sport has to offer. It is important, however, that sport participants from all "walks of life" be afforded a comfortable space so that they can experience these benefits to their fullest. In order to accomplish this goal, changes are required. It is our belief that, instead of mirroring and reproducing the homophobic prejudice and discrimination found in other social institutions, sport can become *the* model for change on a broader sociocultural level. It takes a team, however, of people committed to fostering this change. We hope that you, the reader, will become a team member!

References

Adams, N., Schmitke, A., & Franklin, A. (2005). Tomboys, dykes, and girly girls: Interrogating the subjectivities of adolescent female athletes. *Women's Studies Quarterly, 33*(1-2), 17–34.

Baird, S. (2001). *Femininity on the pitch: An ethnographic study of female rugby players.* Unpublished Master's thesis, Bowling Green State University, Bowling Green.

Barber, H., & Krane, V. (2001, June). *Examining lesbian high school coaches' experiences: A social identity perspective*. Poster presentation at the 10th World Congress of Sport Psychology, Skiathos, Greece.

Barber, H., & Krane, V. (2005). The elephant in the locker room: Opening the dialogue about sexual orientation on women's sport teams. *Sport Psychology in Practice*, 265–285.

Birrell, S., & Cole. C. (1994). *Women, sport, and culture*. Champaign, IL: Human Kinetics.

Blinde, E., & Taub, D. (1992a). Women athletes as falsely accused deviants. *Sociological Quarterly, 33*, 521–533.

Blinde, E., & Taub. D. (1992b). Homophobia and women's sport: The disempowerment of athletes. *Sociological Focus, 25*(2), 151–166.

Blinde, E. M., Taub, D. E., & Han, L. (1994). Sport as a site for women's group and societal empowerment: Perspectives from the college athlete. *Sociology of Sport Journal, 11*, 51–59.

Britzman, D. P. (1995). Is there a queer pedagogy? Or, stop reading straight. *Educational Theory, 42*, 151–165.

Broad, K. L. (2001). The gendered unapologetic: Queer resistance in women's sport. *Sociology of Sport Journal, 20*, 87–107.

Cahn, S. K. (1994). *Coming on strong: Gender and sexuality in twentieth-century women's sport*. New York: The Free Press.

Castelnuovo, S., & Guthrie. S. R. (1998). *Feminism and the female body: Liberating the Amazon*. Boulder: Lynne Rienner Publishers.

Caudwell, J. (2006). *Femme-fatale: Re-thinking the femme-inine*. New York: Routledge.

Caudwell, J. (2007). Queering the field? The complexities of sexuality within a lesbian-identified football team in England. *Gender, Place, and Culture: A Journal of Feminist Geography, 14*(20), 183–196.

Cobhan, L. (1982). Lesbians in physical education and sport. In M. Cruikshank (Ed.) *Lesbian Studies* (pp. 179–186). New York: Feminist Press.

Cox, S., & Gallois, C. (1996). Gay and lesbian identity development: A social identity perspective. *Journal of Homosexuality, 30*, 1–30.

Forbes, S. L., & Lathrop, A. H. (2002). A pervasive silence: Lesbophobia and team cohesion in sport. *Canadian Women's Studies, 21*(3), 32–38.

Greendorfer, S. L., & Rubinson, L. (1997). Homophobia and heterosexism in women's sport and physical education. *Women in Sport and Physical Activity Journal, 6*(2), 189.

Griffin, P. (1992). Changing the game: Homophobia, sexism, and lesbians in sport. *Quest, 44*, 251–265.

Griffin, P. (1993). Homophobia in women's sport: The fear that divides us. In G. Cohen (Ed.), *Women in sport: Issues and controversies* (pp. 193–203). Newbury Park, CA: Sage Publications.

Griffin, P. (1998). *Strong women, deep closets*. Champaign, IL: Human Kinetics.

Guthrie, S. R. (1982). *Homophobia: Its impact on women in sport and physical education*. Unpublished Master's thesis, California State University, Long Beach.

Guthrie, S. R. (2005). Following the straight and narrow: An exploratory study of lesbophobia and eating disorder symptomatology among lesbian athletes. *Women in Sport and Physical Activity Journal, 14*(1), 6–23.

Herek, G. M. (1992). Psychological heterosexism and anti-gay violence: The social psychology of bigotry and bashing. In G. M. Herek & K. T. Berrill (Eds.), *Hate crimes. Confronting violence against lesbians and gay men* (pp. 149–169). Thousand Oaks, CA: Sage.

Hogg, M. A., & Abrams, D. (1988). *Social identifications: A social psychology of intergroup relations and group processes*. New York: Routledge.

Jagose, A. (1996). *Queer theory.* University of Melbourne Press: Melbourne.

Kauer, K. J., & Krane, V. (2006). Scary dykes and feminine queens: Steeotypes and female collegiate athletes. *Women in Sport and Physical Activity Journal, 15*(10), 42–53.

Krane, V. (1996). Lesbians in sport: Toward acknowledgment, understanding and theory. *Journal of Sport and Exercise Psychology, 18,* 237–256.

Krane, V. (1997). Homonegativism experienced by lesbian collegiate athletes. *Women in Sport and Physical Activity Journal, 6*(2), 141.

Krane, V. (2001). We can be athletic and feminine, but do we want to? Challenging hegemonic femininity in women's sport. *Quest, 53,* 115–133.

Krane, V., & Barber, H. (2003). Lesbian experience in sport: A social identity theory perspective. *Quest, 55,* 328–346.

Krane, V., Barber, H., & McClung, L. (2002). Social psychological benefits of Gay Games participation: A social identity theory explanation. *Journal of Applied Sport Psychology, 14,* 27–42.

Krane, V., & Waldron, J. (2000). The Gay Games: Creating our own culture. In K. Schaffer & S. Smith (Eds.), *The Olympics at the millennium: Power, politics, and the Olympic Games* (pp. 147–164). Piscataway, NJ: Rutgers University Press.

Lenskyj, H. (1986). *Out of bounds: Women, sport, and sexuality.* Toronto, Ontario. The Women's Press.

Lenskyj, H. (1991). Combating homophobia in sport and physical education. *Sociology of Sport Journal, 8,* 61–69.

Lenskyj, H. (1994). Femininity and sexuality. *Journal of Sport and Social Issues, 18,* 356–376.

Lenskyj, H. (1997). No fear? Lesbians in sport and physical education. *Women in Sport and Physical Activity Journal, 6*(2), 7–17.

Leyens, J., Yzerbyt, V., & Schadron, G. (1994). *Stereotypes and social cognitions.* London: Sage.

Messner, M. (2002). *Taking the field: Women, men, and sports.* Minneapolis: University of Minnesota Press.

Messner, M., & Sabo, D. (Eds.). (1990). *Sport, men and the gender order: Critical feminist perspectives.* Champaign, Illinois: Human Kinetics.

Pitts, G. (1997). From leagues of their own to an industry of their own. *Women in Sport and Physical Activity Journal, 6*(2), 109–127.

Riemer, B. A. (1997). Lesbian identity formation and the sport environment. *Women in Sport and Physical Activity Journal, 6*(2), 83–97.

Sykes, H. (1996). Constr(i)(u)cting lesbian identities in physical education: Feminist and poststructural approaches to researching sexuality. *Quest, 48,* 459–469.

Sykes, H. (1998). Of gods, money, and muscle: Resurgent homophobias and the narcissism of minor differences in sport. *Psychoanalysis and Contemporary Thought, 24,* 203–225.

Vealey, R. S. (1997). Transforming the silence on lesbians in sport. *Women in Sport and Physical Activity Journal, 6*(2), 165–178.

Veri, M. (1999). Homophobic discourse surrounding the female athlete. *Quest, 51,* 355–368.

Vigorito, A. J., & Curry, T. J. (1998). Marketing masculinity: Gender identity and popular magazines. *Sex Roles, 39,* 135–152.

Walters, S. D. (1996). From here to queer: Radical feminism, post-modernism, and the lesbian menace (or, why can't a woman be more like a fag?). *Signs, 21,* 830–869.

Wellman, S., & Blinde, E. (1997). Homophobia in women's intercollegiate basketball. *Women in Sport and Physical Activity Journal, 6*(20), 63–75.

Worshel, S. (1998). A developmental view of the search for group identity. In S. Worshel, J. F. Morales, D. Paez, & J. C. Deshamps (Eds.), *Social identity: International perspectives* (pp. 53–74). Thousand Oaks, CA: Sage.

Internet Resources

It Takes a Team: *http://www.womenssportsfoundation.org/Issues-And-Research/Homophobia/Resources.aspx*

National Center for Lesbian Rights Sports Project:
   http://www.nclrights.org/site/PageServer?pagename=issue_sports

Discussion Questions

1. Why has homophobia been a prominent issue in women's sport for a long period of time?

2. What are some of the negative consequences of homophobia in women's sport? How does homophobia in women's sport impact heterosexual and lesbian athletes differently? What can athletes, coaches, and other athletic personnel do to reduce the negative effect of homophobia in women's sport? What can you, as an American citizen, do to improve the situation?

3. Why did the early female physical educators argue for a separatist strategy and how were their behaviors linked to homophobia and heterosexist ideology?

4. It is easy for most people to see the downside to being a lesbian in sport; however, what benefits might a lesbian athlete have experienced if she participated prior to Title IX, or might she experience during contemporary times?

5. What do you believe to be the roots of homophobia and homonegativity in American society?

6. Compare and contrast the three theoretical models presented in this chapter: feminism, social identity theory, and queer theory. That is, what do they have in common and how are they different?

7. How does theory help us understand the consequences of homophobia in women's sport and society at large? How does theory help provide the tools to work toward social change?

6

Fear of Feminism

Why Young Women Get the Willies

Lisa Maria Hogeland

I began thinking about young women's fear of feminism, as I always do in the fall, while I prepared to begin another year of teaching courses in English and women's studies. I was further prodded when former students of mine, now graduate students elsewhere and teaching for the first time, phoned in to complain about their young women students' resistance to feminism. It occurred to me that my response—"Of course young women are afraid of feminism"—was not especially helpful. This essay is an attempt to trace out what that "of course" really means; much of it is based on my experience with college students, but many of the observations apply to other young women as well.

Some people may argue that young women have far less to lose by becoming feminists than do older women: they have a smaller stake in the system and fewer ties to it. At the same time, though, young women today have been profoundly affected by the demonization of feminism during the 12 years of Reagan and Bush—the time when they formed their understanding of political possibility and public life. Older women may see the backlash as temporary and changeable; younger women may see it as how things are. The economic situation for college students worsened over those 12 years as well, with less student aid available, so that young women may experience their situation as extremely precarious—too precarious to risk feminism.

My young women students often interpret critiques of marriage—a staple of feminist analysis—for centuries—as evidence of their authors' dysfunctional families. This demonstrates another reality they have grown up with: the increased tendency to pathologize any kind of oppositional politics. Twelve years of the rhetoric of "special interests versus family values" have created a climate in which passionate political commitments seem crazy. In this climate, the logical reasons why all women fear feminism take on particular meaning and importance for young women.

To understand what women fear when they fear feminism—and what they don't—it is helpful to draw a distinction between gender consciousness and feminist consciousness. One measure of feminism's success over the past three decades is that women's gender consciousness—our self-awareness as women—is extremely high. Gender consciousness takes two forms: awareness of women's vulnerability and celebration of women's difference. Fear of crime is at an all-time high in the United States; one of the driving forces behind this fear may well be women's sense of special vulnerability to the epidemic of men's violence. Feminists have fostered this awareness of violence against women, and it is to our credit that we have made our analysis so powerful; at the same time, however, we must attend to ways this awareness can be deployed for nonfeminist and even antifeminist purposes, and most especially to ways it can be used to serve a racist agenda. Feminists have also fostered an awareness of women's difference from men and made it possible for women (including nonfeminists) to have an appreciation of things pertaining to women—perhaps most visibly the kinds of "women's culture" commodified in the mass media (soap operas and romance, selfhelp books, talk shows, and the like). Our public culture in the U.S. presents myriad opportunities for women to take pleasure in being women—most often, however, that pleasure is used as an advertising or marketing strategy.

Gender consciousness is a necessary precondition for feminist consciousness, but they are not the same. The difference lies in the link between gender and politics. Feminism politicizes gender consciousness, inserts it into a systematic analysis of histories and structures of domination and privilege. Feminism asks questions—difficult and complicated questions, often with contradictory and confusing answers—about how gender consciousness can be used both for and against women, how vulnerability and difference help and hinder women's self-determination and freedom. Fear of feminism, then, is not a fear of gender, but rather a fear of politics. Fear of politics can be understood as a fear of living in consequences, a fear of reprisals. The fear of political reprisals is very realistic. There are powerful interests opposed to feminism—let's be clear about that. It is not in the interests of white supremacy that white women insist on abortion rights, that women of color insist on an end to involuntary sterilization, that, all women insist on reproductive self-determination. It is not in the interests of capitalism that women demand economic rights or comparable worth. It is not in the interests of many individual men or many institutions that women demand a nonexploitative sexual autonomy—the right to say and mean both no and yes on our own terms. What would our mass culture look like if it didn't sell women's bodies—even aside from pornography. It is not in the interests of heterosexist patriarchy that women challenge our understandings of events headlined MAN KILLED FAMILY BECAUSE HE LOVED THEM, that women challenge the notion of men's violence against women and children as deriving from "love" rather than power. It is not in the 'interests of any of the systems of domination in which we are enmeshed that we see how these systems work—that we understand men's violence, male domination, race and class supremacy, as systems of permission for both individual and institutional exercises of power, rather than merely as individual pathologies. It is not in the interests of white supremacist capitalist patriarchy that women ally across differences.

Allying across differences is difficult work, and is often thwarted by homophobia—by fears both of lesbians and of being named a lesbian by association. Feminism requires that we confront that homophobia constantly, I want to suggest another and perhaps more subtle and insidious way that fear of feminism is shaped by the institution of heterosexuality. Think about the lives of young women—think about your own. What are the arenas for selfhood for young women in this culture? How do they discover and construct their identities? What teaches them who they are, who they want to be, who they might be? Our culture allows women so little scope for development, for exploration, for testing the boundaries of what they can do and who they can be, that romantic and sexual relationships become the primary, too often the only, arena for selfhood.

Young women who have not yet begun careers or community involvements too often have no public life, and the smallness of private life, of romance as an arena for selfhood is particularly acute for them. Intimate relationships become the testing ground for identity, a reality that has enormously damaging consequences for teenage girls in particular (the pressures both toward and on sex and romance, together with the culturally induced destruction of girls' self-esteem at puberty, have everything to do with teenage pregnancy). The feminist insistence that the personal is political may seem to threaten rather than empower a girl's fragile, emergent self as she develops into a sexual and relational being.

Young women may believe that a feminist identity puts them out of the pool for many men, limits the options of who they might become with a partner, how they might decide to live. They may not be wrong either: how many young men feminists or feminist sympathizers do you know? A politics that may require making demands on a partner, or that may motivate particular choices in partners, can appear to foreclose rather than to open up options for identity, especially for women who haven't yet discovered that all relationships require negotiation and struggle. When you live on Noah's ark, anything that might make it more difficult to find a partner can seem to threaten your very survival. To make our case, feminists have to combat not just homophobia, but also the rule of the couple, the politics of Noah's ark in the age of "family values." This does not mean that heterosexual feminist women must give up their intimate relationships, but it does mean that feminists must continually analyze those pressures, be dear about how they operate in our lives, and try to find ways around and through them for ourselves, each other, and other women.

For women who are survivors of men's violence—perhaps most notably for incest and rape survivors—the shift feminism enables, from individual pathology to systematic analysis, is empowering rather than threatening. For women who have not experienced men's violence in these ways, the shift to a systematic analysis requires them to ally themselves with survivors—itself a recognition that it could happen to me. Young women who have not been victims of men's violence hate being asked to identify with it; they see the threat to their emergent sense of autonomy and freedom not in the fact of men's violence, but in feminist analyses that make them identify with it. This can also be true for older women, but it may be lessened by the simple statistics of women's life experience: the longer you live, the more likely you are to have experienced men's violence or to know women who are survivors of it, and thus to have a sense of the range and scope of that violence.

My women students, feminist and nonfeminist alike, are perfectly aware of the risks of going unescorted to the library at night. At the same time, they are appalled by my suggesting that such gender-based restrictions on their access to university facilities deny them an equal education. It's not that men's violence isn't real to them, but that they are unwilling to trace out its consequences and to understand its complexities. College women, how ever precarious their economic situation, and even despite the extent of sexual harassment and date rape on campuses all over the country, still insist on believing that women's equality has been achieved. And, in fact, to the extent that colleges and universities are doing their jobs—giving women students something like an equal education—young women may experience relatively little overt or firsthand discrimination. Sexism may come to seem more the exception than the rule in some academic settings—and thus more attributable to individual sickness than to systems of domination.

Women of all ages fear the existential situation of feminism, what we learned from Simone de Beauvoir, what we learned from radical feminists in the 1970s, what we learned from feminist women of color in the 1980s: feminism has consequences. Once you have your "click!" moment, the world shifts, and it shifts in some terrifying ways. Not just heterosexism drives this fear of political commitment—it's not just fear of limiting one's partner pool. It's also about limiting oneself about the fear of commitment to something larger than the self that asks us to examine the consequences of our actions. Women fear anger, and change, and challenge—who doesn't? Women fear taking a public stand, entering public discourse, demanding and perhaps getting attention. And for what? To be called a "feminazi"? To be denounced as traitors to women's "essential nature"?

The challenge to the public-private division that feminism represents is profoundly threatening to young women who just want to be left alone, to all women who believe they can hide from feminist issues by not being feminists. The central feminist tenet that the personal is political is profoundly threatening to young women who don't want to be called to account. It is far easier to rest in silence, as if silence were neutrality, and as if neutrality were safety. Neither wholly cynical nor wholly apathetic, women who fear feminism fear living in consequences. Think harder, act more carefully; feminism requires that you enter a world supersaturated with meaning, with implications. And for privileged women in particular, the notion that one's own privilege comes at someone else's expense—that my privilege is your oppression—is profoundly threatening.

Fear of feminism is also fear of complexity, fear of thinking, fear of ideas—we live, after all, in a profoundly anti-intellectual culture. Feminism is one of the few movements in the U.S. that produce nonacademic intellectuals—readers, writers, thinkers, and theorists outside the academy, who combine and refine their knowledge with their practice. What other movement is housed so substantially in bookstores? All radical movements for change struggle against the antiintellectualism of U.S. culture, the same anti-intellectualism, fatalism, and disengagement that make even voting too much work for most U.S. citizens. Feminism is work—intellectual work as surely as it is activist work—and it can be very easy for women who have been feminists for a long time to forget how hardwon their insights are, how much reading and talking and thinking and work produced them. In this political climate, such insights may be even more hard-won.

Feminism requires an expansion of the self—an expansion of empathy, interest, intelligence, and responsibility across differences, histories, cultures, ethnicities, sexual identities, othernesses. The differences between women, as Audre Lorde pointed out over and over again, are our most precious resources in thinking and acting toward change. Fear of difference is itself a fear of consequences: it is less other women's difference that we fear than our own implication in the hierarchy of differences, our own accountability to other women's oppression. It is easier to rest in gender consciousness, in one's own difference, than to undertake the personal and political analysis required to trace out one's own position in multiple and overlapping systems of domination.

Women have real reasons to fear feminism, and we do young women no service if we suggest to them that feminism itself is safe. It is not. To stand opposed to your culture, to be critical of institutions, behaviors, discourses—when it is so clearly not in your immediate interest to do so—asks a lot of a young person, of any person. At its best, the feminist challenging of individualism, of narrow notions of freedom, is transformative, exhilarating, empowering. When we do our best work in selling feminism to the unconverted, we make clear not only its necessity, but also its pleasures: the joys of intellectual and political work, the moral power of living in consequences, the surprises of coalition, the rewards of doing what is difficult. Feminism offers an arena for selfhood beyond personal relationships but not disconnected from them. It offers—and requires—courage, intelligence, boldness, sensitivity, relationality, complexity, a sense of purpose, and, lest we forget, a sense of humor as well. Of course young women are afraid of feminism—shouldn't they be?

Discussion Questions

1. Women in sport owe a debt to the feminist movement because this movement has fostered greater opportunities and resources for participation at all levels. Why, then, do so many women feel uncomfortable calling themselves feminists?

2. How do you feel about feminism? If you were, or have ever been, called a feminist, how would/did you feel (e.g., proud, uncomfortable) and react and why?

Worksheet 5

Defining the "ISMS" in Sport

Name _____ Date _____

Describe the systems of power listed below that have the potential to facilitate privilege and inequality:

Racism (race and ethnicity) _____

_____

Sexism (gender) _____

_____

Classism (social class) _____

_____

Heterosexism (sexual orientation) _____

_____

Ageism (age) _____

_____

Looksism (body size and looks) _____

_____

Ableism (physical and mental ability) _____

_____

Worksheet 6

"ISMS" in Sport-Gender

Name _____ Date _____

1. List adjectives that society typically uses to describe women and men.

Women	Men

2. Now list adjectives that society typically uses to describe female athletes and male athletes.

Female Athletes	Male Athletes

3. What are the similarities between your two lists? What are the differences?

_____

_____

_____

_____

_____

_____

4. How do you prefer to describe female athletes?

_____

_____

_____

_____

_____

_____

Worksheet 7

"ISMS" in Sport-Race

Name _____ Date _____

Describe the ways in which you experience the categories of privilege in sport listed below:

White _____

_____

Male _____

_____

Heterosexual _____

_____

Middle or upper class _____

_____

Young _____

_____

Able-bodied _____

_____

Worksheet 8

"ISMS" in Sport-Body

The Trait Self-Objectification Questionnaire (Fredrickson & Harrison, 2005). This questionnaire is taken from reading #2 in the Psychology Section of the book.

When considering your physical self-concept, how important is . . .

a. physical coordination?
b. health?
c. weight?
d. strength?
e. sex appeal?

f. physical attractiveness?
g. energy level (e.g., stamina)?
h. firm and sculpted muscles?
i. physical fitness level?
j. measurements (e.g., chest, waist, hips)?

Rank each attribute below:

Most important _____
Second most important _____
Third most important _____
Fourth most important _____
Fifth most important _____
Sixth most important _____
Seventh most important _____
Eight most important _____
Ninth most important _____
Least important _____

Assign each attribute a ranking number as follows: most important = 9, second most important = 8, and so on to the least important = 0. Next, sum the apperance items c, e, f, h, and j and competence related items a, b, c, d, g, and i. Then subtract the competence sum for the appearance sum to determine your trait self-objectification score. Scores may range from –25 to 25 with higher scores indicating a greater emphasis on appearance.

Keep your score for the psychology reading #2 discussion questions.

Name _____ Date _____

Do you have a tendency to "objectify" yourself? Were you surprised by your score? Why or why not?

_____

_____

_____

Worksheet 9

"ISMS" in Sport-Sex

Name _____   Date _____

Take the survey below and compare your responses to the general population.
http://sportsillustrated.cnn.com/2005/magazine/04/12/survey.expanded/index.html?cnn=yes

Homosexuality and Sports

Survey conducted for NBC/USA Network by Penn, Schoen & Berland Associates, Inc.
Methodology: Penn, Schoen and Berland conducted 979 interviews among the general population from March 18–21 of this year. The margin of error sampling is +/–3.1 overall and larger for subgroups.

Question	Agree	Disagree	Your Response
It is OK for gay athletes to participate in sports, even if they are open about their sexuality	78%	22%	
It is OK for male athletes to participate in sports even if they are openly gay	86%	14%	
It is OK for female athletes to participate in sports even if they are openly gay	78%	22%	
It's OK for homosexuals to participate in sports provided they are not open about their sexuality	40%	61%	
Having an openly gay player hurts the entire team	24%	76%	
I would be less of a fan of a particular athlete if I knew that he or she was openly gay	24%	76%	
Having an openly gay athlete hurts the entire sport	23%	78%	
I would enjoy the sport less if I knew a player was gay	21%	79%	
Positive portrayals of gay athletes in the media may encourage children to become gay	19%	71%	
Openly gay athletes should be excluded from playing team sports	14%	86%	
Americans are more accepting of gays in sports today than they were twenty years ago	79%	22%	
It would hurt an athlete's career to be openly gay	68%	21%	
Gay athletes are unfairly treated in both their private and professional lives	66%	34%	
Society is more accepting of gays playing sports like golf or tennis and less accepting of gays athletes participating in more contact sports like wrestling and boxing	65%	35%	
Women's sports are typically more accepting of gay athletes	60%	40%	

Question	Agree	Disagree	Your Response
Openly gay athletes cannot receive the same endorsement deals as other athletes regardless of how they perform on the field	51%	49%	
I admire an athlete who is openly gay	48%	52%	
What America needs now is an open discussion about homosexuality and sports	47%	52%	
Many women in professional sports are lesbians	20%	79%	
Lesbians are better athletes than straight women	10%	89%	
Whether they like it or not, professional athletes are role models for children	90%	11%	
What athletes do in their private life is their own business	67%	34%	
What an athlete does off the court does not affect my enjoyment of his/her performance on the court	54%	46%	
It is a sin to engage in homosexual behavior	44%	46%	
Homosexuality is a way of life that should be accepted by society	61%	33%	
Brands and products are unlikely to select athletes as endorsers if the athletes are gay or even have been accused of being gay	64%	11%	
The reason there is so little coverage of gays in sports is because America is not ready to accept gay athletes	62%	13%	
The reason there is so little coverage of gays in sports is because gays in sports are largely in the closet	57%	11%	
If Sports Illustrated put more emphasis on gay athletes, a public buzz would develop and it would be largely negative	52%	15%	
If ESPN created a television special on the accomplishments of gay athletes, viewers would be enraged	42%	22%	
Americans would be less proud of an Olympics gold winning athlete if he/she were gay and "out"	41%	32%	
If Sports Illustrated put more emphasis on gay athletes, in far-ranging editorial features, its readership and the general public would welcome this shift	19%	43%	
The reason there is so little coverage of gays in sports is because so few gays play sports	15%	43%	
Society should not put any restrictions on sex between consenting adults in the privacy of their own home	77%	18%	
Gay and lesbian couples can be as good of parents as heterosexual couples	59%	35%	
Gay marriage would go against my religious beliefs	55%	38%	

Worksheet 10

Film Critic

Name _____ Date _____

Pick a movie from the list below and answer the following, "What does this film tell you about the social construction of gender, race, sexuality, and disability in American society?"

Women in Sport Films:

Bend It Like Beckham
Million Dollar Baby

Love and Basketball
Little Girls in Pretty Boxes

Additional Films on Women in Sport/Gender Issues

A League of Their Own
On Edge
Personal Best (with Mariel Hemingway)
Crouching Tiger: Hidden Dragon
Billy Elliot
Blue Crush

Girl Fight
Pat and Mike (with Katharine Hepburn)
Whale Rider
The Loretta Claiborne Story
Ma Vie En Rose

Documentaries

- BILLIE JEAN KING: PORTRAIT OF A PIONEER

- DARE TO COMPETE: THE STRUGGLE OF WOMEN IN SPORTS is an historic documentary chronicling women athletes and their drive for recognition in professional and Olympic sports.

- DARE TO DREAM: THE STORY OF THE U.S. WOMEN'S SOCCER TEAM explores the unrivaled phenomenon largely created by five individuals who played together for 17 years on the U.S. National Team: Mia Hamm, Julie Foudy, Brandi Chastain, Kristine Lilly and Joy Fawcett. Their enduring perseverance and success reshaped the American sports landscape, empowering millions of young girls to dream and achieve their goals.

- GIRL WRESTLER follows a year in the life of Tara Neal, a Texas teenager who rocks the establishment by insisting that girls and boys should be able to wrestle on the same mat.

- HITLER'S PAWN: THE MARGARET LAMBERT STORY is the life story of Margaret Lambert, a German athlete who wasn't allowed to compete at the 1936 Olympic games because of her religion.

- PLAYING THE FIELD: SPORTS AND SEX IN AMERICA is a documentary that traces the intimate relationship between professional athletics and sexuality over the past century.

- ROCKS WITH WINGS tells the remarkable story of a Navajo girls basketball team and the unlikely coach who instills in them a new-found self belief.

- THE HEART OF THE GAME captures the passion and energy of a Seattle high school girls' basketball team, the eccentricity of their unorthodox coach, and the incredible true story of one player's fight to play the game she loves.

SECTION 3

Psychological Perspectives on Women in Sport and Physical Activity

© PhotoDisc

"It (soccer) made me who I am. I was given a tremendous gift in terms of athleticism. Maybe it was because I wasn't so confident in other areas."

Mia Hamm, Soccer Player

Section 3
Introduction

T. Michelle Magyar

It's all the time Tiger Woods, Tiger Woods, Tiger Woods. I am better than
he is. I've been on top longer, and I am younger. I'm just better.

Martina Hingis, Tennis Player

In this section of the book you will be presented with a glimpse of some of the most current research on the psychology of women in sport and physical activity. The discipline of psychology focuses on the study of the individual and, in particular, her thoughts, feelings, and behaviors. Sport psychologists examine the psychological predictors of sport and physical activity performance in addition to the psychological processes that are affected by sport and physical activity participation. For example, sport and physical activity participation introduces girls and women to optimal challenges, moments of uncertainty, and even periods of great frustration and disappointment. Thus, sport psychologists want to know how to maximize the positive psychological benefits and minimize the negative psychological effects in an effort to improve women's overall experiences in the sport and physical activity context.

As Mia Hamm's quote at the beginning of this section shows, participation in sport can foster positive psychological development perhaps unlike any other context in life (e.g., school, family, etc.) and sport psychologists have investigated ways that athletes, coaches, and parents can maximize this positive development. For example, research shows that when coaches structure the sport environment to emphasize collaboration, effort, and personal improvement, their athletes rely on constructive sources of information to build their confidence (Magyar & Feltz, 2003). Eventually, the athlete becomes accustomed to a healthy and stable sport environment that puts her in control and empowers her (e.g., she learns to rely on personal mastery rather than on physical self-presentation to feel confident). Unfortunately, not all sport and physical activity contexts lead to positive development, and sport psychology has documented some of the negative experiences which can lead to unhealthy behaviors and harmful outcomes. In this section, we will explore both the positive and negative psychological predictors and consequences of sport and physical activity.

The majority of research that is reviewed in this section is grounded within social cognitive theory and examines the reciprocal influences between cognitive/personal factors, social influences, and behaviors to explain human functioning and motivation in sport. Central to social cognitive theory is the notion of human agency, or the intentional thoughts and behaviors which ultimately reflect an individual's desire to generate actions relative to a specific goal or objective (Bandura, 1997). Individuals can create cognitive representations of past, present, and future experiences to anticipate the possible consequences of future actions. By using symbols or internal representations of behavior, individuals create a personal standard, one they wish to achieve, which serves as a motivator and regulator for their behavior. Bandura (1997) has asserted that once these agency-related beliefs are formed, they will influence whether an individual chooses to perform a certain activity, the amount of effort one will expend, and the degree to which one will persist on a task.

One of the strongest forms of agency is human movement. Girls and women alike may form representations of what it means to be physically strong, powerful, agile, and flexible, ultimately reflecting what it means to be an athlete, exerciser, or someone who adopts a physically active lifestyle. Relying on these standards, women will then make choices about engaging in a sport or physical activity, the amount of effort to put forth in training and competing, and the degree of persistence required to continue participation, particularly when having to overcome obstacles (e.g., pain and fatigue). Thus, by adopting a social cognitive framework, sport psychology research can begin to examine the interactions between the motivational components of choice, effort, and persistence in female athletes/exercisers.

Embedded within social cognitive theory is the notion of triadic reciprocality, or the interrelationship between personal, behavioral, and environmental factors that are believed to influence agency beliefs. Although Bandura (1997) hypothesized that these factors influenced each other bi-directionally, he also proposed that they did not influence human agency equally, but rather that each component prompted cognition and behavior with varying levels of strength and degree. It is this interplay of self-generated (previous behavior, desired standards) and external sources of information that helps a person define his or her self-capabilities and influences future actions. Thus, sport participation is not solely dictated by thoughts and behaviors, but may also be influenced by environmental factors (e.g., access to facilities, significant others).

This section begins with an article by Weise-Bjornstal (2007) on girls' experiences in physical activity settings (e.g., competitive sport, physical education, and exercise class) and serves as the foundation of the psychology section because it advances our understanding of the significant relationships (e.g., parents, coaches, and peers) that influence girls' participation in sport and physical activity, and imparts a greater appreciation for what they think and feel when performing motor skills. For example, current research has identified changes in the use of peer influences from late childhood to adolescence that reflect changes in cognitive abilities in addition to changes in the social environment. As athletes mature, peer comparison and evaluative feedback from peers and coaches increases in importance, while feedback from parents declines in importance. In essence, peer comparison becomes more advanced through the distinction of "near" peers such as teammates, versus "extended" peers or opponents (Horn, 2004). As athletes' cognitive abilities mature, they learn to differentiate task difficulty, effort, and ability, and through this differentiation rely on a greater number of sources, weighting and combining multiple sources simultaneously. Parallel to this cognitive maturation, athletes become more motorically advanced through growth and experience, and with an increase in physical skill levels, athletes broaden their repertoire or awareness of the various sources of information available to them in the sport environment.

Next, we venture along the developmental continuum to explore the impact of competitive sport participation on college-aged and older adult female athletes. These articles represent empirical research that examines the relationship between sport participation and the social behaviors of leadership (Magyar, 2008) and negotiation (Guthrie, Magyar, Eggert, & Kain, 2008). When coaches are successful in developing personal improvement, teaching athletes to work with each other, and providing consistent and accurate positive feedback, the development of leadership skills becomes more salient and relevant to athletes. Similarly, when female athletes internalize positive and empowering athletic experiences, they develop a sense of confidence that transcends the sport context and positively influences other areas of their life through the courage to negotiate.

Finally, we conclude this section with research that shifts attention from the sport context to exercise/physical activity. In an effort to encourage girls and women to be more physically active, researchers have investigated the personal and social barriers to exercise. Some of the more common personal barriers to exercise include low confidence about one's ability to perform physical skills or the dislike of physical exertion, sweating, and enduring pain and fatigue associated with moderate to vigorous exercise. Thus, women who are insecure about their fitness ability, are overly critical of their body, and do not enjoy physical demands, are less likely to seek out exercise opportunities, invest high levels of effort when exercising, or persist when exercise becomes difficult. Some of the significant social barriers to physical activity include lack of social support and lack of facilities or community resources that promote exercise and fitness. When women perceive all of these barriers to be greater than the benefits of exercise (e.g., improve aerobic fitness and bone mass, enhance self-esteem, reduce depression and anxiety) they lose confidence in their ability to overcome these barriers in order to keep up with a regular exercise program (Gill, 2008).

Overall, the collection of readings presented in this section captures how girls and women may encounter both positive and negative experiences in sport and physical activity. While sport may develop positive psychological beliefs such as confidence, leadership, and self-esteem, the opportunity for this development is lost when there are various environmental factors that downplay women's role in sport. When women become too concerned with what they look like when they are moving, these self-perceptions function as a barrier to enhanced sport performance and physical well-being (Greenleaf, 2005). By understanding the integration between society and the athlete, we can begin to realize ways to improve this unfortunate predicament for female athletes and exercisers.

References

Bandura, A. (1997). *Self-efficacy: The exercise of control.* New York: W. H. Freeman.

Gill, D. (2008). Gender, diversity, and cultural competence. In Diane Gill and Lavon Williams (Eds.). *Psychological dynamics of sport and exercise* (3rd ed.), pp. 267–333.

Greenleaf, C. (2005). Self-objectification among physically active women. *Sex roles, 52,* 51–62.

Hall, R. L., & Oglesby, C. A. (2002). *Exercise and sport in feminist therapy: Constructing modalities and assessing outcomes.* Binghamton, NY: Haworth Press.

Horn, T. S. (2004). Developmental perspectives on self-perceptions in children and adolescents. In M. R. Weiss (Ed.), *Developmental sport and exercise psychology: A lifespan perspective* (pp. 101–143). Morgantown, WV: Fitness Information Technology Inc.

Magyar, T. M., & Feltz, D. L. (2003). The influence of dispositional and situational tendencies on adolescent girls' sport confidence sources. *Psychology of Sport and Exercise, 4,* 175–190.

Note

All quotes are from Jay, M. (2001). *The Winning Woman: 500 Spirited Quotations about Female Athletes and their Sport.* Running Press: Philadelphia, PA.

1

Psychological Dimensions of Girls' Physical Activity Participation

Diane M. Wiese-Bjornstal

© PhotoDisc.

Wiese-Bjornstal, Diane M. (2007). Chapter 2. *Psychological dimension of girls' physical activity particiaption.* In M.J. Kane & N.M. LaVoi (Eds.), The 2007 Tucker Center Research Report, "Developing physically active girls: An eveidence-based multidisiplinary approach "(pp. 7–27). Minneapolis, MN: The Tucker Center for Research on Girl's & Women in Sport, University of Minnesota.

This chapter on psychological dimensions is based on research on girls' physical activity within the last 10 years and updates the 1997 President's Council on Physical Fitness and Sports Report, *Physical Activity & Sport in the Lives of Girls: Physical & Mental Health Dimensions from an Interdisciplinary Approach*. The original report called for much needed research specific to dimensions of physical activity for girls and detailed what was known about motivation, self-perceptions, moral development, emotional well-being, stress and anxiety, body image, and disordered eating. In the 10 years following the original report, a considerable amount of research has been conducted that advances psychological understanding of girls' participation in physical activity. In short, psychology research verifies the following important facts about girls and physical activity:

- Girls love physical activity experiences and through them develop important relationships.
- Girls enjoy the challenges of sport and gain confidence through being physically active.
- Girls like the camaraderie and fun inherent in sport, but they rely on adult physical activity leaders to create high quality, positive experiences.
- Girls suffer negative psychological consequences if those leaders do not use their power wisely to meet girls' developmental needs.

Sport psychology research examines the thoughts, feelings, and actions of people in physical activity contexts. It considers how sport and the person reciprocally influence each other through social, cognitive, affective, and behavioral mechanisms. In the present chapter we look at how the social climates of physical activity experiences affect individual girls, and how the psychology of individual girls influences their physical activity experiences. Increasing the quantity and quality of physical activity is a goal in and of itself for the promotion of physical and mental health, but physical activity is also an important medium through which positive psychological development can be promoted. This chapter details how social, cognitive, and affective factors enhance or detract from girls' physical activity behaviors that were outlined in Chapter 1.

Physical Activity Social Climate: People Who Influence Girls

The social climates surrounding physical activity as established by parents, coaches, teachers, and peers affect girls psychologically as well as physically (Saunders, Motl, Dowda, Dishman, & Pate, 2004). Climates are changeable, and with an understanding of how climates influence individual girls they can be structured and controlled in ways that maximize the positive outcomes and minimize the negative outcomes.

Parents and Family Climate

By virtue of the beliefs that they hold, parents offer differing opportunities to their daughters. Parents are the ones who typically make the choice to enter their child into sport and physical activity opportunities. If physical activity is not seen as valuable—or if parents do not believe their daughters to be competent at physical activity—parents are less likely to offer physical activity participation opportunities to them. A developmental continuum of organized sport involvement often looks like the following scenario (Côté, 1999; Wylleman & Lavallee, 2004). The sampling years (3 to 6 years of age) are those in which parents enroll their children in a variety of sports programs; in the specializing years (7 to 12 years of age) parents become more committed supporters of their child's involvement in a limited number of sports. During the investment years (13 to 18 years of age) the demands and expectations on children and parents increase, and an optimal and productive performance environment is expected. Why do parents enroll their children in these sport programs? Parents have multiple reasons for wanting their daughters to be involved in sport programs, including such motives as physical and social development, learning life skills, achievement and rewards, and family bonding (Bzdell, 2001). In spite of wanting their girls to be physically active, it is also the case that from early ages parents allow girls to take fewer physical risks in their active play than boys, thus perhaps instilling in girls a conflicting belief that they are more vulnerable to injury than are boys (Wiese-Bjornstal, 2001).

Aside from their role in tangibly supporting their daughter's involvement in organized sport, parents influence how girls view their own physical abilities. Children are very aware of how their parents appraise their physical abilities (Bois, Sarrazin, Brustad, Chanal, & Trouilloud, 2005), and girls' perceptions of parent appraisals predict belief in their own abilities (Fredricks & Eccles, 2005) as well as their actual participation in physical activity. Girls' perceptions of their sport competence change over time, with one study showing an overall decline in these perceptions from first through twelfth grade (Fredricks & Eccles, 2002). Fathers in this study were found to hold more influence over their daughter's sport competence and value beliefs than mothers; these authors also noted that fathers typically invested more time in their child's athletic participation. But the types of influence wielded by fathers affect consequences for their daughters. For example, female soccer players who perceived their fathers to be involved but exerting lower amounts of pressure reported greater enjoyment and motivation for their soccer participation than girls who perceived higher pressure and involvement from their fathers (Babkes & Weiss, 1999).

Other research suggests that mothers are more often the parent most closely associated with a child's sport participation (e.g., Green & Chalip, 1997; Weiss & Hayashi, 1995; Wolfenden & Holt, 2005) and are typically the ones to first enroll their daughters in sport programs (Davison, Cutting, & Birch, 2003). Perhaps the involvement of fathers takes a more stereotypically direct and active role (e.g., as coach) while the involvement of mothers more often takes the equally stereotypic supportive role (e.g., for provision of transportation, uniforms and apparel, snacks). Data from Fredricks and Eccles (2005) indicated that whereas over 27% of fathers coached their child's sport team, the percentage of coaching mothers was less than 4%. Davison et al. (2003) found that mothers reported engaging in significantly more logistic support whereas fathers reported engaging in significantly more explicit modeling through their own physical activity engagement. Mothers and fathers who are perceived as active role models affect positive psychological outcomes for their daughters (Babkes & Weiss, 1999; Davison et al., 2003; Ransdell, Dratt, Kennedy, O'Neill, & DeVoe, 2001), and yet girls often report on the limited number of active female role models in their lives (Ehlinger & Katz, 1995; Garcia et al., 1998). It would be productive for girls' participation and satisfaction if both mothers and fathers would share the varied joys, opportunities, and responsibilities of valuing and supporting their daughters in physical activity settings through both the active and supportive roles.

Family support for more general physical activity is important as well (Saunders et al., 2004). Among a national sample, Sallis, Prochaska, Taylor, Hill, and Geraci (1999) found that the most powerful predictors of physical activity participation among children in grades 4 to 12 were use of afternoon time for sports and physical activity, enjoyment of physical education, and family support for physical activity. In a study of inactive adolescent girls, one of the strongest predictors of increased physical activity was support from parents, peers, and teachers (Neumark-Sztainer, Story, Hannan, Tharp, & Rex, 2003). Parents who believe in the physical competence of their girls and enact those beliefs through supportive actions provide the groundwork upon which girls will be more likely to value and feel good about physical activity participation throughout their developmental years (Brustad, 1996). Parental encouragement, direct support and facilitation, positive expectations, valuing physical activity and believing it important, fostering physical activity climates that focus on learning and enjoyment, and role modeling physical activity are all powerful means by which parents can facilitate the physical activity engagement of their daughters (Davison, Downs, & Birch, 2006; Fredricks & Eccles, 2004; Welk, 1999; White, 1996).

Coaches and Competitive Sport Climate

The coach-athlete social relationship is central to girls' adherence to organized sport programs and their satisfaction with these experiences. The coach-athlete relationship and associated interactions progress through stages (Bloom, 1985; Wylleman & Lavallee, 2004). In the initiation stage (3 to 9 years of age), coaches typically reward athletes for effort extended rather than results. In the development stage (10 to 15 years of age) coaches become more involved, more personally invested, and more dominant in their role. They expect athletes to advance their sport performance and achievement through discipline and hard work. Athletes at this age, however, prefer that coaches accomplish this through allowing them greater participation in decision-making, and developing warm interpersonal relationships and a positive group atmosphere. In the mastery stage (16 to 18 years of age), a more equal partnership develops between coaches and athletes, and athletes typically become more responsible for their personal training and progress (Wylleman & Lavallee, 2004).

The motivational climate within an organized sport team is most directly affected by the philosophies and practices of coaches. A consistent body of literature supports that coaches should create task-involving climates—climates that characteristically include a focus on mastering skills, reinforcement for effort and improvement, supportive peer relationships, and an inherent belief in the value and unique role of each individual athlete—because they are superior in producing desired psychological outcomes such as more enjoyment, greater satisfaction, intrinsically motivated behavior, positive relationships with others in the sport environment, and less anxiety (Galloway, 2003; Smith, Fry, Ethington, & Li, 2005). Female high school basketball players perceived a task-involved climate when their coaches used positive and encouraging feedback following both successful and unsuccessful performances, and when they did not ignore mistakes (Smith et al., 2005). Adolescent female soccer players (Allen & Howe, 1998; Wilco, 2004) and swimmers (Black & Weiss, 1992) accrued more positive psychological benefits when their coaches used praise and information after good performances, and encouragement and corrective information following errors. Adolescent volleyball players who adopted a higher task orientation and perceived a mastery climate in their training were more confident in their own abilities, more responsive to the coaches' expertise, and more open to other sources of information about their competence (Magyar & Feltz, 2003).

Ego-oriented climates—characterized by a focus on outperforming others, differential treatment of and favoritism toward high-ability team members, competitive peer relationships, and an inherent belief in the superiority of higher skilled athletes—lead to undesirable psychological outcomes such as greater anxiety, lower enjoyment and satisfaction, and more negative relationships with others in the sport environment (Smith et al., 2005). Female basketball players perceived an ego-involved climate as one in which their coaches gave less positive feedback and used more punishment feedback (Smith et al.). Hayashi (1998) found that female youth gymnasts who perceived their coaches as providing more punitive feedback were more likely to discontinue their participation.

Girls want coaches to provide good technical instruction and contingent positive feedback; allow them to participate in decision-making about goals, practices, and games; create positive team atmospheres; and develop warm interpersonal relationships with them (Mageau & Vallerand, 2003; Martin, Jackson, Richardson, & Weiller, 1999; Weiss, Ebbeck, & Horn, 1997). These characteristics of social relationships with coaches affect girls' continued participation through increasing their satisfaction with, and confidence in, their sport experiences.

Physical Education Teachers and School Climate

Adult physical activity leaders and school climates (Birnbaum et al., 2005) play influential roles in girls' attitudes (Silverman, 2005) and behaviors (Trudeau & Shephard, 2005). Research in physical education classrooms shows that student perceptions about the motivational climate, and the reward structure of the classroom created by teachers, affect their physical activity beliefs and interests. Students that perceive the physical education classroom climate to be more task- and mastery-oriented—with emphasis on learning, effort, and improvement—are more likely to give their best effort and persist in the face of difficulty than when the climate is perceived to be ego-oriented. Indicators of an ego- or performance-oriented environment in the physical education classroom would include more emphasis on the use of social comparison, demonstration of personal superiority, and public displays of prowess. Physical education students in ego-oriented climates typically demonstrate more negative attitudes, greater focus on outcomes rather than process, and have lower confidence beliefs (Magyar & Feltz, 2003). Treasure (1997), for example, found that 10- to 12-year-old children who perceived a higher-performance/lower-mastery climate in physical education class believed ability (rather than effort) caused success, experienced boredom, and had a negative attitude toward physical education. Children who perceived a higher-mastery/moderate-performance climate in physical education class experienced satisfaction in physical education, held positive attitudes toward physical education, believed both ability and effort caused success, and had high levels of perceived ability. Likewise, children who perceive autonomy-supportive behaviors from physical education teachers and mastery-involved climates in their classes have been found to be more likely to engage in self-directed leisure activity outside of physical education class (Standage, Duda, & Ntoumanis, 2003).

The ways in which physical activity leaders give feedback about motor performances affect girls' psychological responses as well. Informational feedback provides skill-relevant information in response to a physical attempt, and can provide descriptive feedback, which "describes" what just happened, or prescriptive feedback, which "prescribes" how to fix an error or how to maintain good performance for the future. Evaluative feedback places a judgment of approval or disapproval on the performance (such as praise or criticism). How girls interpret these types of feedback and the consequences for their perceptions of competence and ability appears to be moderated by a variety of factors such as age and sport experience. In general, however, feedback affects girls' perceptions of physical ability, effort, and future expectations for success (Amorose & Smith, 2003). Evidence shows that physical activity leaders—including physical education teachers, coaches, and exercise instructors—best encourage girls' participation through the use of positive, contingent, supportive, informational feedback combined with low punitive feedback (Horn, 2002). These leaders can also detract from girls' participation with an overemphasis on ignoring (no feedback), negative, and punitive feedback (Horn, 2002). Thus the message for physical education teachers is to establish a task-focused and positive environment to generate longer-term commitment to physical activity among girls. Beyond this, characteristics of a physical education classroom climate related to increased physical activity among adolescent girls includes not only developing an enjoyable and motivating environment but also providing a broader range of physical activity offerings such as aerobics, self-defense, and weight training in addition to competitive sports and other traditional physical education activities (Pate et al., 2005).

Peers and Social Climate

Among the most important social influences for girls is their peer group. Research on friendships and peer relationships in physical activity contexts provides us with substantial information that helps us understand girls' behaviors as friendships are related to self-perceptions, enjoyment, and motivated behavior in physical activity (Smith, 2003; Weiss & Stuntz, 2004). Dimensions of sport friendships include factors such as self-esteem enhancement and supportiveness, loyalty and intimacy, things in common, companionship and pleasant play, conflict resolution, and conflict (McDonough & Crocker, 2005; Weiss & Smith, 1999).

Qualities of friendships and other peer relationships vary with age, and, to a certain extent, with gender (Weiss & Smith, 2002). Weiss, Smith, and Theeboom (1996) found in interviews with children and youth about the positive and negative characteristics of their sport friendships that younger children (8 to 12 years of age) talked more about the importance of attractive physical qualities of their friends, prosocial behavior, and loyalty than did the older youth. Adolescents (13 to 16 years of age) more frequently mentioned the attractive personality attributes of their sport friends. Weiss and Smith (2002) found that children (10 to 13 years of age) cited companionship and pleasant play as more important sport friendship qualities than did adolescents (14 to 18 years of age), who rated loyalty and intimacy, things in common, and conflict more highly.

With respect to gender, in many ways boys and girls are similar in the qualities of their best sport friendships (Weiss & Smith, 2002). The only gender difference noted by Weiss et al. (1996) in their interviews was that girls, to a much greater extent than boys, cited emotional support as an important dimension of friendship quality. Weiss and Smith (2002), however, found that female junior tennis players (10 to 18 years of age) rated the qualities of self-esteem enhancement and supportiveness, loyalty and intimacy, and things in common as more characteristic of their sport friendships than did male players, who rated conflict as more typical in theirs.

Beyond dyadic interaction patterns with sport friends, the role of the broader sport peer group has consequences for girls' achievement motivation (Smith, 1999). Ntoumanis and Vazou (2005) identifi ed five dimensions of the peer motivational climate in youth sport clustered around task-involving peer climates (with dimensions of improvement, relatedness support, effort) and ego-involving peer climates (with dimensions of intra-team competition/ ability, intra-team conflict). The task-involving dimensions of the peer motivational climate positively influence girls' enjoyment, satisfaction, and competence beliefs (Vazou, Ntoumanis,

& Duda, 2006). Allen (2003) reported on three social motivational orientations among female adolescents in physical activity: affiliation, social status, and social recognition. These orientations were all important to the girls, and were positively related to their interest in and enjoyment of sport. Adherence to sport and exercise teams and groups is in part a function of the social environment within those groups, and the cohesion of the group. Spink (1995), for example, found among female participants 16 to 22 years of age in a recreational ringette league that those who perceived higher social cohesiveness within their team showed greater intention of returning the next season. Feelings of cohesion and belongingness were very important to their retention.

In the process of learning physical activity skills, peers are very important. Peer-assisted learning involves peers helping each other to acquire knowledge or skills. Peers in this sense serve as coping resources for each other during this learning process. In physical activity settings, girls are somewhat different than boys in their peer interactions during peer-assisted learning. Compared to boys, girls in dyadic situations such as peer-assisted learning are more sensitive to their partner and engage in more tutoring and cooperation (d'Arripe-Longueville, Gernigon, Huet, Winnykamen, & Cadopi, 2002). The results of their study (d'Arripe-Longueville et al.) involving peer-assisted learning of a swimming skill supported general developmental findings that "interactive mechanisms among boys are mainly centered on personal appropriation of knowledge, whereas those observed among girls focus more on transmitting and sharing knowledge" (p. 233). In other words, boys wanted to gather knowledge for themselves whereas girls shared their knowledge with others.

It is clear that peers and families are important sources of social support to children and youth for physically active lifestyles. Among children and youth 10 to 14 years of age, Duncan, Duncan, and Strycker (2005) found that social support was positively related to physical activity. The strongest finding was that young people who perceived greater support for physical activity from their friends were more active. Having parents, siblings, and friends watching their participation was another important source of support. Evidence that most children want their parents to watch them play was also found by Shields, Bredemeier, LaVoi, and Power (2005) in their study of youth in grades five through eight. Understanding the important role of peers in enhancing physical activity participation is essential to successful adherence efforts among girls.

Social Influences on Physical Expertise and Talent Development

Coaches and other adults play a critical social role in influencing girls' efforts toward developing expertise in sport performance. In order to achieve elite levels of sport skill performance, some researchers have demonstrated that athletes must accumulate thousands of hours of "deliberate practice"—described as effortful practice usually guided by a coach with the goal of facilitating performance improvements (Ericsson, Krampe, & Tesche-Romer, 1993; French & McPherson, 2004)—over at least a 10-year period (Ericsson, 1996). It is characterized by increasing amounts of practice time invested as athletes move up to higher levels of competition and age (Côté, Ericsson, & Law, 2005). Although intense commitment and preparation is necessary to achieve world-class sport performance, researchers in this area also say that coaches should provide sufficient periods of mental and physical rest allowing time for mental and physical recuperation, tissue regeneration, and avoidance of injury (Baker, Côté, & Deakin, 2005).

Intrinsic motivation for improvement also is inherent in the development of expert levels of sport skill. Retrospective evidence (French & McPherson, 2004) demonstrates that early in their careers, many elite athletes spent more time outside of organized practice sessions working on their individual motor skills than did their ultimately less-elite counterparts. A composite of research on sport practice (derived from reviews by scholars such as French & Thomas, 1987; Starkes, Deakin, Allard, Hodges, & Hays, 1996) would lead to a rough estimate of approximately 4 to 6 practice hours per week outside of organized practices spent by these future elite young athletes on their individual motor skills from about 8 to 12 years of age. Additive to the physical practice effects, these unstructured child-centered times are driven by intrinsic motivation and behavioral choice, and they allow opportunity for the development of creative play-making and decision-making skills required in so many sporting activities.

Recently, scholars studying talent development suggest that talent identification cannot be achieved by discrete measures such as coach-judged tryouts, but rather must be viewed through a lens that sees talent as a complex and dynamic system that changes as the athlete develops (Abbott, Button, Pepping, & Collins, 2005). Under this system, the emphasis is on sport leaders continuously assessing the changing learning potential of young sport participants rather than relying on time-isolated, genetically driven indicators of sport performance that are heavily influenced by physical maturity alone. Current systems of identifying sport talent early are limited by their emphases on isolated observations by adults, such as through sport tryouts, making cuts, and emphasizing coaching practices that invest more time with the "high talent" young athletes. The consequence is that many potentially talented girls are prematurely eliminated from organized sport. These authors (Abbott et al.) emphasize that youth sport talent identification strategies should focus on assessments of physical, motor, and psychological dispositions, and their capacity to develop across transitions in individual athletes. The powerful social influence exerted by the evaluations of coaches during such talent identification processes should be focused on maximizing opportunity for development and improvement.

Many elite athletes evidence a pattern of broad-based physical activity participation throughout their childhood years that lays a foundation for their later expertise, rather than intense and exclusive foci on sport specialization at early ages (Baker, Côté, & Deakin, 2005; Côté et al., 2005). Parents play an important role in providing these varied early opportunities for girls. This pattern, though, is somewhat dependent on the specific sport. The fact that success in sports such as gymnastics and figure skating requires intense early training and a career that peaks in puberty is a function not only of the demands of the sport and the physical and psychological capacities of girls at certain ages, but also of the social influence of governing boards, which choose to adopt rules and reward physical maneuvers that force girls to excel early before their bodies grow, specialize early, and accept and play with injuries (Hartman Nippert, 2005; Wiese-Bjornstal, 2001, 2004), and to follow the dictates of often authoritarian and overbearing coaches (Krane, Greenleaf, & Snow, 1997; Ryan, 1995; Whitney, 2005).

Not all sport skill practice can and should be adult structured, even for the development of sport talent. There are varying patterns of development and windows of time and experience within which elite levels of sport skill can be achieved. Adults who establish rules and standards for elite sport talent development programs are encouraged to use that power in ways that advantage and benefit girls' physical, mental, and social development.

Physical Activity Cognitions: What Girls Think

Maturational processes oblige girls to operate in a continually changing personal psychological climate as they move from early childhood through adolescence. Major components of girls' personal psychological climate include their cognitions or thoughts (such as beliefs and self-perceptions) and emotions or affect (such as anxiety and enjoyment). These interrelated and dynamic mechanisms become points at which practitioners can invest intervention efforts that can influence positive changes in the physical activity habits and experiences of girls. We fi rst consider the cognitions that girls have about physical activity.

Values, Interest, and Importance of Physical Activity

What girls think and believe about the value of physical activity and how much interest it holds for them affects their feelings and actions. Social cognitive theory (Bandura, 1986) and the large body of literature exploring its premises in the physical activity environment supports that beliefs about self and environment influence affect and behavior. Research indicates that girls are interested in sports and physical activity, but see them as less important than do boys. Elementary school girls report less interest in and believe sports to be less important and useful than do boys of the same age, but compared to other domains of interest (including math, reading, and music), girls rate their interest highest in sports (Wigfield et al., 1997). The interest and importance that children place on sport influences current and future activity choices, such as participating in sport or exercise (Fredricks & Eccles, 2004). Adolescents who place higher value on sport and health improvement are more physically active (Vilhjalmsson & Thorlindsson, 1998), but the question remains as to whether they learn to value these domains more highly because they participate, or whether they participate because they value them more highly.

A community survey in Canada found that girls, more so than boys, were interested in initiating or increasing their physical activity participation in a variety of sports (Varpalotai & Doherty, 2000). Girls in their community, however, had fewer sports program opportunities than boys. Certain aspects of sport participation such as social, fitness, and group dynamics were particularly valued by the girls (Varpalotai & Doherty), but their opportunities to meet these motives were limited by the lack of available programs. Expanded community opportunities for physical activity programming would be welcomed by the girls in this sample. One wonders how many other such inequities exist based on unchallenged misconceptions about what girls are interested in and what they value and seek in physical activity opportunities.

Ratings of sport importance become somewhat lower as girls move into adolescence, although their interest in sport remains high (Fredricks & Eccles, 2002). Garcia et al. (1998) found that the transition from elementary to junior high school was a time at which girls' physical activity beliefs changed. They found that following this transition girls reported less support for physical activity, lower exposure to physically active role models, and perceptions that the benefits of physical activity did not outweigh the barriers. Since perceived importance of a particular domain such as physical activity is a stronger predictor of participation than interest (Fredricks & Eccles, 2002, 2005) it is essential that girls perceive physical activity as important in their lives.

Motivation

Participation motivation refers to why people are motivated to engage in particular activities, in this case sport and physical activity. Weiss and Ferrar-Caja (2002) report on three consistent reasons why youth participate in sport: 1) physical competence or adequacy, 2) social acceptance and approval, and 3) enjoyment. Consistent reasons for stopping are the converse of these: not developing or demonstrating competence, not feeling socially accepted, not enjoying the experience or having fun, as well as being harmed (e.g., injury, hurt esteem, hurt feelings) (Weiss, 2000; Weiss & Ferrar-Caja, 2002).

Competence motivation (Harter, 1987) refers to the degree to which individuals are motivated from within to master challenging skills and demonstrate competence. In the physical domain, children inherently want to move, to be active and playful, to be challenged, and to master physical tasks. Unfortunately, factors in the physical activity social environment can cause them to lose this innate intrinsic motivation, and they instead adopt an extrinsic (outward) motivational focus guided by preference for easy skills, rewards, and a dependence on teacher or coach approval for performing skills (Weiss & Williams, 2004).

Children's motivation for physical activity is affected by their perceptions of their own ability in relation to the difficulty of the physical task (Weiss & Williams, 2004). If they believe the tasks to be too hard for their perceived abilities, they will be somewhat less likely to perform them. According to Weiss and Williams, preschool-aged children use egocentric and self-referenced assessments of task difficulty, judging whether a task is hard or not by whether or not it is hard for them personally. They equate high effort with high ability in these preschool years (Fry & Duda, 1997). In the early elementary years, children begin to adopt a more objective level or norm-referenced view of task difficulty, such that they recognize tasks that a few children can do are difficult, and that it takes high ability to complete those tasks. They are beginning to distinguish between ability and effort, but cannot separate them completely. In the later elementary and early middle school years, children begin to believe that performance on tasks can be improved with effort, but they believe that effort is the cause of ability. From about early adolescence on, children typically understand that the effects of effort on performance are limited by one's finite abilities, which indicates their ability to cognitively differentiate between ability and effort. Effort and ability are viewed as negatively related, meaning that if one has to work harder at something one must not have high ability (e.g., Fry & Duda, 1997; Weiss & Williams, 2004). These beliefs affect girls' perceptions of their own competence and potential for future success, and thus affect their motivated behavior in physical activity contexts.

Achievement motivation approaches focus on competence beliefs and subjective task values as predictive of motivated behaviors in achievement situations like sport. Competence beliefs refer to girls' perceptions of how good they are at physical activity and their expectations for future success. Subjective task values refer to the importance that girls place on physical activity participation. This approach to understanding motivation focuses on two orientations: task-involved, in which perceptions of competence are self-referenced with respect to performance and exerted effort (i.e., participants feel competent and successful when they have tried their best and have experienced personal performance improvement and/or task mastery), and ego-involved, in which perceptions of competence are dependent on comparisons with performance and exerted effort of relevant others (i.e., participants feel competent and successful when superior ability is revealed and they have shown more ability than others). Harwood, Hardy and Swain (2000) have suggested that within the ego-involved orientation a distinction should be made between perceptions of competence which are either dependent on demonstrating one's current ability, performance, and effort without comparisons to others ("self-referenced" ego involvement) or on demonstrating one's current ability, performance, and effort to be superior to that of others ("norm-referenced" ego involvement).

A large body of literature investigating goal perspectives and physical activity shows a task-involved perspective to be more strongly linked with positive beliefs and behaviors than an ego-involved perspective. Girls are more task-involved than boys, although some cultural differences have been observed (Guinn, Vincent, Semper, & Jorgensen, 2000). Many girls may be more interested in developing their personal capacities through sport than they are in establishing personal superiority over others (Ryckman & Hamel, 1995).

In terms of physical activity behaviors, looking at the physical activity motivational profiles of 12- to 15-year-olds, Wang and Biddle (2001) found that girls were disproportionately represented in the motivational clusters of "poorly motivated" and "amotivated" (i.e., a complete lack of motivation). Both of the motivational clusters were characterized by low levels of physical activity participation, self-worth, perceived competence, task orientation, and ego orientation. This verifies that something is missing in our efforts to help girls maintain continued motivation for physical activity participation.

Global Self-Esteem

Self-esteem is the evaluative component of believing in, feeling good about, and valuing oneself. Girls' self-esteem influences—and is influenced by—physical activity participation. A study of Mexican American adolescents, for example, found that higher self-esteem was associated with more physical activity involvement (Guinn et al., 2000). Adolescent females participating on sport teams had higher self-esteem than non-participant females (Keane, 2004). Achievement in team sports in early adolescence was associated with increased self-esteem in middle adolescence (Pedersen & Seidman, 2004), and participation by 10- to 12-year-old girls in a four-week sports camp resulted in improvements in their self-esteem (Hoganbruen, 1999). Among a diverse sample of Girl Scouts, nearly one-half reported that participating in an athletic activity made them feel good about, or esteem, themselves (Erkut, Fields, Sing, & Marx, 1996).

High self-esteem is associated with desirable psychological outcomes (such as low anxiety, generalized optimism, and happiness), but it should not come at the expense of esteem for others. Generalized self-esteem may be less important to physical activity participation, however, than more specific components of self-perceptions such as those girls hold about their physical competence.

Physical Competence Self-Perceptions

The perceptions that girls hold about their physical competence affect their physical activity behavior. In general, younger children are more optimistic and older children are more realistic in evaluations of their competence (Wigfield et al., 1997), with an overall trend indicating children's belief in their physical competence declines over time (Fredricks & Eccles, 2002). From early childhood, girls perceive themselves to be less competent in sports than do boys (Wigfield et al., 1997), although it may be that girls are more realistic about their competencies and boys overestimate their physical competence, especially in the early years. The global gender gap in physical competence beliefs and the value/importance placed on sport remains relatively constant from childhood to adolescence (Fredricks & Eccles, 2002). Adolescent female athletes in competitive sport, however, share with male athletes similar levels of competence perceptions, interest in sport, and valuing of sport as important and useful (Cox & Whaley, 2004).

Girls rely on a variety of sources to gather information about their physical competence. These sources change with age and as a function of certain psychological factors (for reviews, see Horn, 2004; Weiss & Amorose, 2005; Weiss & Williams, 2004). Preschool and early elementary aged children rely to a greater extent than do older youth upon parent and spectator feedback and game outcome as information sources for knowing how good they are at physical activities. During late elementary and early adolescent ages, children demonstrate greater reliance on peer comparison and evaluation from peers and coaches. Later adolescence finds greater dependence on self-referenced information about physical competence (e.g., effort exerted, goal achievement, skill improvement) and on a wider variety of information sources than at earlier ages. Halliburton and Weiss (2002), for example, found that among adolescent (12 to 14 years of age) female gymnasts, reliance on physical competence information sources varied as a function of skill level. Lower-level gymnasts relied more on perceptions of effort and enjoyment as sources of information, whereas higher-level gymnasts relied on feelings of nervousness and spectator feedback. Social comparison processes are also in operation affecting girls' self-concepts in physical settings (Chanel, Marsh, Sarrazin, & Bois, 2005). In adolescence, girls may use different sources than boys for competence judgments, with girls more focused on using attraction toward physical activity, goal achievement, and adult and peer feedback and evaluation as bases for their judgments (Weiss, 2000).

Weiss et al. (1997) reported that psychological factors also affect use of physical competence information sources. In their study, children with high anxiety and low competence self-perceptions were more reliant on external sources for physical competence information than were children with the opposite profile. The consequence was that the high anxious/low competence self-perception children were more psychologically vulnerable to coach and parent criticism. In other words, children who did not think they were very good at physical activity and who were anxious as a result of that belief relied more on what adults told them about their physical abilities. If adult comments reinforced their belief that they were not very good then they were more likely to believe it and thus be poorly motivated for future physical activity.

Physical self-perceptions and the associated self-confidence can be changed through experience. A physical activity program for 5- to 12-year-olds resulted in improvements in physical fitness and overcoming exercise barrier self-efficacy among girls (Annesi, Westcott, Faigenbaum, & Unruh, 2005), and a 12-week physical activity program for 11- to 14-year-old urban minority girls led to improvements in physical fitness and self-perceptions that included athletic competence and social acceptance (Colchico, Zybert, & Basch, 2000). Physical activity programs should identify strategies that enhance girls' physical self-perceptions and consequently encourage their participation.

Physical Appearance Self-Perceptions

How girls view and experience their bodies is central to understanding their physical activity behaviors. Body image can be appearance and/or performance focused. Girls, unlike boys, typically associate body image dissatisfaction with self-esteem (Furnham, Badmin, & Sneade, 2002), and low body image has been linked with risk behaviors in girls (Wild, Flisher, Bhana,

& Lombard, 2004). Girls as young as age five who participate in aesthetic sports (e.g., gymnastics, dance) show more concern about their weight (reflective of appearance-related concerns) than girls in no sports or non-aesthetic sports (Davison, Earnest, & Birch, 2002). This may be a function of the culture and sport-specific expectations (see Sociological Dimensions chapter), as other research has found that aesthetic sport girls' body images do not differ from controls at the outset of their participation (Poudevigne et al., 2003). For developing girls, early maturation relative to peers can relate to lower physical self-worth for girls (Smith, 2004). Perceived and ideal body size discrepancies predict weight management motives for exercise participation among adolescent girls (Ingledew & Sullivan, 2002), and in general weight and appearance concerns are primary motivators for physical activity participation among adolescent girls (McConnell, 1998; Strelan, Mehaffey, & Tiggemann, 2003).

Girls' thoughts about their bodies have emotional consequences. For example, social physique anxiety refers to feeling anxious about the evaluations others hold about one's body. High social physique anxiety causes girls to feel more anxious about how their bodies look, and relates to lower self-perceptions, disordered eating attitudes, and motives for exercise that focus on participating for appearance reasons and to look better to others (Eklund, Mack, & Hart, 1996; Smith, 2004). For these girls, exercise participation becomes a tool for impression management rather than something of inherent or intrinsic value for their mental and physical health, and as such anxiety and eating restrictions can make it difficult to limit excessive exercise even when contraindicated by health status (e.g., such as among adolescents with eating disorders) (Holtkamp, Hebebrand, & Herpertz-Dahlmann, 2004). Social physique anxiety tends to be higher in adolescent girls than boys (Eklund et al., 1996), and is in part related to the standards that the media conveys for the ideal female physique. One study of girls 9 to 16 years of age showed that 46% of girls made some attempt to look like female media figures, and higher physical activity levels were associated with the desire to look like these media figures (Taveras et al., 2004). Some researchers have found, however, that less body satisfaction in adolescents is related to lower levels of physical activity participation (Neumark-Sztainer, Goeden, Story, & Wall, 2004) and to disturbed eating (Strelan et al., 2003). The goal is to help girls have realistic and healthy body images and recognize the importance of physical activity for overall health and well-being—not just for appearance-focused reasons.

Moral Reasoning and Sportsmanship Attitudes

Sport morality is concerned with the beliefs, judgments, and actions surrounding what is deemed ethical or unethical in a sport context (Shields & Bredemeier, 1995). Moral development is the growth and experiential process through which girls learn to reason and act morally. Moral reasoning refers to the cognitive process of deciding between what is right and wrong, ethical or unethical. During the elementary years, children engage in "parallel" reasoning about moral issues in sport and in life; in other words, they use similar reasoning processes in both contexts. As they move toward the early adolescent years, however, they begin to engage in "divergent" reasoning (Bredemeier, 1995); they reason at a higher moral level about daily life issues than they do about competitive sport life issues. Thus, for example, while they might see pushing, elbowing, or punching someone as wrong in daily life, they may view those same actions as acceptable in a sport context because they are "part of the game" or because they serve a goal of getting the ball or scoring the goal. They engage in more "egocentric" reasoning in sport, termed "game reasoning" or "bracketed morality" (Bredemeier, 1995). The longer they stay in competitive sports—in particular sports involving contact—the more they use lower levels of reasoning about moral dilemmas in sport (Beller & Stoll, 1995). When faced with having to choose between displaying concern for an opponent and losing a contest, the pre-eminent choice is to maximize personal gain (Vallerand, Deshaies, & Cuerrier, 1997).

Children in the elementary years who reason about moral issues at a lower level are more accepting of aggressive acts in sport as legitimate (Duquin & Shroeder-Braun, 1996; Shields & Bredemeier, 1995; Solomon, 2004; Stephens, 2001). This pattern continues through the later elementary years, with team norms related to tolerance for aggressive behaviors beginning to predict the aggressive actions of girls and boys. Some researchers have also noted gender differences beginning at this time and continuing through the early adolescent years such that females tend to use higher levels of moral reasoning (Beller & Stoll, 1995; Shields & Bredemeier, 2001) and are more concerned about coach improprieties than are males (see review by Solomon, 2004). By early adolescence those children who find aggressive actions in sport more legitimate are more likely to actually commit aggressive acts in sport contexts. The same appears to hold true for later adolescence, with older adolescents rating coach improprieties as less problematic than they did at younger ages (Duquin & Shroeder-Braun, 1996; Solomon, 2004). Stephens (2001) found that among girls in grades 4 to 12 attending a sports camp, girls' perceptions of what their teammates do and their willingness to injure others at the request of the coach were the major predictors of their aggressive behavior tendencies. Stephens defined aggression as an intentional verbal or physical action intended to cause injury to another person.

Even though girls may reason from a more mature perspective than males, many girls are socialized to accept aggression and questionable ethical behavior through their years in competitive sport, rather than learning the oft-claimed lessons of good sportsmanship. It is true that there are semantic and confusing distinctions that need to be made in what is meant by "aggressiveness." "Aggressiveness" is encouraged, developed, and applauded in many sports. For example, adolescent female ice hockey players speak of "the importance of being aggressive, which they define as being powerful and sometimes fearless in use of the body" (Theberge, 2003, p. 497). Th e difficulty is that coaches, parents, and other adults in youth sport environments often fail to distinguish semantically or otherwise between "good" aggression—using bodies in powerful ways within the rules of play and spirit of the game and not intended to harm opponents—and "bad" aggression—using bodies in ways that are against the rules, harmful to others, self-injurious, or unnecessary.

With respect to sportsmanship attitudes, a substantial number of girls, parents, and coaches report that significant ethical problems, manifested in poor sportsmanship attitudes and behavior, exist in some youth sport cultures. For example, Shields et al. (2005) found among youth sport participants in grades 5 to 8 that 27% report that they had acted like "bad sports." Fourteen percent of parents admit to yelling at or arguing with sport officials, and 8% of coaches make fun of their athletes, which indicates the behavioral patterns of adults have room for improvement. Four percent of children in this sample described having been kicked, hit, or slapped by their coaches. Sportsmanship programs relying on prosocial behavior theories (e.g., Wells, Ellis, Paisley, & Arthur-Banning, 2005) can be one step toward working to rectify this culture, although systemic change in the philosophical grounding of youth sport structures is essential before meaningful progress toward improved moral climates can be made. Girls must be given explicit opportunities to develop their moral reasoning capacities through physical activity and organized sport experiences.

Physical Activity Affect: What Girls Feel

What girls believe about physical activity, their attitudes toward physical activity and their physical competence, and their previous experiences in physical activity settings influence their affective or emotional experiences in sport. In turn, the affective experiences associated with participation influence future physical activity behaviors. Thus, affect is an important component of physical activity participation because it serves both as an impetus for and a consequence of participation. Both positive and negative affective components are part of physical activity experiences.

Enjoyment

The positive affective states of enjoyment and fun are central to girls' participation in physical activity, and have been common themes in other sections of this report. Fun is the most prevalent reason girls give for participating in sport (e.g., Ehlinger & Katz, 1995; Center for Research on Girls & Women in Sport, 1997; Shields et al., 2005). Enjoyable aspects of sport and physical activity participation encompass a broad spectrum, such as optimal challenges, social connection, intrinsic pleasure in activity, mastery-focused climates, skill improvement, and positive reactions from important adults. Enjoyment in school-based physical activity programs relates to overall level of physical activity (Dishman et al., 2005). Enjoyment is a key component of the sport commitment model (Scanlan, Simons, Carpenter, Schmidt, & Keeler, 1993), and is the strongest predictor of commitment to organized sport (Weiss, 2003; Weiss, Kimmel, & Smith, 2001). When sport is enjoyable, girls are more likely to stay involved (Crocker, Hoar, McDonough, Kowalski, & Niefer, 2004). A task orientation—as opposed to an ego orientation—is more explicitly linked to greater enjoyment, positive engagement, and revitalization (Vlachopoulos, Biddle, & Fox, 1997). Among 11- to 14-year-olds in physical education class, Vlachopoulos et al. (1997) found a positive relationship among task involvement, perceptions of success, and positive emotion. They found an inverse relationship between perceived success and negative affect. Unstructured physically active play, such as that afforded by school recess periods and after-school free play, is a very enjoyable and underestimated source of exercise for girls (Jarett, 2002; Pellegrini & Bohn, 2005; Pellegrini & Smith, 1998). Again, this reinforces that for best retention and adherence to physical activity programs, creating a task-oriented climate that leads to enjoyment is essential.

Stress, Anxiety, and Burnout

Excessive stress leads to physical and mental consequences, such as fatigue, injury, decreased enjoyment, and emotional control problems. Anxiety, an emotional response to a perceived threat that comprises cognitive and physiological responses, is another one of these consequences. Researchers in sport psychology have explored competitive trait anxiety, a relatively stable personality disposition toward anxiety, and competitive state anxiety, an anxiety response in a specific competitive sport situation. Both interpersonal and situational factors affect competitive state anxiety (Crocker et al., 2004; Hall & Kerr, 1997). High trait anxiety, low self-esteem and confidence, and low perceived ability are interpersonal factors predictive of higher state anxiety, as are situational factors such as individual sports, losses, more parental pressure, greater situation importance, and ego-oriented climates. Understanding these antecedents of anxiety can direct coaches and parents toward ways of alleviating anxiety in those under their purview.

The pressures of excessive sport performance expectations, limited control over one's sport participation, and perceptions of stress and anxiety can result in burnout. It is a condition characterized by physical and psychological exhaustion, perceptions of a reduced sense of accomplishment, and no longer caring about sport (Raedeke & Smith, 2004). An array of personal and situational factors affects young athlete burnout, as illustrated in a series of studies on burnout in junior tennis by Gould and colleagues (Gould, Tuffey, Udry, & Loehr, 1996a; 1996b; 1997). Personal factors affecting the burnout of the tennis players included more perfectionist tendencies and less motivation. Situational factors affecting burnout included negative parental influences and unhelpful coaches. Raedeke's (1997) study of 13- to 18-year-old senior level swimmers showed that those whom he labeled "malcontents"—who were swimming because they felt obligated or pressured to and who were unhappy with their participation—scored much higher on burnout than did the other swimmers. Higher burnout among a second sample of 14- to 19-year-old senior level swimmers was related to greater perceived stress, fewer general coping behaviors, and lower satisfaction with social support (Raedeke & Smith, 2004). Burnout is related to coaching behaviors such as less social support, positive feedback, training and instruction, and democratic behavior (Wylleman & Lavallee, 2004) and higher levels of autocratic behavior (e.g., Raedeke & Smith, 2004). Negative consequences of anxiety and burnout include a number of factors such as reduced interest and positive affect, performance decrements, and discontinuation.

Coping consists of those cognitive, emotional, and behavioral efforts that people use to manage difficult life situations. Three dimensions of coping with the stress and anxiety of sport situations have been identified: 1) problem-focused coping (trying to change the situation), 2) emotion-focused coping (managing the emotions associated with the situation), and 3) avoidance coping (removing oneself from the situation). General evidence suggests that girls use emotion-focused coping (in particular, social support) and avoidance coping (in particular, resignation) more frequently than do boys. Minimizing perceptions of excessive stress by providing a more positive and task-involved climate and developing coping and social resources among girls are important mechanisms by which continued participation in physical activity can be achieved.

Mental Health

Regular exercise is of benefit to many psychiatric and mental health conditions such as depression and anxiety. Thomson, Pangrazi, Friedman, and Hutchinson (2003) reported a strong association between depression and level of physical activity and health-related fitness among 8- to 12-year-old children. Greater depression was associated with lower levels of physical activity. What is not clear is whether depression leads to inactivity, or whether inactivity is a contributor to depression among these children. Crews, Lochbaum, and Landers (2004) found that low-income, fourth-grade children in a six-week aerobic fitness program reported less depression and higher self-esteem at the completion of the program. Motl, Birnbaum, Kubik, and Dishman (2004) observed that changes in physical activity among seventh and eighth grade youth were related to depressive symptoms. Steiner, McQuivey, Pavelski, Pitts, and Kraemer (2000) found that adolescents participating in sports reported fewer mental and physical health problems than did their peers. Better psychosocial functioning has been associated

with participation in physical activity among children and youth with developmental disabilities (Block, Griebenauw, & Brodeur, 2004), including decreases in aggression and off-task
behaviors, and increases in self-esteem, social competence, and peer relationships (Dykens,
Rosner, & Butterbaugh, 1998), and improved social and sport skills (Bernabe & Block, 1994).
Physical activity has also been linked to improved general cognitive functioning (Etnier et al.,
1997). More research exploring the relationships between physical activity and mental health
among girls is needed to help us understand these important connections.

Summary and Implications

What is psychologically good for girls in physical activity contexts is very consistent with the
tenets of a positive youth development approach. This general approach focuses on how we
can use important mechanisms like physical activity to help young people strengthen their
perceptions of competence, usefulness, belonging, and empowerment (Minnesota
Commission on Out-of-School Time, 2005; U. S. Department of Health and Human Services
[U.S. DHHS], 2006). The objectives of a positive youth development approach to offering programs for young people involve the following: promoting social, emotional, cognitive, behavioral, physical, and moral competence; fostering resilience, self-efficacy, and identity; and
developing connection and civic engagement (Catalano, Berglund, Ryan, Lonczak, &
Hawkins, 1998). These are the same objectives conveyed by the psychology of physical activity literature just reviewed.

Experiences and qualities central to positive youth development include building specific
Developmental Assets® (Search Institute®, 2005). Developmental Assets are clusters of positive
external assets received via the social climate and social institutions (e.g., support, empowerment, boundaries and expectations, and constructive use of time) and internal psychological
assets generated through positive experiences (e.g., commitment to learning, positive values,
social competencies, and positive identity) (Search Institute, 2005). Having more
Developmental Assets is associated with more positive and successful youth development
(Search Institute, 2005). Girls can develop these assets through properly structured physical
activity opportunities as one important avenue for positive youth development (Petitpas,
Cornelius, Van Raalte, & Jones, 2005). These opportunities should help girls avoid risk behaviors (Search Institute, 2005), develop healthy lifestyles (Carnegie Corporation of New York,
1996), and strengthen themselves for the challenges of adolescence (Henderson & King, 1998).
Targeted programs with institutional and organizational support are key elements contributing to the success of physical activity interventions with girls (Vescio, 2003), and initiatives and
programs intended to use sport as a means of inspiring and motivating girls for success in
other areas of life such as academics also make valuable contributions to positive youth development (Cadwallader, 2001; Sharp, Kendall, & Schagen, 2003).

In sum, demographic, psychological, behavioral, social, and environmental factors all
affect girls' physical activity participation (Motl, Dishman, Saunders, Dowda, & Pate, 2004).
This review has focused on establishing what we know about the psychological and social correlates of physical activity participation among female children and youth to serve as a foundation for the next step, which is to identify how ideal physical activity opportunities might
be structured for girls in a way that takes into account these multiple influences and builds
positive attitudes and competencies. Many of the common recommendations for how to
increase girls' physical activity participation are tied to an understanding of the psychological

factors that motivate, attract, and retain girls' interest and energy. These recommendations revolve around stimulating interest, promoting engagement, creating a motivating climate, and ensuring success. Our goal is that professionals invested across a broad spectrum of physical activity participation opportunities employ this knowledge in creating psychologically ideal approaches for diverse girls of varied ages and skill levels.

Why is this essential? When we concern ourselves with finding more ways to attract girls to physical activity, facilitate their activity, and keep them motivated and interested throughout their formative years we promote a lifetime pattern of healthy living. Physical activity in the childhood and adolescent years relates to the level of physical activity later in life (Telama, Laakso, Yang, & Viikari, 1997). Sport psychology research findings help us better understand how to sustain the motivation and involvement of those girls who already participate, as well as define how to develop and improve the motivational climate and participation incentives and reduce the barriers for those girls who are inactive.

Further Reading

Schnieder, M., Fridlund Dunton, G., & Cooper, D. M. (2008). Physical activity and physical self-concept among sedentary adolescent females: An intervention study. *Psychology of Sport and Exercise, 9,* 1–14.

Discussion Questions

1. What are some of the positive benefits female athletes experience when participating in sport?

2. Compare and contrast the influence of coaches, parents, and peers on female sport participation? Which socializing agent has the most influence on the initiation stage of sport involvement? Is this the same agent that has the most influence on the maintenance stage and keeping girls involved in sport?

3. Based on the findings presented in this article, what is one research question on the psychological dimension of girls' sport participation that would be worth exploring? For example, are there any relationships that would be important to research that were not addressed in this review article?

2

Teaching Athletes to Connect and Collaborate

The Power of Peer Leadership in Sport

T. Michelle Magyar

I'm becoming comfortable with who I am and the way I look.
I like my muscles now. I look this way for a reason;
my body has a purpose—it helps me achieve my goals.

Jenny Thompson, Swimming

Drawing from the sport psychology literature, leadership is traditionally thought of as a behavioral process in which coaches can influence their athletes toward the accomplishment of established goals (Chelladurai, 1984; Chelladurai & Riemer, 1998). By focusing only on the behavioral mechanisms of leadership, this common approach neglects to consider the social and cognitive dimensions of the leadership process. Furthermore, the inherent hierarchical power structure of a sport team positions the coach in the central leadership role exceedingly above his/her athletes, and thus, the less clearly defined leadership role of the athlete receives little empirical scrutiny.

217

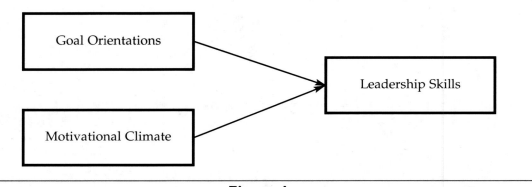

Figure 1

Hypothesized model of achievement goal theory and leadership skills in athletes.

The purpose of this study is to adopt a social cognitive approach in the examination of peer leadership by testing the relationships between achievement goals and leadership skills in athletes (Duda, 2001; Nicholls, 1984, 1989). A summary of the research on leadership specific to athletes is presented, followed by a brief introduction to a current trend in industrial/organizational leadership research that emphasizes skill development. A synthesis of the theoretical tenets of achievement goal theory is then provided as the backdrop from which a social cognitive conceptual model is proposed to test the hypothesized personal and situational achievement goal determinants of leadership skills in athletes (see Figure 1).

Leadership in Athletes

Initial research on leadership in athletes associates formal leadership with the centrality of position, or the actual location of the athlete relative to his/her teammates (Gill & Perry, 1979; Loy, Curtis, & Sage, 1978; Tropp & Landers, 1979). With formal leadership, athletes are typically designated as the "team captain" by their teammates and coaches. Researchers that examine the relationship between group structure and leadership demonstrate that positions requiring more interaction, for example, baseball and softball infielders and catchers, significantly predict team captain selection over the positions that require less interaction, such as, pitchers and outfielders. However, Tropp and Landers (1979) counter this hypothesis in the sport of field hockey, finding that formal leaders are individuals that display "leadership," have more years experience playing at the varsity level, and are well liked by their teammates.

Additional research on leadership in athletes focuses on informal leadership and identifies performance ability, gender roles, starter status, age/grade level, and interpersonal attraction as attributes of effective emergent leaders (Glenn & Horn, 1993; Rees, & Segal, 1984; Yukelson, Weinberg, Richardson, & Jackson, 1986). Opposing the concept of the designated leader is the notion of emergent leadership in which an athlete may be perceived as a leader but does not receive a formal title such as team captain. For example, athletes receiving high peer scores on leadership ability self-reported higher scores on masculinity, perceived soccer competence, and competitive trait anxiety, whereas, the coaches' ratings of leader ability were associated with only the athlete's skill ranking (Glen & Horn, 1993).

While the findings from these investigations distinguish behavioral characteristics of peer leaders that are identified as meaningful by their peers, this research is a theoretical and descriptive in nature. Initial attempts to operationalize leadership specific to the athlete's responsibilities were marginal at best. For example, Tropp and Landers (1979) asked athletes to rate each teammate on leadership by responding to the question "How much of a team leader is she?" While Yukelson et al. (1986) assessed leadership with the question "Who do you look to with admiration or for leadership within the group during practice or competitive situations?" Given the divergent perspectives regarding the conceptual definition and essential features of effective leadership, this descriptive approach is problematic.

Additional empirical research on the social, emotional, and behavioral dimensions of leadership in athletes is necessary to understand the pertinent skills and abilities that reflect athletes' conceptions regarding the definition and meaning of the leadership process. In order to assess and understand individual differences in leadership, researchers must determine the conception and expectations of athlete leadership (i.e., "What is an athlete leader supposed to do to lead the group?") and the mechanisms behind leader conduct (i.e., "What skills are necessary to engage in this leadership?"). More importantly, the hypothesized relationships between meaning and construction with the mechanisms of influence should be derived from theory that allows for researchers to test proposed determinants and mechanisms of athlete leadership. Beyond the implications of improved performance, researchers must discern the positive psychological benefits of leadership, so that parents, coaches, and practitioners may continue to foster the holistic development of athletes (Kretchmar, 2005; Larson, 2000).

Leadership Skill Development

Recent trends in leadership research in the organizational/industrial and military settings assess the process of leadership by adopting a skill-based model of leadership development (Day, 2000; Mumford et al., 2000a, 2000b; Marta, Leritz, & Mumford, 2005). Day (2000) refers to leadership development as a collectivist approach that enhances interpersonal skills (e.g., social awareness and social skills) in all group members and prepares everyone for informal leadership opportunities. He contrasts leadership development from the traditional notion of leader development, or the individualistic perspective that promotes intrapersonal skills (e.g., self-awareness, confidence, and regulation) in only formal leaders. Leadership skills may be partially distinguished from personality traits in that they are not always inherent attributes of the leader, but rather can be learned and developed over time (i.e., complex problem solving skills, creative thinking, etc.), and their use may fluctuate given certain situations. By examining the skills and abilities of leadership, this conceptualization provides a more inclusive social, emotional, and developmental approach that engages everyone in the leadership process and can delineate the developmental processes that may be involved in teaching people how to become leaders. Furthermore, by attending to both individual leader and collective leadership development, sport teams may maximize their leadership capacity.

Mumford and his colleagues examined the developmental differences in the multi-dimensionality of skill acquisition and leadership patterns among military officers as a function of experience and timing of leadership opportunities (Mumford et al., 2000a, 2000b). Specifically, they examined the development of the following leadership skills: complex problem solving, solution construction, social judgment, creative thinking, and leadership expertise. As expected, the senior-level leadership positions, by nature, required multi-dimensional leadership patterns and skills. Senior level officers were better at translating new ideas into actions, and spent more time appraising the implications of a novel situation, which ultimately resulted in a higher quality solution to the problem.

Similar to the military setting, athletes may also experience meaningful transitions in leadership skill development. In the same manner in which skills were identified as leadership skills in the military setting, future research on leadership in athletes should identify skills that are pertinent to the individual and collective conceptions of leadership in sport. Further exploration of individual differences in athletes' perceptions regarding the importance of certain leadership skills may reflect important transitions in the acquisition and underlying mechanisms of leadership in athletes.

This skills-based approach to leadership is relevant for sport teams, particularly for athletes performing a skill in which they are greatly dependent on each other. One sport that embodies this dependency dynamic is rowing. According to Steiner's (1972) task typology, rowing may be classified as a unitary additive task, meaning all rowers perform the same aspects of the task at the same time, and the sum of each individual rower's output determines the group outcome. Therefore, to limit the leadership skill development to only one athlete as opposed to all athletes contradicts the performance requirements inherent in the sport of rowing and denies the athletes the feelings of empowerment from the sense of responsibility and control associated with leadership.

Achievement Goal Theory

The social cognitive framework of achievement goal theory describes how individuals define personal ability, successful experiences, and task difficulty using two primary achievement goals, task/mastery and ego/performance (Ames, 1992a, 1992b; Bandura, 1997; Duda, 2001; Dweck & Leggett, 1988; Nicholls, 1984, 1989). With task/mastery goals, the objective is to acquire skills and knowledge, exhibit effort, and experience optimal challenges and personal improvement. Ego/performance goals, however, represent a preoccupation with personal ability, or more importantly, the desire to demonstrate superior ability relative to others.

Achievement goal theory provides the framework from which to study variations in goal perspectives at the individual level through personal goal orientations (e.g., task and ego) and at the situational level through perceptions of motivational climate (e.g., mastery and performance). Research establishes an empirical link between goal orientations and perceptions of the motivational climate with achievement-related beliefs such as sources of confidence, collective efficacy beliefs, enjoyment, interest, and satisfaction in sport (Duda & Whitehead, 1998; Magyar & Feltz, 2003; Magyar, Feltz, & Simpson, 2004; Newton & Duda, 1999; Treasure & Roberts, 1998).

Personal and situational goal perspectives not only reveal athletes personal beliefs regarding achievement, but also conceptions of knowledge, fairness, justice, and general views about the world (Nicholls, 1989, 1992). Therefore, through the assessment of achievement goals, researchers may explore how people construct meaning of social conventions in sport and how these conceptions are regulated by one's goal perspective while engaged in a sport task. For example, Nicholls (1989) postulated that an emphasis on normative comparison (ego orientation) is likely to correspond with a lack of concern with fairness and justice. Whereas, the perceived importance of self-referenced criteria (task orientation) will likely coincide with the value of effort, collective engagement, respect for rules, and proper conduct.

Research provides empirical evidence Nicholls (1989) postulation through the relationships between achievement goals and beliefs regarding social conventions such as the purpose of sport (Duda, 1989; White, Duda, & Keller, 1998) and sportspersonship (Gano-Overway et al., 2005). Specifically, task orientation aligns with intrinsic, pro-social, and cooperative views about the purpose of sport (e.g., master a skill, work well with others); while ego orientation correlates with more extrinsic and self-serving motives (e.g., outperform others to gain recognition).

Duda and Balaguer (1999) examined athletes' goal orientations, and perceptions of the motivational climate in relation to their perceptions of their coach's leadership style and found that the climate created by the coach was significantly related to athletes' preferred and perceived facets of leadership behavior. When the players perceived that their coach created a mastery climate, they were more likely to perceive their coach as demonstrating positive leadership behaviors. Whereas, athletes who perceived a predominately performance climate were less likely to view their coaches as leaders. These findings further reinforce the relevance of the perceived climate reflecting the opinions that athletes may adopt about their coach, and, in particular, the significance of the motivational climate in the display of leadership.

To date, research in sport psychology has yet to link achievement goal theory to the social dimension of leadership specific to athletes. For example, leadership requires skills that represent the underlying dimensions of both task/mastery and ego/performance achievement goals. If the situation calls for collaboration, such as solving interpersonal conflict among members of the team, one would expect task orientation and mastery motivational climate to emerge as a strong correlate. On the other hand, a situation that calls for exerting power over others to lead a team would have a stronger association with ego/performance personal and situational goal structure. Therefore, both task/mastery and ego/performance goal dimensions may be related to leadership in some capacity.

Based on the tenets of achievement goal theory, task orientation was hypothesized to positively predict performance-execution skills, motivational-interpersonal skills, and respect-communication skills, and negatively predict negative tactics. Ego orientation was hypothesized to positively predict performance-execution skills and negative tactics.

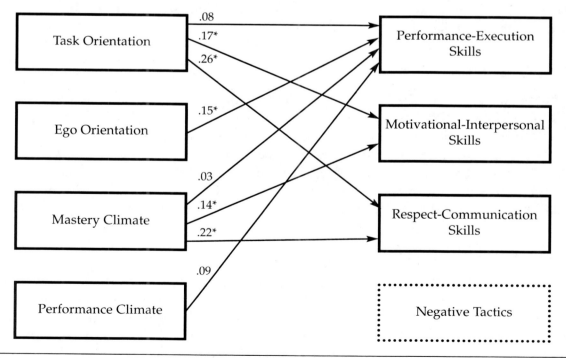

Figure 2
Path model of achievement goal theory and leadership skills in athletes.

Perceptions of mastery climate were hypothesized to positively predict performance-execution skills, motivational-interpersonal skills, and respect-communication skills, while perceptions of performance climate were hypothesized to positively predict performance-execution skills and negative tactics and negatively predict motivational-interpersonal skills, and respect-communication skills.

Method

Participants

Participants were 375 female intercollegiate rowers, however eight athletes were classified as "spares" and were removed, resulting in 367 rowers, ages 18–37 years ($M = 19.63$, $SD = 1.56$), from 17 collegiate rowing programs located in the Western, Midwestern, and Eastern regions of the United States. A total of 54 boats were included in the current sample (coxed eight $8 + n = 47$ and coxed four $4 + n = 7$). The rowers had an average of 2.3 years' experience rowing in college ($SD = 1.8$) and viewed the sport of rowing to be very important ($M = 8:21$, $SD = 1.36$). A total of 199 athletes (54.2%) rowed varsity, 43 (11.7%) rowed junior varsity, and 125 (34.1%) rowed novice.

Measures

Demographic

All participants completed a demographic background questionnaire. This questionnaire packet included a series of items that assessed athletes' years of experience in rowing (e.g., "How long have you rowed in a competitive program?") and experience as leaders (i.e., "Have you ever held a leadership role of any kind?").

Goal Orientations in Sport

A modified version of the Task and Ego Orientation in Sport Questionnaire (M-TEOSQ; Duda & Nicholls, 1992) was used to assess individual differences in goal orientation within the sport context. Certain items within the task and ego dimensions were modified to reflect the nature of the sport of rowing.[1] Athletes were asked to respond to the stem "I feel most successful in rowing when . . ." and respond to each item on a 5-point Likert scale ranging from 1 (strongly disagree) to 5 (strongly agree). The final M-TEOSQ was a 15-item measure with eight items for the task dimension ($a = .80$) seven items for ego ($a = .81$).

Perceived Motivational Climate

The motivational climate of each team was measured using a modified version of the Perceived Motivational Climate in Sport Questionnaire-2 (MPMCSQ-2). The original 33-item inventory developed by Newton and Duda (1999) that assesses the extent to which athletes perceive the situationally emphasized goals on their current team as mastery or performance was reduced to 12 items. This reduced version was based on previous research that employed the PMCSQ-2 in a study of rowers (Magyar, Feltz, & Simpson, 2004). Five items represented mastery climate (i.e., "each rower contributes in some important way"), and seven items assessed perceptions of performance climate (i.e., "coach favors some rowers more than others"). Athletes were asked to respond on a 5-point Likert scale and indicate the degree to which he/she strongly disagrees (1) to strongly agrees (5) with each item. Both performance and mastery subscales demonstrated reliability with Cronbach alphas of .70 and .78.

Leadership Skills

The Athlete Leadership Skills in Sport Questionnaire (A-LSSQ) measure was developed for the purpose of this study. This measure was constructed in line with achievement goal theory (Nicholls, 1984) to represent the cognitive, behavioral and affective leadership skills within the task and ego dimensions and assessed the perceived importance of skills used by athlete leaders. This is a 26-item measure with the following four subscales: Performance-Execution (ten items; e.g., "Be one of the best athletes on the team"), Motivational-Interpersonal (seven items; e.g., "Be sensitive to the needs of every teammate"), Respect-Communication (five items; e.g., "Communicate effectively with teammates"), and Negative Tactics (four items; "Encourage teammates to win at all cost"). All subscales except the negative reached acceptable levels of reliability (a = .72, .73, .73, and .60, respectively). After removing the items "Intimidate others to get the work done" and "'Call someone out' who is not giving 100%" negative tactics achieved an alpha level of .76.

Results

Descriptive Statistics

Two hundred eighty-six athletes (77.9%) reported having previous leadership experiences. Among this group who occupied leadership roles, 128 (34.9%) reported having leadership experience in sport (e.g., team captain in high school). The majority of the entire sample considered themselves to be leaders in crew (n = 241, 65.7%) while only 26 athletes (7.1%) were current team captains. On average, this sample of athletes considered leadership to be fairly important (M = 7.45, SD = 2.0).

Task orientation was significantly correlated with all of the leadership skills, while ego orientation and mastery motivational climate were significantly correlated with performance-execution, motivational-interpersonal, and respect-communication, and performance climate was not associated with any of the leadership skills (see Table 1).

Predictive Utility of Achievement Goals

Partial support for the hypothesized relationships was found as multiple regression analysis revealed that task orientation (β = .21, p < .001), ego orientation (β = .14, p < .01), mastery climate (β = .15, p < .01), and performance climate (β = .12, p < .05) significantly predicted and explained 10% of the variance in performance-execution leadership skills. Related to motivational-interpersonal skills, task orientation (β = .17, p < .01) and mastery climate (β = .17, p < .01) significantly predicted and explained 5% of the variance. Task orientation (β = .25, p < .001) and mastery climate (β = .25, p < .001) also emerged as significant predictor of respect-communication explaining 14% of the variance, while task orientation (β = −.15, p < .01) and ego orientation (β = .11, p < .05) significantly predicted and explained 3% of the variance in negative tactics.

TABLE I   Means, Standard Deviations, and Correlations Among Conceptual Model Variables

	1	2	3	4	5	6	7	8
1. Task	1.0							
2. Ego	.15**	1.0						
3. Mastery Climate	.28***	−.03	1.0					
4. Performance Climate	−.11*	.11*	−.46***	1.0				
5. Performance-Execution	.27***	.21***	.17**	.05	1.0			
6. Motivational-Interpersonal	.20***	.04	.19***	−.004	.56***	1.0		
7. Respect-Communication	.32***	.10	.29***	−.08	.50***	.44***	1.0	
8. Negative Tactics	−.14**	.10	−.05	.09	.09	.09	−.15**	1.0
M(SD)	4.38 (.43)	2.84 (.73)	4.06 (.59)	2.82 (.70)	4.00 (.45)	4.03 (.52)	4.60 (.43)	1.40 (.71)

Note: *$p < .05$, **$p < .01$, ***$p < .001$

To test the hypothesized predictors simultaneously and examine the fit of the conceptual model, a recursive path analysis on the estimated covariances of directly observed variables (e.g., subscale scores) was conducted with LISREL 8.52 (Scientific Software International, Inc, Chicago, IL). The negative tactics subscale was not included in the model because it consisted of only two items (see Figure 2). The overall hypothesized model demonstrated an acceptable fit to the data X2 (15) = 59.77. Root Mean Square Error of Approximation = .09, Goodness of Fit Index = .96, Normed Fit Index = .87, Comparative Fit Index = .90. Examination of the amount of variance explained in the endogenous variables ranged from 6% of the variance in motivationalinterpersonal skills measure, 14% in respect-communication skills measure, and 38% in performance-execution skills measure. Task orientation emerged as a significant predictor of motivational-interpersonal skills ($\beta = .17$, $p < .05$) and respect-communication skills ($\beta = .26$, $p < .05$), while ego orientation significantly predicted performance-execution ($\beta = .15$, $p < .05$). Mastery motivational climate significantly predicted motivational-interpersonal skills ($\beta = .14$, $p < .05$) and respect-communication skills ($\beta = .22$, $p < .05$). Both mastery motivational climate and performance climate failed to predict performance-execution skills.

Discussion

Regardless, of how it is designated, or how it emerges, it is apparent that leadership is an integral part of athletic performance. A leaderless group will often become a frustrated group with no guidance or direction. The current findings provide an important contribution to the understanding of leadership specific to athletes. The primary purpose of this study was to develop and test a conceptual model of leadership in athletes based on achievement goal theory (Duda, 2001; Nicholls, 1984, 1992). Results from the correlation and regression analyses demonstrate support for the integration of achievement goals with skills that emulates athletes' beliefs about leadership in sport. Specifically, individual differences in goal perspectives reflect individual differences in beliefs about leadership. The observed differences among goal orientations highlight the contrast between task and ego orientation and the appraisal of information and beliefs that has been established consistently in previous research (Duda, 2001; Magyar & Feltz, 2003). Task orientation aligns with the belief that it is important for athlete leaders to endorse a range of adaptive skills and strategies that emphasize performance ability, motivation, respect, and communication when leading teammates. In contrast, ego orientation relates only to performance execution (e.g., has the ability to identify performance related problems, performs with confidence, etc.).

A significant pattern of beliefs regarding conceptions of leadership also emerged relative to individual differences in the subjective appraisal of the motivational climate. Achievement goal theory suggests (Ames, 1992a; Nicholls, 1992) that the way in which adults organize their environment will increase the likelihood that a particular achievement behavior or goals will be adopted. In other words, the environment can be structured to increase the probability that athletes will choose a more adaptive approach to leadership. The current findings suggest that one way coaches can develop leadership in their athletes is through the situational goal structure of their sport team. Specifically, mastery motivational climate demonstrates a consistent and significant relationship with all leadership skills, whereas performance climate failed to significantly influence any of the leadership skills. The emphasis of a mastery climate will encourage manageable leadership strategies that foster collaboration, learning, and effort, all of which are in control of the athlete at both the individual and group levels. However, perceptions of favoritism and an emphasis on normative comparison will not only decrease the salience of leadership skills but may also render a perception of uncontrollability both for the individual athlete, and the collective group working toward a common goal. Therefore, the perceived climate in which athletes are performing directly influences the types of skills and strategies that were used in leadership situations.

Implications for Coaches

An important finding for coaches pertains to the association between mastery motivational climate and leadership skills. With an emphasis on a mastery goal structure, coaches may make the use of leadership skills more obvious and accessible to the athletes. Coaches can initiate and manage the development of leadership skills by mentoring athletes and encourage the athletes to connect and collaborate during the process of acquiring and refining the various skills that foster leadership behavior. Therefore, coaches may groom future leaders by establishing a mastery motivational climate making the use of leadership skills available to athletes, by providing teachable moments and opportunities that develop mastery experiences and enhance leadership.

The current findings not only fill a significant void in the sport psychology literature, but also contribute to better understanding of how athletes perceive leadership in sport and what characteristics they value in a leader. This information can be used by coaches, parents, and sport psychology practitioners to improve the teaching and development of leadership through experiences in sport.

The development of effective leadership demands time and involvement from the coach to teach athletes to think for themselves and develop a sense of independence while at the same time, learning to work with each other. By using team sport participation to emphasize the development of the fundamental skills that result in leadership, coaches can provide athletes with the opportunity to acquire interpersonal and relation-management skills. Coaches who make an effort not only to develop the physical competence but also to foster social competence may provide their athletes with long lasting skills that could beneficially impact their lives beyond sport.

Implications for Future Research

The method of learning, developing, and exercising leadership skills in sport represents a dynamic process, which is difficult to measure and operationalize. As with any complex and dynamic intra-team interaction, it is important to acknowledge that there are other variables that may influence the leadership process that will not be included in the current investigation. Furthermore, with a one-time assessment the dynamic process of leadership over time was not taken into account. In order to explore the dynamic changes in leadership, future research should examine leadership over the entire course of a competitive season in order to assess the emergent patterns that may occur.

References

Ames, C. (1992-a). Achievement goals, motivational climate, and motivational processes. In G. Roberts (Ed.), *Motivation in Sport and Exercise* (pp. 161–176). Champaign, IL: Human Kinetics.

Ames, C. (1992-b). Achievement goals and classroom motivational climate. In J. Meece & D. Schunk (Eds.), *Students' perceptions in the classroom* (pp. 327–348). Hillsdale, NJ: Erlbaum.

Bandura, A. (1997). *Self-efficacy: The exercise of control.* New York: W. H. Freeman.

Chelladurai, P. (1984). Discrepancy between preferences and perceptions of leadership behavior and satisfaction of athletes in varying sports. *Journal of Sport and Exercise Psychology, 6,* 27–41.

Chelladurai, P., & Reimer, H. A. (1998). Measurement of leadership in sport. In J. L. Duda (Ed.), *Advances in Sport and Exercise Psychology Measurement* (pp. 227–256). Morgantown, WV: FIT Press.

Duda, J. L. (1989). Relationship between task and ego orientation and the perceived purpose of sport among high school athletes. *Journal of Sport and Exercise Psychology, 11,* 318–335.

Duda, J. L. (2001). Goal perspective research in sport: Pushing the boundaries and clarifying some misunderstandings. In J. G. C. Roberts (Ed.), *Advances in motivation in sport and exercise* (pp. 129–182). Champaign, IL: Human Kinetics.

Duda, J. L., & Balaguer, J. (1999). Toward an integration of models of leadership with a contemporary theory of motivation (pp. 212–230). In R. Lidor & M. Bar-Eli (Eds). *Sport Psychology: Linking Theory to Practice.*

Duda, J. L., & Nicholls, J. G. (1992). Dimensions of achievement motivation in schoolwork and sport. *Journal of Educational Psychology,* 84, 290–299.

Duda, J. L., & Whitehead, J. (1998) Measurement of goal perspectives in the physical domain. In J. L. Duda (Ed.), *Advances in Sport and Exercise Psychology Measurement* (pp. 21–48). Morgantown, WV: FIT Press.

Dweck. C. S., & Leggett, E. (1988). A social-cognitive approach to motivation and to personality. *Psychological Review,* 95, 256–273.

Gano-Overway, L., Ewing, M., Guivernau, M., Magyar, T. M., & Waldron, J. (2005). Understanding the role of the coaches' motivational climate and female athletes' goal orientations in predicting sportspersonship. *Psychology of Sport and Exercise,* 6, 215–232.

Glenn, S. D., & Horn, T. S. (1993). Psychological and personal predictors of leadership behavior in female soccer athletes. *Journal of Applied Sport Psychology,* 5, 17–34.

Loy, J. W., Curtis, J. E., & Sage, J. N. (1978). Relative centrality of playing position and leadership recmitment in team sports, *Exercise and sport sciences reviews,* 6, 257–284.

Magyar, T. M., & Feltz, D. L. (2003). The influence of dispositional and situational tendencies on adolescent girls' sport confidence sources. *Psychology of Sport and Exercise,* 4, 175–190.

Magyar, T. M., & Feltz, D. L., & Simpson, I. P. (2004). Individual and crew level determinants of collective efficacy in rowing. *Journal of Sport and Exercise Psychology,* 26, 136–153.

Marta, S., Leritz, S. L. E., & Mumford, M. D. (2005). Leadership skills and the group performance: Situational demands, behavioral requirements, and planning. *The Leadership Quarterly,* 16, 97–120.

Mumford, M. D., Zaccaro, S. J., Johnson, J. F., Diana, M., Gilbert, J. A., & Threlfall, K. V. (2000a). Patterns of leader characteristics: Implications for performance and development. *Leadership Quarterly,* 11(1), 115–133.

Mumford, M. D., Marks, M. A., Connelly, M. S., Zacarro, S. J., & Reiter-Palmon, R. (2000b). Development of leadership skills: Experience and timing. *Leadership Quarterly,* 11(1), 87–114.

Newton, M. & Duda, J. L. (1999). The interaction of motivational climate, dispositional goal orientations, and perceived ability in predicting indices of motivation. *International Journal of Sport Psychology,* 30, 63–82.

Nicholls, J. G. (1984). Achievement motivation: Conceptions of ability, subjective experience, task choice, and performance. *Psychological Review,* 91(3), 328–346.

Nicholls, J. G. (1989). *The competitive ethos and democratic education.* Cambridge, MA: Harvard University Press.

Nicholls, J. G. (1992). The general and the specific in the development and expression of achievement motivation. In G. C. Roberts (Ed.), *Motivation in sport and exercise.* (pp. 31–55). Champaign, IL: Human Kinetics.

Rees, C. R., & Segal, M. W. (1984). Role differentiation in groups: The relationship between instrumental and expressive leadership. *Small Group Behavior,* 15, 109–123.

Riemer, H. A., & Chelladurai, P. (1995). Leadership and satisfaction in athletics. *Journal of Sport and Exercise Psychology,* 17, 276–293.

Treasure, D. C., & Roberts, G. C. (1998). Relationship between female adolescents achievement goal orientations, perceptions of the motivational climate, belief about success and sources of satisfaction in basketball. *International Journal of Sport Psychology,* 29, 211–230.

Tropp, K., & Landers, D. (1979). Team interaction and the emergence of leadership and interpersonal attraction in field hockey. *Journal of Sports Psychology,* 1, 228–240.

Yukelson, D., Weinberg, R., Richardson, P., & Jackson, A. (1981). Interpersonal attraction and leadership within collegiate sport teams. *Journal of Sport Behavior,* 6, 29–36.

Endnotes

1. The notion of learning the skill or a new skill is a rather restricted notion at the collegiate level. Therefore, "I learn a new skill and it makes me want to practice more" was changed to "I make improvements and it makes me want to practice more." Also, "I learn a new skill by trying hard" was changed to "I make improvements by trying hard." An additional item, "I work together with my teammates," was also included in the task dimension. For ego orientation, the concept of outperforming others is also rather restricted given the nature of the sport. For example, "I'm the only one who can do the play or skill" does not apply; everyone on the team knows how to perform the skill of rowing. Therefore, this item was changed to "I outperform everyone else on my team." A second item, "I score the most points/goals/hits, etc.," was changed to an equivalent concept in the sport of rowing—"I outperform others on the erg."

2. The A-LSSQ was piloted on 317 undergraduate students enrolled in either activity or lecture classes in the Department of Kinesiology (*M* age = 20.11 years, *SD* = 2.04). The sample included 136 female and 174 male students (seven failed to identify their gender) with athletic experience in a variety of sports (*M* years = 12.44, *SD* = 4.03). Participants were asked to think about the importance of leadership and identify the skills that were important for athlete leaders to use and respond to the stem "It is important for an athlete leader to . . ." on a 5-point Likert scale (not at all important = 1 to very important = 5). To determine the factor structure of the A-LSSQ, an exploratory principal component factor analysis with varimax rotation was conducted. This analysis revealed 13 factors with eigenvalues greater than 1.0. However, only four factors were interpretable and reliable and were kept in the final solution. Items with .40 or higher were retained on any given factor. In order to generate a more parsimonious measure, corrected item-total correlations were examined to determine which of the remaining items maximized internal consistency.

Further Reading

Damon, A. (2007). Perspectives of leadership behavior in women's collegiate tennis from leaders and followers: A test of social role theory. *Women in Sport & Physical Activity Journal, 16,* 21–31.

Holt, N. L., Black, D. E., Tamminen, K. A., Fox, K. R., & Mandigo, J. L. (2008). Levels of social complexity and dimensions of peer experiences in youth sport. *Journal of Sport and Exercise Psychology, 30,* 411–431.

Moran, M. M., & Weiss, M. R. (2006). Peer leadership in sport: Links with friendship, peer accep-tance, psychological characteristics, and athletic ability. *Journal of Applied Sport Psychology, 18,* 97–113.

Discussion Questions

1. Specific to team sports, is it more effective to have one designated "team captain" or should all athletes have the opportunity to emerge as a leader of the team?

2. In addition to establishing mastery motivational climate, what are some other ways coaches can create an environment that supports leadership development in all athletes?

3

Female Athletes Do Ask! An Exploratory Study of Gender Differences in the Propensity to Initiate Negotiation among Athletes

Sharon R. Guthrie, T. Michelle Magyar,
Stephanie Eggert, and Craig Kain

© JupiterImages

© JupiterImages

Image Copyright Stephen Coburn, 2009
Used under license from Shutterstock, Inc.

There is a boldness when you declare your purpose with your anatomy,
when size is your design, your weapon, and you carry your body around
without any shame

Alexis Roberson, Fencing

Over the past 50 years, federal laws, including Title IX, have been passed with the intent of prohibiting discrimination and promoting equitable economic and educational opportunities for all persons, regardless of gender. The result has been an impressive increase in the number of women pursuing higher education degrees and entering professional fields historically dominated by men (e.g., business). This increase of women in the workplace has led to a shift in America's male-dominated corporate culture and a rise in women's economic empowerment. Despite these enhanced opportunities for advancing economically and professionally, there remains a significant pay gap relative to gender, regardless of occupation; that is, women, on average, do not yet earn salaries equal to their male counterparts in comparable positions and are less likely to be promoted at similar rates (Babcock & Laschever, 2003; Babcock, Gelfand, Small, & Stayn, 2006; Bowles, Babcock, & Lei, 2007; Bowles, Babcock, & McGinn, 2005; Dey & Hill, 2007).

Moreover, when women begin their professional careers, their salaries are generally lower than those of men. Research has shown that these salary differentials are due, at least in part, to the varying perceptions between men and women regarding the negotiation process. For example, women applying for jobs have been found to ask for less money than men because they feel less entitled to do so (Babcock & Laschever, 2003; Kray & Thompson, 2005). They also tend to be less confident than men in their ability to negotiate successfully (Babcock & Laschever, 2003; Babcock, Gelfand, Small, & Stayn, 2006) and less comfortable with the prospect of negotiation because they often view it as a form of competition requiring confrontation (Gelfand & McCusker, 2002). Additionally, women, more often than men, report being concerned that negotiating in the workplace, particularly with persons in superior positions, will damage or disrupt their relationships and that requesting increases in salary or other resources may imply that they are elitist and/or self-serving (Babcock & Laschever, 2003; Babcock et al., 2004, 2006). These gender differences make their mark over time, often resulting in a half-million dollar difference in earnings by retirement age (Babcock & Laschever, 2003). In addition to a decrease in lifetime earnings, starting salary may also negatively affect initial job status and career advancement (Dey & Hill, 2007; Gerhart & Rynes, 1991; Martel, Lane, & Emrich, 1996; Stevens, Bavetta, & Gist, 1993).

The vast majority of studies examining differences in negotiation behavior between males and females have been conducted in laboratory settings with individuals who are instructed to negotiate in an artificial situation. This type of research misses a critical step in the negotiation process, that is, the decision to bargain in the first place. Noting this limitation, Babcock et al. (2004, 2006) investigated gender differences in what they have termed the "propensity to initiate negotiation" (PIN).

To make a decision to negotiate, a person must be aware that opportunities to do so are available. Multiple factors likely influence this awareness and the subsequent choice to negotiate. Based on a review of the negotiation and psychological literature, Babcock and her colleagues examined three variables (i.e., recognition of negotiation opportunities, sense of entitlement, and feelings of apprehension), which they predicted would mediate gender differences in PIN. In their 2006 study, the propensity to initiate negotiation was operationalized as the participants' two most recent negotiations and their next anticipated negotiation. The researchers found significant gender differences for all three predictors; however, only recognition of opportunities significantly predicted the propensity to initiate negotiation.

Ultimately, negotiation is critical in achieving success in the work force, whether it influences who moves up the job ladder quickest or who earns the most salary initially and over time. This is particularly true now that opportunities to negotiate the terms of one's work experience have increased due to changes in the labor market and its organizational structure (e.g., decline in unionism, fewer standardized contracts, increases in employee turnover, hierarchical flattening, reduced formalization, more mergers and acquisitions). Because research has shown that women operate at a disadvantage on the "negotiation playing field," when compared to men, and that this difference contributes to the ongoing salary gap between the genders, further investigation of this phenomenon is needed. It is important, however, to take into account historical, demographical, and sociocultural variations among women rather than treating them as a homogeneous group.

This study investigated women and men with extensive athletic experience. In particular, we were interested to see whether the gender differences commonly found in negotiation studies would exist among those who had competed in sport for many years. Previous studies have shown that traditional gender belief systems advantage men over women in negotiations as women tend to report lower levels of confidence and attribute success to more external reasons (e.g., luck) than men (Babcock et al., 2006; Kray & Thompson, 2005). Research in the physical domain, however, has shown that females derive psycho-emotional benefits from sport participation such as enhanced self-confidence, esteem, and assertiveness (e.g., Heywood & Dworkin, 2003; Magyar & Feltz, 2003, 2005; Messner, 2003). Each of these sport-derived benefits is likely to be useful in negotiation contexts, but whether they transfer as characteristics that influence negotiation at the bargaining table is currently unknown.

In 2003, Babcock and Laschever published a book entitled, "Women Don't Ask: Negotiation and the Gender Divide." The title was based on their findings that women are less likely than men to ask for what they want—whether it is pay raises, promotions, better job opportunities, or more help at home—because they feel less comfortable and capable when confronted with the prospect of negotiation. This study was designed to determine whether this reticence to ask for what one wants existed among a sample of female athletes. More specifically, we examined: a) the difference between female and male athletes in their propensity to negotiate, and b) whether the cognitive and emotional factors associated with the Babcock et al. (2006) Propensity to Initiate Negotiation (PIN) Model (i.e., recognition of opportunity, entitlement, and apprehension) explained and mediated these differences. Propensity to negotiate was operationally defined as self-reported responses to a series of hypothetical negotiation scenarios, as well as recent and anticipated future negotiation experiences. Consistent with Babcock et al.'s previous work, we hypothesized that there would be gender differences in the timing of recent and future negotiations, hypothetical scenario responses, and the three Babcock et al. predictors.

Method

This study was conducted in accordance with the policies and procedures of a university Institutional Review Board.

Participants

The research participants were 228 male ($n = 77$) and female ($n = 151$) current and former athletes ranging in age from 22–70 with the majority of participants within the 22–34 age category ($n = 151$, 66%). To qualify for participation, all participants must have competed in sport for a minimum of 10 years and obtained at least a baccalaureate degree. The academic degree requirements were established to increase the likelihood that participants would be employed at the time of the study or have work experience.

The sample included persons who had competed in a variety of individual and team sports with the majority having been former college or university athletes (n = 145, 64%). All participants had participated in sport for at least 15 years and many for 30 years or more (n = 81, 36%). The majority (n = 130, 57%) had participated after Title IX went into effect (1978 or later). In terms of racial/ethnic status, the vast majority of participants were Caucasian (n = 181, 79%), followed by Spanish/Hispanic/Latino (n = 14, 6%), Black/African American (n = 9, 4%), multiracial (n = 9, 4%), American Indian/Alaskan Native (n = 7, 3%), Asian/Pacific Islander (n = 4, 2%), Middle Easterner (n = 3, 1%), and "other" or no response (n = 1, < 1%).

Measures

A four-part survey instrument, based on that developed by Babcock et al. (2004, 2006), was used to collect the data. Content validity was established by the instrument developers.

Part I: Propensity to Initiate Negotiation (PIN): Timing of Recent and Anticipated Future Negotiations

Two assessments of PIN were made. The first was a free-recall measure in which participants were queried about their negotiation experiences. First, they were asked questions about their two most recent negotiations (i.e., "How long ago was your most recent and second most recent negotiation that you initiated?") and responded to a 9-point category scale ranging from 1 (over one year ago) to 9 (today). They were then asked to anticipate when they would initiate their next negotiation experience using a 9-point category scale ranging from 1 (a year from now) to 9 (today). The time to most recent and second most recent negotiations was averaged to determine a scale score producing a Cronbach alpha of .90.

Part II: Propensity to Initiate Negotiation (PIN): Hypothetical Scenarios

In the second measure of PIN, participants were given 12 hypothetical negotiation scenarios (see Appendix). The scenarios, which were identical to those used in Babcock et al.'s (2004) research, assessed the participants' propensity to initiate negotiation in various work and social situations. For example, participants reviewed a statement such as, "You believe you deserve a salary increase" or "You believe that you are overdue for a promotion," and responded to the following four questions regarding the given scenario using a 5-point category scale: "How often have you encountered a situation similar to this?" (occurrence); "Do you think of this situation as one involving negotiation?" (identification); "How likely would you be to negotiate in this situation?" (initiation); and "How anxious would you feel if you negotiated in this situation?" (anxiety). As demonstrated in Table 1, all of the hypothetical scenario subscales reached an acceptable level of internal consistency except that associated with occurrence (alpha = .61).

Table 1 Correlations, Means, Standard Deviations, and Internal Consistencies of Independent and Dependent Variables for the Entire Sample

Variables	1	2	3	4	5	6	7	8	9
1. Recent Negotiation	1.0								
2. Next Negotiation	.74***	1.0							
3. Hypothetical-occurrence	.10	.14*	1.0						
4. Hypothetical-identification	.21**	.22**	.25**	1.0					
5. Hypothetical-initiation	.21**	.20**	.25**	.65***	1.0				
6. Hypothetical-anxiety	−.20**	−.11	.07	−.03	−.39***	1.0			
7. Opportunity	.09	.07	.11	.32***	.38***	−.20**	1.0		
8. Entitlement	.03	.13*	.10	.22**	.37***	−.18**	.38***	1.0	
9. Apprehension	−.20**	−.12	.03	−.11	−.44***	.63***	−.34***	−.24**	1.0
M	5.55	6.16	2.52	3.12	3.03	2.62	5.79	4.54	3.95
SD	2.19	2.33	.44	.64	.58	.83	.83	1.06	1.42
α	.91	---	.61	.75	.71	.88	.64	.72	.87

*p < 0.05 level, **p < 0.01 level, ***p < 0.001 level, two-tailed.

Part III: Predictors of the Propensity to Initiate Negotiation (PPIN)

An 18-item instrument consisting of three subscales: a) *Recognition of Opportunities* measures the extent to which respondents view situations as being amenable to change via negotiation (e.g., "Most things are negotiable"), b) *Entitlement* assesses the extent to which individuals feel entitled to have the things they want (e.g., "I think situations should be changed to fit my desires"), and c) *Apprehension* measures the degree to which respondents feel uncomfortable about asking for resources for themselves (e.g., " I experience alot of stress when I think about asking for something I want").[1] Responses were rated on a 7-point Likert scale ranging from strongly disagree to strongly agree. Scores for each subscale were calculated as the mean score of the designated items for each of the three dimensions. Cronbach alphas were satisfactory for entitlement (.72) and apprehension (.87) and approached an appropriate level of internal consistency for recognition of opportunity (.64).

Part IV: Demographical Information

Participants were asked to provide their gender, race/ethnicity, age, education, income, and time of sport participation (e.g., before or after Title IX was in effect).

Procedure

Participants who fit the study criteria (i.e., minimum baccalaureate degree and 10 years of athletic competition) were recruited through word of mouth, professional networks of the researchers, and Internet listserves and surveyed over a one-year period. An online survey, which could be accessed from a website, was used to collect the data. Links on the website directed prospective respondents to a cover letter explaining that the study concerned their beliefs about themselves and their work environment and to a consent form. If agreeing to participate in the study, respondents were linked to the survey and asked to think about their current (or most recent) work experience and to reflect on their work experiences as they were responding to questions. If not currently employed, they were requested to think about their most recent work experiences. After completion of the survey, an e-mail address was provided so that participants could contact a researcher if they had any questions or wished to receive the results of the study.

Analysis of Data

Preceding statistical analysis, the raw data were inspected to ensure reliable data entry and test assumptions related to normality, linearity, and homogeneity. Basic statistics were calculated, including internal reliabilities of measurements, means, standard deviations, and simple correlations among observed variables (see Table 1). Gender differences in recent and anticipated future negotiation experiences, hypothetical negotiation scenario responses (i.e., occurrence, identification, initiation, anxiety), and the three PIN predictors (i.e., recognition of opportunity, entitlement and apprehension) were determined using independent *t*-tests.

Relationships between the three predictors and the time since the last two negotiations, the time until the next anticipated negotiation, and responses to the hypothetical scenario questions were examined using Pearson Product-Moment correlations. Multiple linear regression was also performed with recognition of opportunity, entitlement, and apprehension as predictor variables and time since the last two negotiations, time until the next anticipated negotiation, and hypothetical-occurrence, identification, initiation, and anxiety as criterion variables. Due to the exploratory nature of the study, there were no specific a priori hypotheses regarding the order of entry of the predictor variables; thus, all predictor variables were examined simultaneously.[2] Finally, a test to determine whether gender differences in the propensity to negotiate were mediated by recognition of opportunity, entitlement, and apprehension was performed, based on the methods proposed by Barron and Kenny (1986).

Results

Table 1 presents the descriptive statistics, correlation coefficients, and internal reliabilities for all independent and dependent variables used in this study.

Gender Differences in the Propensity to Initiate Negotiation (PIN): Timing of Recent and Anticipated Future Negotiations

Statistically significant gender differences were present for recent experiences ($t = 2.53$, $p < .05$) with men reporting significantly more recent negotiations than women: 1–2 weeks ($M_{male} = 6.06$, $SD = 2.23$) and 3–4 weeks ($M_{female} = 5.30$, $SD = 2.14$), respectively. There was no significant difference, however, between men and women in their anticipated time to next negotiation ($M_{male} = 6.52$, $SD = 2.38$; $M_{female} = 5.98$, $SD = 2.29$). Thus, the hypothesized gender difference in the timing of negotiation experiences was partially supported.

Gender Differences in the Propensity to Initiate Negotiation (PIN): Hypothetical Scenario Responses

There were no significant differences between men and women in reporting the occurrence of the hypothetical scenarios ($M_{male} = 2.50$, $SD = .42$; $M_{female} = 2.52$, $SD = .43$), in identifying these scenarios as requiring negotiation ($M_{male} = 3.07$, $SD = .42$; $M_{female} = 3.15$, $SD = .61$), and the likelihood that they would initiate negotiation in these situations ($M_{male} = 3.05$, $SD = .55$; $M_{female} = 3.01$, $SD = .60$). There was, however, a significant gender difference in anticipated anxiety if negotiation in a particular situation were to occur ($t = 2.52$, $p = .01$), that is, men reported "a little" anxiety ($M = 2.43$, $SD = .74$) while women reported that they would be "somewhat" anxious ($M = 2.72$, $SD = .85$). The hypothesis of gender difference in hypothetical scenario responses was therefore only partially supported.

Gender Differences in Predictors of the Propensity to Initiate Negotiation (PIN)

The hypothesis of gender difference in predictor variables was only partially supported as a significant gender difference was found in apprehension ($M_{male} = 3.62$, $SD = 1.43$; $M_{female} = 4.12$, $SD = 1.38$; $t = 2.57$, $p = .01$), with women reporting more apprehension when negotiating than men, but not in recognition of opportunity ($M_{male} = 5.71$, $SD = 1.00$; $M_{female} = 5.82$, $SD = .71$;

Table 2 Comparison of Mean Scores on the Propensity to Initiate Negotiation variables with Babcock et al.'s (2006) sample (N = 227)

Predictor	Babcock Male	Babcock Female	Current Male	Current Female
Recognition of opportunities	5.43 (.91)	5.17 (1.01)	5.71 (1.0)	5.82 (.71)
Entitlement	3.59 (1.24)	3.26 (.95)	4.42 (1.07)	4.60 (1.06)
Apprehension	3.78 (1.65)	4.26 (1.67)	3.62 (1.43)	4.12 (1.38)

$t = .98$, $p = .33$) or entitlement ($M_{male} = 4.42$, $SD = 1.07$; $M_{female} = 4.60$, $SD = 1.06$; $t = 1.34$, $p = .18$). In fact, the female athletes had higher mean scores on recognition of opportunities and entitlement subscales than their male counterparts.

A comparison of the current sample's mean scores on all three predictors to those of Babcock et al.'s sample (2006) is shown in Table 2. In the Babcock study, there were significant gender differences in all three variables with men recognizing more negotiation opportunities, feeling more entitled, and reporting less apprehension associated with negotiation than women, whereas in the present study, the only significant gender difference was in apprehension.

Relationships Between PIN Predictors and Timing of Recent and Anticipated Future Negotiations and Hypothetical Scenario Responses

Pearson Product-Moment correlations were calculated to determine relationships between the three predictor variables (i.e., recognition of opportunity, entitlement, and apprehension) and PIN variables (i.e., recent and future negotiation experiences, hypothetical scenario responses) (see Table 1). Positive relationships of "opportunity recognition" and "entitlement" to recent and future negotiation experiences and to hypothetical scenario identification and initiation were hypothesized. Conversely, a negative relationship was predicted between apprehension and the PIN dependent variables.

Findings provided partial support for these hypotheses. Entitlement correlated positively with next anticipated negotiation, but not with recent experiences, both recognition of opportunity and entitlement were positively related to hypothetical-identification and hypothetical-initiation, and apprehension was negatively associated with recent negotiation experiences and hypothetical-initiation, but not with anticipated future negotiations or hypothetical-identification.

Additionally, the multiple regression analysis revealed a significant relationship between the three PIN predictors and timing of recent negotiation experiences, $F (3, 224) = 3.14$, $p < .05$; however, the apprehension main effect emerged as the only significant predictor of the dependent variable ($\beta = -.19$, $p = .006$, Adj. R2 = .03). Moreover, none of the variables predicted next anticipated negotiation.

PIN predictor variables also demonstrated a significant relationship with hypothetical-identification of negotiation [$F (3, 224) = 9.56$, $p < .001$] and explained 10% of the variance in this dependent variable. Recognition of opportunity ($\beta = .27$, $p = .000$) was the only significant predictor, however. In contrast, all three predictors were significant in explaining 28% of the variance in hypothetical-initiation [F (3,224) = 31.01, p < .001] with apprehension (β = −.33, p = .000) being the strongest factor, followed by entitlement (β = .23, p = .000) and opportunity (β = .18, p = .005). The three variables also demonstrated a significant relationship with hypothetical-anxiety [F (3, 224) = 49.07, p < .001] and explained 39% of the variance in anxiety a person might feel when negotiating; however, apprehension was found to be the only significant predictor (β = .63, p = .000).

Test of Mediation

The potential mediation effects of gender were examined using the methods of Barron and Kenny (1986). Gender differences in recent negotiation experiences were partially mediated by apprehension whereas the relationship between gender and hypothetical-anxiety was completely mediated by apprehension (see Table 3). Specifically, in Model 1, the mediating effect of apprehension on the relationship between gender and recent negotiation experiences was examined. In step 1 of the Model, gender significantly predicted apprehension with women reporting greater levels of apprehension with the prospect of negotiation. In step 2, gender significantly predicted recent negotiation experiences with men reporting more recent experiences than women.

When gender and apprehension were examined simultaneously, the standardized beta weight and p-value for gender were reduced (i.e., β = .17, p = .01 to β = −.14, p = .04). Thus, apprehension partially explains the gender difference in recent negotiation experiences. Specific to the direction of the observed relationships, men who reported less apprehension had more recent negotiation experiences than women who reported greater apprehension when having to negotiate. In Model 2, the same relationships emerged except the dependent variable was hypothetical-anxiety. In this case, gender became a non-significant predictor of anxiety after apprehension was included in the model (i.e., β = .17, p = .01 to β = .06, p = .24).

Table 3 Significant Mediator Model for the Propensity to Initiate Negotiation Based on Recent Negotiation Experiences and Hypothetical Apprehension to Negotiation

Predictor	Criterion	Beta	Adj. R2	P
Recent Negotiation Experiences				
Step 1. Gender	Apprehension	.17	.02	.01
Step 2. Gender	Recent Negotiation Experiences	−.17	.02	.01
Step 3. Gender and	Recent Negotiation	−.14		.04
Apprehension	Experiences	−.18	.05	.008
Hypothetical Apprehension to Negotiation				
Step 1. Gender	Apprehension	.17	.02	.01
Step 2. Gender	Hypothetical Apprehension	−.17	.02	.01
Step 3. Gender and	Hypothetical Apprehension	.06		
Apprehension		.62	.39	.000

Therefore, apprehension completely mediated the relationship between gender and anticipated anxiety associated with negotiation in the hypothetical scenarios.

Differences in the Propensity to Initiate Negotiation Between Athletes who Participated Pre- and Post-Title IX

Because Title IX has been instrumental in advancing educational and sport opportunities for women, differences between athletes who competed in sport prior to 1978 and those who competed in a post-Title environment (1978 or later) were examined (see Table 4). Findings revealed that both females and males who competed in sport post-Title IX scored significantly higher on hypothetical anxiety ($M_{post\text{-}Title IX} = 2.71$, $SD = .77$; $M_{pre\text{-}Title IX} = 2.38$, $SD = .77$; $t = 2.08$, $p = .04$) than those who competed pre-Title IX.

Discussion

This study contributes to the body of research examining gender differences in negotiation perceptions and performance. Both empirical studies and anecdotal accounts have documented that women have less confidence in their negotiation skills and are less comfortable with the negotiation process than men. This difference may be due to the fact that negotiation historically has been portrayed as a masculine arena involving competition between adversaries. Because women, more often than men, express discomfort with confrontation and combative styles of communication, it is not surprising that they report less confidence when negotiating to enhance their professional and economic status, and may avoid negotiation all

Table 4 Comparison of Means and Standard Deviations on the Propensity to Initiate Negotiation Variables Between Pre-Title IX and Post-Title IX Participants

Variables	Before Title IX (Before 1978)	After Title IX (1978–present)
1. Recent Negotiation	5.60 (2.29)	5.57 (2.106)
2. Next Negotiation	6.43 (2.36)	6.07 (2.29)
3. Hypothetical-occurrence	2.52 (.46)	2.47 (.44)
4. Hypothetical-identification	3.23 (.58)	3.10 (.65)
5. Hypothetical-initiation	3.15 (.53)	2.97 (.56)
6. Hypothetical-anxiety	2.38 (.77)	2.71 (.77)*
7. Opportunity	5.74 (1.09)	5.78 (.76)
8. Entitlement	4.26 (1.22)	4.64 (.96)
9. Apprehension	3.68 (1.26)	4.11 (1.36)

*p < 0.05 level, two-tailed

together. This study examined whether women and men who had competed in sport for many years would differ in their perceptions regarding negotiation.

Gender Differences in Timing of Negotiation Experiences and the Propensity to Initiate Negotiation in Hypothetical Scenarios

Consistent with Babcock et al.'s (2006) findings, gender differences in the timing of recent negotiations existed, that is, men reported more recent negotiations than women, 1–2 weeks vs. 3-4 weeks, respectively. In contrast to Babcock et al.'s findings, however, gender differences were not revealed in participants' estimation of future negotiation experiences. In fact, the females in this study anticipated that their next negotiation experience would arrive 1–2 weeks sooner than males. In addition, no gender differences were found in terms of participant responses to the hypothetical scenarios with the exception of hypothetical-anxiety, that is, the women in this study reported significantly greater anxiety than men when contemplating negotiation in the hypothetical situations.

PIN Predictors

Similar to the Babcock et al. study, the women in this study reported significantly more apprehension associated with negotiation than men. The test for mediation also demonstrated apprehension as an inhibitory factor in negotiation for this group of women. These results suggest that traditional gender beliefs that diminish women's confidence when confronted with negotiation opportunities, regardless of athletic experience, are still well entrenched.

Of particular relevance, however, women did not differ significantly from men in their recognition of opportunities and sense of entitlement to negotiate. In fact, their scores on these two subscales were higher than those of their male counterparts. This finding is in contrast to Babcock et al.'s study where men were found to recognize significantly more negotiating opportunities than women and felt more entitled to negotiate when an opportunity was available. It is also interesting to note that the female participants in the present study had higher mean scores on recognition of opportunity and entitlement subscales than both the women and men in the Babcock et al. study (see Table 2).

Due to the design of this study, a claim cannot be made that sport participation caused the greater recognition of negotiation opportunities and sense of entitlement among this sample of women. The findings are consistent, however, with previous research demonstrating that sport participation enhances physical and global self-perceptions of females and that self-perception changes can transfer to other contexts (Castelnuovo & Guthrie, 1998; Krane, 2001; Krane, Choi, Baird, Aimar & Kauer, 2004). It is quite possible, therefore, that competition in sport, particularly if sustained over time, may help minimize gender differences in negotiation attitudes and behaviors that disadvantage women. This possibility is worthy of further study as it has been shown that high-powered individuals display a greater propensity to initiate negotiation (Magee, Galinsky, & Gruenfeld, 2007).

Still, the test for mediation demonstrated that apprehension associated with negotiation was an inhibitory factor for this group of women. Thus, although sporting participation may have fostered some of the characteristics that ultimately resulted in enhanced negotiation perceptions among this sample (i.e., opportunity recognition, entitlement), their greater apprehension related to negotiation suggests that they also lack a degree of negotiation efficacy.

Differences between Pre- and Post-IX Participants in PIN Predictors and Propensity to Initiate Negotiation

Only one significant difference between pre- and post-Title IX athletes was found, but none related to gender. Both females and males who competed in sport after Title IX went into effect reported significantly more anxiety when contemplating negotiation in the hypothetical situations than those who participated before 1978. This finding may be due to different developmental experiences among sample participants. It is likely that the pre-Title IX participants, due to their older ages, had more actual negotiating experience in the situations described in the hypothetical scenarios (e.g., asking for a promotion, negotiating for a new car, hiring someone to work on your house) than their younger counterparts, and thus less reported anxiety.

Limitations and Recommendations for Future Research

Although the findings of this study suggest a possible relationship between sport participation and two predictors of negotiation success, there were a number of limitations that must be taken into consideration. First, non-probability sampling was used, prohibiting generalization beyond the current data set. A second limitation, which may have influenced the results, is the large difference in female and male sample sizes (i.e., 69% female, 33% male). It is important to note, however, that the same difference in gender distribution was observed in the Babcock et al. (2006) study (i.e., 63% female, 37% male). In addition, this study did not include a comparison of female athletes and non-athletes. Although Babcock et al.'s (2006) female sample was used as a non-athletic comparison group, it may be that some individuals in their sample had athletic experience similar to the participants in this study. It was not possible to determine whether this was the case as Babcock and her colleagues did not assess athletic background. Finally, the vast majority of participants in this study were Caucasian. Different findings might emerge with a more diverse sample in terms of race/ethnicity.

Despite the aforementioned limitations, this study provides initial data supporting the possibility that athletic training and competition for women may help reduce the gender gap in negotiation attitudes and behaviors, which in turn may empower women in the workplace. The fact that the females in this study, all of whom had extensive sporting experience (i.e., 15 years or more), scored much higher on entitlement and recognition of opportunity than both the men and women in Babcock et al.'s (2006) study and were not significantly different from their male counterparts who also had extensive athletic training, is intriguing and worthy of further study.

Additional research with prospective (longitudinal) designs are required before conclusions regarding the intersection of high-involvement sporting participation and negotiation attitudes and behaviors can be drawn. Within the sport and business world, goal setting has become an integral element of performance. Researchers have found that training in goal-setting increases goal attainment and leads to improvements in the negotiation performance of both women and men (Babcock & Laschever, 2003). Longitudinal studies examining the relationship between goal-setting practices and the propensity to initiate negotiation may be helpful in this regard. Research designs that employ qualitative and mixed-methods are also recommended so that the complexities of negotiation attitudes and behaviors can be more fully understood.

Conclusions

In conclusion, the women in this study exhibited two of the perceptual characteristics that contribute to negotiation success (i.e., recognition of opportunity and entitlement). They also expressed more apprehension than men about the negotiation process, similar to the female participants of previous research studies. This finding suggests the power of gender in shaping self-perception, which in many cases works against women when they are confronted with negotiation opportunities.

Although negotiation has always been an important professional skill, changes in the workplace have made it critical that women develop their negotiating expertise and exercise greater control over their careers than in the previous times. Both negotiation and sport have long been viewed as arenas in which men excel and women are less capable. Just as changes have occurred in sport, giving females greater freedom to advance their mind-body capabilities, notions of what constitutes a successful negotiation are also in flux. Rather than being perceived uniformly as a battle between adversaries, negotiation is increasingly viewed as a collaborative process (Babcock et al., 2003, 2006). Such changes, if materialized on a broad scale, will likely enable women, particularly those who are uncomfortable in highly competitive situations and/or prefer collaborative forms of communication and decision-making, to negotiate more comfortably and successfully.

Competition is still pervasive in the capitalist workplace, however, and many persons continue to negotiate in a competitive and confrontational manner. Thus, the ability to perform confidently in a variety of competitive environments is a useful skill for females to acquire, particularly at young ages. It is hoped that this research will serve as a catalyst for further examination of how sport participation may contribute to the enhancement of women's negotiation efficacy, and ultimately socioeconomic advancement. The persistence of pay inequity between men and women in the workplace, regardless of occupational choice, calls both researchers and professionals who advocate for gender equity to action.

References

Babcock, L., Gelfand, M., Small, D., & Stayn, H. (2004). Propensity to initiate negotiations: A new look at gender variation in negotiation behavior. Unpublished manuscript, Carnegie Mellon University, Pittsburgh, PA.

Babcock, L., Gelfand, M., Small, D., & Stayn, H. (2006). Gender differences in the propensity to initiate negotiations. In De Cremer, M. Zeelenberg, & J. K. Murnighan (Eds.), *Social psychology and economics* (pp. 239–262). Mahway, NJ: Lawrence Erlbaum Associates.

Babcock, L., & Laschever, S. (2003). *Women don't ask*. Princeton, NJ: Princeton University Press.

Barron, R. M., & Kenny, D. A. (1986). The moderator-mediator variable distinction in social psychological research: Conceptual, strategic, and statistical considerations. *Journal of Personality and Social Psychology*, 51(6), 1173–1182.

Bowles, H. R., Babcock, L., & Lei, L. (2007). Social incentives for gender differences in the propensity to initiate negotiations: Sometimes it does hurt to ask. *Organizational Behavior and Human Decision Processes*, 103, 84–103.

Bowles, H. R., Babcock, L., & McGinn, K. L. (2005). Constraints and triggers: Mechanics of gender in negotiation. *Journal of Personality and Social Psychology*, 89(6), 951–965.

Castelnuovo, S., & Guthrie, S. R. (1998). *Feminism and the female body: Liberating the amazon within.* Boulder, CO: Lynne Rienner Publishers.

Dey, J. G., & Hill, C. (2007). *Behind the pay gap.* Washington, D.C.: AAUW Educational Foundation.

Gelfand, M. J., & McCusker, C. (2002). Metaphor and the cultural construction of negotiation: A paradigm for theory and research. In M. Gannon & K. L. Newman (Eds.), *Handbook of cross-cultural management* (pp. 292-314). New York: Blackwell.

Gerhart, B., & Rynes, S. L. (1991). Determinants and consequences of salary negotiations by graduating male and female MBAs. *Journal of Applied Psychology*, 76(2), 256–26.

Heywood, L., & Dworkin, S. L. (2003). *Built to win: The female athlete as cultural icon.* Minneapolis: University of Minnesota.

Krane, V. (2001). We can be athletic and feminine but do we want to? Challenging hegemonic femininity in women's sport. *Quest*, 53, 115–133.

Krane, V., Choi, P. Y. L., Baird, S. M., Aimar, C. M., & Kauer, K. J. (2004). Living the paradox: Female athletes negotiate femininity and masculinity. *Sex Roles*, 50(5–6), 315–329.

Kray, L. J., & Thompson, L. (2005). Gender stereotypes and negotiation performance: A review of theory and research. *Research in organizational behavior*, 26, 103-182.

Magee, J. C., Galinsky, A. D., & Gruenfeld, D. H. (2007). Power, propensity to negotiate, and moving first in competitive interactions. *Personality and Social Psychology Bulletin*, 33(2), 1–13.

Magyar, T. M., & Feltz, D. L. (2003). The influence of dispositional and situational tendencies on adolescent girls' sport confidence sources. *Psychology of Sport and Exercise*, 4, 175–190.

Magyar, T. M., & Feltz, D. L. (2005). Self-efficacy and adolescents in sport and physical activity. In F. Pajares & T. Urdan (Eds.), *Self-efficacy beliefs and adolescent development and education* (pp. 161–179). Greenwich, CT: Information Age.

Martel, R. F., Lane, D. M., & Emrich, C. (1996). Male-female differences: A computer simulation, *American Psychologist*, 51, 157–58.

Messner, M. A. (2003). Men as superordinates: Challenges for gender scholarship. In M. S. Kimmel & A. L. Ferber (Eds.), *Privilege: A reader* (pp. 287–298). Boulder, CO: Westview.

Stevens, C. K., Bavetta, A. G., & Gist, M. E. (1993) Gender differences in the acquisition of salary negotiation skills: the role of goals, self-efficacy, and perceived control. *Journal of Applied Psychology*, 78(5), 723–35.

Tabachnik, B. G., & Fidell, L. S. (2001). *Using multivariate statistics*, (4th ed.). Boston: Allyn & Bacon.

Appendix
Hypothetical Scenarios

1. You are buying a new car.
2. Your family is trying to decide where to go on vacation.
3. You and your friends are trying to decide which movie to see.
4. You are eating at a restaurant and the dish you ordered tastes bad.
5. You take your pants to the tailor to get them hemmed.
6. You believe that you are overdue for a promotion.
7. You believe that you deserve a salary increase.
8. At work, you are assigned to a project or task that you feel should be given to someone more junior.

9. You hire someone to work on your house and the job is not done to your satisfaction.

10. You decide to buy a piece of kitchen equipment and the only one left is a floor sample.

11. You take your car to be fixed and when it is ready, the bill is significantly higher than the original estimate.

12. You pull into a gas station hoping to get your car inspected. A sign says inspections don't begin for 20 minutes. There appear to be plenty of employees around.

Endnotes

1. The *PPIN* used in this study is a modified version of the instrument Babcock et al. presented in their 2004 unpublished manuscript. Three items were added to the entitlement subscale, per the recommendation of instrument developers, to increase the reliability of the subscale. Readers may contact the first author for instrument modifications.

2. The block single step entry method was employed in the current investigation mainly because the stepwise method capitalizes on statistical chance that may "overfit" the data (e.g., Tabachnik & Fidell, 2001). As a result, significant predictors that emerge in this sample may not emerge in different samples, making it difficult to interpret across different studies in the future.

Further Reading

Armstrong, K. L. (2007). The nature of black women's leadership in community recreation sport: An illustration of black feminist thought. *Women in Sport & Physical Activity Journal*, 16, 3–14.

It's time to negotiate!

A local high school was recently reported as being non-compliant with Title IX regulations and the athletic department was given six months to rectify this situation. The Athletic Director has contacted you because of your expertise in Title IX and your ability to negotiate. The high school has one male Athletic Director, and the following sports: football, basketball, baseball, and soccer for boys; volleyball and swimming for girls. In addition, the girls' volleyball team must practice later in the evening during season because the boys' basketball team uses the gym for off-season practice immediately following school. What are some of your recommendations to get the athletic department in compliance? What would you do to negotiate for even more than just the minimum requirements to achieve compliance? Based on the negotiation article, what strategies would you use?

_____

_____

_____

_____

_____

_____

4

Cultural Beliefs and Attitudes of Black and Hispanic College-Age Women Toward Exercise

Karen T. D'Alonzo and Natalie Fischetti

© JupiterImages, 2009

© JupiterImages, 2009

From *Journal of Transcultural Nursing,* Volume 19, No. 2, April 2008 by Karen T. D'Alonzo, Natlie FischettiI, & Ruters, New Jersy State University. Reprinted by permission.

Physical inactivity has become a major public health issue in the United States. Although recent data suggest that a significant percentage of Americans do not accrue sufficient amounts of daily physical activity (Centers for Disease Control and Prevention [CDC], 2003), it has been demonstrated that sedentarism is particularly acute among minority women, irrespective of socioeconomic status (Crespo, Smith, Andersen, Carter-Pokras, & Ainsworth, 2000). Differences in levels of moderate to vigorous physical activity are apparent between Black, Hispanic, and White non-Hispanic females as early as 8 years of age (Grunbaum et al., 2004; Kimm et al., 2002; Trost, Pate, Ward, Saunders, & Riner, 1999). These disparities suggest that culture-specific beliefs and attitudes about exercise may influence participation in phyiscal activity among Black and Hispanic females.

There is some empirical evidence that cultural beliefs about the meaning of physical activity and exercise may play a role in the adoption and maintenance of physical activity by minority women. Eyler et al. (1998) conducted a qualitative study using focus groups to explore the physical activity patterns of middle-aged and elderly minority women. Less is known about the perceived importance of physical activity in the lives of younger Black and Hispanic women. D'Alonzo, Stevenson, and Davis (2004) reported that only 16% of those participants who completed a 16-week exercise intervention targeting Black and Hispanic college-age women were Hispanic and that Hispanic subjects were more likely to cite family responsibilities as interfering with exercise plans. There is increased interest in the applicability of theoretical models, e.g., social cognitive theory (SCT; Bandura, 1997), to clarify the influence of culture-specific factors which likely play a key role in exercise intentions among minority populations. Bandura (2004) has addressed the issue of human functioning in cultural embeddedness from the viewpoint that cultural knowledge shapes the development, structure, purpose, and function of efficacy beliefs and outcome expectations. Qualitative methods are ideally suited to uncover this type of culture-specific information.

The purpose of this qualitative study was to examine what cultural knowledge informs the decision to initiate and adhere to a program of exercise among Black and Hispanic college-age women. The investigation was carried out via focus group interviews. Data obtained from this study will be used to inform a culturally appropriate exercise intervention for Black and Hispanic college-age women based on constructs from SCT. This article addresses the focus group process, data analysis techniques, and results.

Background

There is considerable evidence that obesity and sedentarism have reached epidemic proportions in the United States. Less than one half of adults and less than two thirds of children currently meet the minimum recommendations for physical activity (30 or more minutes of moderate activity 5 or more days/week or 20 or more minutes of vigorous activity 3 or more days/week; CDC, 2003). Rates of inactivity are even higher for Black and Hispanic females at all ages and these discrepancies become more pronounced during the college years (Suminski, Petosa, Utter, & Zhang, 2002; Wallace, Buckworth, Kirby, & Sherman, 2000). Therefore, Black and Hispanic young women are particularly at risk for the development of chronic illness, such as cardiovascular disease, cancer, and diabetes, which are associated with a sedentary lifestyle.

These gender-based racial and ethnic disparities in physical activity appear to have their beginnings in childhood, which suggests that culture-specific beliefs about the role of exercise in the lives of females may influence participation in moderate and vigorous physical activity. Few qualitative studies have examined the exercise beliefs and behaviors of minority women. Belza et al. (2004) used focus groups comprised of older Black, Hispanic, Native American, and Asian women to explore beliefs and patterns of physical activity. Social support was a major facilitator for exercise among both Black and Hispanic women. In another qualitative study, Nies, Vollman, and Cook (1999) likewise reported that social support was a major factor in the decision to initiate and continue a program of exercise. Juarbe, Lipson, and Turok (2003) reported that cultural attitudes about exercise influenced the exercise beliefs and behaviors of Mexican immigrant women. Rogers et al. (2004) used focus groups based on SCT constructs to examine exercise beliefs among women with breast cancer. There is a paucity of theory-based research conducted among younger minority women to identify the similarities and differences in exercise beliefs and behaviors for cross-cultural comparison. Qualitative research methods are well matched to this type of investigation.

Method

Study Design

In this descriptive study, focus group interviews were utilized to examine the women's exercise attitudes and beliefs. Focus groups may provide an alternative means of examining communicative phenomena. They also offer a unique opportunity to interview participants as well as to observe their interaction. Focus groups have been used successfully with various groups to uncover attitudes about exercise (U.S. Department of Health and Human Services, 2002). In this study, the SCT framework was selected for the focus group questions because the purpose of the interviews was to inform an SCT-based exercise intervention.

Participants

Female undergraduate students, 18 to 35 years old, who self-identified as Black or Hispanic and were not regular exercisers were recruited for the focus groups from three student organizations at a large public university in the northeastern United States. The student organizations consisted of a Black women's group, a Latina group, and a minority leadership group comprised of both Black and Hispanic female students. A key informant or "culture broker" (Fetterman, 1998) was identified in each organization who assisted with recruitment. These formal and informal group leaders were later trained by the principal investigator (PI) to serve as a comoderator in each focus group. A purposeful sample was sought, specifically Black and Hispanic women who were not regular exercisers. In purposive sampling, the researcher intentionally selects participants according to the needs of the study. The PI and key informants used primary selection to recruit subjects who met the criteria and who would be willing to participate. A total of 26 women participated in one of three focus group interviews. The PI recruited 12 to 15 individuals per group, to allow for no-shows and to target approximately six to eight informants per group (Morgan, Krueger, & King, 1998). This technique was successful for two of the groups, which contained six and eight informants, respectively. All 12 individuals who were approached for the third group participated.

Measures

Prior to beginning the focus group discussions, a semi-structured interview guide was developed by the PI. The questions were constructed based on application of selected SCT constructs for health promotion interventions but were subject to modification as each session progressed. The SCT framework has consistently been found to be the strongest predictor of intention to exercise and maintenance of exercise over time among adolescents and young adults (Cash, Novy, & Grant, 1994). The two SCT constructs that most directly explain intention to exercise are self-efficacy and outcome expectations. Self-efficacy is defined as judgments of one's ability to perform at a particular level when executing a specific behavior, whereas outcome expectations are judgments of the likely consequences such performances will produce (Bandura, 1997). Specifically, exercise self-efficacy is defined as a person's confidence about their ability to perform specific physical activities under specific circumstances. Self-efficacy is influenced by four principal sources of information: performance accomplishments, modeling (vicarious experiences), verbal persuasion, and emotional arousal (physiological states). Outcome expectations include the positive and negative physical, social, and self-evaluative effects that influence the outcomes that flow from a given course of action. The joint influence of self-efficacy and outcome expectancies on human behavior is illustrated in Figure 1. The application of the conceptual framework is outlined in Table 1, and a copy of the interview schedule is presented in Table 2. Three questions were added to stimulate discussion about culture-specific influences on exercise attitudes and beliefs. These were (1) Do you think there should be anything different about exercise programs for minorities? (2) If you could design an exercise program for minority college women, what would it be like? and (3) What do you think is the best way to encourage participation in an exercise program by both Black and Hispanic students? What could be done to keep these students coming on a regular basis?

An outside researcher with extensive experience in conducting qualitative studies among minority women reviewed the proposed questions. Face validity of the interview schedule was subsequently determined prior to the focus group sessions by having key informants review and approve the questions.

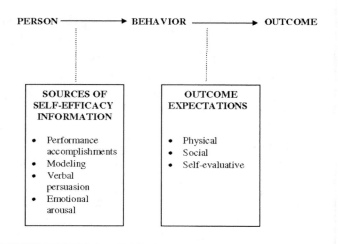

Figure I

The conditional relationships between efficacy beliefs and outcome expectations.

Note: From Bandura, A. (1997). *Self-efficacy: The exercise of control* (p. 22). New York: W. H. Freeman and Company. Adapted with permission.

Table 1 Application of Selected Social Cognitive Theory Constructs to Physical Activity	
Social Cognitive Theory Construct	Definition (Related to Physical Activity)
Expectations	Expected effects of physical activity behavior.
Self-efficacy	Confidence in ability to engage in physical activity.
Behavioral capability	Knowledge of the type of physical activity needed and the skill to perform this activity.
Expectancies	The value of an expected effect of physical activity to the individual.
Environment	Factors influencing physical activity external to the individual.

Note: Adapted from Rogers et al. (2004).

Table 2 Social Cognitive Theory Constructs and Focus Group Questions	
Social Cognitive Theory Construct	Questions
Expectations	Question 1: What is your general impression or thoughts about exercise? Question 2: What do you believe are the benefits of exercising on a regular basis?
Self-efficacy (modeling)	Question 3: Has anyone (e.g., your family or friends) influenced your beliefs about exercise? If so, who and in what ways?
Self-efficacy (performance accomplishments)	Question 4: Have you participated in an exercise program in the past? What did you enjoy about it? What did you dislike?
Behavioral capability	Question 5: What kinds of physical activity do you like to participate in? How important is this for you?
Expectancies	Question 6: Do you refer to exercise alone or in a group? In a structured program (e.g., exercise class) or something else? How important is this for you? Question 7: Would you come to an exercise class if you did not know anyone or no close friends came? Question 8: What do you think are the major facilitators that would keep women like yourself exercising on a regular basis?
Environment	Question 9: What do you think are the major barriers or problems that would keep women like yourself from exercising on a regular basis? Question 10: How important to you are options to exercise (e.g., different types of activities, classes tailored to individual needs/abilities, choice to exercise by yourself or with others)? Question 11: How important is the location where you exercise (e.g., in a gym, in the residence hall, indoors/outdoors)?

Procedure

Following approval from the Institutional Review Board at the university, written consent was obtained from all participants at the beginning of a focus group session. The PI, who has had previous experience in leading focus groups about exercise with minority students, served as the moderator. A key informant for each group worked as the comoderator, and one to two research assistants functioned as recorders. To help foster a naturalistic setting, each focus group was held in the group's regular meeting place in lieu of a regularly scheduled meeting. To promote attendance, a small monetary incentive was offered and pizza and refreshments were provided after each session. The focus groups sessions were audiotaped; two tape recorders were used in the event one malfunctioned. The moderator, comoderators, and trained recorders held a copy of the interview guide during the session and added memos or reflective remarks during the interview process. The moderator followed the interview guide but used the informants' feedback to establish subsequent questions to be posed in the interview. Likewise, the moderator conducted periodic member checks during the interview to summarize or clarify points, gain consensus about emerging patterns, and, when appropriate, to encourage expression of opposing points of view. The focus groups continued until all questions were answered and no new information was provided by the informants. Each focus group session lasted 1.5 to 2.5 hours.

Data Analysis

In this descriptive study, directed content analysis was used to identify repetitive themes regarding exercise. Krippendorff (2004) defines content analysis as ". . . a research technique for making replicable and valid inferences from data to the contexts of their use (p. 18). Berelson (1971) noted that content analysis is a particularly effective technique for uncovering "cultural patterns" of population groups. Directed content analysis, driven by a theoretical framework (in this case, SCT) is a more structured process than conventional content analysis (Hickey & Kipping, 1996). The goal of a directed content analysis is to confirm and conceptually expand the selected conceptual framework (Hsieh & Shannon, 2005). In concept analysis, the use of an a priori theoretical framework with well-defined variables contributes to hypothesis validity (Weber, 1990).

The moderator, comoderator, and recorders debriefed after each focus group session to review the conduct of the session. The audiotapes were transcribed by a paid transcriptionist and the results were reviewed by the research team. To identify errors or incomplete data, the authors replayed the audiotapes while reviewing a copy of the transcript. Each researcher then independently hand-coded "chunks" of words, sentences, and paragraphs and clustered the codes into categories and patterns, using Krippendorff's analytic technique (Krippendorff, 2004). The thematic categories were based on questions from the SCT-based interview guide, but additional culture-specific categories were added that arose during the conduct of the focus groups. To assess reliability, the authors first tested the coding scheme on a sample of the transcript. Intercoder reliability (Weber, 1990) was satisfactory and minor coding, category, and theme discrepancies were discussed and resolved between the researchers. Subthemes were generated from the themes and compared with information in the literature, in an attempt to draw inferences from the data obtained in the focus group sessions. The results were reviewed by both researchers. Theme statements were then formulated and interwoven with the data to obtain a story line.

Results

Fifteen Hispanic women and 11 Black women, ages 19 to 31, participated in the focus group interviews. Twenty-five of the 26 subjects were single women without children. One third of the informants were commuter students. Approximately one third of the subjects were classified by the university as economically disadvantaged; the responses of these subjects to the interview questions were not significantly different from the rest of the group. Demographically, the subjects in the study were very similar to the university's overall Black and Hispanic student populations with regard to age, marital status, residential/commuter status, and socioeconomic position. The women were also evenly distributed with regard to year in college. The responses of the informants were classified into seven thematic categories: (1) general impressions about exercise, (2) exercise role models, (3) social support, (4) benefits of exercise, (5) constraints to exercise, (6) exercise preferences, and (7) cultural issues influencing exercise.

General Impressions About Exercise

Among both Black and Hispanic informants, exercise was overwhelmingly seen in terms of planned, vigorous physical activity—strenuous and uncomfortable: "Getting down and dirty, I mean muscle strain, heart strain, pain." The majority of the informants focused only on aerobic forms of exercise: "Sweating, you know, cardio stuff." Exercise was conceptualized as a means to an end. Most often, the goal was weight loss/appearance enhancement: "You exercise to look good. If you already look good, you don't need to exercise. When you exercise to the point where you look good, you can stop exercising." A few informants saw exercise as a lifestyle choice: "It's walking or normal activities that can be incorporated into what you would normally do in your day." Fewer still conceptualized exercise as a life-long pursuit, "A part of your life plan." Interestingly, none of the women in the focus group interviews associated exercise with either health promotion or prevention of disease.

Exercise Role Models

Black informants were more likely to identify a family member (often a male, but sometimes a female) who influenced them positively to exercise: "My dad and my mom both ran track in high school and that all kind of trickled down to my brothers and me." Another Black informant said, "My mom used to go to the gym a lot and my sister is a body builder—she's very disciplined. So it rubs off a bit."

Hispanic informants were less likely to have role models who exercised. Several women mentioned that they themselves were role models, trying to motivate their family members to exercise with them: "In my family, no one exercises. I'm into sports, I get to exercise, so I'm like the motivator instead of somebody motivating me."

Social Support

Social support was most often conceptualized in the groups as "persons who would go to the gym with you or otherwise encourage you to exercise." Such persons were seen as very important by Black and Hispanic informants, both in terms of initiating and maintaining a program of exercise: "It's easier to go the gym when you have someone who motivates you." One woman noted that her "exercise friends" had become a sort of surrogate family: "People who wanna exercise with you and stuff, its like they become your family."

Social support was also discussed in the context of women's sports. A significant number of Black informants indicated they played team sports in high school and valued the camaraderie of social support. Now that they were in college and no longer active, these women lamented the loss of such support: "When I was in high school, I played for four years . . . and that had to be the best time. You never wanted to let your team down. So that was exercise and you didn't even realize it."

Conversely, a few Black informants indicated they preferred to exercise alone, particularly when running: "When I'm on a treadmill, don't talk to me. I like to run by myself because it's kind of like a personal time. I don't want a lot of people around me." These women also found exercise to be a welcome break from classes and friends: "I like to exercise by myself when it comes to running. I don't like to run with other people because they lower your motivation."

Benefits of Exercise

Both Black and Hispanic informants focused on the immediate "feel-good" effects of exercise: "When you go to the gym, after you are finished, no matter what you did, you don't feel bad. Yeah, hey! I made it! It's so good when you finish." Another informant said, "I used to exercise in the morning. And the rest of the day, I would have so much energy." The Black women in particular emphasized that exercise was a good outlet for their competitive natures: "The person next to you is running five miles and you are only running two, and I want to run as fast as the next person." One woman summarized the feelings of others in the group: "We're all competitive."

Constraints to Exercise

Informants all noted that exercise facilities often cater to experienced exercisers and this sets beginners up to fail: "You will not catch me in advanced classes, 'cause it discourages me. You just don't know if a class says 'cardiovascular exercise' and then you find out it's really hard and then you don't go back." Long waiting lines at the campus gym and sophisticated equipment were also mentioned as barriers to exercise: "There is a long waiting line to get at the equipment at the gym, and there's not enough equipment and so many members. That pretty much turns me off." Another informant said, "I didn't know what the machines were for. You go there and you look like an idiot trying to read the diagrams. Then there are these people who look like they come to the gym all the time and they are looking at you like "You don't know what you are doing."

The Hispanic women (who in this study were more likely to be commuter students) focused more on time limitations as constraints to exercise, including childcare, commuting, and part-time jobs. Even the Hispanic women who were not commuters tended to travel home more frequently and to identify family responsibilities, such as babysitting siblings and assisting grandparents, as barriers to exercise: "You have to budget the time to get there, plus you have to budget the time to exercise, plus you have to budget the time to get yourself cleaned up and maybe to figure out where you're going to be when you get yourself cleaned up." Another informant said, "If I go to the campus gym and work out and I have a large gap of time, I want to go home and take a bath. But if I go home, I won't come back to school."

Preferences

Both groups noted that options, both in terms of specific activities and places to exercise, are preferred. Flexibility was seen as an important factor in adhering to an exercise program: "I don't feel well that day, so maybe I don't want to take an exercise class and I'll just do the treadmill. I just like the option that I could do this for that day and see what happens the next day, how my body feels. If you try to plan, sometimes it just doesn't work out right." Another informant said, "I get bored with the same thing. So I change my activities. Not too different, but never the same thing twice."

Both groups preferred to exercise in places where there were women who looked like themselves, both in terms of body size and race/ethnicity: "I look for someone of my body type." "If I go to a class that seems to be more Caucasian than Hispanic and Black, that gets to be a little weird." Both groups identified musical preferences/dislikes and how they affect their motivation to exercise: "I don't want to go into a class and hear the Dave Matthews Band. I'd like to hear rap music or even a mix of music."

Cultural Issues

Both groups spoke at length about cultural issues relating to exercise and body image. Some topics, such as preferences in the design of classes, have been previously noted. Much of the discussions focused on differences in attitudes about exercise. The Hispanic women focused on adherence to culturally constructed "rules" about what physical activities are appropriate for women and girls. These responses varied according to the women's country of origin and degree of acculturation. Foreign-born women were more likely to feel that certain types of vigorous physical activities were "unfeminine:" "I just came back from Peru and girls over there only play volleyball. I started playing soccer with the guys, and they're like, 'What's she doing?' When I first came to practice, they would say that. They have certain sports for girls."

Several immigrant women noted that parental support for girls who exercise was not as strong in their country of origin as in the United States: "When my sister and I first started playing soccer here, my father would never come to watch us play. He really didn't approve. But once he saw that everyone else does it here and that we are good—now he comes to all the games. It would have been different if he had a son." Dancing was a preferred form of exercise for both groups, but particularly among Hispanic women: "I went to a class and the popular instructor was this Latino guy—it was a dancing Latin aerobics class. There was so much more variety—it was much more of an attraction, I really think so."

As previously noted, both groups conceptualized exercise primarily as a means of appearance enhancement. Both groups emphasized how their bodies were different than those of White non-Hispanic women and that exercise programs designed for minority women should acknowledge and embrace these differences: "My family is from Puerto Rico. I used to hear my father talk. That's what they'd say, 'A little meat here, a little meat there.' They don't like thin—they don't marry thin—they like a little bit of curves and stuff like that."

Another woman from Puerto Rico described the cultural conflict associated with female body image in the mainland United States and in Puerto Rico: "Jennifer Lopez, she looks like an American now. Yeah and she's lost her uniqueness." Black women expressed similar feelings about their bodies: "I walk into the gym, and they all look like Workout Barbie— blonde-haired, ultra slim, big chest, super thin thighs. Only I don't look like Workout Barbie. If anything, I want to look like Halle Berry. She's got a nice little shape, she's got hips." In one focus group in particular, the Black informants reported they often felt pressured (particularly by their mothers) to stay physically active to avoid becoming overweight. Being overweight did not fit with (White) society's expectations for a successful young woman. Many of the Black women felt bitter about exercising only to comply with the expectations of White people: "This is a country that values appearances."

Some of the women noted the pressure to conform to societal standards of beauty was particularly acute for young Black women who are aspiring to highly visible careers: "And so because I want to be a lawyer, she's like 'How are you going to walk around the courtroom in like (that body)?'" Another informant responded, "Ooh, but you can't be fat on the news. You gotta be skinny. You know what I mean? So it's always been this thing of how like, people are gonna respond to you."

Discussion

The responses of the focus group informants to many of the 10 SCT-based questions were consistent with those reported by majority populations (Cash et al., 1994; Tiggerman & Williamson, 2001). Among adolescents and young adults, exercise is most often conceptualized as a means of weight control/appearance enhancement. Both Black and Hispanic informants in this study expressed similar such opinions. Few informants mentioned the health benefits of exercise, which suggests that it is likely not a major motivator in this age group. Time constraints were cited by a number of the respondents as barriers to exercise, along with environments that did not support neophyte exercisers (Ainsworth, 2000; Sallis, Bauman, & Pratt, 1998). Consistent with other studies, social support from family and friends was seen as important by many of the informants (Treiber et al., 1991). The women identified numerous benefits associated with exercise, e.g., renewed energy, and Black women in particular cited a sense of camaraderie and competitiveness as benefits. These findings suggest that these concepts may play an important role as motivators to exercise among some adult minority women.

There were major differences between the Black and Hispanic women's responses with regard to cultural beliefs and influences to exercise. Hispanic informants, particularly those whose who were born outside the United States, were less likely to have participated in competitive sports or vigorous exercise in the past and were less likely to identify family members who were role models for physically active lifestyles. In addition, the foreign-born women were more likely to believe that certain vigorous physical activities were "unfeminine," whereas both foreign-born and American Hispanic women were more likely to cite family responsibilities as constraints to exercise. In the empirical literature, it has been noted that Latinas are often socialized into placing family needs above their own throughout their lives (Alvarez, 1993), which can serve as a barrier to participation in exercise. This phenomenon is referred to as *marianismo* (Comas-Diaz, 1988; Stevens, 1973) and may contribute to low self-efficacy for exercise, either directly or indirectly, by contributing to feelings of depression. There is evidence to suggest that level of acculturation strongly influences *marianismo* beliefs in Hispanic women (Gil & Vasquez, 1996).

Both Black and Hispanic subjects saw their body types as distinctly different from those of White women and acknowledged that they felt uncomfortable comparing their bodies to those of White non-Hispanic women. This is in contrast to the findings from previous studies which noted that Black subjects were not influenced by idealized images of White women (Frisby,

2004). These concerns reflected their conceptualization of exercise as a means of weight control. The Black women were more vocal in describing exercise in terms of a dichotomy. Although they had many positive exercise experiences, they simultaneously felt "pressured" to exercise to conform to "White" standards of beauty. In the past, some of these women had intentionally avoided comparisons with White women in exercise and sport by either (1) participating in "color-blind" sports, e.g., track and swimming, where performance is measured objectively, or (2) gravitating to activities, such as basketball, where there are larger numbers of Black women. As college students, they were now revisiting some of these issues and struggling with how to reconcile two competing value systems.

The impact of these culturally related beliefs and attitudes on intention to exercise using SCT is illustrated in Figures 2 and 3. As depicted in Figure 2, *marianismo* beliefs may directly impact exercise self-efficacy through limited performance accomplishments, few vicarious experiences (*modeling*), and a lack of verbal persuasion. Women who have had less positive exercise experiences and have had few familial role models for physical activity are unable to devise effective "self-talk" strategies to initiate and sustain exercise behaviors. Consequently, women with strong *marianismo* beliefs are more likely to have low exercise self-efficacy and are less likely to participate in physical activity. *Marianismo* beliefs may also influence exercise self-efficacy indirectly, because satisfaction with *marianismo* beliefs may contribute to feelings of depression and self-efficacy beliefs operate as mediators to depression. In these women, exercise is seen as a selfish indulgence, rather than a health-promoting lifestyle behavior.

The Black women in this study experienced negative outcome expectations in the form of negative social reactions, which discouraged them from participation in exercise. Bandura (1997) has noted that individuals resist goals that are externally imposed and when they see no personal benefit. Conversely, individuals will willingly adapt and stick to a goal when their self-interests are linked to goal attainment. In this instance, the women's responses indicated that they personally exercised for reasons other than weight control. The proposed impact of

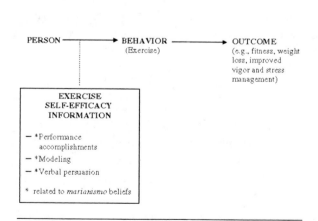

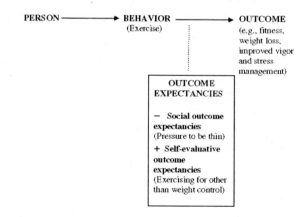

Figure 2

The proposed impact of cultural beliefs and attitudes of Hispanic women on intention to exercise.

Note: From Bandura, A. (1997). *Self-efficacy: The exercise of control* (p. 22). New York: W. H. Freeman and Company. Adapted with permission.

Figure 3

The proposed impact of cultural beliefs and attitudes of Black women on intention to exercise.

Note: From Bandura, A. (1997). *Self-efficacy: The exercise of control* (p. 22). New York: W. H. Freeman and Company. Adapted with permission.

the outcome expectations on intention to exercise is illustrated in Figure 3. Smith, Thompson, Raczynski, and Hilner (1999) have suggested that Black women may possess a source of influence that allows them to feel attractive and satisfied with their appearance, even when at a higher body weight. Thus, their self-evaluative outcome expectations may override the negative social reactions. There is evidence that self-image is a more multifaceted concept for Black women than for White women (Parker et al., 1995; Thomas & James, 1988). One informant in this study echoed these beliefs: "My concept of beauty has to do . . . with what you feel is healthy for you, the individual. It's not just about your looks. It's like a total package deal."

Implications for Nursing Practice

The findings of this study support Bandura's (2004) assumption that cultural knowledge shapes efficacy beliefs and outcome expectations and provide support for the use of SCT as a framework for exercise interventions among Black and Hispanic young women. Moreover, these findings have important and distinctly different implications for the design of culturally appropriate exercise intervention studies. When working with Hispanic women, nurses need to address the balance between meeting responsibilities toward others (*marianismo*) and self-care activities, such as exercise, particularly among immigrant women. Because women need to be healthy and strong to care for their families, it may be useful in this group to emphasize the health benefits and enhanced vigor that are the outcomes of regular physical activity. Likewise, Hispanic women can be encouraged to engage their family members in the process of establishing regular exercise programs. The responses of the informants in this study suggest that dancing may be an appropriate form of exercise for young Latinas. When working with young Black women, it may be helpful to place less emphasis on weight loss as an outcome of exercise and focus instead on "color-blind" outcomes, such as feeling good and making friends. There is growing evidence that as more social and economic opportunities arise for women of color, Black women may become more susceptible to body image dissatisfaction and eating disorders (Root, 1990). By emphasizing their own positive physical and self-evaluative reactions, Black women can learn to use the self-efficacy skills they acquire through exercise to overcome the negative social pressures to conform to maladaptive aspects of what they perceive as "White" behavior.

Limitations

Limitations to this study include a limited period of contact between the PI and the informants. The PI met with the comoderators in advance of the focus group sessions, but did not interact with the informants until the night of the interview. Nonetheless, the informants were eager to participate. The moderator and comoderator monitored the participation of the informants at each session to ensure that everyone had the opportunity to speak and also periodically interacted with informants to foster discussion of opposing points of view. Two focus group sessions ran longer than expected, with the richest discussion coming toward the end and often continuing after the formal meeting. These two groups consisted of only Black and only Hispanic women. Participants in the session involving both Black and Hispanic women were somewhat more reluctant to share their experiences. For future research, it is recommended that the focus groups be kept as homogenous as possible. It is advisable to have smaller numbers of participants with similar racial and ethnic backgrounds and similar exercise histories in each group. This may require additional focus group sessions, each with the use of a moderator and a key informant as comoderator. Although the literature suggests that overrecruitment strategies are recommended to account for no-shows, our experience has been that contingency plans are needed in the event of snowballing or otherwise larger-than-expected numbers of individuals at the focus group sessions. Lastly, care must be taken that the cultural themes identified are not based only on the researcher's view of the cultural system. In addition to the periodic member checks of the informants' responses, it would have been helpful for the moderator and comoderator to have the informants validate the specific cultural categories derived from the data.

The results of this study suggest that there are distinct differences between Black and Hispanic young women in their cultural beliefs and in the attitudes that inform decisions about exercise. Further identification and explication of these cultural beliefs will be valuable for designing future culturally appropriate exercise intervention studies among minority women based on constructs from SCT.

REFERENCES

Ainsworth, B. E. (2000). Issues in the assessment of physical activity in women. *Research Quarterly in Exercise and Sport*, 71(2), S37–S42.

Alvarez, R. R. (1993). The family. In N. Kanellos (Ed.), *The Hispanic American almanac: A reference work on Hispanics in the United States*. Detroit, MI: Gale Research, 151–173.

Bandura, A. (1997). *Self-efficacy: The exercise of control*. New York: W.H. Freeman and Company.

Bandura, A. (2004). Social cognitive theory in cultural context. *Applied Psychology: An International Review*, 51(2), 269–290.

Belza, B., Walwick, J., Shiu-Thornton, S., Schwartz, S., Taylor, M., & LoGerfo, J. (2004). *Preventing chronic diseases. Older adult perspectives on physical activity and exercise: Voices from multiple cultures*. Retrieved September 24, 2005, from http://www.cdc.gov/pcd/issues/ 2004

Berelson, B. (1971). *Content analysis in communication research*. New York: Hafner.

Cash, T. F., Novy, P. L., & Grant, J. R. (1994). Why do women exercise? Factor analysis and further validation of the Reason for Exercise Inventory. *Perceptual and Motor Skills*, 78(2), 539–544.

Centers for Disease Control and Prevention. (2003). *Behavioral Risk Factor Surveillance Survey (BRFSS) Data*. Atlanta, GA: U.S. Department of Health and Human Services, Centers for Disease Control and Prevention.

Comas-Diaz, L. (1988). *Feminist theory with Hispanic/Latina women: Myth or reality?* Binghamton, NY: The Hayworth Press.

Crespo, C. J., Smith, E., Andersen, R. E., Carter-Pokras, O., & Ainsworth, B. E. (2000). Race/ethnicity, social class and their relation to physical inactivity during leisure time: Results from the Third National Health and Nutrition Examination Survey, 1988–1994. *American Journal of Preventive Medicine*, 18, 46–53.

D'Alonzo, K. T., Stevenson, J. S., & Davis, S. E. (2004). Outcomes of a program to enhance exercise self-efficacy and improve fitness in Black and Hispanic college-age women. *Research in Nursing and Health*, 27, 357–369.

Eyler, A. A., Baker, E., Cromer, L., King, A. C., Brownson, R. C., & Donatelle, R. J. (1998). Physical activity and minority women: A qualitative study. *Health Education Behavior*, 25(5), 640–652.

Fetterman, D. M. (1998). *Ethnography step-by-step* (2nd ed.). Thousand Oaks, CA: Sage.

Frisby, C. M. (2004). Does race matter? Effects of idealized images on African American women's perceptions of body esteem. *Journal of Black Studies*, 34(3), 323–347.

Gil, R. M., & Vasquez, C. I. (Eds.). (1996). *The Maria paradox.* New York: G.P. Putnam & Son.

Grunbaum, J. A., Kann, L., Kinchen, S., Ross, J., Hawkins, J., Lowry, R., et al. (2004). Youth risk behavior surveillance—United States, 2003. *Morbidity and Mortality Weekly Report (MMWR)* 53(SS-2), 1–95.

Hickey, G., & Kipping, C. (1996). Issues in research. A multi-stage approach to the coding of data from open-ended questions. *Nurse Researcher,* 4, 81–91.

Hsieh, H. S., & Shannon, S. E. (2005). Three approaches to content analysis. *Qualitative Health Research.* 15(9), 1277–1288.

Juarbe, T., Lipson, J. G. & Turok, X. P. (2003). Physical activity beliefs, behaviors and cardiovascular fitness of Mexican immigrant women. *Journal of Transcultural Nursing,* 14(2), 108–116.

Kimm, S. Y., Glynn, N. W., Kriska, A. M., Barton, B. A., Kronsberg, S. S., Daniels, S. R., et al. (2002). Decline in physical activity in Black girls and White girls during adolescence. *New England Journal of Medicine,* 347, 709–715.

Krippendorff, K. (2004). *Content analysis: An introduction and its methodology* (2nd ed.). Thousand Oaks, CA: Sage. Morgan, D. L., Kreuger, R. A., & King, J. A. (1998). *Focus group kit.* Thousand Oaks, CA: Sage.

Nies, M. A., Vollman, M., & Cook, T. (1999). African American women's experiences with physical activity in their daily lives. *Public Health Nursing,* 16(1), 23–31.

Parker, S., Nichter, M., Nichter, N., Vockovic, N., Sims, C., & Ritenbaugh, C. (1995). Body image and weight concerns among African American and White adolescent females: Differences that make a difference. *Human Organization,* 54, 103–114.

Rogers, L., Matevey, C., Hopkins-Price, P., Shah, P., Dunnington, G., & Courneya, K. S. (2004). Exploring social cognitive theory constructs for promoting exercise among breast cancer patients. *Cancer Nursing,* 27(6), 462–473.

Root, M. P. (1990). Disordered eating in women of color. *Sex Roles,* 22, 525–536.

Sallis, J. F., Bauman, A., & Pratt, M. (1998). Environmental and policy interventions to promote physical activity. *American Journal of Preventive Medicine,* 15(4), 379–397.

Smith, D. E., Thompson, J. K., Raczynski, J. M., & Hilner, J. E. (1999). Body image among men and women in a biracial cohort: The CARDIA study. *International Journal of Eating Disorders,* 25, 71–82.

Stevens, E. D. (1973). Marianismo: The other side of machismo in Latin America. In A. Decastello (Ed.), *Female and male in Latin America.* Pittsburgh, PA: University of Pittsburgh Press.

Suminski, R. R., Petosa, R., Utter, A. C., & Zhang, J. J. (2002). Physical activity among ethnically diverse college students. *Journal of American College Health,* 51(2), 75–81.

Thomas, V. G., & James, M. D. (1988). Body image, dieting tendencies and sex role traits in urban Black women. *Sex Roles,* 18(9), 523–529.

Tiggerman, M., & Williamson, S. (2001). The effect of exercise on body satisfaction and self-esteem as a function of gender and age. *Sex Roles,* 43, 199–227.

Treiber, F. A., Baranowski, T., Braden, D. S., Strong, W. B., Levy, M., & Knox, W. (1991). Social support for exercise: Relationship to physical activity in young adults. *Preventive Medicine,* 20(6), 737–750.

Trost, S. G., Pate, R. R., Ward, D. S., Saunders, R., & Riner, W. (1999). Determinants of physical activity in active and low-active sixth grade African-American youth. *Journal of School Health, 69,* 29–34.

U.S. Department of Health and Human Services. (2002). *Physical activity evaluation handbook.* Atlanta, GA: U.S. Department of Health and Human Services, Centers for Disease Control and Prevention.

Wallace, L. S., Buckworth, J., Kirby, T. E., & Sherman, W. (2000). Characteristics of exercise behavior among college students. *Preventive Medicine, 31,* 494–505.

Weber, R. P. (1990). *Basic content analysis* (2nd ed.). Newbury Park, CA: Sage.

Further Readings

Raedeke, T. D. (2007). The relationship between enjoyment and affective responses to exercise. *Journal of Applied Sport Psychology, 19,* 105–115.

Discussion Questions

1. You have been asked to design an exercise intervention that will strengthen women's self-efficacy to exercise. What are the four sources of information you will use to do this? Please provide specific examples with your activity of choice.

2. Compare self-efficacy beliefs to outcome expectations. Which belief is the most influential in changing exercise behavior?

3. Identify one or two findings from this article that you find interesting, maybe something that surprised you or that you were not expecting to find among African American and Latina college-aged women?

4. A fitness professional from 24-Hour Fitness is seeking your advice on ways to make exercise programs more culturally appropriate for ethnically diverse college-aged women. Using the findings from this study, what would you recommend?

5. Specific to Hispanic/Latina women, what is marianismo and what are the implications of this term for exercise psychologists attempting to design interventions that will foster adherence to exercise in Hispanic/Latina women? Is it possible to establish a healthy balance between marianismo and exercise?

5

Psychosocial Mediators of a Walking Intervention among African American Women

Mary Z. Dunn

© photos.com

© photos.com

From *Journal of Transcultural Nursing,* Volume 19, No. 1, January 2008 by Mary Z. Dunn. Reprinted by permission.

The goals of Healthy People 2010 include increasing participation in physical activity and eliminating health disparities related to race and ethnicity, socioeconomic status, sex, disability, and sexual orientation (Centers for Disease Control & Prevention [CDC], 2003; Levin, Mayer-Davis, Ainsworth, Addy, & Wheeler, 2001; Sheppard, Senior, Park, Mockenhaupt, & Chodzko-Zajko, 2003). In 2001, Behavioral Risk Factor Surveillance System data showed that 46% of adults reported low levels of activity and 33% reported no moderate activity (CDC, 2003). Increasing levels of physical activity to 30 minutes of moderate activity most days of the week would significantly reduce the adverse effects of a sedentary lifestyle on health (American College of Sports Medicine, 1998).

The Harvard Nurses' Studies of 72,000 women, ages 45–65 years, indicated that 3 hours of moderate walking per week (15-min mile or 4 miles/hr) would reduce the annual incidence of coronary heart disease and Type 2 diabetes by one third. Women with a body mass index greater than 29 were more likely to have coronary events unless they were physically active on a regular basis. Physically active people have lower rates of mortality at any age compared with physically inactive peers, independent of percentage and distribution of body fat (Katzmarzyk, Janssen, & Ardern, 2003).

People in minority groups, especially those with lower incomes, self-report low PA. Minority groups have a higher prevalence of overweight individuals and exhibit a greater probability of living in neighborhoods that are not conducive to physical activity because of a lack of safety or comfort or simply for aesthetic reasons (CDC, 2002). Inactivity rates are higher among women than men (CDC, 2003). In studies using conventional measures that favor sporting activities, African American women reported the least physical activity. A high percentage of African American women are obese, and they are twice as likely to have other risk factors that predispose them to heart disease, including hypertension and diabetes (CDC, 2003).

In the United States, obesity is increasing among all age groups, racial and ethnic groups, and educational levels and in both sexes. It is a major health problem, especially among older women, who typically have age-related increases in body weight, an important risk factor for coronary heart disease (CHD), diabetes, and cancer. The prevalence of overweight and obesity among 20- to 74-year-olds increased from 47% to 65% in 2 decades (CDC, 2003). Among African American women, overweight and obesity increased 60%, moving from 31% of the population to 50% between 1995 and 2000 (CDC, 2003). Of African American women in their childbearing years (18–44), 35% are overweight, and 50% of women older than 45 are overweight (Crespo, Smit, Andersen, Carter-Pokras, & Ainsworth, 2000).

The effectiveness of exercise in reducing risk factors in overweight and obese people is seen in improved lipid profiles, lower blood pressure, reduced body fat, and increased metabolic rate. Physical activity improves glucose uptake and insulin sensitivity, increases high-density lipoproteins, and lowers blood pressure (Crespo et al., 2002). Among women in particular, body fat distribution, overweight, and obesity are independent predictors of cardiovascular disease (Sharma, 2004). A 1998 survey of Texas adults indicated that 70% of adults were sedentary. Of that percentage, 60% were older women in their middle years and 77% were African American (CDC, 2003). Women who are overweight or obese often experience disparities in health care such as differential and delayed treatment for elevated cholesterol and blood pressure, poor outcomes following myocardial infarction, and a shortened life span with more chronic disease and disability (CDC, 2003).

Both epidemiological and experimental studies support the hypothesis that regular physical activity is associated with lower morbidity and mortality rates from CHD and better levels of several major CHD risk factors. The greatest health benefits appear to occur between low and moderate levels of activity and cardiorespiratory fitness (Blair et al., 1996; Blair, Kohl, & Barlow, 1993; Kampert, Blair, Barlow, & Kohl, 1996). In a longitudinal cohort study of almost 40,000 women 45 and older, investigators found that active women had a significantly lower risk for events related to CHD than inactive women (Lee, Cook, Rexrode, & Buring, 2001). Epidemiological studies indicate some protective effects of physical activity for other chronic disease conditions including Type 2 diabetes, osteoporosis, colon cancer, anxiety, and depression (Pate et al., 1995). Physical activity is a leading health indicator in Healthy People 2010. It is first-line therapy for reducing disease risk factors and delaying or preventing the development of chronic conditions (U.S. Department of Health & Human Services, 1996). Physical activity preserves function during aging, improves mood, controls weight, and maintains muscle and joint integrity (American College of Sports Medicine, 1998).

Despite what is already known about the benefits of physical activity and intervention methods designed to increase activity, we have much to learn about the relative importance of factors in the domains of the individual, the social milieu, and the physical environment as predictors of physically active behavior (Lewis, Marcus, Pate, & Dunn, 2002). With regard to the individual, we must consider capacity, attitudes, preferences, values, and time demands. For the social milieu, we must evaluate social and cultural norms and support networks. Finally, for the physical environment, we must gauge safety, walking trails, and parkland. Previous research indicates that behavioral changes in physical activity relate to intention, a minimum number of obstacles, level of self-efficacy, congruence with social norms and cultural group values, images of health, frequency of encouragement, and the built environment (Elder, Ayala, & Harris, 1999; Mayo, 1992; Perry & Woods, 1995).

Studies that have examined adherence to physical activity in adults have shown a variety of results: poor physical activity adherence for women (Bautista-Castano, Molina-Cabrillana, Montoya-Alonso, & Serra-Majem, 2004), increased physical activity when the activity is associated with social cognitive theory variables (McAuley, Jerome, Elavsky, Marquez, & Ramsey, 2003; Wilbur, Chandler, Dancy, & Lee, 2003), and increased adherence to physical activity when the group relied on telephone communication for reminders to walk and general encouragement (Heesch, Masse, Dunn, Frankowski, & Mullen, 2003). For the primary study (Keller, Robinson, & Pickens, 2004), adherence to physical activity was low and the factors affecting women's participation in sustained physical activity were not well defined. Therefore, the current study, in which psychosocial factors that hinder or promote adherence to physical activity are explored, was warranted

Method

This descriptive, exploratory study used semistructured focus-group interviews with a group of African American women (Krueger & Casey, 2000) to elicit the women's perceptions of factors that encouraged or inhibited adherence to physical activity during a 9-month period. Before the focus-group interviews, these same women were enrolled in a walking intervention study that was reported elsewhere (Keller et al., 2004).

Investigators recruited participants by personal conversation, letter, telephone, and announcements made at area churches. The invitation to participate described the purpose of the focus groups, provided directions to the meeting room, and explained the time commitment and compensation for the time these discussions required. On the day before each focus-group discussion, participants were telephoned to remind them to attend the group and assess their need for transportation. All groups met at a university conference room. Before consent, the purpose of the focus group and procedures were again explained to all participants. A facilitator and recorder were present at each focus group.

Sample

The sample included 14 postmenopausal African American women between 45 and 66 years of age, all of whom were either overweight or obese (see Table 1). The investigators earned approval from the university Institutional Review Board and obtained signed consent forms from each study participant.

Focus-Group Discussions

Three focus groups were formed, each of which lasted 1.0 to 1.5 hour. An interview guide with stimulus questions was developed to ensure that the study's purpose was addressed fully, but latitude in the content and direction of conversation was allowed. Discussions elicited (a) personal experiences as study participants, (b) perceived motivators and barriers to participation in a walking routine, (c) strategies for maintaining a walking routine, and (d) ideas regarding the salutary effects of exercise. An African American facilitator who served as a research assistant and was known to the women either conducted or was present at each focus group. If women exhausted their discussion of one topic, the facilitator redirected the conversation to another pertinent area. Each discussion began with the facilitator setting expectations that the women could speak freely and express diverse viewpoints. The facilitator used probing questions to elicit expanded explanations of meaning, events, and behavior. Refreshments were served to create a comfortable and socially pleasant atmosphere. A recorder at each group took extensive notes. The discussions were audiotaped and transcribed verbatim.

Table 1 Characteristics of Participants (*N* = 14)		
Characteristic	Range or Frequency (%)	M
Age (years)	56–66	60.1
Height (inches)	61–68.5	65.2
Weight (pounds)	143.4–11	218
% body fat	34.8–56.4	46.5
Body mass index	26–52	52.5

Marital status
  Married
  Divorced
  Widowed
	10 (71.4)
	3 (21.4)
	1 (7.1)	

Data Analysis

In the first step of the data analysis process, the congruity of recorder notes and transcripts of tape-recorded discussions, was assessed. Next, the transcripts were read systematically and iteratively to identify narrative relevant to broad categories of physical activity facilitators, barriers, and social processes. Coding validity was assessed by providing these first-level data categories and their definitions to doctoral nursing students who coded transcripts independently. Next, the graduate students' coding was compared with the coding system, thereby achieving a coding interrater reliability of 98%.

In second-level coding, analytic induction and domain and theme analysis were used to examine processes associated with beginning, stopping, and maintaining a walking routine as prescribed by the intervention (Miles & Huberman, 1994; Spradley, 1979). The integrity of the interpretations of participants' ideas was evaluated during focus groups by paraphrasing women's statements and later by contacting participants for confirmation. Demographic and anthropometric means, ranges, frequencies, and percentages describe the sample.

Findings

Study findings reflected individual, social, and environmental attributes that influenced women's ability to sustain PA. Initially, women characterized their decisions to enroll in the primary study as being underpinned by good intentions; they began with motivation, great hopes, and commitment. However, many found that maintaining a walking program was difficult. Descriptions of the women who were, and were not, able to maintain their walking program; the barriers and facilitators identified in the women's narratives; and the comments expressed by the women in their own words illustrating their experiences are included below.

Women Who Stopped Walking

Women knew walking was what they needed, but they could not manage everything going on in their lives. Most were able to develop tactics and strategies to manage simple barriers, such as schedule changes and weather, to continue regular walking. Those who stopped walking could not do so and stated their reasons without hesitation or self-consciousness: (a) multiple situational factors including family demands, lack of time, and lack of support to continue and (b) personal perspectives, such as devaluing walking and giving over control of behavior to God (see Table 2).

I Wanted to Walk, but My Family Needed Me

Family demands were the most frequently reported reason for not walking. One participant summarized it this way:

> We are always putting other people, our family, and friends first. They always have problems, and they call me, and I'll listen. Even though other people care about you, but they're not thinking that they are drawing energy away from you the whole time, and it wears you down.

Table 2 Barriers and Facilitators to Walking among African American Women	
Barrier Category Exemplars	Facilitator Category Exemplars
Perceiving family needs—"My family needed me"	*Feeling optimistic and enjoyment*—"Walking is challenging and refreshing"
Needing presence of others—"Without others, I couldn't keep it up"	*Having meditative time*—"It was my time with God"
Lacking a routine—"I didn't have a time to walk"	*Feeling better about self*—"I felt and looked good"
Feeling helpless—"Walking is what I need, but can't do"; "I had health problems"	*Achieving better health*—"I have better health (with walking)"
Avoiding accountability—"I dodged responsibility"	*Keeping self foremost*—"Walking is a priority"
Holding potential—"I can change what I do"	*Experiencing reciprocity*—"I can help others"; "Others help me by walking with me"
Unwilling mindset—"I cannot or will not walk"	

I Didn't Have a Time to Walk

The second most frequently cited reason for not walking was not having a regular time to walk. Thanksgiving and Christmas holidays, irregular work schedules, and unanticipated demands on time were perceived as expected and acceptable, but they interfered with walking. Regular walking required setting a goal, developing a routine, and adapting to changing circumstances. Nonwalkers did not have a personal objective in mind when they chose to participate and thought their motivation would come from other participants. One woman said, "I participated because I thought it would be more of a group thing, and I needed the motivation. I enjoy that part."

I Cannot or Will Not Walk

Numerous women made references to God and the devil when they described being committed to their promise to walk. "I promised God I would do this" but "was unable to manage a routine [because of] the devil." Health problems were viewed by 4 women as sufficient reasons for remaining sedentary. One woman stated, "I was so tired. I went to the doctor and they found three thyroid nodules. I think part of the time it might have been from the thyroid." Other women complained of arthritis in the knees, heel ligament damage, or side effects of medication as reasons for not walking.

Women Who Continued Walking

Women who continued to walk claimed exercise was "challenging and refreshing." Comments were made reflecting "I have potential" as women described their initiation of a walking routine. They gave priority to walking, helping others, and altering lifestyles. The most important motivator was having someone who expressed interest in their activity and either acknowledged their efforts or walked with them.

Interjecting Walking into Life as a Priority

There was general acknowledgment that a walking routine had to take priority. One woman described it this way:

> We need to interject walking into our lives, just like cooking dinner for our families. We don't think about it; we just do it for ourselves. We each one of us has to do it in our own way to make it right for ourselves.

Keeping a focus on the self seemed to be the most difficult shift in thinking for women. They spoke of keeping "time for myself" and making walking a "must-do" activity.

Changing What I Do

Walkers experienced changes that were beneficial, unexpected, and joyful and that they described as being for "better health." One woman described her husband's involvement:

> I like to walk with people. My husband said, "I'll walk with you" and I said, "You don't even like to walk." He said, "You said you'd walk. I'll walk with you." So we walked at Fort Sam. We did the track. We did the mall. We had a great time walking together.

Another woman spoke about changes in her cooking style:

> Walking made me change the way I cook. I use ground chicken and turkey. I eat a lot of vegetables. I eat a lot of fish. I eat a lot of salad. And my job at the health promotion center, there is a library where I can read books and pamphlets about health. I collect recipes. That taught me to read labels.

It Was My Time with God

Spirituality and a connection to God were prevalent topics of discussions. Women described feeling meditative during walks, praying while walking, and the happiness this created within them. A woman noted, "I took the time to get close with God and during my walk, especially when I walked by myself. I would just talk to God, like we were having a conversation." One woman equated walking with relief from worry and stress. Walking improved her home life by improving her responsiveness to family members. She said,

> [Walking provided] time to reflect on what was going on in my life. It's a stress relief, and it helped me unwind after work before I get home. It's easier to get along when everybody walks in the evening before they get home.

I Looked Good and Felt Good!

Regular walking yielded positive results for body shape and size. One woman reported that she lost 12 lb, and another said, "My chin disappeared." Not all women were successful in losing weight, but their body shapes were altered.

I Changed and then Helped My Family

The primary motivator for regular walking was the pleasure women got from having a positive impact on their families, family support, and someone to "goad" them. In addition, they liked being able to use their new knowledge, attitudes, and experience to encourage family members and others to begin walking.

Women who walked regularly developed goals and could make changes in their lives and their thinking to accommodate their walking goals. They found a way to weave their focus on their own fitness into their family's lives so that everyone could benefit from the experience. In so doing, they met their family obligations, found time to focus on their personal needs and goals, and generated a sense of personal satisfaction. Contributions to their family's health provided the women with a reciprocal exchange they appreciated and found important to justify their desire to continue walking. The findings indicated that if women lacked an ambition to help others and a reciprocal relationship with others, they found that walking seemed superfluous and selfish. A woman who experienced reciprocity described it this way:

> I enjoy people. I met two new ladies at the mall, and they said, "You seem to be losing weight and you're walking so slow." They started walking slowly with me and then on their own. So when I finished with them, I started with somebody else.

Women consistently reported that they viewed their primary roles as caretaker of the family and those in close social networks. These roles were often extended by responsibility for rearing grandchildren, caregiving for older parents and sick spouses, and obligations within the church. The value of physical activity was secondary to their roles as family women.

Discussion

This study concerned information derived during discussions in three focus groups of older African American women who had participated in an intervention program to promote physical activity. The discussions yielded the women's personal perspectives on factors that increased or hindered adherence to a 9-month walking routine. These findings have implications for future intervention research studies, primary care, and the psychosocial processes of being physically active.

Because of physical activity's well-documented beneficial effects on a variety of health outcomes, it has received considerable attention. It is a national health goal and a growing area of research. No conclusive evidence supports the idea that counseling by primary care providers to promote physical activity is effective, but the U.S. Preventive Services Task Force (2004) has recommended that primary care providers consistently suggest that their patients become physically active.

Becoming active requires certain personal qualities. One of these, self-efficacy, is important as a predictor of behavior, as are motivation, health status, and social support (Boyette et al., 2002; Juarbe, Turok, & Perez-Stable, 2002; Laffrey, 2000; McCauley, Jerome, Elavasky, Marquez, & Ramsey, 2003; Nies & Kershaw, 2002). Physical activity self-efficacy involves having a concept of self that fits with being active, successful experience, positive evaluation of the social environment of activity, and a pleasant emotional response.

Bandura (1997) suggested that the primary predictors of self-efficacy are verbal persuasion, primary experience engaging in a behavior, vicarious experience, and satisfying physiological responses. Whaley and Ebbeck (2002) used the term *self-schemata*, described as "cognitive generalizations about the self that regulate the processing of self-related information as well as behavior" (p. 246). Although it was not a frequent occurrence, some women made self-effacing comments that decreased their motivation. Women who described themselves as walkers were more likely to walk than women who had negative self-images or primary self-schemata as mothers, wives, daughters, and friends.

Individual motivation is strongly associated with self-efficacy and routine physical activity (McCauley, Jerome, Marquez, Elavsky, & Blissmer, 2003). Through motivational interviewing, changes can be made in one's intention and readiness to be active (Prochaska & DiClemente, 1984). More difficult for health providers to address is the value women place on family over self. Family demands may dampen women's motivation to be active, and leisure time may be used for family responsibilities rather than to fulfill personally significant activities, even if such activities would be necessary for health promotion (Oman & King, 2000). The meaning and value of health is both personal and subjective and influences women's physical capacity and desire to exercise.

Conn, Tripp-Reimer, and Maas (2003) suggested that overcoming barriers to exercise would increase women's confidence and foster increased levels of activity. However, overcoming environmental barriers, such as neighborhood constraints, to enhance a woman's ability to engage in physical activity may not transmute to barriers tied to gender role expectations such as family responsibility. On the basis of an analysis of physical activity intervention studies, the Task Force on Community Preventive Services developed recommendations for health care providers to counsel their patients to increase physical activity (Kahn et al., 2002). Strengthening social networks was strongly recommended for its effectiveness in increasing minutes spent in activity and frequency of exercise episodes. As part of the context of physical activity, social network interventions include setting up a buddy system, contracting with another person to complete activity, and developing groups to enhance activity, social relationships, and support.

Perceived barriers and facilitators to activity act as confounders, mediators, and moderators between individual attributes and behavior (Castro, Sallis, Hickman, Lee, & Chen, 1999). They may have a considerable effect in studies of causal relationships between physical activity determinants and outcomes. Investigators planning studies of individual interventions directed toward changing activity behavior should assess individual histories of physical activity and especially subjective perceptions of psychosocial and environmental factors that influenced changes in their physical activity patterns historically. If individuals are strongly influenced by family and friends, group-level interventions directed toward women's social networks may be warranted.

Physical inactivity is one of the leading causes of preventable death, morbidity, and disability in the United States (McGinnis & Foege, 1993). Therefore, interventions designed to increase physical activity must (a) assess knowledge and skills necessary for physical activity,

(b) create an inventory of health-promoting behaviors from which people can choose, (c) teach participants how to gauge their exertion, (d) establish goals for moderate exercise, and (e) assess personal and environmental barriers that are likely to hinder or promote adherence to physical activity.

Broman (1995) and Belza et al. (2004) also found that some women felt health problems kept them from walking. This could be an indication that the meaning of the term *risk* and its association with physical activity needs further assessment. Women need specific information regarding the manner in which physical activity reduces risks for diabetes, hypertension, and other chronic illnesses; how physical activity contributes to cardiorespiratory and metabolic fitness; and how to use equipment and kinesthetic practices for reducing injuries. Exercise diaries that record activity, duration, and frequency with parallel documentation of exertion using the Borg (1998) scale could enhance women's levels of activity and their sense of goal accomplishment.

Researchers who are developing exercise interventions should consider participants' stated preferences for engaging in physical activity with others, particularly with friends. It was worthwhile to recruit participants from churches, because participants knew one another, and these established relationships facilitated adherence to physical activity. Other community settings, such as neighborhood centers, women's social groups, and schools and colleges provide established social networks and affiliations that could increase participants' adherence to exercise regimens. If the physical activity intervention is to be conducted in the participants' neighborhoods, then the need to manage potential barriers to outdoor activity by identifying workplace and community facilities for exercising in inclement weather should be addressed (Eyler et al., 2002). In addition, if investigators assess participants' entry-level fitness before allowing them to embark on an exercise program, then they have an opportunity to match participants who exhibit similar characteristics, such as health status, body size, functional capacity, and exercise goals.

Given the high attrition of women in exercise studies in general, including those that incorporate social networks, further research is needed to examine the relationship between personal facilitators, barriers, and social relationships among these women. This research study suggests that prospects for individual success increase when programs augment individual facilitators, mitigate personal and social barriers, assess individual health status, and design exercise programs that are appropriate for the individuals. The findings support the need to include family-focused interventions and methods that include family activities to encourage compliance among women participating in walking programs. Family support was key to increased physical activity for the African American women who participated in this research study.

References

American College of Sports Medicine. (1998). The recommended quantity and quality of exercise for developing and maintaining cardiorespiratory and muscular fitness, and flexibility in healthy adults. *Medicine and Science in Sports and Exercise, 30,* 975–991.

Bandura, A. (1997). *Self-efficacy: The exercise of control.* New York: Freeman.

Bautista-Castano, I., Molina-Cabrillana, J., Montoya-Alonso, J. A., & Serra-Majem, L. (2004). Variables predictive of adherence to diet and physical activity recommendations in the treatment of obesity and overweight, in a group of Spanish subjects. *International Journal of Obesity & Related Metabolic Disorders, 28*(5), 697–705.

Belza, B., Walwick, J., Shiu-Thornton, S., Schwartz, S., Taylor, M., & LoGerfo, J. (2004). Older adult perspectives on physical activity and exercise: Voices from multiple cultures. *Preventing Chronic Disease,* 1, (4), 1–12.

Blair, S. N., Kampert, J. B., Kohl, H. W., 3rd, Barlow, C. E., Macera, C. A., Paffenbarger, R. S., Jr., & Gibbons, L. W. (1996, July 17). Influences of cardiorespiratory fitness and other precursors on cardiovascular disease and all-cause mortality in men and women. *JAMA,* 276, 205–210.

Blair, S. N., Kohl, H. W., 3rd, & Barlow, C. E. (1993). Physical activity, physical fitness, and all-cause mortality in women: Do women need to be active? *Journal of the American College of Nutrition,* 12, 368–371.

Borg, G. (1998). *Borg's perceived exertion and pain scales.* Champaign, IL: Human Kinetics.

Boyette, L. W., Lloyd, A., Boyette, J. E., Watkins, E., Furbush, L., Dunbar, S. B., & Brandon, L. J. (2002). Personal characteristics that influence exercise behavior of older adults. *Journal of Rehabilitation Research and Development,* 39, 95–103.

Broman, C. L. (1995). Leisure-time physical activity in an African American population. *Journal of Behavioral Medicine,* 18, 341–353.

Castro, C. M., Sallis, J. F., Hickmann, S. A., Lee, R. E., & Chen, A. H. (1999). A prospective study of psychosocial correlates of physical activity for ethnic minority women. *Psychological Health,* 14, 277–293.

Centers for Disease Control & Prevention. (2002). *Physical activity and health: A report of the Surgeon General, 1996.* Atlanta, GA: U.S. Department of Health & Human Services.

Centers for Disease Control & Prevention, National Center for Health Statistics. (2003). *Health, United States.* Retrieved December 1, 2006, from *http://www.cdc.gov/nchs/hus.htm*

Conn, V. S., Tripp-Reimer, T., & Maas, M. L. (2003). Older women and exercise: Theory of planned behavior beliefs. *Public Health Nursing,* 20, 153–163.

Crespo, C. J., Palmieri, M. R. G., Perdomo, R. P., Mcgee, D. L., Smit, E., Sempos, C. T. , I-Min, & Sorlie, P. D. (2002). The relationship of physical activity and body weight with all-cause mortality: Results from the Puerto Rico heart health program. *Annals of Epidemiology,* 12, 543–552.

Crespo, C. J., Smit, E., Andersen, R. E., Carter-Pokras, O., & Ainsworth, B. E. (2000). Race/ethnicity, social class and their relation to physical inactivity during leisure time: Results from the Third National Health and Nutrition Examination Survey, 1998–1994. *American Journal of Preventive Medicine,* 18, 46–53.

Elder, J. P., Ayala, G. X., & Harris, S. (1999). Theories and intervention approaches to health-behavior change in primary care. *American Journal of Preventive Medicine,* 17, 275–284.

Eyler, A. A., Matson-Koffman, D.,Vest, J. R., Evenson, K. R., Sanderson, B., Thompson, J. L., et al. (2002). Environmental, policy, and cultural factors related to physical activity in a diverse sample of women: "The Women's Cardiovascular Health Network Project." *Women & Health,* 36(2), 1–15.

Heesch, K. C., Masse, L. C., Dunn, A. L., Frankowski, R. F., & Mullen, P. D. (2003). Does adherence to a lifestyle physical activity intervention predict changes in physical activity? *Journal of Behavioral Medicine,* 26, 333–348.

Juarbe, T., Turok, X. P., & Perez-Stable, E. J. (2002). Perceived benefits and barriers to physical activity among older Latina women. *Western Journal of Nursing Research,* 24, 868–886.

Kahn, E. B., Ramsey, L. T., Brownson, R. C., Heath, G. W., Howze, E. H., Powell, K. E., et al. (2002). The effectiveness of interventions to increase physical activity: A systematic review. *American Journal of Preventive Medicine,* 22(4, Suppl. 1), 73–107.

Kampert, J. B., Blair, S. N., Barlow, C. E., & Kohl, H. W., III. (1996). Physical activity, physical fitness, and all-cause and cancer mortality: A prospective study of men and women. *Annals of Epidemiology,* 6, 452–457.

Katzmarzyk, P. T., Janssen, I., & Ardern, C. I. (2003). Physical inactivity, excess adiposity and premature mortality [review]. *Obesity Reviews, 4*, 257–290.

Keller, C., Robinson, B., & Pickens, L. (2004). Comparison of two walking frequencies in African-American postmenopausal women. *Association of Black Nursing Faculty Journal, 15*(1), 3–9.

Krueger, R. A., & Casey, M. A. (2000). *Focus groups: a practical guide for applied research* (3rd ed.). Thousand Oaks, CA: Sage.

Laffrey, S. C. (2000). Physical activity among older Mexican-American women. *Research in Nursing and Health, 23*, 383–392.

Lee, I. M., Cook, N. R., Rexrode, K. M., & Buring, J. E. (2001). Lifetime physical activity and risk of breast cancer. *British Journal of Cancer, 85*, 962–965.

Levin, S., Mayer-Davis, E. J., Ainsworth, B. E., Addy, C. L., & Wheeler, F. C. (2001). Racial/ethnic health disparities in South Carolina and the role of rural locality and educational attainment. *Southern Medical Journal, 94*(7), 711–718.

Lewis, B. A., Marcus, B. H., Pate, R. R., & Dunn, A. L. (2002). Psychosocial mediators of physical activity behavior among adults and children. *American Journal of Preventive Medicine, 23* (2, Suppl. 1), 26–35.

Mayo, K. (1992). Physical activity practices among African American working women. *Qualitative Health Research, 2*, 318–333.

McAuley, E., Jerome, G. J., Elavsky, S., Marquez, D. X., & Ramsey, S. N. (2003). Predicting long-term maintenance of physical activity in older adults. *Preventive Medicine, 37*, 110–118.

McAuley, E., Jerome, G. J., Marquez, D. X., Elavsky, S., & Blissmer, B. (2003). Exercise self-efficacy in older adults: Social affective and behavioral influences. *Annals of Behavioral Medicine, 25*(1), 1–12.

McGinnis, J. M., & Foege, W. H. (1993, November 10). Actual causes of death in the United States. *JAMA, 270*, 2207–2212. Miles, M. B., & Huberman, A. M. (1994). *Qualitative data analysis: An expanded sourcebook.* Thousand Oaks, CA: Sage Publications.

Nies, M. A., & Kershaw, T. C. (2002). Psychosocial and environmental influences on physical activity and health outcomes in sedentary women. *Journal of Nursing Scholarship, 34*, 243–249.

Oman, R. F., & King, A. C. (2000). The effect of life events and exercise program format on the adoption and maintenance of exercise behavior. *Health Psychology, 19*, 605–612.

Pate, R. R., Pratt, M., Blair, S., Haskell, W. L., Macera, C. A., Bouchard, C., et al. (1995, February 1). Physical activity and public health: a recommendation from the Centers for Disease Control and Prevention and the American College of Sports Medicine. *JAMA, 273*, 402–407.

Perry, J., & Woods, N. F. (1995). Older women and their images of health: A replication study. *Advances in Nursing Science, 18*, 51–61.

Prochaska, J. O., & DiClemente, C. C. (1984). *The transtheoretical approach: Crossing traditional boundaries of therapy.* Melbourne, FL: Krieger.

Sharma, A. M. (2004). Mediastinal fat, insulin resistance, and hypertension. *Hypertension, 44*, 117–118.

Sheppard, L., Senior, J., Park, C. H., Mockenhaupt, R., & Chodzko-Zajko, W. (2003). Strategic priorities for increasing physical activity among adults age 50 and older: The National Blueprint Consensus Conference Summary Report. *Journal of Aging and Physical Activity, 11*, 286–292.

Spradley, J. P. (1979). *The ethnographic interview.* New York: Holt, Rinehart & Winston.

U.S. Department of Health & Human Services. (1996). *Physical activity and health: A report of the surgeon general, 1996.* Atlanta, GA: U.S. Department of Health & Human Services, Centers for Disease Control & Prevention, National Center for Chronic Disease Prevention & Health Promotion.

Whaley, D. E., & Ebbeck, V. (2002). Self-schemata and exercise identity in older adults. *Journal of Aging and Physical Activity*, 10, 245–259.

Wilbur, J., Chandler, P. J., Dancy, B., & Lee, H. (2003). Correlates of physical activity in urban Midwestern African-American women. *American Journal of Preventive Medicine*, 25(3, Suppl. 1), 45–52.

Further Reading

Sit, C. H. P., Kerr, J. H., & Wong, I. T. F. (2008). Motives for and barriers to physical activity participation in middle-aged Chinese women. *Psychology of Sport and Exercise*, 9, 266–283.

Discussion Questions

1. If you had to design a physical activity intervention for elderly African American women, what activities (besides walking) would be most culturally appropriate and appealing?

2. In addition, what are some ways you could incorporate family and spirituality into these activities?

3. Using the response from the women who successfully completed the walking intervention, what advice would you give to the women who were unable to successfully adhere to the physical activity intervention?

Worksheet 11

Link Up!

Name _____ Date _____

Log on to the Tucker Center for 2007 research report on girls and women in sport:
http://cehd.umn.edu/tuckercenter/projects/TCRR/default.html

Define the following terms:

Anxiety: _____

_____

Burnout: _____

_____

Competence: _____

_____

Confidence: _____

_____

Identity: _____

_____

Moral Reasoning: _____

_____

Motivation: _____

_____

Self-esteem: _____

_____

Sportsmanship: _____

_____

Worksheet 12

What's Missing

Name _____ Date _____

In chapter two, Magyar (2008) focused on the sport of rowing and the majority of participants were White. What do you think the results would be if the sample was more diverse and performing a different sport? Are there any important leadership skills that are missing? Review the leadership skills questionnaire below and add skills that are important for leadership in ethnically diverse female athletes performing different team sports (e.g., basketball, volleyball, field hockey, etc).

Directions: Please think about **leadership in rowing** and rate the importance of each statement below.

It is important for an athlete leader to . . .

	Not at all Important		Somewhat Important		Very Important
1. Be the "go to" person in a time of need	1	2	3	4	5
2. Be sensitive to the needs of every teammate	1	2	3	4	5
3. Set performance goals for the team	1	2	3	4	5
4. Do anything to win (e.g., jump the start, or cheat)	1	2	3	4	5
5. Make others perform better through example	1	2	3	4	5
6. Display 100% effort	1	2	3	4	5
7. Console teammates when they are frustrated	1	2	3	4	5
8. Be respected by teammates	1	2	3	4	5
9. Have confidence in his or her ability to lead others	1	2	3	4	5
10. Keep teammates calm before competition	1	2	3	4	5
11. Intimidate others to get the work done	1	2	3	4	5
12. Resolve conflict between teammates	1	2	3	4	5
13. Be one of the best athletes on a team	1	2	3	4	5
14. Foster "togetherness" or cohesion	1	2	3	4	5
15. Handle pressure situations	1	2	3	4	5
16. Communicate effectively with teammates	1	2	3	4	5
17. Be respected by coaches	1	2	3	4	5
18. Have the ability to identify performance related problems	1	2	3	4	5
19. Provide external motivators (e.g., foster team-bonding situations, develop team identity, etc.)	1	2	3	4	5
20. Encourage teammates to win at all cost (e.g., jump the start or cheat)	1	2	3	4	5

What skills would you add to this list for a different sample of athletes performing a different team sport?

_____

_____

Worksheet 13

Gold Medal Body

Name _____ Date _____

Wall of Fame
- Photos of male and female Olympians featured in *Vanity Fair* (1996)
- Olympic female track athletes pose in nude calendar (1999)
- Brandi Chastain, USA World Cup champion soccer team member, poses nude behind a soccer ball in *Gear Magazine* (1999)
- Jenny Thompson, Olympic swimmer, shirtless in *Sports Illustrated*, her breasts covered only by her own clenched fists (2000)

Listed above are just a few of the notable Olympic pin-ups. Conduct your own research to determine the Olympic athletes who have posed in magazines more recently. Some of the more popular magazines are *FHM* and *Maxim*.

Magazine: _____

Olympic athlete who posed: _____

_____

How do the photos portray the athlete? _____

_____

Was there an article on the athlete? If so, what was the content? _____

_____

Why do you think the athlete chose to pose for this particular magazine?_____

_____

Do you believe that female athletes become more empowered when they decide to take their clothes off to get greater exposure, or do you feel that these efforts to promote the sport are demeaning to female athletes?

_____

_____

_____

Worksheet 14

"ISMS" in Sport-Age

Name _____ Date _____

How do we typically view elderly women in our society? _____

_____

How do you think body image changes for women as they transition across the lifespan?

Youth	High School	Young Adult	Middle Age	Older Adult

Worksheet 15

"Who's Your Role Model?"

Name _____   Date _____

Martin, Richardson, Weiller, and Jackson (2004) surveyed 426 family units to identify their athlete role models. Their results are presented in the table below.

	Athletes		Parents	
	Boys	Girls	Fathers	Mothers
Female Model	2 (1%)	74 (57%)	1 (.05%)	33 (24%)
Male Model	207 (99%)	56 (43%)	142 (95.5%)	103 (76%)
Total	209	130	143	136

1. Why do you think 43% of girls identified a male role model while only 1% of boys identified a female role model?

   _____

   _____

2. A majority of girls identified with a female role model (57%) rather than a male role model (43%). In contrast, the majority of mothers identified with a male role model (76%) rather than a female role model (24%). What do you attribute this difference to?

   _____

   _____

3. Do you think we will ever see a time when men will identify with a female athlete rather than a male athlete as their role model in sports? Why or why not?_____

   _____

4. Who was your role model growing up who inspired you to become physically active and/or involved in sport?

   _____

   _____

Martin, S. B., Richardson, P. A., Weiller, K. H., & Jackson, A. W. (2004). Role models, perceived sport encouragement, and sport expectancies of United States adolescent athletes and their parents. *Women in Sport and Physical Activity Journal*, 13, 18–27.

SECTION 4

Biomedical
Issues

© Goodshoot

Section 4
Introduction

Ann F. Maliszewski

As the participation of women and girls in sport increased following the passage of Title IX in the 1970s, scientific research on the effects of physical activity and exercise in women has expanded considerably. This section of the text provides an overview of some of the most critical scientific and medical issues related to women and sport and physical activity today. The primary focus of the research is in the area of exercise physiology and health, so the information applies to most women, not just athletes. Physiology is the study of how the cells and organ systems of the body function, how they respond to different stimuli, how they can be improved, and how they can fail (i.e., disease). Research on the physiology of women and physical activity is vast and ranges from epidemiological studies on how physical inactivity relates to various diseases to biochemical studies on how exercise stimulates molecular changes within the body's cells.

Physiological research on physical activity examines responses or adaptations of the body to physical stress, or lack thereof. *Physiological responses* are the changes that occur during and immediately following physical activity. *Physiological adaptations*, on the other hand, are the changes that take place over weeks or months of participation in an activity program. For example, the increase in heart rate during a workout is a physiological response. The decrease in resting heart rate that occurs when someone participates regularly in an aerobic training program is a physiological adaptation. The studies in this section will include both types of research.

Generally, physical activity is used to achieve one of three main goals. The first and most basic goal is *physical activity for health*, in which minimal requirements of daily activity reduce the risk of various diseases. The second goal is *physical activity for fitness*. Meeting the recommendations for this category leads to improved measures of cardiorespiratory endurance, body fatness, flexibility, and/or muscular strength and endurance. The highest achievement goal is *physical activity for athletic competition*. Exercise in this category is prescribed to meet the specific demands of a given sport and is designed to maximize athletic performance. The physiological and medical issues related to women and physical activity span the range of these goal categories.

In Chapter 1, *Physical Activity: The Magic Bullet for Chronic Disease*, Lamont and Maliszewski provide an overview of these issues ranging from the leading causes of death for women, what those diseases actually entail, and how physical activity can help to prevent those diseases. Differences across racial and ethnic groups for these topics are also discussed. The current recommendations for physical activity for health are clearly outlined in this chapter, and finally the authors discuss how well women are doing in achieving those recommendations.

Besides being among the top 10 leading causes of death for women in the United States, cardiovascular disease and type 2 diabetes have other things in common, namely their risk factors. In the study of chronic disease, a cluster of pre-disease risk factors, which together increase the risk for cardiovascular disease and type 2 diabetes, has been identified. There has been some debate in the scientific and medical communities about the name for this cluster of risk factors, but the most commonly used term is *metabolic syndrome*. The components of metabolic syndrome include high blood pressure, elevated blood sugar and cholesterol measures, and increased fat storage in the abdominal region of the body. The more of these risk factors that are present in one individual, the greater the risk of developing cardiovascular disease and/or type 2 diabetes. Fortunately, physical activity has beneficial effects on the risk factors that make up metabolic syndrome. In *Metabolic Syndrome & Physical Activity: Move to Better Health* (Chapter 2), the facts about metabolic syndrome, how it affects women of various ethnic and racial backgrounds, and what women can do to avoid it are discussed.

Although most of the biochemical processes of the body are identical for men and women, one clear difference is in the amount of the different reproductive hormones. Women and men can make all three major reproductive hormones: estrogen, progesterone, and testosterone. But women have more estrogen and progesterone because these hormones are made in large quantity by the ovaries. Men have a lot more testosterone, because this hormone is produced in large quantity in the testes.

Hormones are molecules that are secreted from the body's glands into the blood. The blood delivers the hormones to cells throughout the body where they will have a variety of effects. Insulin, for example, is a hormone secreted by the pancreas. It travels through the blood and binds to muscle cells, causing them to take sugar out of the blood. Similarly, when the ovaries secrete estrogen and progesterone, they will bind to and have effects on various tissues in the body.

When studying physiological effects of exercise in women, the menstrual cycle must be taken into consideration. This is because the reproductive hormone levels change throughout the cycle, and therefore have the potential to vary the responses of the tissues and cells being studied. Chapter 3, titled *Exercising with "Your Friend": Exercise and the Menstrual Cycle*, provides an overview of how the reproductive hormone levels change throughout the menstrual cycle, what the target tissues are for the hormones, and what the effects of those hormones are on those tissues during exercise.

The hormone and tissue changes that take place during the menstrual cycle are sometimes associated with physical and emotional symptoms. Likewise, when the menstrual cycles cease in a woman's life (i.e., menopause) the absence of the hormones has it own side-effects. Women who are physically active have a different experience with these symptoms compared with women who are inactive. These issues are also examined in Chapter 3.

During pregnancy, the normal monthly hormone cycles cease. The woman's body experiences increasing levels of estrogen and progesterone throughout the nine months. Accompanying the increases in the reproductive hormones are other changes including weight gain, increased nutritional demands, changes in body temperature, joint laxity, etc. During pregnancy, the mother shares nutrients and oxygen in the blood with her fetus. When the woman is physically active, the muscles require more oxygen and fuels to supply energy. During exercise, blood is shunted away from the internal organs and out to the working muscles. The concern is that the mother's tissues and the fetus will compete for the fuels and oxygen. Fortunately, research on the effects of physical activity during pregnancy consistently demonstrates a positive role of exercise in both the mother and the fetus. In Chapter 4, *Pregnancy & Exercise*, Little provides an overview of the role of exercise during pregnancy, including an examination of the effects of different types of exercise on various measures. She also provides the current recommendations for exercising during and after pregnancy.

What most of the research included in this section demonstrates is that physical activity has many health benefits for women. But because exercise places physical stress on the body's systems and cells, it must be managed carefully and applied in moderation. Moderation is rarely seen in highly competitive athletes, however, and there are physical complications associated with extremely high levels of training. It has long been known that some women athletes, especially those involved in endurance (e.g., distance runners) and aesthetic activities (e.g., ballet dancers), sometimes experience a loss of the menstrual cycle. *Amenorrhea*, the absence of normal menstrual cycles, used to be considered a perk for women athletes. Now there is a better understanding of the negative physiological consequences of this condition.

Amenorrhea is accompanied by reductions in the female reproductive hormone levels. Because tissue growth and maintenance depend on normal levels of these hormones, the absence of the menstrual cycle may be a sign of malfunctioning organ systems. As research in this area intensified in the 1980s, a pattern emerged in which amenorrhea was related to low bone density levels. Because amenorrhea and bone loss had been observed in women with anorexia nervosa, the influence of dietary status also became a primary area of focus. *The Female Athlete Triad* is the label applied to this combination of symptoms and conditions. This, and other complications of pushing the body too far with exercise are discussed in Chapter 5, *Too Much of a Good Thing: Overtraining & The Female Athlete Triad*.

Activities related to physical activity, health, and hormone status are presented at the end of this section on *Biomedical Perspectives*. Some of these activities may be used as part of your course on women in sport and physical activity. The activities are designed to help you understand more about your own physiology, health status, and physical activity patterns, or that of female friends and family members. You are encouraged to use these tools to enhance your learning.

1

Physical Activity

The Magic Bullet for Chronic Disease

Linda S. Lamont & Ann F. Maliszewski

Disease and Death Among Women in the U.S.

Chronic disease is defined by the World Health Organization as "diseases of long duration and generally slow progression." Chronic diseases are responsible for over 70% of the deaths in the United States (US) and Table 1 lists the top 10 leading causes of death of women in this country. The good news is that many chronic diseases are preventable. This chapter focuses on the influence of physical activity and exercise on the prevention and treatment of these diseases, however, it should be understood that other factors such as genetics, diet, and environmental factors influence the risk and progression of these diseases as well.

The statistics from the Centers for Disease Control and Prevention (CDC) outlined in Table 1 show that heart disease is the leading cause of death among all U.S. women, accounting for approximately 350,000 deaths each year. When asked, however, only half of women are aware that heart disease is number 1. According to one survey, only 31% of Black women (and 29% of Hispanic women) know that heart disease is the leading cause of death, even though Black women are at the highest risk for the disease among all racial/ethnic groups! According to the American Heart Association (AHA), only 1 in 5 physicians knows that more women die of heart disease each year than men. It's clear that both the lay public and health-care professionals are misinformed about heart disease—and disease—risk in general. Getting this information out is especially important because heart disease is preventable through proper diet and physical activity.

Cancer is the second leading cause of death among women in the U.S. All racial/ethnic groups have cancer as the second leading cause of death except for Asians or Pacific Islanders for whom cancer is the leading cause. Most women think that breast cancer is the leading cause of cancer deaths among women. Although breast is the most common form of cancer, lung cancer kills about 4 times as many women. Smoking accounts for 85% of all cases of lung

	Table I Leading Causes of Death of Women in the U.S. all Women and by Racial/Ethnic Group. (CDC Statistics for 2004, http://www.cdc.gov/women/lcod/04females_by_race.pdf)					
Rank	All Women	White Women	Black Women	Native American	Asian or Pacific Islander	Hispanic
I	Heart Disease	Heart Disease	Heart Disease	Heart Disease	Cancer	Heart Disease
2	Cancer	Cancer	Cancer	Cancer	Heart Disease	Cancer
3	Stroke	Stroke	Stroke	Accidental Injury	Stroke	Stroke
4	CLRD*	CLRD*	Diabetes	Diabetes	Diabetes	Diabetes
5	Alzheimer's Disease	Alzheimer's Disease	Kidney Disease	Stroke	Accidental Injury	Accidental Injury
6	Accidental Injury	Accidental Injury	Accidental Injury	Liver Disease	Influenza or Pneumonia	Influenza or Pneumonia
7	Diabetes	Diabetes	CLRD*	CLRD*	CLRD*	CLRD*
8	Influenza or Pneumonia	Influenza or Pneumonia	Septicemia	Influenza or Pneumonia	Alzheimer's Disease	Alzheimer's Disease
9	Kidney Disease	Kidney Disease	Alzheimer's Disease	Kidney Disease	Kidney Disease	Perinatal
10	Septicemia	Septicemia	Influenza or Pneumonia	Septicemia/ Suicide	Hypertension	Kidney Disease

*CLRD = Chronic Lower Respiratory Disease; Data from Centers for Disease Control & Prevention (http://www.cdc.gov/Women/lcod.htm)

cancer, making it a very preventable disease. Breast and colorectal cancers are the second and third leading causes of cancer among women, and as you will learn in this chapter the risk of these cancers can be influenced by lifestyle.

For all women and for each racial and ethnic group except for Native Americans, stroke is the 3rd leading cause of death (5th for Native American women). Diabetes is the 7th leading cause of death for all women combined and for White women only, however, it is the 4th leading cause of death for all other groups (Black, Native American, Asian/Pacific Islander and Hispanic). Alzheimer's disease (AD) and chronic lower respiratory disease (CLRD) are also among the top 10 causes of death among women. What many of these diseases (heart disease, cancer, stroke, CLRD, diabetes and AD) have in common is that they may be influenced by lifestyle, specifically physical activity and diet.

Of the ten leading causes of death in the United States, six can be affected by physical activity. The risk of developing heart disease, cancer, stroke, and diabetes can all be reduced by participation in a regular exercise program. Being physically active can also affect the development and progression of Alzheimer's disease and chronic lung diseases. Although it is not among the top leading causes of death, osteoporosis impacts many women late in life. This is another chronic disease that can be influenced by physical activity. We will take a closer look at each of these diseases and examine what the research shows us about the relationship between physical activity and the disease.

Chronic Disease and Physical Activity in Women

Heart Disease

The cardiovascular system consists of the heart and the blood vessels. The heart is a 4 chambered, fist sized muscle that is located beneath the breast bone. It pumps oxygen poor blood to the lungs in order to pick up oxygen, and it pumps oxygen rich blood to the rest of the body to feed oxygen to our working cells. Interestingly, the blood that is being pumped by the heart does not reach the individual cells of the heart. Therefore, the heart must obtain its own supply of oxygen rich blood through a network of blood vessels. There are two large vessels that branch into smaller and smaller vessels around the heart to feed it with blood. These two vessels are known as the right and left coronary arteries. A blockage to either of these arteries, or their smaller branches, can cause a reduction in the oxygen supply to the heart. When a reduction in oxygen occurs it is known as *ischemia*. A prolonged lack of oxygen-rich blood to the heart causes a heart attack and the proper medical term for this is a *myocardial infarction* (MI). An MI is the result of a long-term process of narrowing in the coronary arteries. It damages the heart muscle itself and can leave the heart unable to pump blood effectively. There are many types of diseases of the heart, but the specific type of disease that affects the arteries that supply blood to the heart is known as *coronary artery disease* (CAD).

CAD is the leading cause of death in this country. Although more men than women have this disease, it kills more women than it does men. Nearly 1 in 3 women die of heart disease. But when asked what they're most likely to die of, women will significantly underestimate their risk for heart disease and overestimate their risk for breast cancer. It is important that women are educated about this misconception, because they are much more likely than men to die within a year of sustaining a heart attack. Scientists believe that women develop heart disease at an older age in life because their sex-specific hormones are protecting them from its development. The hormone estrogen is thought to protect women from heart disease until menopause. Estrogen levels decrease at menopause, usually around the age of 50 years, and at this time a woman's risk for heart disease climbs. Another reason women are more likely to die of a heart attack is that their hearts and their arteries are smaller than men's. Of concern is that women who have heart disease are evaluated and treated for this disease less aggressively when compared with men. This may be because women have different symptoms when having a heart attack than do men. *Women are just as likely to say that they are having chest pain; but they are much more likely to have non-chest pain symptoms such as fatigue, weakness, nausea, breathing difficulties, and vomiting. Furthermore, women may report pain in areas other than the chest, such as in the back, stomach or jaws.* Women, therefore, need to be persistent when seeking medical care and realize that hospital personnel can also be deceived by these "atypical" heart attack symptoms.

Symptoms of a heart attack can be sudden and intense, but most attacks start slowly with a mild pain or discomfort. If heart attack symptoms are experienced the individual should call 911 and go to the nearest hospital emergency room. Unfortunately, half of all heart attack victims wait too long (more than 2 hours) before going for help. This delay can prolong the time in which necessary medical treatment can be started.

A program of regular exercise will reduce the chances of a woman developing heart disease. An expert panel of the National Institutes of Health states that this activity does not need to be structured or vigorous to reduce your risk. But exercise must be regularly performed at a moderate intensity for at least 30 minutes or more on most days of the week. Aerobic (e.g., "cardio") activities such as walking, jogging, swimming, bicycling, or rowing are all excellent forms of exercise that will lower heart disease risk. Exercise is thought to be the closest thing to a magic bullet in the arsenal available to prevent the onset of CAD. One study found that women who accumulate around 3 hours of brisk walking each week can cut their risk of a heart attack by half. Regular aerobic exercise helps to decrease the risk for CAD by lowering blood pressure, increasing "good cholesterol" levels (HDL cholesterol), improving the condition of the blood vessels themselves, and helping to maintain a desirable body weight. Many feel that more research is needed in women, but that a sedentary lifestyle affects a woman's risk for CAD to the same extent that it does in men. Women also can benefit from a resistance exercise program (i.e., weight lifting). Although aerobic activities are most effective for developing cardiorespiratory fitness and lowering risk for heart disease; muscle strengthening exercises are important because activities of daily living require some amount of muscle strength to complete.

Exercise is also being prescribed for people as a rehabilitative tool after sustaining a heart attack. Generally, exercise is included in a program that emphasizes lifestyle change, vocational counseling, smoking cessation, and the optimization of drug therapy. This program is known as *cardiac rehabilitation* and it is staffed by various health-care professionals including: nurses and physicians, social workers, psychologists, dietitians, and exercise physiologists. These types of programs were developed in the 1950s when the epidemic of heart disease was growing rapidly in this country. The medical procedure used to treat someone who had sustained a heart attack in the 1950s was to have them stay in bed for a minimum of two to three weeks. Early rehabilitation programs demonstrated that physical activity was helpful to the recovery process for the cardiac patient. Today, however, only a small percentage of eligible cardiac patients actually participate in a cardiac rehabilitation program. Heart attack patients should be encouraged to enroll in a safe exercise program at their local cardiac rehabilitation facility. The benefits to them include an increase in their endurance, a reduction in their chest pain symptoms, an increase in their sense of well-being, and a reduction in their chances of death. The value of enrolling in cardiac rehabilitation is that an exercise prescription can be written specifically for that patient and their heart rate, blood pressure, and electrocardiogram can be monitored for safety.

Cancer

There are more than 100 known types of malignant tumors or *neoplasms*: a disease of uncontrolled growth and spread of abnormal cells. Cancer is a general term used to indicate any one

Table 2 Mortality Rates for Cancer Deaths in the U.S. by Racial/Ethic Group (American Cancer Society, Surveillance Research, 2007; http://www.cancer.org)

Rank	White Women	Black Women	Native American	Asian or Pacific Islander	Hispanic/Latina
1	Lung & Bronchus	Lung & Bronchus	Lung & Bronchus	Lung & Bronchus	Breast
2	Breast	Breast	Breast	Breast	Lung & Bronchus
3	Colon & Rectum	Colon & Rectum	Colon & Rectum	Colon & Rectum	Colon & Rectum
4	Kidney or Liver	Stomach	Liver	Stomach or Liver	Stomach

of these 100 types. Normally, cells reproduce and divide in an orderly manner. However, some environmental, hormonal, immune, or inherited factors appear to contribute to the process by which cells experience abnormal changes and eventually become cancer cells. The formation of cancer is known as *carcinogenesis* and it is a long process that can often take more than 10 years. Cancer is the second leading cause of death in this country and the lifetime risk of its development is slightly greater in men than in women (46% versus 38%). Scientists believe that cancer will replace heart disease as the leading killer of Americans sometime after the year 2010. This is because the death rates for heart disease have steadily fallen for the past 60 years, whereas those for cancer have not. Table 2 ranks the most common types of cancer in women.

People who exercise regularly have less of a cancer risk than do individuals who have a sedentary lifestyle. The most significant protective effect of exercise has been shown for three of the most common types of cancer: colorectal, breast, and prostate and we will discuss in detail the first two types. Colorectal cancer appears to be 40–50% more likely to occur in sedentary compared with physically active individuals. When 90,000 female nurses were studied over a 12–year period of time, regular physical activity was shown to have a protective effect against the appearance of colon cancer in these nurses. The reason for this protective effect remains unknown but there are many theories. One theory is that physical activity stimulates muscle movement in the large intestines. This increased intestinal movement shortens the time that cancer-causing substances actually stay in contact with the cells that line the gut. That is, fecal matter moves through the gut faster with exercise. Some liken the effect of exercise to the effects that dietary fiber has on the intestines. Interestingly, those who exercise report fewer symptoms of constipation than do sedentary individuals. Other theories for the reduction in colon cancer in active people is an enhancement in immune function, an improvement in diet in those who are active, or a more favorable change in energy balance.

The other major form of cancer that demonstrates a protective effect with exercise in women is breast cancer. Three out of 4 published studies indicate that physically active women have a 30–40% reduced risk for the development of breast cancer. It should also be underscored that this research indicates that those who engage in vigorous exercise from early in life appear to gain the best protection against this disease. The theories for why breast cancer risks are reduced with regular exercise include: a reduction in the exposure to the female hormones, alterations in the menstrual cycle, changes in hormonal or immune factors, or a decrease in the body's fat stores.

Exercise therapy is also being used as a rehabilitative tool after the cancer diagnosis. Although it has not been shown to influence tumor growth, disease progression, or patient survival, it is promoted for its benefits on quality of life issues. In these types of rehabilitation programs, the exercise is often modified based on the patient's treatment schedule and tolerance. It is being recommended for cancer patients to improve their level of aerobic fitness, their quality of life, and their morale.

Stroke

Stroke is the 3rd leading cause of death in the United States and it is caused by an insufficient supply of blood going to the brain. It is a form of cardiovascular disease that affects the blood vessels to the brain. Most strokes are due to arterial narrowing from fatty buildup. The underlying causes for this fatty buildup are similar to that found in the heart. However, when the arteries that supply blood to the brain become blocked, a stroke occurs. The interruption of blood supply to the brain prevents the nerve cells from functioning and can cause death. Of the 700,000 Americans who suffer a stroke each year, nearly one-third will die within a year, and of those who survive most will have some lasting disability.

Effective treatment requires that the symptoms of stroke be recognized and that therapy is started promptly. Stroke symptoms include: a sudden numbness or weakness of the face, arm or leg (especially on one side of the body), a sudden confusion, trouble speaking or understanding, a sudden problem seeing in one or both eyes, a sudden severe headache of unknown origin. If any of these symptoms occur 911 should be called and the individual transported to the nearest emergency room.

Physical inactivity is not recognized by the American Heart Association as a primary risk factor for stroke but it is classified as a *potentially modifiable risk factor* for this disease. In essence this means that there are fewer research studies available to link physical inactivity with an increased risk of stroke or that the relationship between inactivity and stroke is not as strong as it is for CAD. But a growing number of studies in recent years are establishing a link. In one study the risk of a stroke fell by 56% in individuals who engaged in regular and vigorous exercise from the ages of 15–25 years, and an additional protective effect was experienced in those who exercised throughout adulthood. Another current study found a strong protective effect against strokes in both men and women with a regular exercise program. It seems likely that future research will indicate that regular physical activity is useful in the prevention of this form of cardiovascular disease as well.

Diabetes

Diabetes is in the top ten leading causes of death in this country. Table 1 indicates that the disease risk for African American, Native American, Asian or Pacific Islander, and Hispanic women places this disease at 4th place, but it remains the 7th leading cause of death for Caucasian women and for women as a whole. The development of diabetes has been on the increase in recent years: for instance during the decade of 1990–2000, the prevalence rose by 29%. This statistic has many health care providers alarmed because diabetes has many long-term complications including: heart disease, stroke, high blood pressure, blindness, kidney disease, nervous system disease, risk for amputations, dental disease, and complications of pregnancy. Common symptoms of diabetes include: excessive urination, thirst, and hunger. Other common symptoms are weight loss, fatigue, weakness, blurred vision, slow healing times, and an increased risk of infection. The symptoms vary depending on which type of diabetes the individual has.

Diabetes impairs the body's ability to use a simple sugar known as *glucose* for fuel. Glucose is carried throughout the body in the blood, but insulin is needed to move this glucose from the blood into the cells. Insulin is a hormone made by the pancreas gland and sometimes diabetes is caused by a lack of this hormone; but it also can occur because the patient's cells are insensitive to the insulin hormone that is produced. There are 2 common types of diabetes.

The first type is known as *type 1 diabetes* and the risk factors for its development include: autoimmune, genetic and environmental factors. The autoimmune process that causes type 1 diabetes is the body's own immune system destroys the cells that make insulin. The cells of the pancreas that produce insulin are known as the *beta cells*. This type of diabetes generally requires: daily insulin injections or treatment with an insulin pump in order to maintain blood insulin levels, as well as a diet and exercise plan. Fewer than 1 million Americans have type 1 diabetes.

Another common type of diabetes is known as *type 2 diabetes*. In the past, type 2 diabetes was considered to be a disease primarily of adults. Now the incidence of this type of diabetes is increasingly being diagnosed in children and this is of major concern to health-care providers. The incidence of this type of diabetes is highest among ethic minority children. Type 2 diabetes is caused by the body's inability to use insulin properly. That is the body's cells are insensitive to the insulin hormone. More than 17 million Americans have type 2 diabetes and that makes it the most common type of this disease. It is noteworthy that rates for this type of diabetes have dramatically risen as a modern lifestyle is adopted. In China for instance the rates of diabetes increased by 3–times as their culture moved from a traditional to a more modern society. Scientists report that 90% of type 2 diabetes can be linked with poor lifestyles: obesity, unhealthy diet, smoking, and physical inactivity. Another example of the link between lifestyle and diabetes risk can be found in the Pima Indians in Arizona. As this group moved away from their traditional culture which included a healthy diet and lots of physical activity, they now have a large incidence (50% of adults) of obesity and type 2 diabetes. Treatment of type 2 diabetes usually includes: diet control, exercise, home glucose testing, and in some cases oral medications with or without insulin injections.

Physical activity is helpful in both type 1 and type 2 diabetes. In the type 1 diabetic, a regular activity program can reduce the amount of insulin that will be needed to control this disease. In the type 2 diabetic regular exercise can improve insulin sensitivity. Improving insulin sensitivity means that the body does not require as much insulin in order to move the glucose from the blood into the exercising muscle cell. It should be highlighted that the increase in insulin sensitivity found after physical activity (1 hour of running) continued for at least one day after the exercise. Therefore, a *regular consistent exercise program* is necessary in the treatment of the type 2 diabetic person. Most importantly, scientists are finding that an active lifestyle can actually delay or prevent the onset of type 2 diabetes. The American Diabetes Association now recommends that individuals at high risk for developing diabetes participate in a regular exercise program (30 minutes or more daily) in order to reduce their risk for the onset of this metabolic disease.

Another issue on diabetes risk specific to women is that there is a form of diabetes that develops during pregnancy. This type of diabetes is called *gestational diabetes* and it is more common in African American, Hispanic/Latino American, Native American, obese women, and those women with a family history of diabetes. Pregnant women with gestational onset diabetes require treatment to normalize their blood glucose levels in order to avoid complications for their infant. Risk assessment for this type of diabetes should occur at the first prenatal visit to the physician's office. Women at high risk for the development of this disease should be screened for it at this time. After the pregnancy that individual will also have a higher risk for the development of type 2 diabetes.

Alzheimer's Disease

Alzheimer's disease (AD) is the fifth leading cause of death among all women in the United States. It is among the top 10 leading causes of death in each racial/ethnic group with the exception of Native Americans (see Table 1). AD is a complicated disease of the central nervous system that leaves its victims unable to care for themselves. AD is most often a disease of the elderly (late-onset AD), however it begins to develop years before the symptoms appear.

According to the National Institute on Aging, *dementia*, a permanent loss in cognitive function and memory, is characterized by a group of symptoms including:

- Repeatedly asking the same questions,
- Getting lost, even in places that should be familiar,
- Inability to process and follow directions,
- Disorientation or lack of recognition of locations, time, and people,
- Failure to maintain proper hygiene and nutrition, and
- Placing oneself in a dangerous situation due to loss in judgment.

Alzheimer's disease is one cause of dementia. AD directly affects the cells of the brain called neurons. These cells make up the lines of communication among the various regions of the brain. Neurons are activated when the brain is taking in and processing new information, integrating new information with old, or calling up old information when needed. In AD, neurons are destroyed in certain regions of the brain and the size of the brain actually decreases.

The areas of the brain most affected by AD include the cerebral cortex and the hippocampus. The *cerebral cortex* makes up the bulk of the higher brain centers where information processing takes place. It is the site of thinking, sensory processing (i.e., sight, sound, smell), integration of information, and storage of memories. The *hippocampus* is essential in the formation of new memories. Destruction of cells in these regions can have severely debilitating consequences.

At the cellular level, the changes in the brain observed with AD include a build up of proteins on the outside of the neurons. The protein masses are specifically called *Beta-amyloid plaques*. Another symptom associated with AD is the formation of *tangles* in dying and dead cells. These cellular factors are thought to interfere with the communication that takes place between neurons in the brain. Preventing the ability of these cells to communicate with each other essentially shuts down function in the affected regions. When neurons are unable to send signals to each other, a thought, memory, or incoming information from the outside world gets lost, unable to reach its destination within the brain.

Alzheimer's disease usually begins by affecting regions of the brain involved in learning and memory, and thinking and planning. As the disease progresses, the speech centers of the brain may become affected. This not only limits the person's ability to speak, but also the ability to understand words being spoken by others. In advanced stages of the disease, much of the cerebral cortex has been affected. The individual will not be able to recognize words or people, will lack the ability to access memories, and will be unable to take care of themselves.

While death from cardiovascular disease and certain cancers has decreased between the year 2000 and 2005, the rate of death from AD increased by approximately 45% during that same time period. Based on data from the Framingham Heart Study, Alzheimer's disease will affect almost twice as many women (17%) as men (9%) who live beyond 55 years of age. This difference between the sexes may, in part, be due to the fact that women live longer than men. Because women will spend more years in old age (life expectancy for U.S. women is 80.4 years as compared with 75.2 years for men), there are more years over which the disease is likely to develop. As life expectancy continues to increase, the number of people affected by AD also will increase. Because the number of people affected by the disease is increasing, more research is being conducted to gain a better understanding of Alzheimer's disease. In addition to trying to identify the actual causes of the disease, some research has begun to identify risk factors for it.

Age is the number one risk factor for AD. Past the age of 65 years, the risk of developing AD doubles every 5 years. *Family history* and *genes* also play critical roles in the risk for AD. However, having a gene that is related to AD does not guarantee one will develop the disease. Like any other predisposition to disease, the gene may exist, but something must "turn on" that gene. Therefore, environmental factors are likely to influence the probability of developing AD. How much control we really have in reducing the risk of developing AD is not fully understood, but information in this area is accumulating.

The National Institute on Aging (NIA) reports that AD has some common risk factors with cardiovascular disease. For example, hypertension, type 2 diabetes, and elevated levels of cholesterol and the amino acid homocysteine in the blood increase the risk of both of these diseases. Given the well-documented benefits of physical activity in fighting heart disease, similar benefits may exist for AD. However, research in this area is limited.

The NIA and Alzheimer's Association do not identify physical inactivity as a direct risk factor for Alzheimer's disease, however new research suggests that active lifestyles help to reduce the risk for and/or rate of developing Alzheimer's disease, and dementia in general.

Because access to brain tissue in humans is limited, most of the research on cellular changes in the brain has been conducted on animals (e.g., mice). There is a growing body of research showing that exercise stimulates growth of neurons (dendrites and axon terminals) in juvenile and adult animals. These findings illustrate the potential of physical activity in keeping brain tissue healthy. But can physical activity influence neurons that are or will be affected by AD?

Research examining direct effects of exercise on the Alzheimer's disease-affected tissue has also been examined in animal models. Mice that are genetically destined to develop Alzheimer's disease have been used to study exercise effects. The findings thus far have been promising. When compared with sedentary, genetically-matched mice, those that exercise regularly on running wheels have significantly less Beta-amyloid plaque in the cortex and hippocampus regions of the brain. These findings support the idea that exercise can slow the progression of AD. Furthermore, the exercising AD animals learned tasks more quickly than the sedentary animals. If this finding applies to humans, an improved quality of life with better cognitive function would be an expected benefit of exercise in AD patients.

Research on humans has had somewhat mixed results, but in some well-designed studies, physical activity appears to have beneficial effects on cognitive function, as well as positive outcomes related to dementia and Alzheimer's disease. One often-cited study by Laurin et al. (2001) examined the link between physical activity and the development of (a) cognitive impairment without dementia, (b) dementia, and (c) AD in an elderly population. In that study, physical activity was divided into 4 categories: sedentary, low (intensity less than walking, frequency $\geq$ 3 times per week), moderate (intensity equal to walking, frequency $\geq$ 3 times per week) and high (intensity greater than walking, frequency $\geq$ 3 times per week). Regardless of activity level, those who were physically active had lower risk for cognitive impairment without dementia, as well as lower risk for dementia and AD than those who were sedentary. Generally, the benefits were greater with higher intensities of exercise. The authors reported that, when compared with their sedentary counterparts, the women who were most active had a 50% reduction in cognitive impairment without dementia and a 60% reduction in Alzheimer's disease. These findings strongly support a link between physical inactivity and the development of AD.

There is limited research on the effect of exercise on the progression of AD in elderly patients who have already been diagnosed with the disease. However, a recent study by Rolland, et al. (2007) on nursing home patients suggests that participating weekly in two 1-hour exercise sessions (walking, strength, balance and flexibility training) may slow the decline in daily functioning in AD patients.

These studies and others suggest that physical activity is beneficial in reducing the risk, development, and progression of Alzheimer's disease. However, recommendations on how much and how intense the exercise needs to be to protect against or slow the progression of AD have not yet been established.

Chronic Obstructive Pulmonary Disease

Chronic lower respiratory disease (CLRD) is the 4th leading cause of death for all women combined and for White women as a subgroup. CLRD is the 7th leading cause of death for Hispanic, Native American, Asian/Pacific Islander, and Black women. CLRD is a term that encompasses many lung diseases including emphysema, chronic bronchitis, and cystic fibrosis.

Chronic obstructive pulmonary disease (COPD) is a narrower grouping, which includes emphysema and chronic bronchitis. *Chronic bronchitis* involves the inflammation of the bronchial tubes, which direct air into and out of the lungs. Excess mucus forms and must be coughed up to clear the airway. The build-up of mucus and eventual scarring of the lung tissue reduce the ability of air to move through the passage-way, leading to shortness of breath. Bacterial infections are common in the irritated bronchial tubes, increasing the risk for further damage.

Emphysema affects the tissue where gas exchange takes place in the lungs. Tiny sacs, called *alveoli*, are made up of a thin and delicate membrane through which oxygen and carbon dioxide move. Oxygen moves from the lungs into the blood so it can be transported to the cells of the body where it plays a role in energy production. Carbon dioxide is a waste product that must be removed, so it moves from the blood, across the alveolar membrane into the lungs in order to be exhaled. Too much carbon dioxide in the blood is dangerous, and too little oxygen in the cells can lead to cell failure. Because this disease reduces gas exchange in the lungs, the person with emphysema experiences shortness of breath and muscle weakness. As the disease progresses, the ability to perform minimal physical activity is compromised.

The primary causes of COPD include smoking, exposure to pollutants, asthma, genetics, and infections of the respiratory tract. According to the CDC, more women than men are hospitalized for and more die from COPD. Changing rates of COPD reflect trends in smoking. For example, the rate of women affected by COPD nearly tripled between 1980 and 2000, reflecting a large increase in smoking in the previous quarter-century. The good news is that as smoking rates have been on the decline in recent years, COPD in the younger population also appears to be lower.

The most obvious ways to avoid COPD is to avoid smoking tobacco and breathing unhealthy air, including second-hand smoke, pollutants in the workplace and environment. Next, it is important to have respiratory infections diagnosed and treated early. Once a person has COPD, the treatments include drugs to enhance lung function and oxygen supplementation, which involves carrying a tank and inhaling oxygen through a tube. In the most severe, late stages of COPD, lung transplants or surgery to remove damaged tissue may be required. Lung tissue damage due to COPD is irreversible.

So can physical activity help someone with COPD? Although limited, the research in this area suggests that physical activity can be beneficial for COPD patients. One study by Garcia-Aymerich and coworkers (2006) reported that COPD patients that were physically active (those performing activities such as walking or cycling at least 2 hours per week) were 28% less likely to be hospitalized and were 30% less likely to die from respiratory complications than the sedentary COPD patients. This was true for women and men.

In a follow-up study the same researchers examined the effectiveness in *preventing* COPD. They reported that there were 21% fewer cases of COPD in smokers who were moderately or highly active as compared with those with low activity levels. They also reported that through the course of this 10+ year study, those who increased their activity level had lower declines in lung function, while those who decreased their physical activity had greater declines in lung function. The authors proposed that, because COPD has a strong inflammatory component, the benefit from physical activity lies in its anti-inflammatory effects.

Aerobic exercise is considered the most important form of physical activity in the rehabilitation of COPD patients. Stressing cardiorespiratory endurance through training leads to improved lung function and reduces the degree to which the patient is breathless. Resistance training (weight lifting) may also be beneficial for COPD patients. Focus on strengthening of the skeletal muscles is important because COPD patients tend to experience muscle weakness and thereby lose the ability to function optimally during daily activities. In 2002, the American College of Sports Medicine published guidelines for prescribing exercise for patients with COPD that included both forms of exercise.

Although physical activity is not seen as a preventive measure for COPD, regular physical activity appears to reduce the risk of developing and the rate of progression of the disease among those most at risk for the disease (i.e., smokers, etc.). Because aerobic exercise stresses the muscular, cardiovascular and respiratory systems of the body, it is likely to have benefits for lung function in healthy individuals. However, expanding our understanding of just how effective exercise is in maintaining lung health will require more research.

Osteoporosis

Although osteoporosis is not among the top 10 diseases leading to death in U.S. women, it is a debilitating disease that afflicts 8 million women, according to the National Osteoporosis

Foundation. Osteoporosis is a disease in which bone ("osteo-") becomes porous ("-porosis"), weakened and fragile.

Bone health is determined by the amount of mineral (e.g., calcium) there is in the bone, as well as the architecture of the bone (i.e., how the mineral is structured). The greater the bone mineral density (BMD) the stronger will be the bone. BMD is measured using low-level X-ray in a method called *dual-energy X-ray absorptiometry* (DEXA or DXA). Although this method can be used on the entire skeleton, it is used clinically to examine the vertebrae of the lower region of the spine (lumbar region) and the hip. Along with the wrists, these are the areas most often affected by osteoporosis. BMD and architecture together determine bone strength and the likelihood that the bone will fracture. Unfortunately, there is no easy or routine method to examine bone architecture at this time.

Under normal conditions, bone is maintained through a process called "bone remodeling." Every 3 to 4 months bone is turned over in cycles of *resorption* (breakdown of bone mineral) and *formation* (adding new mineral). The degree to which bone is built-up or maintained during each cycle reflects the demands placed on the bone. This is similar to what we see with skeletal muscle. If someone works out with weights (strength/resistance training), the muscle will continue to grow stronger and larger as the weight is progressively increased. If the same weight is lifted week after week, the muscle will simply maintain its size and strength. On the other hand, if the weight lifting program ceases and the demands are no longer placed on the muscle, it will get smaller and weaker. Similarly, if the bone experiences more stress during one cycle, it will receive a greater stimulus for growth than during a cycle in which it receives less stimulus.

The type of stress that bone responds to includes impact forces, like that experienced while landing from a jump. Also, the force that a contracting muscle places on bone helps to stimulate the bone. There's recent evidence in humans that applying vibration to bone will also stimulate its growth. At the low end of the mechanical stress scale is bed rest. Following an injury that requires bed-rest, BMD can be significantly reduced because the stress applied to bone is minimal or even absent during that period of time. It is interesting to note that astronauts experience loss in bone mass during space flight in which they are exposed to a low-gravity environment. The stress on the bone in space is much lower than that on Earth. That's one reason why astronauts must exercise while in space.

Osteoporosis is often thought of as a disease of the elderly, and most people with osteoporosis are elderly women. However, it's a disease that has its roots beginning in childhood. Peak rate of skeletal growth occurs during childhood—especially around puberty. Bone can continue to develop more slowly until a woman reaches her peak bone mass in her early 20s. During adulthood and up to about age 40 years, bone can be maintained or lost, but there is little evidence that it will continue to grow. After the age of 40 years, bone mass will be lost, and the rate of that loss accelerates following menopause. Bone loss in post-menopausal women is due to the absence of estrogen, a hormone that is essential for maintaining bone health. In the post-menopausal years ($\geq$ 50 years), it is essential to try to reduce the rate of bone loss. So how does one maximize bone mass early in life and work to maintain it throughout adulthood? There are several factors that can benefit the health of bone, and others that can contribute to its loss.

The risk factors for osteoporosis include *age* (risk increases as we get older), *sex* (women are at greater risk than men), *family history*, *low body weight* (more weight means heavier load carried by the bones, which makes them stronger), *small skeletal frame* (smaller bones, in terms of diameter, are weaker than larger ones), *race/ethnicity* (women of African decent have stronger bones than White, Asian/Pacific Islander, and Hispanic), *low levels of sex hormones* (low estrogen levels, missed menstrual periods, menopause), *nutritional factors* (levels of vitamin D and calcium must be sufficient, eating disorders lead to the loss of bone mineral density), *smoking*, *alcohol consumption*, and *physical inactivity*. Although some factors cannot be changed (i.e., skeletal frame size, race/ethnicity, family history, age), many can be modified (i.e., diet, smoking, physical activity level). Physical activity's affect on bone health varies depending on age and hormone status of women.

The primary goal during childhood and adolescence should be to maximize the development of bone. Youth who participate in impact activities (e.g., gymnastics, jumping, basketball, soccer, running) will likely have the greatest benefits to bone health. These activities apply mechanical stress to the bone, which, theoretically, will stimulate bone growth. Studies support the idea that girls who participate in high impact sports (i.e., gymnastics) have higher BMD measures than those who do not. The American College of Sports Medicine (ACSM) recommends that these bone-loading activities be performed for 10–20 minutes 2 or more times per day, 3 days per week.

Once peak bone mass has been achieved through childhood and adolescence, *the goal for adult women should be to maintain what they have.* During adulthood, women should be involved in weight-bearing endurance activities such as jogging and tennis (3–5 times per week). Activities that require jumping such as volleyball and basketball are also strongly recommended (2–3 times per week). ACSM also recommends participation in a weight lifting program that targets most muscle groups of the body. The bones to which the active muscles are attached are the ones that will benefit from weight lifting exercise. The goal of a program that combines these different types of activities is to maximize the mechanical load or stress on the bone. The duration of the combined exercise workout should be between 30 and 60 minutes per day.

Without pharmaceutical intervention, post-menopausal women will lose bone mass, but the rate at which it is lost may be reduced through physical activity. *The goal for post-menopausal women is to reduce the rate of loss of bone mass.* Again, exercise programs for women in this age group should be weight-bearing. However, because fractures often occur when a person with low bone mass falls, performing exercises that focus on balance and fall-prevention are also recommended. Once diagnosed with osteopoenia (low bone mass) or osteoporosis, however, a woman should work closely with her physician to determine the best approach for treatment.

Although age, genes, and family history play an important role in osteoporosis risk, lifestyle choices such as physical activity, especially early in life, can help to achieve and maintain bone health in women.

Physical Activity Goals—Are Women Meeting Them?

As we examine the benefits of physical activity in the prevention of chronic diseases, it is easy to see why exercise can be seen as a "magic bullet." No drug comes close to the range of benefits of physical activity, and none is as easily accessed. Yet it is still unclear exactly how exercise is so beneficial. Many of the chronic diseases that lead to death in U.S. women have a relationship to the body's inflammatory processes. These diseases include COPD, cardiovascular, and Alzheimer's disease. The anti-inflammatory actions of aerobic exercise may be the basis for it being considered a "magic bullet" in reducing risk of disease and increasing life-expectancy. Different modes of physical activity have other benefits as well. Strength training helps build and maintain muscle and bone mass, which are important for performing tasks in everyday life and for the prevention of osteoporosis. And because exercise stresses the metabolic processes of the body, there are clear benefits when it comes to reducing the risk for and treating type 2 diabetes. Because the risk for so many diseases that lead to death among U.S. women can be significantly reduced by regular physical activity, it is important to understand exactly what is required to reap these benefits.

In 1995, scientists from the American College of Sports Medicine (ACSM) and the Centers for Disease Control and Prevention (CDC) developed guidelines for physical activity that were directed at reducing the rate of disease and early death in Americans. The guidelines were updated in 2007 by a team of scientists from the ACSM and the American Heart Association (AHA). The current physical activity guidelines for healthy adults include:

1. Accumulate 30 minutes of moderate-intensity physical activity through the course of most days of the week.

   The term *"accumulate"* means that the 30 minutes do not have to be performed at one time, but each bout should last for *at least* 10 minutes. For example, brisk walking for 10 minutes 3 times per day would meet this recommendation.

   "Moderate-intensity" activities would include brisk walking and equivalent aerobic activities in which the heart rate is elevated. This might include gardening, washing the car, carpentry work, etc., (as long as it lasts a minimum of 10 minutes).

   "Most days of the week" means 5 or more days per week.

   AND/OR

2. Perform vigorous-intensity activity for at least 20 minutes 3 or more days per week.

   "Vigorous intensity" activities include jogging and other activities that elevate breathing and heart rates substantially.

   The duration (20 minutes) and frequency (3 days) are *minimum* recommendations. The American College of Sports Medicine recommends 20–60 minutes per session and 3–5 sessions per week for optimum cardiorespiratory fitness.

   OR

3. A combination of #1 and #2.

   AND

4. Perform 8–10 muscular strength and endurance exercises at least 2 days per week.

   "Muscular strength and endurance" exercises include weight lifting, resistance bands, and calisthenic-type activities (e.g., sit-ups, push-ups, jumping-jacks).

   Gains in strength and muscular endurance require working out a minimum of *2 days per week*. These exercises can be performed more often, but 1 day of rest is recommended between strength-training sessions on a particular muscle group.

Table 3 Percentage of women meeting U.S. Health & Human Services (*Healthy People 2010*) recommended physical activity levels for health/fitness by age.

Age (y)	Meeting Recommendations (%)*
18-24	52.7
25-34	50.5
35-44	49.7
45-64	45.5
≥ 65	36.3

*Statistics from *Behavioral Risk Factor Surveillance System, U.S.*, 2001–2005; 2005 values.

Table 4 Percentage of U.S. women meeting U.S. Health & Human Services (*Healthy People 2010*) recommended physical activity levels for health/fitness by race/ethnicity.

Race/Ethnicity	Meeting Recommendations (%)
White, non-Hispanic	49.6
Black, non-Hispanic	36.1
Hispanic	40.5
Other	46.6

*Statistics from *Behavioral Risk Factor Surveillance System, U.S.*, 2001–2005; 2005 values.

Recent statistics from the CDC indicate that *less than half* of the U.S. population is achieving these basic recommendations for physical activity for health (30 minutes, moderate intensity, 5+ days/week, ≥ 20 minutes vigorous-intensity, ≥ 3 days/week, or a combination of both). Table 3 outlines that as we age our physical activity level decreases. Also, there are some disparities across racial and ethnic groups (Table 4). The good news is that the percentages are up since the previous survey (4 years prior). Yet, 25% of U.S. women are still not getting any physical activity!

How can these trends in physical activity be changed? Let's face it, most people associate exercise with pain and discomfort. However, what most people don't realize is that very strenuous activity is not necessary to gain the benefits of exercise. Here are some hints from The National Women's Health Information Center to help women get started in a physical activity program.

- Choose an activity that's fun.

- Change your activities, so you don't get bored.

- Doing housework may not be fun, but it does get you moving! So does gardening, yard work, and walking the dog.

- If you can't set aside one block of time, do short activities during the day, such as three, 10-minute walks.

- Create opportunities for activity, such as parking your car farther away, taking the stairs instead of the elevator, or walking down the hall to talk to a coworker instead of using e-mail.

- Don't let the cold weather keep you on the couch! You can still find activities to do in the winter like exercising to a workout video or joining a sports league. Or get a head start on your spring cleaning by choosing active indoor chores like window washing or reorganizing closets.

- Use different jogging, walking, or biking paths to vary your routine.

- Exercise with a friend or family member.

- If you have children, make time to play with them outside. Set a positive example!

- Make activities into social occasions—have dinner after you and a friend work out.

- Read books or magazines to inspire you.

- Set specific, short-term goals, and reward yourself when you achieve them.

- Don't feel badly if you don't notice body changes right away.

- Make your activity a regular part of your day, so it becomes a habit.

- Build a community group to form walking clubs, build walking trails, start exercise classes, and organize special events to promote physical activity.

From: http://www.womenshealth.gov/faq/exercise.htm#5

For sedentary women, the message is simple: *anything is better than nothing*. Identify activities that can be incorporated into daily life (e.g., walking or biking to school or work, walking around the block a few times each morning). For women who have risk factors for disease or are over the age of 50 years, a physical activity plan should be discussed with a physician prior to beginning an exercise program. The important thing is to get women moving. Take another look at the chronic diseases listed in Table 1 and remember that being physically active, along with a healthy diet, can help prevent or reduce the risk and severity of many of those diseases.

References

Alzheimer's Association. (2008). Inside the Brain: An Interactive Tour. (*http://www.alz.org/brain/overview.asp*).

Alzheimer's Association. (2008). *2008 Alzheimer's Disease Facts and Figures.* (*http://www.alz.org/national/documents/report_alzfactsfigures2008.pdf*).

Alzheimer's Association. Inside the brain: an interactive tour. (*http://www.alz.org/brain/overview.asp*).

American Cancer Society, (2005). Cancer Facts & Figures–2005. Atlanta: Author, 2005. (*http://www.cancer.org/docroot/STT/stt_0_2005.asp?sitearea=STT&level=1*).

American Cancer Society. (2007). Cancer facts and figures for Hispanics/Latinos 2006–2008. (*http://www.cancer.org/downloads/STT/CAFF2006HispPWSecured.pdf*).

American Cancer Society. (2007). Cancer facts and figures for African Americans 2007–2008. (*http://www.cancer.org/downloads/STT/CAFF2007AAacspdf2007.pdf*).

American Heart Association. (2007). *Heart Disease and Stroke Statistics–2007 Update. Circulation 115*:e69-e171.

Bernstein L., Henderson, B.E., Hanisch R, Sullivan-Halley J., & Ross R. K. (1994). Physical exercise and reduced risk of breast cancer in young women, *J Natl Cancer Inst 86*: 1403–1408.

CDC. (2003). Facts about Chronic Obstructive Pulmonary Disease. (*http://www.cdc.gov/nceh/airpollution/copd/copdfaq.htm*).

CDC. (2007). Leading causes of death in females, U.S. 2004. (*http://www.cdc.gov/Women/lcod.htm*).

CDC. (1999) Physical Activity and Health: a report of the Surgeon General (Women). *http://www.cdc.gov/nccdphp/sgr/women.htm*

Fahey T. D., Insel P. M., & Roth, W. T. (2009). Cardiovascular Health in *Fit & Well*. New York: McGraw-Hill Co. 2009, pages 331–348.

Folsom, A R., Arnett, D. K., Hutchinson, R. G., Liao, F., Clegg, L.X. & Cooper, LS. (1997). Physical activity and incidence of coronary heart disease in middle-aged women and men. *Med Sci Sports & Exercise 29*: 901–909.

Garcia-Aymerich, .J, Lange, P., Benet, M., Schnohr, P., & Anto, J. M. (2006). Regular physical activity reduces hospital admission and mortality in chronic obstructive pulmonary disease: a population based cohort study. *Thorax 61*(9):772–778.

Garcia-Aymerich, J., Lange, P., Benet, M., Schnohr, P., & Anto, J. M. (2007). Regular Physical Activity Modifies Smoking-related Lung Function Decline and Reduces Risk of Chronic Obstructive Pulmonary Disease: A Population-based Cohort Study. *American Journal of Respiratory and Critical Care Medicine 175*: 458–463.

Martinez, M. E., Giovannucci E., Spiegelman D., Hunter D..J, Willett W.C., & Colditz G.A. Leisure-time physical activity, body size, and colon cancer in women. *J Natl Cancer Inst 89*: 948–955, 1997.

Mayo Clinic Staff. (2007). Women's Health Risks. Mayo Foundation for Medical Education and Research. (*http://www.mayoclinic.com/health/womens-health/WO00014*).

National Center for Health Statistics. (2008). *Life Expectancy data from:* Kung HC, Hoyert DL, Xu JQ, Murphy SL. (2008). Deaths: Final data for 2005. *National Vital Statistics Reports* 56 (10). Hyattsville, MD.

National Institute on Aging. (2006). Genes, lifestyles and crossword puzzles: Can Alzheimer's Disease be prevented? NIH Publication No. 06-5503. *(http://www.nia.nih.gov/NR/rdonlyres/63B5A29C-F943-4DB7-91B4-0296772973F3/0/CanADbePrevented.pdf)*.

National Institute on Aging. *(http://www.niapublications.org/agepages/forgetfulness.asp)*.

National Osteoporosis Foundation. (2008). Prevention. Who is at Risk. *(http://www.nof.org/prevention/risk.htm)*.

Nelson ME, Lichenstein A. 2006. *Strong Women, Strong Hearts*. New York: Perigee Trade.

Nieman, D. C. *Heart Disease in Exercise testing and Prescription. A Health-Related Approach*. New York: McGraw Hill Co. 2007 pages 369–446.

NIH Consensus Development Panel on Physical Activity and Cardiovascular Health. Physical Activity and Cardiovascular Health. (1996). *JAMA* 276: 241–246.

Rolland, Y., Pillard, F., Klapouszczak, A., Reynish, E., Thomas, D., Andrieu, S., Rivière, D. & Vellas, B. (2007). Exercise Program for Nursing Home Residents with Alzheimer's Disease: A 1-Year Randomized, Controlled Trial. *Journal of the American Geriatrics Society* 55: 158–165.

U.S. Department of Health and Human Services. (1996). *Physical Activity and Health: A Report of the Surgeon General*. Atlanta, GA: U.S. Department of Health and Human Services, Centers for Disease Control and Prevention, National Center for Chronic Disease Prevention and Health Promotion. *(http://www.cdc.gov/nccdphp/sgr/sgr.htm)*.

Further Reading

Healthy People 2010. Leading Health Indicators. *http://www.healthypeople.gov/document/html/uih/uih_4.htm*

Physical Activity and Good Nutrition: Essential Elements to Prevent Chronic Diseases and Obesity, at a Glance 2008. *http://www.cdc.gov/nccdphp/publications/aag/dnpa.htm*

Diabetes & Women's Health Across the Life Stages: A Public Health Perspective. *http://www.cdc.gov/diabetes/pubs/pdf/womenshort.pdf*

Discussion Questions

1. What are the effects of physical activity on chronic diseases such as heart disease, diabetes, and Alzheimer's disease?
2. What are the current recommendations for physical activity for health? Are women in the United States meeting these recommendations?
3. How do the rates of chronic diseases differ by race and ethnicity?
4. What is osteoporosis and how does exercise affect bone health? What are the specific recommendations for physical activity for bone health during the different stages of a woman's life?

2

Metabolic Syndrome & Physical Activity: Move to Better Health

Ann F. Maliszewski

What Is Metabolic Syndrome?

Metabolic syndrome is a term applied to individuals who have a combination of risk factors that puts them at an increased risk for type 2 diabetes, heart disease and stroke. These 3 diseases are among the top 10 leading causes of death for women in the United States. Understanding the factors that increase the risk for these diseases and identifying ways to reduce or eliminate them may improve morbidity and mortality rates.

Being diagnosed with the risk factors of metabolic syndrome indicates abnormal metabolic (energy processing) activity in the body. The components of metabolic syndrome are listed and briefly described in Table 1.

Although all of the factors listed in Table 1 are components of metabolic syndrome, only the first 4 are used clinically for diagnosis. The last two are not yet routinely tested. Each of the first four risk factors is discussed in detail below.

Insulin Resistance

During and after a meal or snack, food molecules are broken down by the digestive system (mouth, stomach and small intestine) and then are moved into the blood. The pancreas detects these food molecules and is stimulated to secrete the hormone *insulin* into the blood. Insulin travels to different cells of the body and "tells" them to take food molecules out of the blood and either use them for energy or put them into storage for later use. One type of food molecule that increases in the blood after a meal is *glucose,* which is a form of carbohydrate or sugar. Muscle and liver cells, insulin's "target" cells, are primarily responsible for taking glucose out of the blood when it gets high. Under normal conditions, when insulin interacts with these cells, glucose is closely regulated and does not accumulate in the blood, but remains within a narrow, "normal" range. Under abnormal conditions, target cells fail to transport glucose out of the blood effectively, and glucose levels in the blood are elevated, a condition called "*hyperglycemia*" (*hyper* = more, above normal; *glycemia* = glucose levels in blood).

Table 1 The Risk Factors Included in the Diagnosis of Metabolic Syndrome	
Risk Factor	Description
Insulin Resistance	Reduced ability of insulin to function in the body
Abdominal Obesity	Fat stored in the torso or abdominal region of the body
Atherogenic Dyslipidemia	Abnormal blood lipid or lipoprotein levels that lead to the formation of atheromas, or fatty masses on the walls of blood vessels
Hypertension	Blood pressure that's elevated above normal healthy levels
Proinflammatory State	Presence of certain molecules that are associated with an immune response to damaged tissue in the body. *C-Reactive protein* is measured in the blood to identify risk.
Prothrombic State	Content of the blood that increases the likelihood of forming blood clots. Clotting factors (e.g., *fibrinogen* or *Plasminogen activator inhibitor*) are measured in the blood to identify risk.

Note: Metabolic syndrome is also referred to as "Cardiometabolic Risk," "Syndrome X," "Dysmetabolic Syndrome," and "Insulin Resistance Syndrome."

The term "insulin resistance" refers to ineffective action of insulin. Insulin may be present in normal or even high levels, so the message to remove glucose from the blood is getting out by the pancreas. The problem is that the target cells are not responding. Insulin has to bind to receptors (i.e., specialized molecules in the cell membrane) on the muscle or liver cells in order to communicate the message. If there is an insufficient number of these receptors, or the receptors are not working properly, the message is not communicated effectively, and the muscle and liver cells do not "hear" the message. In this way, there is resistance to insulin's message (*insulin resistance*). In advanced states of hyperglycemia or in type 1 diabetes, the pancreas will decrease or even cease its output of insulin, making the situation much worse. If there is no insulin being secreted by the pancreas, there is no message going out to the cells, and glucose accumulates to dangerously high levels. In these cases, the person will have to have injections of insulin. If left untreated, extremely high (or low) levels of glucose in the blood can lead to diabetic coma and death.

Insulin resistance can be assessed by different clinical tests, including the *fasting blood glucose test* and the *glucose tolerance test*. After an 8-hour fast (no food, no beverages other than water), the fasting blood glucose level is measured. To complete the glucose tolerance test, following the fast, the person would eat a certain amount of glucose and the blood glucose levels would be monitored over a 2-hour period. Under normal conditions, the fasting level of blood glucose will be less than 100 mg/dL. Following consumption of glucose, there will be an initial, small increase in glucose (usually during the first half-hour) followed by a reduction back to the fasting level (usually within 1–2 hours). In someone who has insulin resistance, the baseline fasting blood glucose value will be above 100 mg/dL and there will be an increase well above normal following the consumption of glucose. The blood glucose levels will fail to return to baseline levels within the 2-hour test period.

The fasting blood glucose measure is simple and inexpensive. Because it does not require the 2-hour follow-up that is used in the glucose tolerance test, fasting glucose is used in the clinical setting to evaluate insulin resistance. If the fasting measure is greater than or equal to 110 mg/dL, it is referred to as *impaired fasting glucose,*" which is a critical component of metabolic syndrome.

Abdominal Obesity

The medical establishment has declared that there is an "obesity epidemic" in this country. The measure used in population studies to categorize people as underweight, normal, overweight or obese is the *body mass index* (BMI). See Table 2. Body mass index is calculated from height and weight (BMI = weight (kg)/ height (m^2)), so it is a measure of the relative amount of weight a person has for their frame size (i.e., height). BMI is *not* a measure of body fatness, however, it is correlated with measures of fatness, so it is used to classify weight and obesity status in large populations-studies. Other methods that actually measure body fatness are more accurate, but also more costly in terms of time and money.

The usefulness of BMI to estimate body fatness is suspect, and recent evidence suggests that this measure does not necessarily predict risk of metabolic disorders or chronic disease as accurately as once thought. *Where* fat is stored on the body may be a better predictor of disease and mortality than *how much* weight there is on the body. Specifically, fat that is stored in the abdominal region of the body, and thus around the internal organs (i.e., *visceral* fat), is more dangerous than fat stored elsewhere (e.g., the hips). People who store fat in the abdominal region are said to have an "apple" or *android* body shape, whereas those who store it in the hip region are said to have a "pear" or *gynoid* shape.

The distribution of fat on the body can be detected easily by measuring *waist circumference* or calculating the *waist to hip circumference ratio*. Having a waist circumference greater than 35 inches puts a woman at higher risk for CVD. The waist-to-hip ratio is calculated by dividing the waist circumference by hip circumference. If that ratio is greater than 0.85, she is at greater risk for CVD. Both of these circumferences can be measured with a cloth measuring tape. For the waist measurement, the tape should be placed in line with the smallest girth around the waist, usually just about the navel. The hip circumference is placed at the widest circumference in line with where the buttocks protrude. Although the circumference measures do not

Table 2 Classification of Weight Status Based on the Body Mass Index	
BMI	Weight Status
Below 18.5	Underweight
18.5–24.9	Normal
25.0–29.9	Overweight
30.0 and Above	Obese

actually measure fat, they reflect the relative amount of fat stored in the underlying area (e.g., waist circumference represents the amount of visceral fat).

Because waist circumference requires a single measurement, and because it is strongly related to the amount of visceral fat, it is used as a key measure of abdominal obesity for determining this component of metabolic syndrome.

Atherogenic Dyslipidemia

Commonly referred to as "cholesterol levels," the amount and type of lipids (fats) and lipoproteins (fat and protein complex molecules) measured in the blood are used to reflect the health of the cardiovascular system. The term *dyslipidemia* means abnormal lipids or lipoproteins levels in the blood. *Atherogenesis* refers to the formation of fatty plaques on blood vessel walls, which are associated with atherosclerosis. These plaques can protrude into the center of the blood vessel, and can interfere with blood flow, thereby restricting the delivery of blood to the tissues.

Triglyceride is a type of fat that is transported through the blood stream and is thought to contribute to the development of atherosclerosis. High-density lipoproteins (i.e., "good cholesterol"), on the other hand are thought to be "cardio-protective" because they are associated with a reduced risk of cardiovascular disease (CVD). Both of these measures are used to identify atherogenic dyslipidemia. If triglyceride levels are at or over 150 mg/dL or HDLs fall below 50 mg/dL for women, there is an increased risk of atherogenesis. Therefore, these measures, which are included in routine blood cholesterol tests, are used to test for metabolic syndrome.

Hypertension

Hypertension is chronically elevated blood pressure. In clinical settings, blood pressure is measured with an inflatable cuff over the brachial artery in the upper arm. Blood pressure is reported as two numbers, systolic over diastolic pressures (e.g., 120 mmHg/ 65 mmHg; the units of measurement are millimeters of mercury or mmHg). These numbers indicate the amount of pressure that the blood vessels withstand as blood moves through them. When the heart contracts (*systole*) and forces blood into the arteries, a great deal of force is applied against the walls of the vessels as the blood passes through. This high pressure is the *systolic blood pressure*. Between beats (contractions), the heart is at rest (*diastole*) and there is no strong force pushing the blood through. The pressure in the arteries during this restful stage is called the *diastolic blood pressure*. Logically, the higher the pressure the higher the number, and the lower the pressure the lower the number.

A high blood pressure reading while a person is seated at rest indicates that the cardiovascular system is withstanding a great deal of stress on a regular basis. As you might guess, when a person is under emotional or physical stress, the work of the heart increases—and so does blood pressure. The blood pressure measured at rest is the lowest it will be during the course of the day. So when a physician sees a high resting BP, there will be concern that it will be even higher as the person moves through the daily routine or faces stressful situations. High levels of stress within the cardiovascular system, noted by hypertension, are strongly related with risk of heart disease, stroke, and kidney failure. The higher the pressure, the greater the risk for these conditions. In fact for resting blood pressures over 115/75, there is a doubling of the risk of CVD with every 20 mmHg for systolic and 10 mmHg for diastolic!

Blood pressure should be evaluated during annual routine doctor visits. Automated blood pressure machines can usually be found near the pharmacy in drug stores and department stores. So blood pressure is easy to monitor and should be monitored on a regular basis, especially if an individual is at risk or has a family history of hypertension or kidney or heart disease. Normal blood pressure is systolic < 120 mmHg and diastolic < 80. Systolic blood pressure ≥ 140 mmHg or diastolic ≥ 90 indicates hypertension and should be addressed with a physician.

Diagnosis of Metabolic Syndrome

According to the National Heart, Lung, and Blood Institute, if a person tests positive for three of the five clinical tests listed in Table 3 or is currently on medication for any of these factors, she will diagnosed with metabolic syndrome. When compared with women who are not diagnosed with metabolic syndrome, a woman who is has three times the risk of developing cardiovascular disease (heart disease or stroke) and 9 to 30 times the risk of developing type 2 diabetes! Each of the risk factors for which a woman tests positive must be addressed and treated. Fortunately, each of the 5 factors listed in Table 1 can be positively affected by lifestyle, including exercise and diet. Because metabolic syndrome risk factors are lifestyle-related, most individuals have some control over them.

Women and Metabolic Syndrome

According to the American Heart Association, approximately 47 million women and men in the U.S. have metabolic syndrome. In some racial groups (African-American and Mexican-American) more women than men are affected. White women and men are affected similarly. The occurrence of risk factors and diagnosis of metabolic syndrome is different among racial/ethnic groups.

Table 3 Clinical Measures and Critical Cut-off Values for Diagnosing Metabolic Syndrome in Women (Criteria from the National Cholesterol Education Program's Adult Treatment Panel III Report)	
Clinical Measure	Diagnostic Cut-off Values
Fasting blood glucose	≥ 110 mg/dL or 100 mg/dL*
Waist circumference	> 35 inches
Triglycerides	≥ 150 mg/dL
High Density Lipoproteins	< 50 mg/dL
Blood pressure	Systolic ≥ 130 mmHg and/or Diastolic ≥ 85 mmHg
*Criteria by the American Diabetes Association	

Table 4 Ranking Among Racial/Ethnic Groups of Women (1 = highest prevalence, 4 = lowest) and Percent Prevalence by Existing Risk Factor (in parentheses) and Metabolic Syndrome Diagnosis. Data from NHANES III, 1988–1994 (Ford et al., 2002).

Risk Factor	White	African-American	Mexican-American	Other
Fasting blood glucose ($\geq$ 110 mg/dL)	4 (8.5)	2 (15.5)	1 (18.5)	3 (14.4)
Abdominal Obesity (WC > 35 in)	3 (43.5)	2 (62.1)	1 (62.7)	4 (40.0)
Triglycerides ($\geq$ 150 mg/dL)	3 (25.0)	4 (14.4)	1 (35.2)	2 (26.0)
HDL ($\leq$ 50 mg/dL)	3 (39.3)	4 (34.0)	1 (46.3)	2 (39.6)
Hypertension ($\geq$130/85 mmHg)	3 (27.8)	1 (43.3)	2 (32.4)	4 (23.7)
Metabolic Syndrome ($\geq$ 3 risk factors)	3 (22.8)	2 (25.7)	1 (35.6)	4 (19.9)

In studies on metabolic syndrome in women, the prevalence of risk factors varied by racial/ethnic group. The percent of each group testing positive for each risk factor and the ranking among the racial/ethnic groups is presented in Table 4. The highest prevalence of metabolic syndrome was seen in Mexican-Americans. This group of women had highest percentage testing positive for four of the five risk factors, including impaired fasting blood glucose, abdominal obesity, elevated triglycerides and low HDL. African American and White women came in distant second and third places, respectively, with $\geq$ 10 percentage points less than the Mexican American women. African American women had the highest percentage with hypertension, and second highest percentage with impaired fasting glucose and abdominal obesity. However, African American women had the best ranking for blood lipids and lipoproteins among the different racial/ethnic groups. Although the women who fell into the "Other" racial/ethnic group (e.g., Asian/Pacific Islander, Native American) ranked second for the blood lipid/lipoprotein measures, they had the lowest percentage of women with metabolic syndrome. This finding indicates that, although women in the "Other" racial/ethnic group had a high prevalence of some components, they were less likely than other women to have 3 or more risk factors at the same time.

Unfortunately, there is little population-based information about metabolic syndrome in Asian American/Pacific Islander and Native American women. Although these groups are likely represented within the "Other" category, trends unique to each group have not been reported.

Physical Activity and Metabolic Syndrome Risk Factors

Because the components of metabolic syndrome are strongly influenced by lifestyle, there is an abundance of research on how each is affected by physical activity and exercise. Let's take a look at the effect of physical activity/exercise on each of the risk factors.

Impaired Fasting Glucose (IFG)

When fasting glucose test results meet or exceed 100 or 110 mg/dL (depending on the specific criteria used), an individual is diagnosed with *impaired fasting glucose*. Insulin resistance is argued by some to be the most important, and possibly the underlying factor and cause of metabolic syndrome. Some experts claim it causes all of the other metabolic disorders of metabolic syndrome. In fact, elevated insulin levels and the inability to correctly process glucose is strongly related to obesity, dyslipidemia, and the chronic diseases type 2 diabetes and CVD.

Impaired fasting glucose is considered a pre-diabetic state. In other words, the individual is showing signs of developing type 2 diabetes, but has not crossed the critical threshold of being diagnosed as such.

Exercise is shown to have beneficial effects on the processing of glucose in diabetics and non-diabetics. In individuals with type 2 diabetes, exercise has been shown to reduce fasting glucose levels by 10–20%—even following a *single* exercise session. In diabetics, glucose tolerance tests also show that the ability of the cells to remove added glucose from the blood is improved immediately after exercise and up to 48 hours, and maybe even as long as 72 hours, following the exercise. In non-diabetic middle-aged, sedentary, and overweight women, regular exercise programs have reportedly led to significant improvements in the body's ability to handle glucose. It is important to note that the benefits of exercise to blood glucose levels were seen in the research studies to work independently of weight loss. In other words, even though weight did not significantly decrease, the body was able to metabolize glucose more effectively when women were more active. Reduction in visceral fat and improvements in glucose tolerance do tend to occur together. Therefore, to reduce risk of metabolic syndrome and the associated diseases (CVD, diabetes), it is more important to focus on improvements in insulin resistance and abdominal obesity than focus simply on changes in body weight (and BMI).

Aerobic exercise, by itself or in combination with dietary changes (e.g., reduced caloric intake), is highly recommended to treat or avoid impaired fasting glucose and glucose intolerance. Following the American College of Sports Medicine (ACSM) guidelines of 30 minutes of moderate intensity activity on most days of the week appears to be sufficient for reaping benefits. However, some research also suggests that increasing the intensity of the activity (more vigorous, e.g., jogging instead of walking) may provide even greater benefits.

Resistance training (i.e., weight lifting) also has been found to be beneficial to glucose tolerance in diabetics and non-diabetics. A minimum of 2 days per week of resistance/weight training is recommended by ACSM. In those sessions, 8–10 exercises for the major muscle groups of the body should be performed. Each exercise should involve 10–15 repetitions with a weight that will lead to near-fatigue. There should be at least one day between resistance workouts for a muscle group.

Abdominal Obesity

There is strong evidence linking physical activity to (1) reductions in waist circumference (WC) and (2) fewer gains in waist circumferences when they would normally occur (e.g., during aging and menopause). Exercise, even at moderate intensities, leads to reductions in waist circumference, and the more intense the exercise, the greater the reductions. The good news is that following the recommendations for physical activity for health (30 minutes of moderate intensity activity on most days of the week) will lead to reductions in this risk factor for metabolic syndrome. It should be noted, however, that the reduction in WC may or may not be matched with reductions in overall body weight or BMI. In other words, every woman may not lose weight from being more physically active, yet she could still lose abdominal fat. Activity recommendations for weight loss include a minimum of 60 minutes, instead of 30 minutes, of moderate intensity activity on most days of the week. But anyone undertaking an exercise program should keep in mind that if there is a loss in fat with a simultaneous gain in muscle, there may be no weight loss- and maybe even a little gain. It depends on the type of training one is performing. Generally, aerobic training—with no increases in food intake— is more effective at reducing weight than resistance training. But both are beneficial for maintaining health.

As one might expect, the changes in waist circumference seen with exercise reflect actual changes in the underlying visceral fat. Research that involves the more expensive procedures of imaging the fat that is stored around the internal organs demonstrates that exercise leads to a reduction. Furthermore, the more exercise a person performs, the greater the loss in visceral fat. This finding is very important to avoiding the development of metabolic syndrome.

Atherogenic Dyslipidemia

High triglyceride and low HDL levels are components of metabolic syndrome and are related to other factors including abdominal obesity and insulin resistance. Because of the negative effects on blood vessels in the body, these atherogenic components are linked to increased rates of heart disease and stroke.

There is overwhelming evidence showing that physical activity improves cholesterol levels. However, the picture is somewhat less clear when women are evaluated separately from men. Although there are consistent findings that HDL levels increase with increasing levels of aerobic exercise for women, the reductions in triglycerides are smaller. One of the reasons the research findings for women are less consistent is the effect of hormones on blood lipid levels. As reproductive hormone levels shift, so too do blood lipid and lipoprotein levels. Unfortunately, few studies on the effects of exercise and physical activity on blood lipid/lipoprotein profiles have focused solely on women, and even fewer included hormone status in the design.

Although women tend to have better blood lipid profiles than men throughout young adulthood and middle age, post-menopausal women have profiles more in line with men their same age. Research focusing on women suggests that young, pre-menopausal women have benefits in blood lipid profiles with relatively high levels of physical activity. However, in post-menopausal women, only HDL levels seem to benefit from exercise. Because the results on women are mixed, additional well-controlled research is needed that focuses specifically on women while taking hormone status (e.g., pre- vs. post-menopause, hormone replacement therapy, birth control, etc.) into account.

Hypertension

About one-third of women in the United States have or are being treated for hypertension. 43.5% of African American women over the age of 20 years of age are hypertensive. In comparison, 28.5% of White and 28.9% of Mexican American women are hypertensive. Elevated blood pressure significantly increases the risk of stroke, coronary heart disease and kidney disease. In mixed-gender studies, lifestyle changes (diet, exercise) have been found to be as effective as pharmaceuticals in lowering blood pressure.

As seen with some other components of metabolic syndrome, there is limited research that focuses specifically on the relationship between exercise/physical activity and hypertension in women. In one study, women with hypertension who participated in an exercise program had reductions in both systolic and diastolic pressures (~4 mmHg each). When weight loss is added to the equation, larger reductions in blood pressure were seen (SBP decreased by 7 mmHg, DBP decreased by 5 mmHg). Other studies have reported that exercise leads to significant reductions in blood pressure in post-menopausal women and young African American women. The reductions in blood pressure from physical activity are not large, however they are similar to those seen with medications for hypertension (~5–6 mmHg).

There is little evidence suggesting that more, or higher intensity exercise, is better for blood pressure than low to moderate intensity exercise. Therefore, the general recommendations of physical activity for health by the American College of Sports Medicine appear to be sufficient in lowering blood pressure. Combining exercise with changes in diet, as recommended by the American Heart Association (i.e., decrease saturated fat, cholesterol, and salt intake, reduce total calories in the diet if overweight, and limit alcohol consumption to no more than 1 drink per day), will have added benefits. The changes in blood pressure from these lifestyle changes can significantly reduce the risk for metabolic syndrome and related diseases.

Summary

Attention to metabolic syndrome is increasing because each of its components is related to increased risk for three of the top 10 causes of death in the U.S. Research in the area of metabolic syndrome and the individual components is increasing. Hopefully more attention will be given to women, who have higher death rates from cardiovascular diseases and diabetes than men.

There are many factors that influence the risk for metabolic syndrome and the related diseases, including genetics, family history, environment, and lifestyle. The influence of lifestyle, specifically physical activity, is one area in which individual women have some control. Following the basic guidelines for physical activity as recommended by the American College of Sports Medicine is a first step for women who are currently sedentary. Those guidelines are *30 minutes of moderate intensity exercise (equivalent to brisk walking) on most days of the week.* The 30-minute duration can be accumulated in 10+ minute bouts rather than be completed all at once. (See Chapter 1, *Chronic Disease*, for more information).

For women who are already meeting these basic physical activity goals for health, increasing the duration to *60 minutes per day* is the next level to achieve. Try adding 5 minutes to your daily activity every few weeks or months. More intense activity may be beneficial to some, but not all of the components of metabolic syndrome. For women who choose more *vigorous exercise (e.g., jogging), a minimum of 20 minutes 3 or more days per week* is recommended.

The evidence is clear—any activity is better than none, and the benefits apply to most systems of the body. Metabolic syndrome can be controlled or completely avoided by most women without having to rely on medications. Getting annual medical examinations that include evaluation of the different components of metabolic syndrome is important. All women—and men—should be encouraged to do so.

References

American Heart Association. (2008). How Can I Reduce High Blood Pressure? *(http://www.americanheart.org/presenter.jhtml?identifier=3004847).*

American Heart Association. (2004). Statistical Fact Sheet: Metabolic Syndrome. *(http://www.americanheart.org/downloadable/heart/1136819875357META06.pdf).*

American Heart Association. (2008). Statistics: Women and Cardiovascular Diseases. *(http://www.americanheart.org/downloadable/heart/1199816973854FS10WM08.pdf).*

Blumenthal, J.A., Sherwood A., Gullette, E.C.D., Babyak, M., Waugh, R., Georgiades, A, Craighead, L.W., Tweedy, D., Feinglos, M., Appelbaum, M., Hayano, J., & Hinderliter, A. (2000). Exercise and weight loss reduce blood pressure in men and women with mild hypertension. *Arch Intern Med* 160: 1947–1958.

Centers for Disease Control and Prevention. (2007). Facts and Statistics: High Blood Pressure Facts. *(http://www.cdc.gov/bloodpressure/facts.htm).*

Centers for Disease Control and Prevention. (2008). National Diabetes Fact Sheet 2007. *(http://www.cdc.gov/diabetes/pubs/pdf/ndfs_2007.pdf).*

Centers for Disease Control and Prevention. (2007). Summary of Health Statistics for US Adults, National Health Interview Survey 2006. *(http://www.cdc.gov/nchs/data/series/sr_10/sr10_235.pdf).*

Chobanian, A.V., Bakris, G.L., Black, H.R., Cushman, W.C., Green, L.A., Izzo, J.L. Jr., Jones, D.W., Materson, B.J., Oparil, S., Wright, J.T. Jr., Roccella, E.J. (2003). Seventh report of the Joint National Committee on Prevention, Detection, Evaluation, and Treatment of High Blood Pressure. *Hypertension* 42:1206–52.

Cleveland Clinic Heart and Vascular Institute. Metabolic Syndrome (Women). *(http://my.clevelandclinic.org/heart/women/metabolic.aspx).*

Ford ES, Giles WH, Dietz WH. (2002). Prevalence of the Metabolic syndrome among U.S. adults. Findings from the third National Health and Nutrition Examination Survey. *JAMA* 287: 356–359.

Janiszewski, P.M., Saunders, T.J. (2008). Themed Review: Lifestyle treatment of the metabolic syndrome. *Am J Lifestyle Med* 2: 99–108.

National Heart Lung and Blood Institute of the National Institutes of Health. Metabolic Syndrome. *(http://www.nhlbi.nih.gov/health/dci/Diseases/ms/ms_diagnosis.html).*

Slentz, C. A., Duscha, B. D., Johnson, J. L., Ketchum, K., Aiken, L. B., Samsa, G. P., Houmard, J. A., Bales, C. W., & Kraus, W. E. (2004). Effects of the Amount of Exercise on Body Weight, Body Composition, and Measures of Central Obesity. *Arch Intern Med* 164: 31–39.

Slentz, C. A., Aiken, L. F., Houmard, J. A., Bales, C. W., Johnson, J. L., Tanner, C. J., Duscha, B. D., & Kraus, W. E. (2005). Inactivity, exercise, and visceral fat. STRRIDE: a randomized, controlled study of exercise intensity and amount I: 1613–1618.

Wildman, R. P., Muntner, P., Reynolds, K., McGinn, A. P., Rajpathak, S., Wylie-Rosett, J., & Sowers, M. F. R. (2008). The Obese Without Cardiometabolic Risk Factor Clustering and the Normal Weight With Cardiometabolic Risk Factor Clustering. Prevalence and Correlates of 2 Phenotypes Among the US Population (NHANES 1999–2004). *Arch Intern Med* 168: 1617–1624.

Zoeller, R. F. (2008). Lifestyle and the risk of cardiovascular disease in women: is physical activity an equal opportunity benefactor? *Am J Lifestyle Med* 2: 219–226.

Further Readings

Diet & Nutrition Recommendations by the American Heart Association. (*http://www.americanheart.org/presenter.jhtml?identifier=1200010*).

American Heart Association's "Choose to Move" Free 12-Week Physical Activity Program for Women. (*http://www.choosetomove.org/*).

High Blood Pressure: A Special Message for Women: The American Heart Association. (*http://www.americanheart.org/presenter.jhtml?identifier=2123*).

Discussion Questions

1. How do the risk factors for metabolic syndrome vary among racial and ethnic groups? Why do you think these differences exist?

2. Which of the risk factors is considered the foundation of metabolic syndrome and each of the other risk factors? Why is this risk factor so dangerous?

3. What type of exercise is recommended for individuals with risk factors of metabolic syndrome? Which risk factors are positively affected by participation in physical activity?

3

Exercising with "Your Friend"

Exercise and the Menstrual Cycle

Ann F. Maliszewski

The focus of this chapter is the relationship between exercise and women's reproductive hormones as they change through the menstrual cycle or diminish in menopause. Hormones are signal molecules that serve to turn-on or turn-off actions of different tissues in the body. Because of the fluctuations in the reproductive hormones through the menstrual cycle, it has long been thought that exercise performance might be negatively affected during certain phases of the cycle. In this chapter, we're going to take a close look at (1) exactly what happens to hormone levels and the reproductive system during a typical menstrual cycle; (2) how different organ systems contribute to exercise performance; and (3) how the changes in hormone levels during the menstrual cycle might affect exercise performance. Additionally, we will examine how exercise is used to alleviate symptoms associated with changing hormone levels during the menstrual cycle and menopause.

The Menstrual Cycle

Young and adolescent girls can have their first menstruation (i.e., *menarche*) as early as 8 years of age or as late as 16 years (average age = 12.5 years). In normal, healthy conditions, the reproductive years last until menopause, which typically occurs when a woman is in her 40s or 50s (average age = 51 years). The "cycling" of the menstrual cycle means that a woman's body repeatedly prepares itself for pregnancy about 13 times per year throughout the reproductive years. A woman who reaches menarche at age 12 and menopause at 52 years would have 40 reproductive years, which adds up to as many as 520 menstrual cycles in her lifetime. Given the number of times a woman will have a menstrual cycle, it is important to understand what's really going on in her body. Women often have negative feelings about their period, but menstruation actually reflects an amazing sequence of physiological changes in the female body, which if understood can be empowering.

The menstrual cycle is a normal process that prepares a woman's body for pregnancy. It involves the building of the tissue in the uterus (i.e., *endometrium*) that will house a fertilized egg and provide it with nutrition if the woman becomes pregnant. If pregnancy does not occur during a cycle, the prepared tissue is broken down and removed as menstrual flow (*menses*), and the monthly process begins again. Throughout each monthly cycle, the levels of reproductive hormones, *estrogen* and *progesterone*, change systematically. *Hormones* are chemical molecules released by glands into the blood. Once in the blood, hormones travel to their "target" cells where they stimulate the cells to perform certain activities. There are receptors for different hormones in all cells of the body, and how one hormone, or combinations of hormones affect different cells is an entire field of study called *endocrinology*. Estrogen receptors are located in the uterus, brain, breasts, liver, heart, and bone. Progesterone receptors are located in the uterus, ovaries, breasts, brain, and bone. Much is known, but as you will see, much is still unknown about the effects of the reproductive hormones on the cells of a woman's body.

On average, a menstrual cycle lasts 28 days, however the duration varies among women, ranging from 21 to 35 days per cycle. The typical hormone changes through the menstrual cycle are illustrated in Figure 1. No matter how long a cycle lasts, day 1 is marked by the onset of *menstruation* or menses (i.e., bleeding). The bleeding normally lasts for 4 to 5 days (±1–2 days). During the first two weeks of the cycle, the ovarian follicle, which contains the egg, grows and gets ready to release the egg from the ovary. As menstruation slows and ceases after a few days, the maturing follicle secretes the sex hormone estrogen (also called *estradiol*). Because of the activity of the ovarian follicle, this first 2-week phase of the menstrual cycle is called the *follicu-*

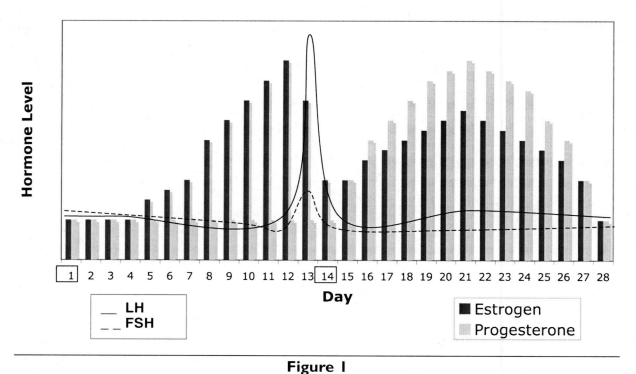

Figure 1

Hormone levels throughout the menstrual cycle. Day 1 = onset of menstruation; Day 14 = ovulation; Days 1–14 = Follicular phase; Days 15–28 = Luteal phase.

lar phase (days 1 to 13). At the middle of the cycle (day 14), the egg is released from the ovary through a process called *ovulation*. Upon release, the egg enters the uterine or Fallopian tube where it will travel to the uterus—and possibly be fertilized by sperm along the way.

The second phase of the menstrual cycle is called the *luteal phase* (days 15 to 28). The follicle that was left behind in the ovary after ovulation is now called the *corpus luteum*. This structure secretes the hormones *estrogen* and *progesterone* during the luteal phase. If pregnancy does not occur, the corpus luteum will disintegrate and stop secreting the hormones after several days, and menstruation will begin. Take another look at Figure 1 to see the different phases of the cycle and how the reproductive hormone levels change through the course of a 28-day menstrual cycle.

In addition to the reproductive hormones, estrogen and progesterone, there are fluctuations in the hormones secreted by the anterior pituitary gland. Located next to the hypothalamus in the brain, the anterior pituitary secretes a class of hormones called *gonadotropins*. As the name suggests, these hormones travel to and have an effect on the gonads (ovaries in women, testes in men). The two gonadotropins are *follicle stimulating hormone* (FSH) and *luteinizing hormone* (LH). As the name suggests, *follicle* stimulating hormone stimulates the development of the ovarian *follicle* during the *follicular* phase. LH initially spikes around day 13, just after the peak estrogen levels during the follicular phase. This spike in LH stimulates ovulation. Following ovulation, LH stimulates the development of the corpus luteum. The gonadotropins directly influence the activities in the ovaries, and therefore indirectly influence the production of reproductive hormones. In turn, the reproductive hormones feedback information to the pituitary and hypothalamus, keeping the gonadotropin secretion in check. This is one example of the typical hormone feedback systems of the body.

Fluctuations in hormone levels throughout the menstrual cycle, although predictable, make the study of exercise physiology in women a complex process. In order to understand the true effects of exercise in women—separate from hormonal influence—research must be conducted in a way to control for the fluctuating hormone levels while examining the effects of exercise. Unfortunately, some research in this area lacks accurate measurement of hormones, and thus lacks precise identification of the menstrual cycle phase. However, there is some well-designed research that sheds light on how different measures of exercise performance are affected by the phase of the menstrual cycle.

The Physiology of Exercise

Muscle Contractions: Endurance versus Power

Before we examine how the reproductive hormones influence exercise, it is important to understand the basic physiological responses to exercise. What all physical activity has in common is the activation of skeletal muscle. In order to have movement, the muscles must contract. The way a muscle contracts depends on the goal of the activity. For example, endurance athletes, such as distance cyclists, runners, and swimmers, depend on the muscles' ability to contract at moderate-to-high levels of force repeatedly for hours. During these repeated contractions, energy must be available to meet the work demands for the long-haul. Power athletes, such as high-jumpers, sprinters, and throwers, need the muscles to generate maximum force once or a few times, as quickly as possible. To perform these powerful contractions, a large amount of energy is required rapidly. Endurance and power-based activities rely on different muscle activation patterns and energy systems within the muscle cells.

Energy Production

The cells of the body have energy pathways that allow them to make the energy-containing molecule called *adenosine triphosphate* (ATP). In one type of energy pathway, muscle cells can use oxygen and fuels from food to make ATP. Because oxygen is used, this process is called *"aerobic"* (aerobic = occurring in the presence of oxygen). The oxygen is taken into the body from the air breathed into the lungs. It must then be transported from the lungs to the cells that need it. These steps will require a few minutes to complete, so time is required to match the oxygen supply with the cell's demand.

Muscles have other ways of making ATP that do not rely on oxygen, and thus are referred to as *"anaerobic."* Because they don't rely on the delivery of oxygen from the lungs to the muscle cells, anaerobic pathways can produce ATP very quickly. Anaerobic energy production takes place in the *cytosol*, which is the fluid part of the cell. Generally speaking, high-power, short duration events primarily rely on the anaerobic energy pathways. Endurance events, on the other hand, reply primarily on aerobic energy production. But no matter what a person is doing, even sitting at rest, the cells are using some combination of the aerobic and anaerobic pathways to provide ATP.

One of the best overall predictors of endurance performance is maximum oxygen consumption (VO_2max). VO_2max reflects the highest (*maximum*) ability of the body to take in and use oxygen (V = *volume*; O_2 = *oxygen*) for the production of energy. VO_2max is dependent on oxygen *delivery*, *uptake* and *use* by the cardiovascular, respiratory, and muscular systems. So it provides a single measure to reflect the effectiveness of all of the systems listed. Terms that are synonymous with VO_2max include *aerobic capacity*, *maximum oxygen uptake*, *maximum oxygen consumption*, and *maximum aerobic power*.

Cardiovascular and Respiratory Systems

Muscle cells cannot store large amounts of oxygen, so they rely on organ systems to constantly deliver it. The more work the cells do, the more energy (i.e., ATP) they need, and thus, the more oxygen is required. The organ systems that are responsible for making oxygen available to the working muscle cells are the *cardiovascular* (blood, heart and blood vessels) and *respiratory* (lungs) systems. When air is breathed into the lungs, oxygen is transported from there into the blood. The heart then pumps the oxygenated blood out to the cells throughout the body. When the oxygen arrives at the cells, it is transported into those cells where it will be used to make ATP.

The cardiovascular system has several components that can affect its ability to carry and deliver oxygen. The blood carries oxygen in its red cells where the oxygen binds to the iron-containing molecule *hemoglobin*. The more red blood cells, hemoglobin, and iron, the better the blood is at carrying oxygen. Assuming the blood content is optimum for carrying oxygen, the next factor in the delivery system is the pump that pushes the blood out to the working cells. The heart is the pump, and its ability to deliver oxygenated blood is dependent on the *rate* at which it pumps (*heart rate*, measured in *beats per minute*). Another factor that can affect delivery is *stroke volume*, which is the amount of blood pumped out with each heart beat. Stroke volume is determined by the size of the heart's chambers that hold the blood before it is pumped. The larger the chamber, the more blood it can hold and then push out when contracting. The product of heart rate and stroke volume is *cardiac output* (HR × SV = CO), which is the volume of blood pumped out of the heart and directed to the body's tissues every minute.

Finally, the blood has to reach the cells that need the oxygen. Large blood vessels called *arteries* direct blood away from the heart. They eventually branch into smaller (*arterioles*) and then tiny blood vessels (*capillaries*). Capillaries surround muscle cells and allow oxygen to be transported from the blood into the cells. The more capillaries there are around a cell, the more oxygen can enter that cell. Once in the cell, the oxygen is delivered to the mitochondria, a small oval-shaped organelle, where it is used to make ATP in the aerobic pathways. In summary, aerobic capacity is a function of capillary density (*oxygen uptake* into the cells); cardiac output (heart rate and stroke volume), and hemoglobin content of the blood (*delivery* to the cells); and mitochondrial density (oxygen *use* in the cells). The ability to carry, deliver, and use oxygen directly influences how well the muscles can work, especially during endurance/aerobic activities.

Because reproductive hormones affect different organ systems of the body, changing levels of estrogen and/or progesterone may affect the cardiovascular and respiratory systems, and thus the ability to make oxygen available to the cells. As the levels of reproductive hormones change through the menstrual cycle, these potential effects could alter a woman's VO$_2$max and her ability to perform endurance activities. Some of the factors identified above are more likely to be influenced by hormones, while others are more stable and longer-lasting. For example, the size of the heart's chambers, which directly influences stroke volume, and the number of capillaries surrounding muscle cells can change, but measurable changes usually require several weeks to months. These measures would not be expected to change significantly in a 28-day menstrual cycle. Measures like ventilation (breathing) rate and heart rate can be changed immediately, and the number of hemoglobin-containing red blood cells can be altered within days. These are variables that are more likely to demonstrate variability during a monthly menstrual cycle.

Fuel Use

Another factor that can influence the production of ATP is the availability of fuels for the aerobic or anaerobic pathways. Fuels are used, with or without oxygen, to provide energy to make ATP. The fuel molecules are broken down so that energy can be removed from them. Then the energy is put into ATP, which in turn provides the cell with that energy. That energy is used by muscle cells to contract, and produce force and movement. Some hormones bind to the tissues that influence the availability of certain fuels (e.g., liver, fat cells), therefore with changing hormone levels, there may be variations in fuel availability at different phases of the menstrual cycle. Let's first take a look at what fuels are normally available for the muscle cells.

Fat and carbohydrate are the primary food-based fuels used in the cell's energy pathways. Although protein can be used for energy, it typically contributes a very small amount (< 5–10%) to the overall energy needed for exercise. As discussed earlier, anaerobic processes can provide a lot of energy quickly, whereas aerobic pathways can provide ATP at a slower rate, but for a longer period of time before fatigue sets in.

Carbohydrate (i.e., sugar), specifically *glucose*, can be used as a fuel for aerobic and/or anaerobic energy production. Through anaerobic processes, glucose can be broken down

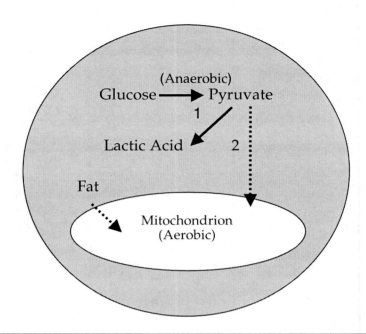

Figure 2

Fuel use (glucose = carbohydrate; fat) in the anaerobic and aerobic pathways of muscle cells.

quickly into pyruvate for energy making a relatively large amount of ATP in a short amount of time. Under anaerobic conditions, however, *lactic acid* is produced when glucose is broken down (See Figure 2). If you've ever experienced lactic acid in your muscles, you know that it makes muscles burn and can be very uncomfortable. As lactic acid builds up, the ability of the muscle to continue contracting is diminished and the muscle cells fatigue. To help alleviate the effects of fatigue, the lactic acid moves out of the muscle cells into the blood, where we refer to it as *blood lactate*.

Under aerobic conditions, glucose can be broken down all the way to carbon dioxide, which you breathe out, and water. In this situation, glucose is still broken down into pyruvate (anaerobically), but then most of the pyruvate enters the mitochondria, where it is further broken down in the aerobic pathways. With minimal accumulation of lactic acid during aerobic activities, the muscle can continue to contract as long as fuel and oxygen are available. There will always be some lactic acid produced when glucose is used as a fuel because the initial breakdown of glucose is always an anaerobic process. However, at a certain point, one of two steps can take place, (1) formation of lactic acid, or (2) continued breakdown in the aerobic pathways (See steps 1 and 2 in Figure 2).

As illustrated in Figure 2, fat can only be broken down aerobically in the mitochondria of the cell. So, when fat is the primary fuel, ATP production is not rapid enough to support a power-event, but it can supply energy steadily for endurance events. In reality, the cells always use combinations of fuels, not carbohydrate or fat exclusively. Furthermore, the cells never solely rely on one energy pathway. Instead they use both the aerobic and anaerobic pathways to make ATP. At any given time, the cells rely more on one type than the other, depending on the demands being placed on the muscle cells. The amount of the fuels available to the cells and the type of contraction being performed determine the amount of energy available for the cells to perform their work. If the reproductive hormones influence fuel availability to the muscle cells, performance of different activities (endurance/aerobic vs. power/anaerobic) also may be affected.

Because the demands of exercise rely on the cardiovascular, respiratory, muscular, and fuel-supplying organs of the body, there are many potential sites of influence of the reproductive hormones during exercise. As a woman participates in exercise, be it power or endurance, the phase of the cycle may influence the factors that determine her performance. In the next section we will examine what the research shows about the effect of the menstrual cycle on exercise performance.

The Effect of the Menstrual Cycle on Exercise

Endurance exercise performance relies heavily on the cardiovascular and respiratory systems, as well as the availability of fuels for making ATP. There are many possible sites of influence for the reproductive hormones. As discussed above, they include blood hemoglobin levels, heart rate, ventilation rate, blood lactate (from the cells' lactic acid), VO$_2$max, and ultimately measures of exercise performance (e.g., endurance time or time to exhaustion). If the reproductive hormones do affect these measures, there should be clear differences in these measures between the different phases of the menstrual cycle. Most studies compare different physiological measures between the follicular (low, then high estrogen) and luteal phases (high estrogen and progesterone). In this section we will examine the research on how the physiological measures related to exercise performance are affected by the two phases of the menstrual cycle.

Hemoglobin is the oxygen-binding molecule in the red blood cells, and is, therefore, critical for carrying oxygen to the working cells during exercise. Reports of changes in hemoglobin levels between the phases of the menstrual cycle are not consistent in the research literature. Some studies report higher hemoglobin levels during the luteal phase when estrogen and progesterone levels are high, while many others report no differences between the phases. *Based on current research, there is no overwhelming evidence to support the idea that the ability of the blood to carry oxygen is significantly affected by the phases of the menstrual cycle.*

Although a few studies have reported higher heart rates in the luteal phase, most studies report no difference between the follicular and luteal phases during rest or exercise. *The pumping of blood, and therefore the delivery of oxygen to the working cells, does not appear to be affected by the hormonal fluctuations of the menstrual cycle.*

In well-controlled studies, progesterone has been shown to directly affect the phrenic nerve, which stimulates breathing or ventilation. Increases in progesterone increase ventilation rate (V_E). Given this hormonal influence, one would expect increases in V_E during the luteal phase of the menstrual cycle when progesterone levels peak. However, when V_E is compared across the phases of the menstrual cycle in women, there are no consistent findings among the research studies. Some studies report elevated V_E during the luteal phase while many other studies report no difference between phases. Because estrogen is also increased during the luteal phase, the interaction of the two reproductive hormones may reduce the individual affect of progesterone on ventilation. *The ability to move air into and out of the lungs does not appear to be altered through the different phases of the menstrual cycle.* More research may be needed in this area to clarify the individual and combined effects of progesterone and estrogen on ventilation rate.

The only measures in which changes across the menstrual cycle have been reported consistently are those of fuel availability. Animal studies, which allow for very controlled manipulation of hormone levels, show that estrogen supplementation increases fat availability and use by muscle cells and decreases carbohydrate use during exercise. Glucose that is stored in body cells as *glycogen* (a long chain of glucose molecules) is conserved when estrogen is present. The practical application to saving glucose is that it is relatively easy to deplete the glucose stores in the body, whereas fat is much more abundant under normal condition. Because glucose can be used up in a matter of hours, the body's attempt to store it is a beneficial response, especially if there's a chance that the female might become pregnant. A growing fetus will rely heavily on carbohydrate for energy. Progesterone has also been shown to stimulate the conservation of glucose and it has been suggested that there is an additive effect between estrogen and progesterone. An interaction of the two reproductive hormones has been supported in an often-cited human study in which muscle glycogen stores, at rest, remain higher during the luteal phase (with elevated estrogen and progesterone) when compared with the follicular phase (elevated estrogen only). Supporting the findings that report higher carbohydrate use during the follicular phase, are higher blood lactate levels during this phase as well. Because lactic acid is a by-product of carbohydrate (i.e., glucose) use, increased levels of lactate would also be expected. Unfortunately, there are just as many studies that report no changes in fuel use during exercise across the phases of the menstrual cycle as those that show a change.

Research studies on fuel use are complicated because they have to control for hormone, as well as nutritional status. Meals consumed in the days prior to testing strongly influence the measures of fuel availability and use. It is very difficult and expensive to control what research study participants eat in the days leading up to the testing session. There are also factors that cannot be controlled by the research, including the interaction of the reproductive hormones with other hormones in the body that influence fuel availability (e.g., epinephrine, insulin, etc.). Clearly this is a complicated field of study.

Maximum oxygen consumption is the ultimate measure that reflects the body's ability carry, deliver, and use oxygen during maximum aerobic exercise. We have seen that none of the individual VO_2max-related physiological measures discussed above are consistently affected by changing hormone levels. Similarly, *studies that examine VO_2max directly across the phases also identify no clear and consistent effects.* This supports the premise that women performing endurance sports and activities will perform similarly throughout the menstrual cycle.

Given there are few obvious physiological effects of the menstrual cycle during aerobic exercise, one would also expect no effects on endurance performance. With few exceptions, the research overwhelmingly demonstrates that there are *no phase-related differences in the performance of endurance activities at low-, moderate-, and high-intensities of aerobic exercise.* Middleton and Wenger (2006) reported improved short-duration power performance in women during the luteal phase compared with the follicular. However, other studies do not support phase difference in muscular strength and power. In summary, there is *little evidence to suggest that athletic performance by women is significantly altered between the follicular and luteal phases.* But the inconsistencies in the research suggest more research is needed.

Anecdotally, many women report having days during their cycle in which they feel sluggish or even super-strong. However, even subjective measures of how difficult exercise feels as its being performed fail to show consistent patterns in groups of women. This finding may be because "feeling" is affected by so many factors including nutritional status, brain chemistry, fitness and physical activity level, drug and alcohol use, and daily stress. The interactions among these various factors and the hormones are likely to affect women differently. Because the fluctuations in hormone levels in the different phases of the menstrual cycle are highly variable among women, it is difficult to make generalized statements about all, or even the majority of women. Such variability is seen in many of the physiological measures. So, although the groups of women who participated in these studies did not demonstrate changes similar to one another, individual women may, in fact, have cyclic shifts in their performance or feelings of difficulty of an exercise depending on the phase of the menstrual cycle. More research is needed that can provide better controls on the testing situation, including control of diet, previous exercise, stress level, etc.

Because of individual differences, it is important for a woman to monitor her own changes (mood, cravings, exercise performance) through the menstrual cycle so she can become familiar with her own patterns. Knowledge is power when understanding your own cycle. For example, if a woman consistently cries at TV commercials on day 14 of her cycle, and then experiences road-rage on day 21, she may begin to recognize the exaggerated feelings and be able to handle them better if she knows the source (i.e., hormone levels). But keep this in mind, women: just because some of you might experience extreme irritability on some days of your cycle doesn't mean you don't have reason to be angry. No one should blame the menstrual cycle for the emotion—but hormones may influence (e.g., exaggerate) the *expression* of the emotion on certain days.

Exercise and Premenstrual Symptoms

Up to 90% of women who are of childbearing age (from the onset of menses to menopause) experience some physical or mental symptoms in the week before menstruation. Women under 30 years of age tend to be most affected. The symptoms occur during the luteal phase of the menstrual cycle and are most often reported to occur from the point of peak progesterone levels and subside soon after menses begins.

Classification of premenstrual disorders is based on the number and severity of the symptoms. Having one symptom among the list of symptoms does not warrant classification of a disorder. Instead, to be classified as *premenstrual syndrome*, a woman must experience at least one *somatic* (physical) and one *affective* (emotional or mental) symptom. Additionally, these symptoms must (a) interfere with social or work-related performance, (b) occur only during the luteal phase, and (c) must be experienced when no drugs (e.g., birth control, mood disorder treatments, etc.) or alcohol are in the system. About 40% of women experience PMS. The symptoms for PMS are listed in Table 1.

A more severe collection of premenstrual symptoms affects about 3–8% of women. This more severe condition is called *Premenstrual Dysphoric Disorder* (PMDD). The symptoms associated with PMDD are outlined in Table 2. Note that a diagnosis of PMDD includes having 5 or more of the symptoms, one of which must be among the first 4 in the list. Again, these symptoms must occur during the week preceding menstruation and subside soon thereafter. Women who are diagnosed with PMDD have impaired work/school function and relationship difficulties, and these impairments must be present for more than one menstrual cycle.

When examining the fluctuations in hormones during the menstrual cycle, the symptoms experienced by women might not seem so surprising. Considering the fact that the body has been preparing for pregnancy since early-follicular phase, the physical symptoms may make

Table 1 Symptoms of Premenstrual Syndrome (American College of Obstetrics & Gynecology, 2000)	
Somatic Symptoms	**Affective Symptoms**
Breast tenderness	Depression
Abdominal bloating	Anger (outbursts)
Headache	Anxiety
Swelling of extremities	Irritability
	Confusion
	Social withdrawal
Source: Mishell, D. R. (2007). Premenstrual dysphoric disorder: A new treatment paradigm. *www.medscape.com*	

Table 2 Symptoms of Premenstrual Dysphoric Disorder (American Psychiatric Association, 2000)
1. Depressed mood or dysphoria (unhappy, hopeless)
2. Anxiety or tension
3. Affective lability (frequent changes in emotional state)
4. Irritability
5. Decreased interest in regular activities
6. Difficulty concentrating
7. Noticeable lack of energy
8. Change in appetite (overeating, cravings)
9. Insomnia, extreme insomnia
10. Overwhelm
11. Other physical symptoms (e.g, bloating, breast tenderness, cramping)
Source: Mishell, D. R. (2007). Premenstrual dysphoric disorder: A new treatment paradigm. *www.medscape.com*

sense. For example, the development of the endometrium, which includes increased storage of glycogen and increased blood and vascularization (growing of blood vessels to feed the endometrium), it might seem more surprising when a woman does NOT feel bloated. Whether a woman experiences occasional minimal or regular severe symptoms, it is important to understand what might be done to reduce these symptoms.

Before pharmacological agents are prescribed, gynecologists might recommend lifestyle changes to treat premenstrual symptoms. Dietary recommendations include vitamin B6, calcium, and/or magnesium supplements. These have been reported to be beneficial for reducing symptoms. Physical activity also has benefits. Women who perform aerobic exercise on a regular basis report fewer premenstrual symptoms, both physical and affective. And women who were sedentary but begin an exercise program report reductions in bloating, breast tenderness, and affective symptoms. The exercise recommendations for premenstrual symptoms include 20 to 30 minutes or more of aerobic exercise on 3 or more days per week. Relaxation exercises (meditation, yoga, etc.) may also be beneficial.

Exercise and Menopause

A woman is officially *post-menopausal* one year after her last period. Menopause occurs, on average, around the age of 51 years. If a woman undergoes a hysterectomy, she is considered "surgically menopausal" and is likely to experience the same symptoms as women who enter menopause naturally.

Menopause is marked by an extreme reduction in levels of the reproductive hormones estrogen and progesterone, and the normal cycling of the hormones ceases. The changes associated with menopause may begin around the age of 40 years even though a woman is still cycling normally. This state is considered *peri-menopause*.

The menopausal reduction in reproductive hormones is associated with a variety of physical and affective symptoms, including irritability, insomnia, difficulty concentrating, incontinence, and hot flashes.

Approximately 75% of post-menopausal women experience hot flashes (i.e., *vasomotor symptoms*). This sudden increase in body temperature and sweating appear to be related to reductions in estrogen. Hot flashes may be accompanied by nausea, anxiety, and/or dizziness, making them very disruptive and difficult to ignore. Because hot flashes can occur at any time of day, it's been suggested that they may increase the likelihood of insomnia when they occur at night, which in turn may contribute to mood disorders and lack of concentration.

Many studies report that women who exercise regularly have fewer hot flashes than women who do not. One study reported that half as many physically active women experienced hot flashes as those who were inactive. In another study, post-menopausal women were assigned to different groups that participated in a regular exercise program with or without nutritional or hormonal supplementation, or into a control, no-intervention group. Groups that included exercise all experienced significant decreases in hot flashes when compared with the women in the control, non-exercising group.

Because of the decreased incidence of hot flashes in post-menopausal women who exercise, it is possible that there are concomitant reductions in mood and sleep disorders. However, the findings on the benefits of exercise on these specific symptoms are not clear. Promising results were observed in one study in which post-menopausal women who increased their physical activity levels also had the lowest increase in stress and depression when compared with women who were less active. But other studies were not as definitive.

Body weight increases with age. But expending calories through exercise can reduce the rate of weight gain over the years, or even reverse it. Studies on women have reported that both pre- and post-menopausal women gain, on average, about 1 to 2 pounds per year. However, the women who gain the most weight are those who are least active. But there's always opportunity to gain the body composition benefits of exercise. When sedentary women in one study increased their activity level over the 3-year study period, they experienced less weight gain than those who did not become active. This indicates that it is never too late to obtain the benefits of exercise.

The issue of weight loss in elderly women must be considered carefully. Unless a woman is obese (extremely high levels of body fat), weight loss may actually be detrimental. Loss in body weight is associated with a loss in bone density, which is an important consideration for women at risk for bone loss or disease. Exercise for the average post-menopausal woman should focus on the maintenance of or increase in muscle mass while keeping body fat in-check. Focus on the scale (i.e., body weight) should be discouraged.

Bone mass is also lost when estrogen is no longer being produced (i.e., menopause). Loss in bone content can lead to a pre-disease state called *osteopoenia*, and continued loss can lead to *osteoporosis*. The disease osteoporosis is associated with weakness of the bone tissue and increased risk of fracture. When elderly women break a hip, quality of life is significantly reduced, and about 20% of women die within a year of experiencing such a fracture. Estrogen is a critical ingredient in the process of bone growth in women. Without estrogen—and without pharmacologic interventions—the best post-menopausal women can do is work to hold onto the bone they have. As discussed in Chapter 1 (Chronic Disease), bone health in old age is highly dependent on bone growth early in life. One study showed that exercise led to increased estrogen levels in both pre- and post-menopausal women. Having elevated estrogen levels during and following exercise may help in the maintenance of bone. Research consistently demonstrates that exercise is beneficial for bone health throughout life.

The research examining the benefits of exercise for physical symptoms related to menopause overwhelmingly report benefits to women who exercise regularly and to those who begin an exercise program. Being physically active throughout life will add to the quality and quantity of a woman's life.

Summary

Although the monthly menstrual cycle involves various fluctuations in the reproductive hormones, the research does not support the idea that women's performance of endurance—or power-based activities will be affected. Studying physiological changes in women during exercise through the menstrual cycle is not a simple task. Because of the variability within and among individual women, it is difficult to identify trends within groups of women if they exist. As research methods and technology improve, the ability to study these changes may begin to explain why there are so many inconsistencies in the existing research. Based on what is currently known, however, performance of work-related or athletic activities is not compromised by the hormone fluctuations of the menstrual cycle.

Exercise is actually beneficial to women who suffer symptoms associated with the menstrual cycle and menopause. Given all of the benefits of living a physically active life, women should be encouraged to participate in a regular exercise program or at least attempt to meet the minimum recommendations of physical activity for health.

References

Ashley, C. D., Kramer, M. L., & Bishop, P. (2000). Estrogen and substrate metabolism. A review of contradictory research. *Sports Med* 9: 21–227.

American College of Obstetricians and Gynecologists. (2008). Menstruation. *(http://www.acog.org/publications/patient_education/bp049.cfm)*.

Bonen, A., Haynes, F. W., & Graham, T. E. (1991). Substrate and hormonal responses to exercise in women using oral contraceptives. *J Appl Physiol* 70: 1917–1927.

Burghardt, M. (1999). Exercise at Menopause: A critical difference. *Medscape General Medicine 1*. *(http://www.medscape.com/viewarticle/408896)*.

Connolly, M. (2001). Premenstrual syndrome: an update on definitions, diagnosis and management. *Advances in Psychiatric Treatment* 7: 469–477.

D'eon, T., & Braun, B., (2002). The roles of estrogen and progesterone in regulating carbohydrate and fat utilization at rest and during exercise. *J Women's Health & Gender-Based Med* 11: 225–237.

Graham J. D., & Clarke C. L. (1997). Physiological action of progesterone in target tissues. *Endocrine Reviews* 18: 502–519.

Hackney, A. C., Effects of menstrual cycle on resting muscle glycogen content. *Hormone & Metabolic Research* 22: 647.

Janse de Jonge, X.A.K. (2003). Effects of the menstrual cycle on exercise performance. *Sports Med* 33: 833–851.

Jurkowski, J. E, Jones, J. L., Walker, W. C., Younglai, E. V., & Sutton, J. R. (1978). Ovarian hormonal responses to exercise. *J Appl Physiol* 44: 109–114.

Lamont, L. S. (2003). Dietary protein needs, endurance exercise, controversies in exercise science/nutrition. *International Sports Journal* 7: 39–45.

Galliven, E. A., Singh, A., Michelson, D., Bina, S., Gold, P, W., & Deuster, P. A. (1997). Hormonal and metabolic responses to exercise across time of day and menstrual cycle phase. *J Appl Physiol* 83: 18–1831.

Marsh, S. A., & Jenkins, D. G. (2002). Physiological responses to the menstrual cycle. Implications for the development of heat illness in female athletes. *Sports Med* 32: 601–614.

Middleton, L. E., & Wenger, H.A. (2006). Effect of menstrual phase on performance and recovery in intense intermittent activity. *Eur. J. Appl. Physiol.* 96: 53–58

Mishell, D. R. (2007). Premenstrual dysphoric disorder: A new treatment paradigm. *(http://www.medscape.com/viewarticle/557445)*.

National Cancer Institute. (2006) Understanding Cancer Series: Estrogen Receptors/SERMs. *(http://www.cancer.gov/cancertopics/understandingcancer/estrogenreceptors)*.

National Institutes on Aging. (2008). Age Page: Menopause. *(http://www.nia.nih.gov/HealthInformation/Publications/menopause.htm)*.

Shephard, R. J. (2000). Exercise and training in women, Part II: Influence of menstrual cycle and pregnancy on exercise responses. *Can J Appl Physiol* 25: 35–54.

Further Readings

Menstrual Cycles: What Really Happens in Those 28 Days?!
(http://www.fwhc.org/health/moon.htm).

Menstrual Cycle Disorders, National Women's Health Resource Center.
(http://www.healthywomen.org/healthtopics/menstrualdisorders).

Nutrition and Exercise Guide for PMS.
(http://www.uihealthcare.com/depts/med/obgyn/patedu/pms/pmsnutrition.html).

Dietary Factors: The PMS-Free Diet? MedicineNet.com.
(http://www.medicinenet.com/script/main/art.asp?articlekey=56086).

Discussion Questions

1. How do hormone levels change during the menstrual cycle and how do these changes affect physical activity and sport performance for women?

2. What's happening in the uterus during the menstrual cycle and which hormone(s) is/are contributing to those changes?

3. What are the symptoms associated with premenstrual syndrome? Is exercise beneficial for reducing or preventing these symptoms? How much physical activity is necessary for the benefits?

4. What are the symptoms/conditions of menopause? Discuss how exercise influences each of these symptoms.

4

Exercise and Pregnancy

Kathleen D. Little

Introduction

The relationship between the menstrual cycle and exercise was discussed in detail in the previous chapter. Normally, the menstrual cycle will occur about every 28 days throughout a woman's reproductive years. However, when a woman becomes pregnant, menstrual cycles will cease for the next nine months as the embryo (i.e., conception to two months) develops into a fetus (i.e., two months to birth) and the baby is born. As discussed in the previous chapter, exercise performance is not negatively affected by cyclic changes in reproductive hormones, and thus, it is safe to exercise throughout the menstrual cycle. However, once a woman becomes pregnant, both her physiological response as well as those of the baby must be considered. As you will learn in this chapter, exercise can be beneficial to both the mother and the baby.

Today, more women are reaping the benefits of exercise during pregnancy as evidenced by a large study of 9,953 women randomly selected from 48 U.S. states in which 42% reported exercising during their pregnancy, with half of them doing so for longer than six months. Walking (43%), swimming (12%), aerobic dancing (12%), and biking (8%) were the preferred types of exercise (Zhang & Savitz, 1996). There have also been a number of documented cases of Olympic athletes who won medals while competing during early pregnancy. Most recently, at the 2008 Beijing Olympics, Dara Torres became the oldest (41 years) Olympic swimmer to ever medal at an Olympic event. Torres started her Olympic comeback by swimming 3–4 days per week while pregnant and broke a world record at the 2006 Masters Nationals just three weeks after her daughter's birth. Other elite athletes have trained and competed during pregnancy, right up until delivery, with no adverse effects reported. In an extreme example, *Runner's World* described a case in which a woman ran a marathon nine days before delivery, and then completed a 24-hour race of 62.5 miles the day before delivering a healthy baby (Nieman, 2007). These examples suggest that with proper diet, training, and no pregnancy complications, well-conditioned women are capable of exercising at high levels during pregnancy without adverse effects.

In light of the above examples, it might seem surprising that until recently, clinical guidelines for exercise during pregnancy were quite conservative in an attempt to avoid any potential risks to either the mother or the baby. For example, in 1985 the American College of Obstetricians and Gynecologists (ACOG) issued guidelines that limited exercise duration to 15 minutes and heart rate to 140 beats per minute. A decade later, the ACOG (1994) guidelines were revised with the duration and heart rate limits removed. However, recommended types of exercise were limited to stretching, stationary cycling, swimming, and walking, still suggesting a somewhat conservative approach. This raises several questions that will be addressed in the following sections. What are the potential risks of exercise during pregnancy? Are there physiological adaptations to pregnancy that minimize these potential risks? What are the benefits of exercise during pregnancy to both the mother and the baby? What are the most recent clinical guidelines for exercise during pregnancy and the post partum period?

Potential Risks of Exercise During Pregnancy

Exercise requires physiological responses in order to optimize the delivery of oxygen and fuel to the exercising muscles, especially as exercise intensity increases. These include: 1) redirecting blood flow from organs that are relatively inactive during exercise (i.e., gastrointestinal tract, kidneys, liver, spleen, and in women, the uterus) to the exercising muscles; 2) increased use of carbohydrate as fuel by the exercising muscles; 3) increased body temperature which is exacerbated during prolonged exercise performed in hot, humid conditions; and 4) release of a variety of hormones including norepinephrine and prostaglandins. While all of these physiological responses are normal during exercise, they pose the following potential risks to the baby when the mother exercises during pregnancy, especially as exercise intensity increases (ACOG, 2002; ACSM, 2006; Artal et al., 1999; Clapp, 2001; Clapp, 2002; Davies et al., 2003; Wolfe, 2005):

1. **Lack of oxygen** (*fetal hypoxia*) due to redirecting the blood to the working muscles and away from the uterus, which may lower the baby's heart rate (*fetal bradycardia*). If chronic, this response can hamper development or be fatal;
2. **Elevated body temperature** (*fetal hyperthermia*) due to the mother's increased body temperature, which in early pregnancy can result in abnormal development of the baby's central nervous system;
3. **Stimulation of uterine contractions** by norepinephrine and prostaglandins released during exercise, which can lead to premature labor;
4. **Reduced carbohydrate availability**, the primary fuel used by the baby, as carbohydrate use by the mother increases during exercise. This limitation of fuel may lead to inadequate growth of the baby;
5. All of the above, as well as **abdominal trauma** associated with some types of exercise (i.e., contact sports, falls, etc.), may contribute to adverse pregnancy outcomes such as miscarriage, premature labor, shortened length of pregnancy, decreased birth weight, and abnormal development of the baby.

In addition to these potential risks to the baby, exercise during pregnancy also poses the following potential risks to the mother (ACOG, 2002; ACSM, 2006; Artal et al., 1999; Clapp, 2001; Clapp, 2002; Davies et al., 2003; Wolfe, 2005):

1. **Low blood sugar** (*hypoglycemia*) during exercise due to (a) reduced liver carbohydrate stores (i.e., glycogen), and (b) increased use of carbohydrate to meet the energy demands of both exercise *and* pregnancy. The higher the intensity of the exercise, the greater the reliance on carbohydrate;
2. **Chronic fatigue** due to the increased energy demands of both pregnancy (approximately 300 kcal/day) *and* exercise;
3. **Musculoskeletal injury** due to joint laxity induced by the release of *relaxin*, a hormone that softens pelvic cartilage to enhance delivery of the baby. Other factors include weight gain, which alters the center of gravity, balance, coordination, and may contribute to backache.

Physiological Adaptations to Pregnancy Which Minimize Potential Risks

As described above, exercise during pregnancy poses potential risks to the baby, with fetal hypoxia (lack of oxygen) and fetal hyperthermia (elevated body temperature) being the most dangerous. Fortunately, there are a number of physiological adaptations during pregnancy that minimize these potential risks to the baby.

Fetal Hypoxia

The potential for fetal hypoxia is minimized by cardiovascular adaptations by the mother's body during pregnancy (Brooks et al., 2005). One of the most important of these adaptations is a 40–50% increase in blood volume (Wolfe, 2005), which increases the amount of blood pumped by the heart each minute, and thus allows increased blood flow to the uterus and placenta (the organ responsible for providing oxygen and nutrients from the mother to the baby). The ability of the placenta to take oxygen out of the blood that is delivered to it is also enhanced during pregnancy. So, even if blood flow to the placenta falls up to 50%, oxygen delivery to the fetus is maintained (Clapp, 2002). In addition, after exercise, blood flow to the placenta is increased in a compensatory fashion. There are also important adaptations by the baby's body that help minimize the risk of fetal hypoxia. One of the most important of these is that the baby's hemoglobin (the oxygen carrying molecule in the blood) can carry 20–30% more oxygen than does the mother's hemoglobin, and it is also more concentrated in the baby's blood (50%). Finally, the oxygen needs of the baby are relatively small because there's little muscle activity and fairly stable body temperature due to the amniotic fluid in which it is suspended (Brooks et al., 2005). Some studies, mostly in pregnant animals exercising at high intensity, have shown reductions in uterine blood flow during exercise. However, a recent study in pregnant women did not find such a reduction immediately after exercise (Ertan et al., 2004). Measuring immediately after exercise is considered to be a good representation of what was taking place *during* exercise. Numerous studies in exercising pregnant women have reported an increase in the baby's heart rate, which is considered a normal response (Clapp et al., 1993), but few have shown a significant decrease (fetal bradycardia), the most common clinical index of fetal hypoxia (Clapp, 2002). Thus, it appears that the physiological adaptations by both the mother and the baby during pregnancy minimize the potential risk of fetal hypoxia during exercise.

Fetal Hyperthermia

The potential for fetal hyperthermia is also minimized by cardiovascular (heart and blood vessels), respiratory (lungs), and thermoregulatory (temperature regulation) adaptations by the mother's body during pregnancy. The increased blood volume described previously, in addition to an increase in ventilation (the amount of air moved into and out of the lungs per minute), results in increased blood flow to the skin. These changes, in turn, enhance heat loss by the mother during exercise (Artal, 1999). Heat is transported by the blood from the exercising muscles to the skin surface. Sweat is secreted onto the surface of the skin and warmed by the blood. The sweat becomes a vapor as it's heated up, and dissipates from the skin surface. The mother's body cools as the sweat evaporates. Heat loss during exercise is further enhanced by thermoregulatory adaptations in which the mother's core body temperature is lower at both rest and during exercise. Furthermore, sweating occurs sooner and at a lower body temperature compared to her non-pregnant state (Clapp, 1991). As no studies have reported fetal hyperthermia during exercise, it appears that the physiological adaptations during pregnancy minimize this potential risk. However, women should avoid prolonged exercise in hot, humid conditions because this makes evaporation of sweat difficult, thereby reducing the ability of the body to cool. Pregnant women should attempt to maintain a core body temperature of less than 102 degrees Fahrenheit, especially during early pregnancy (Clapp, 2002).

Other Potential Risks of Exercise During Pregnancy

As described previously, other potential risks to the baby during exercise, such as stimulation of uterine contractions, reduced carbohydrate availability, and abdominal trauma can potentially have adverse effects on pregnancy outcome. The potential negative effects include miscarriage, premature labor, shortened length of pregnancy, decreased birth weight, and abnormal development of the baby. However, the majority of studies have shown that women who exercise during pregnancy have either similar or better pregnancy outcomes as compared to women who do not exercise during pregnancy (Artal, 1999; Clapp, 2002; Davies et al., 2003).

As described previously, other potential risks to the pregnant mother during exercise include low blood sugar (glucose), chronic fatigue, and musculoskeletal injury. While there have been no reports of an increased incidence of these risks, the clinical guidelines discussed later in this chapter make specific recommendations in order to minimize these risks (ACOG, 2002; ACSM, 2006; Artal et al., 1999; Clapp, 2001; Clapp, 2002; Davies et al., 2003; Wolfe, 2005).

Benefits of Exercise During Pregnancy

Although pregnancy is not a disease, in the past women were often encouraged to rest and refrain from unnecessary physical exertion. However, in the last 20 years, significant health benefits of exercise during pregnancy, both for the mother and the baby, have been well-documented. As many of the physiological adaptations (i.e., cardiovascular, respiratory, and thermoregulatory) to pregnancy that were described earlier are similar to those of exercise training, it is not surprising that there is likely an additive and/or synergistic beneficial effect of exercise during pregnancy (Clapp, 2002).

Benefits to the Mother

Numerous benefits to the mother have been reported with exercise during pregnancy including improved fitness; prevention of excess weight gain, stretch marks, and varicose veins; improved posture and prevention and relief of back pain and leg cramps; improved psychological well-being, self-esteem, and body image; and recovery from childbirth (Brooks et al., 2005). Recent studies have even shown significant reductions in the risk of two of the most common pregnancy complications, gestational diabetes (50% reduction) and preeclampsia or hypertension (40% reduction), in women who exercise during pregnancy (Dempsey et al., 2005; Weissgerber et al., 2006). As women who develop diabetes and hypertension during pregnancy remain at risk for these diseases after delivery, this has important implications for prevention of these and other chronic diseases associated with the metabolic syndrome later in life, as described in Chapter 2 of this section (Exercise and Metabolic Syndrome).

The benefits of exercise will vary depending on a number of factors including the woman's initial fitness level and stage of pregnancy. Generally, the benefits of exercise in early pregnancy are improved growth of the baby and a decrease in pregnancy symptoms in the mother (i.e., nausea, fatigue, etc.), while exercise in mid- to late-pregnancy maintains the mother's fitness and can positively impact labor (Clapp, 2002). In addition, the type, frequency, intensity, and duration of exercise will also likely impact the benefits obtained. For example, while many of the above benefits were attained regardless of the nature of the exercise, only women who performed weight bearing exercise 30 or more minutes, three or more days per week, throughout mid- to late-pregnancy showed less weight and fat gain (Clapp and Little, 1995), enhanced placental growth (which enhances delivery of oxygen and nutrients to the baby), earlier delivery (7-8 days), shorter labor (by 1/3), and significantly less need for medical intervention during labor (i.e., induced labor, forceps delivery, cesarean section) (Clapp, 2002).

The benefits of exercise during pregnancy have become so clear that women are now being encouraged to consider the negative effects of *not* exercising. The adverse effects of being physically inactive during pregnancy include reduced muscular and cardiorespiratory fitness; excess weight gain; varicose veins; shortness of breath; low back pain; poor psychological adjustment to pregnancy; and higher risk of diabetes and hypertension during pregnancy (Davies et al., 2003). These negative effects of inactivity are obviously the opposite of the benefits of exercise.

Benefits to the Baby

While most research has focused on identifying and minimizing risks to the baby when the mother exercises during pregnancy, it turns out there are actual significant benefits. Some of these include improved tolerance to stress before and during labor; leaner at birth (although weight and growth are normal); and improved developmental behavior at birth (i.e., more alert, interested in their surroundings, and less demanding of their mothers). In order to determine if these short term benefits were maintained long term, the children were re-assessed at one and five years of age and were found to still be leaner and developmentally advanced compared to children of women who did not exercise during pregnancy (Clapp, 2002). It was speculated that the developmental improvement may be due to the synergistic effect of the physiological adaptations to pregnancy and exercise described previously. It may also reflect the benefit of stimuli experienced by the baby as the mother exercises, as might occur when the baby is exposed to music during pregnancy (Clapp, 2002). These results have interesting implications for enhancing growth and development of children.

Clinical Guidelines for Exercise During Pregnancy

In general, there is a lack of evidence of harmful effects of exercise during pregnancy. Instead, exercise provides significant health benefits to both baby and mother. Reflecting this, the most recent clinical guidelines issued by two respected U.S. national organizations (American College of Obstetricians and Gynecologists, ACOG, 2002; American College of Sports Medicine, ACSM, 2006), as well as their Canadian counterparts (Society of Obstetricians and Gynecologists of Canada, SOGC; Canadian Society for Exercise Physiology, CSEP—Joint SOGC/CSEP Guidelines, Davies et al., 2003), encourage regular exercise during pregnancy for all women except those with high risk or pregnancy complications (see Tables 1 and 2 for Absolute and Relative Contraindications, ACOG, 2002).

The approach to exercise during pregnancy is similar for all three sets of guidelines, which focus on a "common sense" rather than the previous conservative approach. They all agree that 1) women with any of the contraindications outlined in Table 1 should not exercise during pregnancy; 2) previously sedentary women or those with any of the relative contraindications outlined in Table 2 should consult their physician before engaging in exercise during pregnancy; 3) women who exercised regularly prior to pregnancy can continue their exercise program during pregnancy without major modifications; and 4) athletes who wish to continue a strenuous training program during pregnancy should be advised and monitored by their physician. There is also general agreement on types of exercise that should be avoided during pregnancy, as well as special considerations to keep in mind for any and all exercise performed during pregnancy (ACOG, 2002; ACSM, 2006; Davies et al., 2003). These issues are covered in the following sections.

Table 1 Absolute Contraindications to Aerobic Exercise During Pregnancy (ACOG, 2002)
■ Hemodynamically significant heart disease
■ Restrictive lung disease
■ Incompetent cervix/cerclage
■ Multiple gestation at risk for premature labor
■ Persistent second- or third-trimester bleeding
■ Placenta previa after 26 weeks gestation
■ Premature labor during the current pregnancy
■ Ruptured membranes
■ Preecalampsia/pregnancy-induced hypertension

Table 2 Relative Contraindications to Aerobic Exercise During Pregnancy (ACOG, 2002)
■ Severe anemia
■ Unevaluated maternal cardiac arrhythmia
■ Chronic bronchitis
■ Poorly controlled type 1 diabetes
■ Extreme morbid obesity
■ Extreme underweight (BMI < 12)
■ History of extremely sedentary lifestyle
■ Intrauterine growth retardation
■ Poorly controlled hypertension
■ Orthopedic limitations
■ Poorly controlled seizure disorder
■ Poorly controlled hyperthyroidism
■ Heavy smoker

Exercises Not Generally Recommended During Pregnancy

1. Supine Exercise or Prolonged Standing after the First Trimester

By mid- to late-pregnancy, the increased size and weight of the uterus and baby can compress the mother's inferior vena cava (the large blood vessel that returns blood to the heart) while she is lying supine (face-up, on her back). This blood vessel compression can subsequently result in reduced blood flow to the uterus and the baby, and increase the risk of fetal hypoxia. However, a recent study found a significant decrease in uterine blood flow only during supine *rest*, not during supine *exercise* (Jeffreys et al., 2006). Thus, the "common sense" approach is to keep the legs and torso moving if exercising in the supine position (i.e., stretching, floor exercises, etc.). Because the vena cava is on the right side of the heart, the woman should turn on the left side if she begins to feel dizzy (Clapp, 2002). Prolonged standing has been similarly shown to adversely affect the return of blood to the mother's heart. This occurs because the blood collects or pools in the legs. Because the blood is temporarily blocked or limited in its ability to get back to the heart, the obvious solution for both issues is to keep moving! This will help prevent compression of the blood vessels, and assist in keeping blood moving back to the mother's heart, and consequently, to the fetus.

2. Scuba Diving

In non-pregnant individuals, scuba diving beyond a depth of 40 feet requires decompression (i.e., slow ascent back to the surface of the water) in order to remove nitrogen from the blood. Failure to do so can result in *decompression sickness*, which in some cases can be fatal. Since it is unknown to what extent the baby can eliminate nitrogen from its blood, it has been suggested that pregnant women should not dive beyond 16 feet without doubling their decompression time (Clapp, 2002). However, "common sense" dictates that this activity should probably be avoided during pregnancy.

3. Exercise at Altitudes Exceeding 6,000 Feet

At altitude, oxygen in the atmosphere is reduced, which not only makes exercise more difficult and uncomfortable for the mother, but it may potentially reduce oxygen delivery to the baby and cause fetal hypoxia. This does not appear to be a problem at altitudes up to 6,000 feet.

4. Sports with High Potential for Contact, Falling, or Other Trauma

Although the pelvis, uterus and amniotic fluid are designed to absorb considerable shock in order to protect the baby, trauma to the abdomen can still be hazardous, especially after the first trimester due to the increased size (Brooks et al., 2005). Thus, sports with a high risk of contact (i.e., boxing, hockey, rugby, etc.), falling (i.e., downhill skiing, gymnastics, horseback riding, outdoor cycling, rock climbing, etc.), or other trauma (i.e., pool/lake diving, water skiing—risk of sudden rush of water into the vagina) should be avoided during pregnancy. For some sports (i.e., basketball, racquetball, soccer, tennis, etc.), the manner in which they are performed can be modified to minimize these types of risks.

Special Exercise Considerations

1. Warning Signs to Terminate Exercise

Table 3 lists warning signs, which if apparent during exercise, indicate a woman should discontinue the exercise and consult with her physician as soon as possible (ACOG, 2002).

2. Additional Caloric Needs

Pregnancy requires an additional 300 kcal per day to support the increased energy demands of the mother and baby at rest (National Research Council, 1989). Calories expended in exercise must also be accounted for in order to maintain a normal pregnancy weight gain (i.e. 24-33 pounds). Dietary adjustments must also ensure adequate nutrient supply to both the mother and the baby (Clapp, 2002).

3. Heat Dissipation and Hydration

As noted previously, pregnant women should avoid prolonged exercise in hot, humid conditions and maintain a core body temperature of less than 102 degrees Fahrenheit, especially during early pregnancy (Clapp, 2002). This is easily achieved by exercising at cooler and less humid times of the day (i.e. morning or evening), exercising inside with air conditioning and/or a fan, wearing appropriate clothing (i.e. lightweight, light-colored, poly-

Table 3 Warning Signs to Terminate Exercise while Pregnant (ACOG, 2002)
■ Vaginal Bleeding
■ Dyspnea prior to exertion
■ Dizziness
■ Headache
■ Chest pain
■ Muscle weakness
■ Calf pain or swelling (need to rule out thrombophlebitis)
■ Preterm labor
■ Decreased fetal movement
■ Amniotic fluid leakage

ester "sweat wicking" materials), and most importantly, drinking plenty of fluids before, during, and after exercise (even during cool conditions) to maintain adequate hydration. In addition, women should avoid prolonged swimming in pools that are warmer than 82 degrees Fahrenheit, and sitting in hot tubs or saunas that are 100 degrees Fahrenheit or warmer (Clapp, 2002).

4. Prevention of Hypoglycemia (Low Blood Glucose)

The risk of hypoglycemia in the mother, which can then lead to such in the baby, is increased in the last trimester of pregnancy. This risk is highest when the exercise is prolonged and/or strenuous. Hypoglycemia can be prevented by increasing carbohydrate intake (30–50 grams or 1–2 ounces) before, as well as during and after exercise (ACSM, 2006). Sports beverages are a good way to obtain both adequate carbohydrate and fluid.

5. Weight Training

As you will see in the exercise prescription guidelines in the next section, weight training can be safely performed during pregnancy. However, abdominal exercises are not recommended if the woman has bulging of the connective tissue along the midline of the abdomen, a condition called *diastasis recti*, which occurs in some women. In addition, heavy weight lifting (i.e., <10 repetitions maximum) and breath-holding while lifting weights (i.e., the Valsalva Maneuver), should be avoided as this can increase blood pressure and may adversely affect blood flow to the uterus and the baby. Low (15+ repetitions maximum) to moderate (10–15 repetitions maximum) intensity weight lifting with proper technique and continuous breathing (i.e., exhale on exertion; inhale on recovery) is appropriate. Following these recommendations may promote good posture, prevent back pain and varicose veins, improve breast support, strengthen muscles of labor, and promote good bladder control and prevent urinary incontinence (CSEP, 2002).

6. Breast and Abdominal Support

Exercise is not fun if it hurts! When running, unsupported breast movement can produce 50–100 pounds of force against the chest (Brooks et al., 2005). For obvious reasons, additional breast and abdominal support are needed, especially in late pregnancy. The key for breast support is compression, which can be achieved by wearing two sports bras and/or wrapping a wide Ace bandage or elasticized belt with Velcro attachments snuggly around the chest over a sports bra. The key for abdominal support is upward lift and mild compression which can similarly be achieved by wrapping the Ace bandage or elasticized belt snuggly over the hips and under the abdomen. The elasticized belts can be obtained commercially and are relatively inexpensive (Clapp, 2002).

Exercise Prescription During Pregnancy

Exercise prescription refers to the frequency, intensity, time, and type (FITT) of exercise performed. While most women can and should exercise during pregnancy (see absolute and relative contraindications in Tables 1 and 2, respectively, as well as previously noted exercises to avoid), the FITT principles will vary based on initial fitness level and desired goals. As indicated previously, all women should consult their physicians prior to starting or continuing an exercise program while pregnant. The *Physical Activity Readiness Medical Examination for Pregnancy* (PARmed-X for Pregnancy) is a tool that includes a short screening questionnaire, contraindications for exercise, and exercise prescription guidelines (CSEP, 2002). It is recommended that this form, which can be downloaded for free (http//www.csep.ca/forms.asp), be included in the initial physician consultation, especially for previously sedentary women.

General guidelines for exercise during pregnancy are relatively consistent to those for non-pregnant individuals including warm-up and cool-down, as well as aerobic, flexibility, and weight training exercises (ACSM, 2006). The following guidelines, which are a composite of those issued by national organizations (ACOG, 2002; ACSM, 2006; Davies et al., 2003) and other experts (Clapp, 2002; Paisley et al., 2003) make specific recommendations concerning goals and FITT guidelines for 1) previously sedentary women, 2) women who regularly exercised prior to pregnancy, and 3) athletes.

Previously Sedentary Women

Goal: Attain the health benefits of exercise during pregnancy by performing "30 minutes or more of moderate exercise a day on most, if not all, days of the week" (ACOG, 2002). This is identical to the Surgeon General's guidelines for all Americans (Pate et al., 1995).

Frequency: Start with 3 days and progress to 4–5 days per week

Intensity: Rating of perceived exertion (RPE) of 11–13 (light to somewhat hard) as heart rate may not be a reliable index of exercise intensity during pregnancy

Time: Start with 15 minutes and progress to 30 minutes per session

Type: Low or non-impact aerobic activities (i.e., walking, swimming, stationary cycling, low impact aerobic dance, etc.); low intensity weight training (1 set, 15+ repetitions maximum, major muscle groups, 2–3 non-consecutive days per week)

Regular Exercisers

Goal: Maintain previous fitness, as well as optimize the health benefits of exercise during pregnancy

Frequency: 3–5 days per week

Intensity: Rating of perceived exertion (RPE) of 12–14 (somewhat hard) as heart rate may not be a reliable index of exercise intensity during pregnancy

Time: 30–60 minutes per session

Type: Any prior activities other than those previously not recommended; moderate intensity weight training (1–2 sets, 10–15 repetitions maximum, major muscle groups, 2–3 non-consecutive days per week)

Athletes

Goal: Maintain a reasonably high level of fitness "without trying to reach peak fitness or train for athletic competition" (Davies et al., 2003), as well as optimize the health benefits of exercise during pregnancy

Frequency: 4–6 days per week

Intensity: Rating of perceived exertion (RPE) of 13–15 (somewhat hard to hard) as heart rate may not be a reliable index of exercise intensity during pregnancy

Time: 60–90 minutes per session

Type: Any prior activities other than those previously not recommended, but avoid serious competition; moderate intensity weight training (2–3 sets, 10+ repetitions maximum, major muscle groups, 2–3 non-consecutive days per week)

In all of the above cases, "common sense" should prevail and "If it feels good, it's probably OK" (Clapp, 2002). This chapter concludes with a brief discussion of exercise during the post partum period (i.e., after delivery).

Exercise During the Post Partum Period

In addition to many of the benefits described earlier for exercise during pregnancy, exercise during the post partum period may provide additional benefits such as resumption of pre-pregnancy weight, reduced incidence of post partum depression, reduced risk of urinary incontinence (if pelvic floor exercises are performed), and *an opportunity* for some time away from the baby which may help keep the mother from feeling overwhelmed (ACOG, 2002; Clapp, 2002; Davies, et al., 2003). However, many of the physiological changes of pregnancy persist four to six weeks post partum, and many women choose to breastfeed, which increases the energy demands of the mother. Interestingly, it has been reported that 95% of women who exercise during pregnancy breastfeed, which has well-documented benefits to the baby (Clapp, 2002).

Generally, there are no known complications for the mother associated with exercise during the post partum period, as well as no detrimental effects on breast milk quantity and quality or the baby's growth in women who breastfeed (ACOG, 2002; Clapp, 2002; Davies, et al.,

2003). However, breastfeeding does result in a loss of bone density (due to its induction of estrogen deficiency, as well as calcium loss in the breast milk) which is normally regained once breastfeeding is stopped (Clapp and Little, 1995; Little and Clapp, 1998). Recreational exercise (i.e., aerobic and light to moderate weight training) has not been shown to prevent this bone loss as the effect of estrogen deficiency appears to outweigh it (Little and Clapp, 1998). The potential benefits of moderate to high intensity weight training or other bone stimulating exercises such as plyometrics (Kohrt et al., 2004) have not been studied. Since bone density is usually regained once breastfeeding stops, the only clinical concern is for women who already have low bone density, are at high risk for osteoporosis, or were formerly amenorrheic (i.e., absence of periods which results in estrogen deficiency) with a history of stress fractures. The latter is common in some women athletes. In this case, the woman should consult with her physician who may prescribe low dose oral contraceptives (combination of estrogen and progesterone) as preliminary data suggest this may reduce some of the bone loss associated with breastfeeding (Little, Unpublished Data).

In terms of exercise guidelines during the post partum, *absolute contraindications* include 1) heavy bleeding; 2) pain; and 3) breast infection or abscess, while *relative contraindications* include 1) cesarean or traumatic vaginal delivery; 2) breast discomfort; and 3) heavy urine leakage or pelvic pressure during exercise (Clapp, 2002). Otherwise, "common sense" dictates that exercise should begin slowly and increas gradually. Most of the special exercise considerations during pregnancy (i.e., additional caloric needs, heat dissipation and hydration, prevention of hypoglycemia, weight training issues, and breast and abdominal support) also apply in the post partum period. An additional consideration is the potential appearance of lactic acid in the breast milk after exercise, which may be distasteful to the baby. This usually only occurs with high intensity exercise. However, this potential problem is easily avoided by refraining from breastfeeding immediately after exercise (especially very strenuous). Instead, breastfeeding or pumping milk for the next feeding prior to exercise will have the added benefit of making the exercise more comfortable as well (Clapp, 2002; Quinn and Carey, 1997). The specific exercise prescription guidelines (i.e., FITT) outlined earlier for previously sedentary, regular exercisers, and athletes also apply during the post partum period. Once again, "common sense" should prevail and "If it feels good, it's probably OK" (Clapp, 2002)!

Conclusion

In the absence of pre-existing disease or pregnancy complications, most women can safely exercise during pregnancy and the post partum period, which may provide significant health benefits to both the mother and the baby.

References

American College of Obstetricians and Gynecologists. (ACOG, 1985). *Exercise during pregnancy and the post partum period*. Technical Bulletin 58. Washington, D.C.: ACOG Press.

American College of Obstetricians and Gynecologists. (ACOG, 1994). *Exercise during pregnancy and the post partum period*. Technical Bulletin 189. Washington, D.C.: ACOG Press.

American College of Obstetricians and Gynecologists. (ACOG, 2002). Committee on Obstetric Practice. Exercise during pregnancy and the postpartum period. ACOG Committee Opinion 267. *Obstetrics & Gynecology, 99*, 171–173.

American College of Sports Medicine. (ACSM, 2006). *ACSM's guidelines for exercise testing and prescription (7th ed.)*. Baltimore: Lippincott Williams & Wilkins.

Artal, R., & Sherman, C. (1999). Exercise during pregnancy. Safe and beneficial for most. *The Physician and Sportsmedicine*, 27 (8), 51–60.

Brooks, G. A., Fahey, T. D., & Baldwin, K. M. (2005). *Exercise physiology: human bioenergetics and its applications* (4th ed.). New York: McGraw-Hill.

Canadian Society for Exercise Physiology (CSEP). (2002). *Physical Activity Readiness Medical Examination for Pregnancy (PARmed-X for Pregnancy)*. Available online at http//www.csep.ca/forms.asp.

Clapp, J. F. (2001). Recommending exercise during pregnancy. *Contemporary OB/GYN*, 46, 30–49.

Clapp, J. F. (2002). *Exercising through your pregnancy*. Omaha, NE: Addicus Books.

Clapp, J. F., & Little, K. D. (1995a). Effect of recreational exercise on pregnancy weight gain and subcutaneous fat deposition. *Medicine and Science in Sports and Exercise*, 27, 170–177.

Clapp, J. F., & Little, K. D. (1995b). The interaction between regular exercise and selected aspects of women's health. *American Journal of Obstetrics and Gynecology*, 173, 2–9.

Clapp, J. F., Little, K. D., & Capeless, E. L. (1993). Fetal heart rate response to sustained recreational exercise. *American Journal of Obstetrics and Gynecology*, 168, 198–206.

Davies, G. A. L., Wolfe, L. A., Mottola, M. F., & MacKinnon, C. (2003). Joint SOGC/CSEP clinical practice guideline: exercise in pregnancy and the postpartum period. *Canadian Journal of Applied Physiology*, 28 (3), 329–341.

Dempsey, J. C., Butler, C. L., & Williams, M. A. (2005). No need for a pregnant pause: physical activity may reduce the occurrence of gestational diabetes mellitus and preeclampsia. *Exercise and Sports Science Reviews*, 33 (3), 141–149.

Ertan, A. K., Schanz, S., Tanriverdi, H. A., Meyberg, R., & Schmidt, W. (2004). Doppler examinations of fetal and uteroplacental blood flow in AGA and IUGR fetuses before and after maternal physical exercise with the bicycle ergometer. *Journal of Perinatology Medicine*, 32, 260–265.

Jeffreys, R. M., Stepanchak, W., Lopez, B., Hardis, J., & Clapp, J. F. (2006). Uterine blood flow during supine rest and exercise after 28 weeks of gestation. *British Journal of Obstetrics and Gyncology*, 113, 1239–1247.

Kohrt, W. M., Bloomfield, S.A., Little, K.D., Nelson, M.E., & Yingling, V. (2004). American College of Sports Medicine Position Stand: Physical Activity and Bone Health. *Medicine and Science in Sports and Exercise*, 36, 1985–1996.

Little, K. D. (Unpublished Data). Effect of low dose oral contraceptives on lactation-induced bone loss.

Little, K. D., & Clapp, J. F. (1998). Self-selected recreational exercise has no impact on early postpartum lactation-induced bone loss. *Medicine and Science in Sports and Exercise*, 30, 831–836.

National Research Council, Food and Nutrition Board, Commission on Life Sciences (1989). *Recommended daily dietary allowances* (10th ed.). Report of the Subcommittee on the Tenth Edition of the RDAs. Washington, D.C.: National Academy Press.

Nieman, D. C. (2007). *Exercise testing and prescription: a health related approach* (6th ed.). New York: McGraw-Hill.

Paisley, T. S., Joy, E. A., & Price, R. J. (2003). Exercise during pregnancy: a practical approach. *Current Sports Medicine Reports*, 2, 325–330.

Pate, R. R., Pratt, M., Blair, S. N., et al. (1995). Physical activity and public health: a recommendation from the Centers for Disease Control and Prevention and the American College of Sports Medicine. *Journal of the American Medical Association*, 273, 402–407.

Quinn, T. J., & Carey, G. B. (1999). Does exercise intensity or diet influence lactic acid accumulation in breast milk? *Medicine and Science in Sports and Exercise*, 31, 105–110.

Weissgerber, T. L., Wolfe, L. A., Davies, G. A. L., & Mottola, M. F. (2006). Exercise in the prevention and treatment of maternal-fetal disease: a review of the literature. *Applied Physiology in Nutrition and Metabolism*, 31, 661–674.

Wolfe, L. A. (2005). Pregnancy. In J. S. Skinner (Ed.), *Exercise testing and exercise prescription for special cases: theoretical basis and clinical application* (3rd ed.), pp. 377–391. Baltimore: Lippincott Williams & Wilkins.

Zhang, J., & Savitz, D.A. (1996). Exercise during pregnancy among US women. *Annals of Epidemiology*, 6, 53–59.

Further Readings

Is It Safe to Exercise during Pregnancy?
  (http://www.childbirth.org/articles/pregnancy/safeexercise.html).

Mother's Physical Activity during Pregnancy Likely to Affect Child's Future Energy Level.
  (http://medheadlines.com/2007/12/14/mothers-physical-activity-during-pregnancy-likely-to-affect-childs-future-energy-level/).

Discussion Questions

1. Compare the physiological changes that occur during pregnancy and those that occur during exercise. Discuss how the changes for each of these factors affects the other.

2. What are some of the benefits to women who maintain physically active lifestyles throughout pregnancy?

3. What specific exercise recommendations are given to pregnant women and how do they change based on the stage of pregnancy?

5

Too Much of a Good Thing: Overtraining and the Female Athlete Triad

Ann F. Maliszewski

Introduction

It is commonly accepted that being physically active on a regular basis is a healthy habit. Exercising or incorporating physical activity into one's everyday life reduces the risk for several diseases including heart disease, type 2 diabetes, cancer, and several risk factors for disease (hypertension, obesity, elevated blood cholesterol). Physical activity has also been shown to be beneficial to mental health (i.e., reduction in anxiety, depression, stress). But is there such a thing as too much exercise? As with most things, it turns out that exercise is best used in moderation. Because exercise is a form of stress, *physical* stress, it can be dangerous if not performed in a balanced and reasonable manner.

The ability of the body to have advantageous changes from exercise is based on the adjustments the body's systems make when confronted with the stress. For example, if a woman begins an exercise program that includes jogging at 5 miles per hour for 20 minutes on 3 days per week, she initially might feel like it's a tough workout. But after working out regularly (e.g., a month or so) at this same intensity, it will begin to feel easier. The reason it feels easier is that her body has made adjustments that make it more prepared to face that level of physical stress. Let's say that this woman's heart rate levels out at about 160 bpm during the first few workouts. As she continues her jogging routine over the next several weeks, she will notice that her heart rate drops by a few beats per minute (e.g., 155–157 bpm)—even though she's performing the same activity. The heart makes changes so that it doesn't have to work as hard to supply blood and oxygen to the working muscles. This example demonstrates the body's ability to *adapt* to the stress it faces.

But every system has its breaking point, and if the body undergoes a training program that proves too stressful, it may not be able to withstand that level of stress for long. A rubber balloon can provide an example of a system reaching its breaking point. As you blow more and more air into a balloon, the rubber stretches. Once the maximum strength of the rubber is exceeded the balloon pops. Fortunately, your organs won't pop from too much stress, but they can be pushed to the point of failure. The failure can be extreme, which would mean that the organs can no longer function at all, or less severe, in which the organ systems cannot work at optimum levels. Imagine if you repeatedly blew up the balloon to the volume just under its breaking point and then let the air out. The rubber will eventually lose its ability to return to its original shape. Likewise, when an individual pushes her body through very intense workouts with insufficient recovery-times between, she may begin to see the effects on her body's systems. This state is called *overtraining*.

Overtraining

Overtraining can be associated with a variety of physical and psychological symptoms. The symptoms include general fatigue, lack of motivation, depression, insomnia, muscle soreness, loss of appetite, headaches, loss of concentration, weight loss, elevated resting heart rate, altered menstrual cycle, decreased sex drive, increased rate of illness, increased incidence of overuse injuries, and increased recovery time. For athletes, performance is negatively affected by overtraining. They can suffer reductions in the ability to use oxygen to produce cellular energy. Additionally, loss of muscular strength and endurance, altered coordination of movement, reduced cardiorespiratory endurance, lower maximal heart rate, and blood levels of stress hormones during exercise are also typical symptoms of overtraining. Clearly, overtraining affects many organ systems, and ultimately the function of the entire body.

What's really going on with the body when it's pushed so hard so often? There are a few things to consider. First, when the body's cells are put through a tough workout, they need time to recover afterwards. The recovery period is used to replenish nutrients and fuels, as well as to rebuild any components that might have been damaged. If recovery time is insufficient, the cells will not be in their optimum condition to face the next workout. Additionally, it is critical that the body receive the nutrients required to rebuild and maintain the integrity of the tissues and organs. How much and what the woman eats will directly influence the body's readiness to face physical stress. It is important for athletes and their coaches—and even women who work out recreationally—to be aware of the signs and symptoms of overtraining. Reductions in the amount of exercise and/or adjustments to the diet may be necessary to return the body to its optimum condition.

There is a particular combination of symptoms/conditions that is unique to women and was originally identified in women athletes. The condition is called the *Female Athlete Triad* and is marked by three conditions: a negative caloric balance, menstrual cycle irregularities, and loss in bone mineral density. Although the name would suggest that only athletes are affected by the condition, the Triad also can be present in women who are not competitive athletes.

The Female Athlete Triad

As seen in Figure 1, the three points on the Female Athlete Triad include a negative caloric balance at the top, menstrual dysfunction on the left of the base, and low bone mineral density on the right. The arrows indicate the relationships among these factors. We'll begin our discussion of the Triad with an examination of the factor that appears to be the initial step: negative caloric balance.

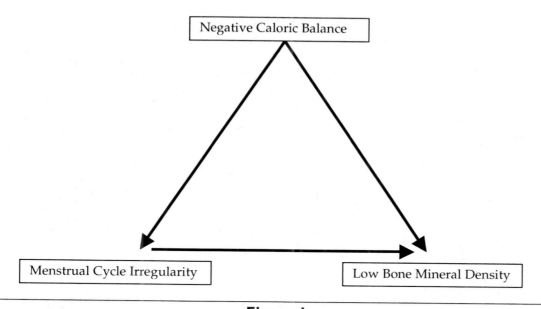

Figure 1

The steps of the Female Athlete Triad and the relationship among the steps (indicated by arrows).

Step 1. Negative Caloric Balance

The concept of *caloric balance* is based on the relationship between the *caloric intake* (i.e., the number of calories consumed in the diet, and thus put *into* the body) and the *caloric expenditure* (i.e., the calories used by the body during the course of the day). The relationship between these components is illustrated in Figure 2.

The concept of caloric balance can be applied to a variety of situations. For example, if someone is trying to lose weight, they need to achieve a *negative caloric balance*. In this case, the caloric intake is *less than* the caloric expenditure. In this state, more energy (measured in *calories*) is used by the body than is taken in through the diet. Thus the body loses energy/calories. Because energy is located inside stored fuel molecules (e.g., sugars and fat), the weight of these stored fuels is lost from the body as the molecules are broken down to provide energy to the cells. The concept of "burning fat" means that fat molecules are being broken down to access the stored energy inside. The remnants from those fat molecules are removed from the body, and consequently, the body loses the weight of those molecules! The more work the cells do, the more energy is required, and the more weight is lost.

There are some situations in which an individual needs to achieve a *positive caloric balance*. In those situations, the caloric intake must be *greater than* the caloric expenditure. Based on what was discussed above, you can assume that this state will lead to an increase in body weight. This would be the case if someone were trying to gain muscle mass (e.g., power athletes) or recover from an illness in which excess weight was lost. To achieve a positive caloric balance, the individual must eat more calories than the body is using during the course of the day.

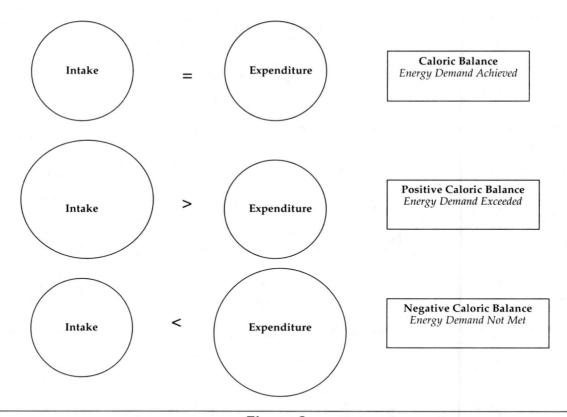

Figure 2
Balance between caloric intake and expenditure and the different caloric states.

Most healthy and active women will focus on maintaining a balance between intake and expenditure. In the state of *caloric balance*, what is consumed in the diet will closely match the energy use by the body. Problems may arise when a woman is not achieving an appropriate balance between the two and inadvertently, or sometimes intentionally, ends up in a negative caloric state. How can that happen?

To understand how someone can end up in a negative caloric state that is potentially dangerous, we need to take a look at what makes up the caloric expenditure side of the equation. Where caloric intake is simply the calories taken into the body through the diet, there are several factors that contribute to caloric expenditure (See Table 1).

Table 1 Components of Caloric Intake and Caloric Expenditure	
Caloric Intake	Caloric Expenditure
■ Food	■ Basal metabolic rate (BMR)
■ Drink	■ Energy required for digestion
■ Supplemental products	■ Physical activity ☐ Exercise ☐ Daily activities

Daily caloric expenditure is the sum of all of the energy the body uses during a 24 hour period. It includes a) basal metabolic rate, b) physical activity, and c) energy used to digest food. The **basal metabolic rate** (BMR) is the amount of energy the body uses while it is completely at rest and between meals (i.e., not digesting food). BMR reflects the amount of energy used by the organs/cells to keep the body alive. For example, the kidneys are constantly working to filter waste from the blood and energy is required for this process. Different regions of the brain are always working, and signals are being sent along neurons from one region of the body to another. The heart and muscles of the respiratory system are constantly working to provide oxygen to the cells. All of these cellular and organ system activities require energy. All systems of the resting body contribute to the BMR, and this baseline amount of energy is the *minimum* amount of energy used during the day.

The other components within the caloric expenditure column build on the BMR. For example, if you rest following a meal, your energy cost would reflect your BMR *plus* the amount of energy the body uses to *digest* the food you just ate. The muscular activity during *exercise* requires energy, and the greater the *volume* of the activity (volume = how hard x how long = exercise *intensity* x exercise *duration*), the more the energy needed. The energy demand on the body is pushed well above the BMR during exercise. One factor that is often overlooked when someone is counting her calories is the energy used during *daily activities*. Included in this category is anything one does that's beyond the resting state, but is not considered exercise. Brushing teeth, ironing clothes, cooking, washing the car, pulling weeds, de-icing the windshield, walking to the mailbox, and throwing the ball for the dog are activities that don't fall into the *exercise* category, but are placing energy demands on the body that are above the BMR level.

When determining the caloric balance, all of the components within the caloric expenditure category must be accounted for. There is little one can do to alter BMR, and digestion contributes minimally to the total daily caloric expenditure. Physical activity, on the other hand, particularly exercise, can contribute hundreds and even thousands of calories to the expenditure side of the caloric balance equation, and lead to a negative caloric balance. But there is another way to tip the scale of caloric balance in the negative direction, and that is by consuming too few calories in the diet.

When a woman participates in a heavy-volume physical training program, she must be careful to match the high energy demand with a high-calorie diet. Sometimes this is difficult, especially for endurance athletes, such as distance runners, cyclists, or triathletes. During heavy training periods, it may be difficult to consume enough calories in the diet to match her training volume, and she may unintentionally end up in a negative caloric balance state.

In athletic events in which appearing thin is emphasized, the negative caloric balance may be intentional. The Female Athlete Triad affects women in some sports more than others. Those sports/activities include gymnastics, swimming, diving, and ballet dancing, activities that considered *aesthetic sports* because of the emphasis on body shape/type or leanness. Women in these sports may attempt to keep the caloric intake side of the equation low in order to achieve the desired body type or fat level. Other athletes in any sport (e.g., volleyball, soccer, basketball, etc.) may be encouraged by their coaches to lose weight because of an out-dated belief that athletes of a specific percent body fat are better at their sport. This is a complicated issue because there's no perfect amount of body fat that fits every woman, and the methods for assessing body fat are often inaccurate—especially for lean women. There are problems with so much focus on keeping body weight/fat low and limiting dietary intake to achieve a certain body size. The primary issue is that the training sessions demand a great deal of energy, and with reduced dietary intake, the body experiences a nutritional deficit. Such deficits are typical in eating disorders.

Women with eating disorders may abstain from food and drink to reduce caloric intake, but they may also try to tip the scale by exercising excessively in order to increase caloric expenditure. There are 3 classifications of eating disorders: *anorexia nervosa*, *bulimia nervosa*, and *eating disorder not otherwise specified* (ED-NOS). See Table 2 for the diagnostic criteria of each.

Supplying the human body with the correct amount and types of nutrients is essential to keep the organ systems and cells of the body functioning. Imagine NOT providing it with what it needs and then pushing it to its maximum capacity over and over through heavy physical exertion. Eventually something is going to give.

Table 2 Diagnostic criteria for eating disorders based on the Diagnostic and Statistical Manual of Mental Disorders, 4th ed: DSM-IV. Washington, D.C. American Psychiatric Association Press	
Eating Disorder	Criteria used in Diagnosis
Anorexia Nervosa	■ Dangerously low body weight (at or below 85% of recommended body weight for her height) ■ Failure to recognize a problem with low body weight ■ Extreme fear of gaining weight or fat ■ Continue to judge body negatively ■ Judges self poorly based on body image ■ Unrealistic body image (physical self-image doesn't match actual state) ■ Amenorrhea (absence menstrual cycles for 3 or more months consecutively)

Bulimia Nervosa	■ Binge eating, in which a more than normal amount is consumed in a relatively short period of time
	■ Feeling of lack of control during binge eating
	■ Attempts to prevent weight gain following binge eating including
	  ☐ Vomiting
	  ☐ Use of laxatives
	  ☐ Excessive exercise
	  ☐ Fasting
	  ☐ Enemas
	■ Sense of self strongly based on physical appearance/size
	
	These behaviors occur 2 times per week or more for 3 consecutive months

Eating Disorder Not Otherwise Specified	■ Meet all criteria for anorexia nervosa EXCEPT
	  ☐ have normal menstrual cycles (**eumenorrhea**) or
	  ☐ still fall within "normal" weight range
	■ Meet all criteria of bulimia nervosa EXCEPT
	  ☐ occurs less frequently
	  ☐ no attempt to offset binging with weight-loss behaviors
	■ Chewing large amounts of food and spitting it out (no swallowing)

Step 2. Menstrual Cycle Irregularity

In the Female Athlete Triad, what appears to "give" is the reproductive and/or the skeletal system. On the left side of the triangle presented in Figure 1, one can see that a negative caloric balance can lead to menstrual cycle irregularities (reproductive system). The right side of the triangle indicates the negative consequence of low bone mineral density (skeletal system).

A negative caloric balance can lead to changes in the menstrual cycle that can range from infrequent (i.e., *oligomenorrhea*) or complete absence of (i.e., *amenorrhea*) menstrual cycles. Because the menstrual cycle is the body's monthly attempt to prepare a woman's body for pregnancy, it should be no surprise that it might shut down if the woman is not in a healthy state. It seems quite logical that nature would have a built-in protection against getting pregnant while the body is in a starvation state. Many women might find the opportunity to avoid having a regular cycle appealing, however, the physiological problems related to that absence can be devastating.

The menstrual cycle is regulated by the hypothalamus and the pituitary gland, which are located in the brain. The hypothalamus stimulates the pituitary gland to release two hormones: *luteinizing hormone* and *follicle stimulating hormone*. These hormones, collectively called the *gonadotropins*, stimulate the gonads (ovaries in females; testes in men). In women, follicle stimulating hormone (FSH), as the name suggests, stimulates the ovarian follicle to grow during the first half of the menstrual cycle. The follicle is what houses the egg and helps it prepare for release. In turn, cells of the follicle release *estrogen*, one of the female steroid/reproductive hormones. When luteinizing hormone (LH) is released in large amounts, *ovulation* (the release of the egg from the ovary) takes place. This takes place right around the middle of the menstrual cycle (day 14). Following ovulation, what remains of the follicle becomes the corpus luteum, which releases estrogen and *progesterone* (the other female steroid/reproductive hormone) during the second half of the menstrual cycle.

Estrogen and progesterone have actions in various locations in the body, including bone. "Normal" levels of these hormones are essential for maintaining healthy bone. When the menstrual cycle is irregular or absent, it is likely that the reproductive hormones are not being produced or secreted at normal levels. So the actions of those hormones on the different organs of the body are also compromised.

Step 3. Low Bone Mineral Density

Bone maintenance includes regular, repeated phases of bone growth (formation) and bone resorption (removal of mineral from bone). This normal fluctuation of formation and removal allows for regular turnover of the bone, which is primarily made up of the mineral calcium phosphate. Estrogen reduces the resorption of bone, thereby helping to maintain the bone's mineral content. Progesterone stimulates bone growth (addition of mineral to bone). As you might guess, if the levels of estrogen and/or progesterone are altered, the skeleton can be adversely affected.

A very clear sign that estrogen and progesterone levels may be compromised is a change in the menstrual cycle. And as you might guess, amenorrhea—the absence of a normal cycle—is a likely sign that the reproductive hormone levels are significantly altered. Because of the role of the reproductive hormones on bone, one might conclude that bone health will eventually be affected. Looking at the right side of the Triad triangle, you'll see that there is a direct link (indicated by an arrow) between menstrual dysfunction and low bone mineral content.

Although in the early stages of the Triad the bone mineral content/density might be *below normal* for the woman's age, it could reach a critical disease state of **osteoporosis**. Most often associated with elderly, post-menopausal women who no longer produce estrogen and progesterone in the ovaries, osteoporosis is marked by porous, brittle bone. When asked to imagine someone with osteoporosis, many people picture an elderly woman hunched over with a Dowager's hump on her back. Elderly women with osteoporosis can lose several inches in height, and the compression of the body that occurs, presses on the internal organs. The cause of the loss in height and compression is fracturing or crushing of the vertebrae of the spine. Likewise, young women with low bone density or osteoporosis are likely to suffer bone fractures, particularly stress fracture. Additionally, the healing time from fractures can be significantly increased.

It might be assumed that getting the hormones back to normal—either by getting the woman out of the negative caloric balance state or prescribing medication to replace the estrogen and progesterone artificially will allow the affected woman to recover.

Although the loss of bone may be stopped, she may not fully recover to a bone mineral density that is normal for her age. This situation may lead to a lifetime of complications. In Figure 3, a possible scenario is presented that compares normal bone growth and loss during a woman's lifetime with that of a woman who has compromised bone growth during adolescence. Under normal conditions (dashed line), bone continues to grow until the early to mid-twenties. Bone mass is maintained until around age 35 years, at which point it begins to decrease. Around age 50 years, when women reach menopause, the decline in bone mass increases, thus the slope of the line is more exaggerated. Note how the woman who experiences the Female Athlete Triad (solid line) experiences normal bone growth through childhood, but no growth during a couple years in late adolescence. Although the condition was corrected around age 20, and the rate of normal bone growth was returned, she remained below what was normal for her age for the rest of her life. She is likely to have low bone den-

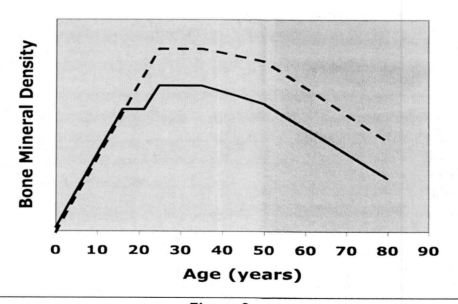

Figure 3

General trend in bone mineral density over age in women. Dashed line represents normal bone growth and loss; solid like represents bone growth and loss in woman who experiences the Female Athlete Triad (marked by no bone growth in late teens).

sity or osteoporosis at a younger age, than if she had not experienced the bone loss in her youth. This simple example illustrates how important it is to recognize the physiological problems related to the Female Athlete Triad as early as possible.

Helping Someone Who Is Overtraining or Falls into the Female Athlete Triad

Women who are experiencing overtraining or have the symptoms of the Female Athlete Triad may be experiencing or heading towards serious health complications. Fortunately, these conditions are well-studied and there are some straight-forward recommendations on how to deal with them.

DeMond (2008) recommends 10 steps to preventing overtraining. They include:

1. Decrease the duration of the workout time
2. Take a day or two off between workout sessions
3. Vary the intensity of the workouts
4. Set realistic fitness goals (this may require input from a coach or trainer)
5. Vary training activities
6. Stop if pain is felt
7. Wear proper footwear
8. If injured, switch to different sports/activities while recovering
9. Exercise with a partner who has a less rigorous workout schedule
10. Develop interests outside of exercise

If someone is already suffering symptoms of overtraining or the Triad, professional intervention may be required. Because disordered eating or involvement of excessive exercise may signal an emotional or mental disorder, working with a mental health specialist may be necessary. The symptoms may suggest malfunctioning or damage to one or more organ systems, so a physician's involvement is essential. To gain a better understanding of nutritional needs of the body and balancing energy demand and supply, dietary counseling with a registered dietician will be highly beneficial. Adjustments to a workout routine will be important, so consulting with a certified fitness specialist or coach who is knowledgeable of the concept of overtraining and the Female Athlete Triad is recommended. The American College of Sports Medicine (ACSM) recommends a team approach, including the professional identified above, for dealing with women who fall into the Female Athlete Triad classification.

ACSM published updated guidelines on the Female Athlete Triad in 2007. Some of the key points in the prevention and treatment include:

- Coaches, fitness professionals, athletes, parents, and school administrators should be educated about the Female Athlete Triad. Knowledge and understanding—and the ability to avoid and recognize the condition—provide a critical starting point.
- Pre-participation screenings for sports and other physical activity programs should include evaluation of signs and symptoms of the Triad.
- If a woman has symptoms that indicate the Female Athlete Triad, the primary treatment goal is to achieve a proper caloric balance. This goal will likely increase the dietary intake and/or reducing the energy expenditure.

- Some women athletes may require coaxing to make the adjustments needed to bring her back to a health state. Denial is often associated with this condition, particularly if there is an eating disorder involved. Sport participation of these athletes should be restricted or reduced until certain health recovery criteria are met. These criteria should be determined and enforced by the treatment team.

Although these recommendations are well supported and provide clear guidelines for professionals dealing with women who fall into the Female Athlete Triad, it is often a friend or teammate who first recognizes there's a problem. Most women with eating disorders are in denial about their situation and are unlikely to get help on their own. Therefore, friends and family members who recognize the problem may need to intervene.

Talking with a Friend Who Has an Eating Disorder

If you suspect a friend might have an eating disorder or is exercising excessively, it is important to know how best to approach her. If she is a close friend, you might be able to get through to her, but don't be surprised or disappointed if she rejects your attempts to help. It's best to prepare yourself before you approach your friend. Here are some suggestions from the Villanova University Counseling Center about how to approach a friend with an eating disorder.

- Educate yourself about eating disorders. There are many sites on the internet that provide valuable information, including the *National Eating Disorders Association*, the *American Psychological Association*, and the *National Institute of Mental Health.*
- Secrecy and denial are two basic characteristics of someone with an eating disorder. If and when you choose to talk with your friend about your concerns, don't be surprised if she rejects your comments initially. Keep in mind that eating disorders are associated with emotional/psychological disorders, and your friend may not be ready to deal with those deeper issues.
- Select a time and place to talk that is low-stress and away from environments that are associated with the unhealthy behavior. For example, you should not bring up the topic of eating and exercising patterns during meals or at the gym.
- Initiate the conversation when she's relaxed and in a tension-free environment.
- Let her know your concerns in a gentle, non-confrontational manner.
- Know ahead of time where she can get help (e.g., contact information for the campus or community health services or counseling center).
- Know that she may respond strongly and negatively to your concerns, especially the first time you address it. Reinforce that you care and want to continue to be her friend.
- Be sure that you speak with your friend at a time when you know you're going to around to support her. Be prepared to spend the next few days or so checking in on her and maybe even accompanying her if she seeks professional help, or when she just needs to talk or have a friend around.
- Make no promises you will regret later. For example, she might ask you to promise you won't tell anyone else. But if her condition worsens, you may want to get others involved. As her friend, you are not responsible for saving—or protecting her from her own actions.

■ Protect yourself by being ready for an angry response or denial. You might consider going to the counseling center ahead of time to get assistance in planning how to handle the situation. It's OK to ask for help from professionals who are trained in dealing with eating disorders—it's a serious illness. In order to help your friend, you must be sure to take care of yourself. This can be a stressful situation for everyone involved.

It is clear that although being physically active is highly beneficial, like anything else, too much of anything can be dangerous. The exercise itself is usually not the problem. Instead, the energy states of what's coming into the body (diet), and what's being used by the body (expenditure) may not be in balance. Being in a negative caloric balance state can lead to hormonal and skeletal problems. In addition to the energy balance, it is important to recognize that the body needs time to recover and rebuild following each workout in order to avoid overtraining. Working out multiple times per day, on most or all days of the week is not a healthy training plan. Unfortunately, there is often not enough information reaching athletes and their coaches about proper training techniques. The "no pain—no gain" concept of training for sports was disproved by sport scientists decades ago. Yet it is not unusual to see coaches placing unhealthy demands on their athletes. With proper and continued education, the world of athletics is progressing and recognizing the need to monitor nutrition and menstrual status of women athletes. Following the lead of various medical and professional organizations, many colleges and universities now have teams of professionals ready to help women with signs of eating disorders, overtraining and the Female Athlete Triad. With these changes, the number of cases of eating disorders, overtraining, and the Female Athlete Triad in women hopefully can be reduced.

References

De Mond, T. E. (1991). Recognizing overtraining: the young, the old, even fitness pros may be at risk". *American Fitness May–June.* (*http://findarticles.com/p/articles/mi_m0675/is_n3_v9/ai_10872997*)

Deshmukh, R. & Franco, K. (2003). Cleveland Clinic Disease Management Project: Eating Disorders. (*http://www.clevelandclinicmeded.com/medicalpubs/diseasemanagement/psychiatry/eating/eating.htm#top*).

Fry, A. C. (2001). Overtraining with Resistance Exercise. *Current Comments American College of Sports Medicine.* (*http://www.acsm.org/Content/ContentFolders/Publications/CurrentComment/2001/overtrain.pdf*).

Loukes, A.B., Manore, M. M., Sanborn, C. F., Sundgot-Borgen, & Warren, M. (2007). American College of Sports Medicine Position Stand: The Female Athlete Triad. *MSSE* 39: 1867–1882.

Makino, M., Tsuboi, K., & Dennerstein, L. (2004). Prevalence of eating disorders: A comparison of Western and Non-Western countries. *Medscape General Medicine* 6: 49.

National Institutes of Health Osteoporosis and Related Bone Diseases National Resource Center. Fitness & Bone Health for Women: The skeletal risk of overtraining. (*www.niams.nih.gov/bone*).

Uusitalo, A. L. T., Huttumen, P., Hanin, Y., Uusitalo, A. J., and Rusko, H. K. (1998). Hormonal responses to endurance training and overtraining in female athletes. *Clinical Journal of Sport Medicine* 8: 178-186.

Villanova University. Eating Disorders: Helping a friend. University Counseling Center. (*http://www.villanova.edu/studentlife/counselingcenter/infosheets/psych_topics.htm?page=friend_eating_disorders.htm*).

World Health Organization. Global strategy on diet, physical activity and health: Physical activity and women. (*http://www.who.int/dietphysicalactivity/factsheet_women/en/index.html*).

Further Readings

ACSM Position Stand: Female Athlete Triad.
   (http://www.acsm-msse.org/pt/pt-core/template-journal/msse/media/mss200785.pdf).

American Psychological Association Help Center: Eating Disorders.
   (http://apahelpcenter.org/articles/article.php?id=9).

National Institute of Mental Health. Eating Disorders.
   (http://www.nimh.nih.gov/health/publications/eating-disorders/complete-publication.shtml).

Overview of Overtraining, Curtin School of Physiotherapy.
   (http://physiotherapy.curtin.edu.au/resources/educational-resources/exphys/00/overtraining.cfm#clinical).

The Female Athlete Triad Coalition. The Triad.
   (http://www.femaleathletetriad.org/faq.html).

Villanova University Counseling Center. Eating Disorders: Helping a Friend.
   (http://www.villanova.edu/studentlife/counselingcenter/infosheets/psych_topics.htm?page=friend_eating_disorders.htm).

US Dept. of Health & Human Services, Office of Women's Health. Eating Disorders.
   (http://www.4woman.gov/owh/pub/factsheets/eatingdis.htm).

Discussion Questions

1. Identify the three components of the Female Athlete Triad and explain how they are related to each other.

2. Discuss the warning signs and symptoms of the Female Athlete Triad. What would you do if you suspected someone you know is experiencing this condition?

3. What are the signs and symptoms of overtraining? What should a woman do to recover from overtraining?

Worksheet 16

Lifestyle—Physical Activity

Name _____ Date _____

List the activities that you **currently** engage in that would be considered *lifestyle* activities. These do not include structured exercise, but instead include activities incorporated into daily life (e.g., walking to school instead of driving the car, taking the stairs instead of the elevator, riding a bike to the store instead of driving, etc.)

List 10 ways you could increase the amount of physical activity you accumulate in the average day. Include daily/lifestyle activities rather than structured exercises.

List the fitness exercises you perform on a regular basis. Also indicate the duration (how long you spend in the activity) and frequency (how many times per week) you spend in each activity.

Based on the physical activities you listed above, are you meeting the minimum requirements for health? (Review recommendations for physical activity for health in Chapter 1 of the Biomedical Perspectives section.)

Go to *http://www.foodandhealth.com/excalc.php* and calculate the number of calories you expend while performing three of the activities you listed above. Enter the information next to each activity.

Worksheet 17

Female Athlete Triad Services

Name _____   Date _____

Make a list of the resources that exist to deal with the Female Athlete Triad on your campus and in your local community. Indicate the name of the facility and its location, as well as what services are provided. How do they let women know about these services? This activity will require that you ask questions of coaches and health care professionals. You might begin with the student health services facility on campus.

Facility Name	Location	Services	Marketing of Services

What was your general impression of the information you gathered? Is the campus and community doing a good job in addressing the health needs of women?

Worksheet 18

Monitoring the Menstrual Cycle

Name _____ Date _____

If you are a normally menstruating female, complete the daily chart (*Monthly Menstrual Cycle Chart*) for three months (make three copies). If you are not, ask a friend or relative to complete the chart for three months.

After the chart has been completed, identify characteristics that may have changed during the course of the cycle. For each segment listed in the table below, indicate any changes that could be identified as different, or more or less frequent than other times during the cycle. For example, if there was more anger experienced between days 20 and 23 than at other time in the cycle, write "angry" next to that segment. Are there any consistencies across the three months?

Segment of the Cycle	Notable Characteristics (e.g., cravings, mood changes, etc.)
Days 1–5	
Days 12–16	
Days 20–23	
Days 26–28 (or within 2 days of the next menstruation)	

For any notable patterns, suggest how hormones may have played a role. (Refer to the hormone fluctuation graph in Figure 1 in Chapter 3.)

Monthly Menstrual Cycle Chart

Month: _____   Date of Day 1: _____   Date of next cycle's Day 1: _____

Day	1	2	3	4	5	6	7	8	9	10	11	12	13	14	15	16	17	18	19	20	21	22	23	24	25	26	27	28
Flow																												
Energy Level																												
Cravings																												
Mood																												
Other																												

Direction: Using the labeling system below, track any or all of these factors through your menstrual cycle. Not every cell must be completed. Complete the cells that are worth noting for the day. For example, each day think about whether you experienced any out of the ordinary feelings.

Flow
H = heavy bleeding
M = moderate bleeding
L = light bleeding, steady flow
S = spotting, irregular or inconsistent flow

Menstrual Symptoms
C = cramps, occasional sharp pains
B = bloated
A = achy, low-back or abdominal muscle ache, but not sharp pain

Energy Level
H = high energy
N = normal, moderate level of energy
L = low energy
W = felt weak or faint

Cravings
C = chocolates
Sw = sweets in general
Sa = salty
Other: _____ =

Mood
H = happy, very good mood
N = normal, no extreme feelings either way
D = depressed, feeling low or blue
A = angry or negatively aggressive
S = sad, easy to cry

Chart used by permission © Ann F. Maliszewski

Worksheet 19

Game Plan to Prevent Type 2 Diabetes

Name _____ Date _____

The risk for type 2 diabetes is increasing across most ethnic and racial groups in the United States. Lifestyle choices, specifically diet and physical activity, can significantly lower the risk of the disease. What are you doing to reduce your risk?

Download the *Game Plan* worksheet from the *National Institute of Health* Web site (*http://www.ndep.nih.gov/diabetes/pubs/GP_FoodActTracker.pdf*) and record your diet and physical activity information for one week.

When you have completed the worksheets, write a summary about how you did and what you learned by monitoring your lifestyle choices. Attach your worksheets and submit the package to your instructor.

Worksheet 20

Know Your Risk

Name _____   Date _____

Determine your risk for chronic diseases. Go to the risk calculator Web sites below and complete the steps to determine your risk for each. Review the results and write a one-page summary about your current health status and risk for the different chronic diseases. Submit the results/reports, your summary, and this page to your instructor.

When you go to each Web site, make sure you fall into the correct age range, sex, etc. If a calculator doesn't apply directly to you, try completing it for a close friend or relative so you can see how it works.

Calculator	Risk Calculator Location
Type 2 Diabetes	http://www.diabetes.org/risk-test.jsp
Heart Disease (Heart attack risk)	http://www.americanheart.org/presenter.jhtml?identifier=3003499
Osteoporosis (Fracture risk)	http://riskcalculator.fore.org/
Breast Cancer (Women only)	http://www.cancer.gov/bcrisktool/
Life Expectancy	http://www.nmfn.com/tn/learnctr--lifeevents--longevity_game

Be sure to complete the life expectancy calculator (*Longevity Game*). It applies to everyone and focuses on many lifestyle factors.

Life expectancy: _____ years